NOT A
KID
ANYMORE

NOT A KID ANYMORE

Canadian Youth, Crime, and Subcultures

Edited by Gary M. O'Bireck
Lakehead University

Nelson Canada

I(T)P An International Thomson Publishing Company

Toronto • Albany • Bonn • Boston • Cincinnati • Detroit • London • Madrid • Melbourne
Mexico City • New York • Pacific Grove • Paris • San Francisco • Singapore • Tokyo • Washington

I(T)P™
International Thomson Publishing
The ITP logo is a trademark under licence

© Nelson Canada
A division of Thomson Canada Limited, 1996

Published in 1996 by
Nelson Canada
A division of Thomson Canada Limited
1120 Birchmount Road, Scarborough, Ontario M1K 5G4

Cover Photo	Susan Ashukian
Interior Design	Kevin Connolly
Page Composition	MacXPress

Canadian Cataloguing in Publication Data

Main entry under title:

Not a kid anymore : Canadian youth, crime, and subcultures

Includes bibliographical references and index.
ISBN 0-17-604875-8

1. Juvenile delinquency —Canada. 2. Teenagers – Canada.
I. O'Bireck, Gary Michael, 1953–   .

HV9108.N67 1996   364.3'6'0971   C95-932545-X

Team Leader and Publisher	Michael Young
Acquisitions Editor	Charlotte Forbes
Senior Production Editor	Bob Kohlmeier
Projects Coordinator	Heather Martin
Cover Design	Liz Harasymczuk
Production Coordinator	Brad Horning
Senior Composition Analyst	Alicja Jamorski

Printed and bound in Canada
1 2 3 4 5 (BBM) 00 99 98 97 96

For Jacqueline

Contents

PART 3: HEARING THE VOICES OF CANADIAN YOUTH: EMPIRICAL STUDIES OF CRIME, DEVIANCE, AND SUBCULTURES   *222*

Prelude

My decision to embark on the development of this volume was influenced by a number of factors worthy of a few words of discussion. Perhaps the most important motivating influence was a discovery I made during the research and preparation of my dissertation in the early 1990s. This ethnographic study of two groups of Canadian youth provided an open platform for these youth to speak and act, largely unencumbered by adult forms of social control. As a result of this forum, I collected reams of data relating to the lived experiences of these actors. However, during the formal writing stage, I quickly discovered that my inquiries into youth in other geographic areas were frustrated by a severe paucity of strictly Canadian data that could be used for cross-country comparisons. Surely, I thought, other Canadian social scientists must have gone into the trenches to observe and hear the voices of the young people that, for a decade at least, our society has complained about so vehemently! But delving further, I realized that current empirical research on Canadian youth is an area that has been largely under-reported by social scientists in Canada.

Later, in my role as professor at both the college and university levels, I was frequently reminded of this paucity of Canadian research on youth. In the first place, locating an exclusively Canadian text of current readings on Canadian youth, to assign as required reading, became a fruitless endeavour year after year. But perhaps more importantly, when assigning essays and research projects, I consistently recommend that students seek out the most current and *Canadian* references to enlighten, localize, and buttress their arguments. In almost every class situation (especially in those dealing with youth), students would become frustrated in their search for literature and sadly report to me that few Canadian references existed. Inevitably, they would ask permission to cite American references instead.

It was the asking of permission that grated on my nerves, not in the context of student requests but in the broader context of comparisons between nations. My hot Canadian blood began to boil when I envisioned Canadian researchers, dedicated to theorizing about their own youth, often having to defer to their American counterparts by asking permission to use American research on American youth. And when applied to youth living in Canada, I wondered, do the American findings (and those of other countries as well) accurately reflect youth on Canadian soil? I concede that American and Canadian youth share many influences, may hold similar attitudes, may engage in similar behaviours, and may encounter similar problems on their journeys toward adulthood. However, are these youth so similar that findings and contentions from the social scientists of one country can be automatically and accurately transposed to the youth of another and largely accepted as social fact?

I battled with this problem because this habit of transposing did not seem entirely appropriate. Having worked as a professional musician for 14 years before returning to academia, I was fortunate to have performed for and interacted with many audiences of youth in both Canada and the United States. Through these experiences I came to believe intrinsically that many differences existed between the youth of these two countries. Discussions with other touring musicians, promoters, and road managers, held both throughout my years in music and after I had retired from the industry, clearly supported my belief that many differences existed. When I consulted academic colleagues for their informal opinions, they offered similar (although largely theoretical) support. Assuming, of course, that differences do exist between the youth of these two countries, some may seem trivial while others appear to loom quite large. Collectively, however, these differences contribute to a uniqueness in Canadian youth (far beyond back bacon and hockey) that I firmly believe should be actively and consistently explored by social scientists living and working in Canada.

Because of this persistent "burr in my saddle," I set out to take a small step toward remedying the lack of current Canadian literature on Canadian youth. At the beginning of 1994 I began contacting social scientists from across Canada and invited them to contribute original papers to this volume. The only restrictions I placed on their work were, first, that their articles be dedicated to any aspect of Canadian youth (with deviance, crime, and subcultures as the primary focus), and, second, that their writing be easily understood by both university undergraduates and college students. In essence, my desire from the outset was that students studying in Canadian colleges and universities be able to read and learn about aspects of themselves and other Canadian youth rather than learn about youth from other countries and be compelled to draw comparisons. Moreover, I wanted this volume to be written especially for students in clearly understandable language, rather than for academic colleagues in the language characteristic of journal articles.

As a result of these invitations, *Not a Kid Anymore* presents 14 original articles about Canadian youth written especially for this volume by scholars who live and work in Canada. These articles address a wide variety of aspects of youth and are arranged in three general sections. Part 1, "Thinking about Canadian Youth," provides both theoretical and methodological approaches to studying youth, addresses the influence of the media in the shaping of youth ideals and behaviours, and wrestles with the conundrum of "doing good" or "doing justice" with those youth who contravene Canadian laws covered under the Young Offenders Act. Part 2, "Talking about Canadian Youth," creates a forum for scholars to develop contentions about youth based on current research in such topic areas as vandalism, unemployment, and the subcultural attraction of funk music. Also in this section are two articles that address the urban Aboriginal youth experience in British Columbia and the rise of Canadian female juvenile offenders. Part 3, "Hearing the Voices of Canadian Youth," presents six examples of empirical research conducted by Canadian scholars on Canadian youth. Topics addressed in this section are youth work camps as correctional facilities, secondary school experiences, black youth–police relations, sports and violence, subcultures and gang violence, and cyberskating on the Internet.

This volume is not intended to serve as the quintessential statement about Canadian youth but rather as a new initiation into the practice of looking at ourselves and attempting to understand our own young people. The scholars from across Canada who contributed original articles to this volume laboured long and hard to provide the most current information available within their own area of inquiry. Many of those scholars wrote with the goals of educating and informing in mind, but the overall thrust of this volume is to encourage others—students and faculty alike—to consider undertaking their own socio-logical inquiries into Canadian youth by whatever means they feel most comfortable with. Only then will we be more equipped to move toward a better understanding of what it means to be an adolescent in Canadian society in the 1990s.

From the outset, I envisioned this volume as a companion to existing comprehensive texts in the areas of youth, deviance, crime, law, social policy, and social/legal reform. From personal experience, the adoption of two volumes (a text and a reader) provides a more balanced overview for students and faculty, especially those who must contend with extremely large classes. Moreover, because the book uses this dual approach, it more easily suggests stimulating ideas for challenging research essays, since this combination inevitably addresses a wider range of topics and includes the most current references available to facilitate further inquiries.

I feel obliged to say one last word about the title of this volume, *Not a Kid Anymore.* Throughout the years of musicianship and songwriting, I found myself creating challenging arrangements, constructing pleasing melodies, and writing fairly expressive lyrics, but when it came to devising song titles I often failed to capture the true essence of the composition. With this track record in mind, deciding what title to place on this volume was a task that I met with increasing trepidation. While preparing the manuscript, however, I had the occasion to screen the classic movie *The Gene Krupa Story*, a fairly accurate Hollywood portrayal of the late "drummer boy's" life. Early in the film, 16-year-old Gene, played by Sal Mineo, gets a chance to play professionally with an array of adult musicians. Though he is eager to become a full-fledged member of the orchestra, his parents detest jazz music and the "immoral" speakeasy settings in which Gene would be obligated to perform. An argument ensues. His parents remind Gene that he is not yet an adult and should not aspire to participate in adult activities. They forbid him to continue to play with the orchestra, even though he is the most inspired and innovative member.

What is Gene's comeback? To his parents he calmly states, "I'm not a kid anymore." By virtue of his age, 16-year-old Gene Krupa was still considered by the state to be of lower status than adult, albeit somewhat higher than a child. In actuality, Gene fell into the large category known as adolescence. However, by virtue of his wide variety of rhythmic gifts, an impeccable sense of timing (a must for all great drummers), and an electrifying stage presence, even a young Gene Krupa was more talented than most adult drummers. This placed Gene in a very difficult position, but he managed to free himself from it by his consistent adherence to perfecting his drumming and performance skills. But the comment to his parents—"I'm not a kid anymore"—really started me thinking, because it contains at least a dual meaning, depending on who says it.

In the context of a young person articulating this phrase to an adult, the term connotes the young person's desire to enter the world of adulthood, perhaps prematurely. The term demands the young person's acceptance by adults on adult terms, and it serves notice to all who listen that the realm of childhood will be abandoned, perhaps permanently. In brief, the term exists as the proclamation that the youth considers him/herself to actually be an adult, regardless of age. On the other hand, when an adult utters this phrase in response to some social or legal infraction committed by a young person, the meaning of the term is severely altered. Now the same term means that the young person has failed (to some degree) to live up to the imagined standards of adulthood and, in the perception of the adult, has reverted to some display of childish behaviour. Taken further, this perceived retroactivity often carries with it some form of negative sanction ranging from verbal putdowns, groundings, and/or physical punishment at the hands of adult figures, to legal sanctions at the hands of police, youth courts, and correctional facilities.

So how should adolescents deal with this dichotomy? If one believes that Canadian youth are "growing up faster these days," then the phrase *not a kid anymore* holds increasing relevance, since it captures the predicament that the vast majority of young people will find themselves in at some point on their journey toward adulthood. For those who reject the notion that youth are developing faster than in previous years, one may consider the cryptic messages contained in *True Lies*, a recent blockbuster action thriller starring Arnold Schwarzenegger, Tom Arnold, and Jamie Lee Curtis.

Viewed by millions of adults and young people throughout the world in theatres and on video, this film offhandedly presents a very strong statement about the youth of today, hidden amid the sensational displays of espionage, technology, and violence. Early in the film, Albert Gibson (played by Tom Arnold) secretly places a hidden camera in the home of Harry Tasker (played by Arnold Schwarzenegger) to guard Gibson's suit jacket and to demonstrate to Tasker his technological brilliance. While they are marvelling at the image that appears in a pair of sunglasses, Tasker's 14-year-old daughter Dana steals $200 in cash from Gibson's jacket in full view of Tasker, who is wearing the glasses. Unable to stop Dana before she rushes off to school on the back of her boyfriend's motorcycle, Tasker demonstrates a state of remorse, since he feels that he and his wife Helen (played by Jamie Lee Curtis) have "taught her better than that." Gibson attempts to contextualize the theft for Tasker:

> Yeah, but you are not her parents anymore, you and Helen. Her parents are Axel Rose and Madonna. The five minutes a day you spend with her can't compete with that type of bombardment. You're outgunned, daddy-o. It's not that you're a bad parent, but kids are ten years ahead of where we were at the same age.

By virtue of its wide dissemination, this socially sanctioned film confirms the perception, in the minds of millions of adults and young people, that today's youth are growing up faster. Since it appears in this socially sanctioned film, the assertion may be adopted as social fact by the millions of viewers who paid to view the film or rent the video. Moreover, Dana is presented as a very contemporary example of a young woman dealing with the difficulties of adolescence. But the film leaves her theft of $200 from a family friend largely unresolved, so viewers are left with the impression that her criminal method of satisfying her material needs is absorbed by the adult world. In effect, even though her birth certificate relegates Dana to the status of adolescent, she appears to believe that she is dealing with social life in adult terms. Could her awkwardness in the transition from child to adult be similar to that of other youth?

The increased demands placed on young people, their desire to escape the throes of childhood and participate in adult activities, their desperate need to feel acceptance by adults—all appear to have increased markedly based on the assumption that "kids are growing up faster" than they ever did before. To my mind at least, the two meanings contained in the frequently used phrase *not a kid anymore* succinctly capture the difficult stage of adolescence. Furthermore, used as the title of this volume, the phrase assumes added significance and increased relevance in that these essays attempt to situate the changing dynamics and lived experiences of contemporary Canadian youth.

Acknowledgments

I would like to extend my appreciation to a number of people who assisted me in the preparation of *Not a Kid Anymore*. Heather Martin, Margot Hanis, Charlotte Forbes, Bob Kohlmeier, and their colleagues at Nelson Canada were invaluable in assisting with the development and production of this volume. Thanks also to Nelson's Chester White. I extend my gratitude to my entire family for giving me support and encouragement. To all of the students I have had the distinct pleasure of teaching, I sincerely hope that this volume helps you in your research interests. To my special friends, the one and only Baby Doll, Skylark, Delicia, Frankiepank, Dudeman, Noogster, Jakester, Hankster and Carole, the Tedders, King and Kath, Biff Steel, Rocko, Old Mill, Kookie, Guzzi, Rocky, Tootsie, Brian, Terri, Tammy, Clint, Stangley, and Speciole, thank you for sharing the high points and supporting me through the trying times.

Gary M. O'Bireck
July 1995

PART 1

Thinking about Canadian Youth: Theoretical and Methodological Perspectives

When sociologists speculate about why events occur or, more specifically, what causes something to happen, they refer to this process as theorizing. Almost everyone holds opinions, feelings, beliefs, and even personal "theories" about a plethora of occurrences in Canadian society, but until these contentions are tested scientifically, supported with existing literature, or buttressed with empirical research, they remain mere opinions and beliefs. It takes rigorous testing and supporting evidence to move personal beliefs into the realm of sociological theory.

To illustrate: As an undergraduate I operated a rehearsal/recording studio in an upper-class area of a large Canadian city. The sound of the music produced in this facility attracted many upper-class youth to the restaurant located directly below. Over time I became quite friendly with a small group of these youth and began to interact with them on a social basis. Through this interaction I was fortunate enough to be allowed to informally observe their behaviour patterns and hear their attitudes in relation to a wide array of topics—school, parents, peers, crime, police, the Young Offenders Act, music, money, sex, films, cars, relationships. By observing and interacting with these young people, I came to believe that the affluent social position they occupied bore some relationship to their attitudes and behaviours. Exactly what that relationship was, I was not completely sure, but I certainly had my opinions.

These opinions may have constituted a personal theory, but I had not yet entered the realm of sociological theory since this "hypothesis" of mine had not been tested scientifically. Not being in the position to run a full-blown study, I attempted to verify my beliefs by consulting other theorists and researchers who had conducted work in a similar area using the variables of youth, socioeconomic status, crime, and deviance. To my surprise my search through a wide variety of theories failed to turn up a consensus.

What I gathered from this literature search was that sociological theories are certainly not "written in stone" but are merely attempted explanations for phenomena. As well, no single theory is completely correct, all-encompassing, or thoroughly accepted by everyone studying the social sciences. Instead, all sociological theories can be revised with current empirical research; all can be questioned, expanded, and even completely rejected, providing one produces substantial evidence to support one's own view.

Moreover, by delving into the research, I became aware that some theoretical perspectives were constructed very rigidly in what sociologists refer to as a "deterministic" or "causal" framework. By contrast, others were much less rigid in their development, their contentions formulated on what sociologists commonly refer to as a "naturalistic" form of inquiry into social life. The more deterministic theories tended to involve research conducted with many subjects over a short period of time. Researchers who conducted this type of examination invariably felt quite confident in extrapolating their results to include large groups of people. Again, by contrast, naturalistic inquiries tended to involve research conducted with a small number of actors in their own settings over relatively long periods of time. For these researchers, gaining the ability to make broad assumptions about some aspect of social life was certainly not their objective. Instead, these researchers and theorists attempted only to understand, in great detail, the life processes their actors passed through in order to reach their current social situations.

Acquiring this theoretical knowledge also made me realize that no universal agreement existed in relation to whether socioeconomic status affected the attitudes and behaviour patterns of youth. While some theorists believed there was a connection, others steadfastly maintained that little evidence supported it. The clarification I sought for my opinions would have to be attained through my own devices—that is, by developing a research instrument that would allow me to study these adolescents more closely. Since theory and methods are very closely linked in sociology, I set out to develop a research strategy that would best serve my needs.

Should I attempt to evaluate this problem quantitatively (using numbers and percentages taken from surveys), qualitatively (using the actual words of the actors from interviews and group discussions, and recording gestures and body language from participant observations), or both? Since the parameters of this inquiry were quite small, I decided to conduct a pilot study—that is, an exploratory endeavour designed to determine whether a more detailed investigation is warranted. Additionally, I decided to adopt both methodological strategies to evaluate my problem.

Armed with a carefully crafted "youth survey," I began contacting these young people and requesting that they complete the questionnaires in my presence so that I could gauge their body language, hear their voices, and offer explanations if need be. Very early on in this process of data collection, I realized that I was more comfortable talking to, interacting with, and observing these young people over time than simply having them complete a survey once and then suspending our association. In short, longer-term interaction seemed more "real" to me.

In an effort to arrive at some level of completeness, I continued to employ both methodological strategies. Quantitatively, I administered questionnaires to all of these young people, tabulated the results, and then used these data to assist in the overall analysis of the problem. Qualitatively, I held open-ended and unstructured interviews, engaged actors in group discussions, observed their behaviour, and recorded all of these findings in field notes. Eventually, this combination of methodological strategies allowed me to arrive at the theoretical conclusion that socioeconomic status does have an effect on youth attitudes and behaviour patterns, at least in this setting. But since this inquiry was only a pilot study, the conclusions are tempered somewhat.

This illustration serves the purpose of offering a brief, albeit cursory, overview of how students may conceptualize and employ sociological theory and methods in their own research endeavours. In Chapter 1 of this section, an increasingly more detailed and sophisticated agenda is provided by Robert Prus. "Adolescent Life-Worlds and Deviant Involvements: A Research Agenda for Studying Adolescence as Lived Experience" provides the reader with an organizational template for conducting sociological inquiries of youth from the symbolic interactionist theoretical perspective. Moreover, this author details the process of conducting research ethnographically and addresses the emergent study of youth subcultures within the social context of community life.

In Chapter 2, Livy Visano presents a thorough examination of the overwhelming effects of youth crime statistics, routinely projected by various forms of media, and how this process shapes the perceptions and self-perceptions of young people. "What Do 'They' Know? Delinquency as Mediated Texts" offers a postmodernist argument that develops the idea that Canadian delinquency is constituted by relations of power that are mediated by cultural forms of the media, thereby marginalizing Canadian youth.

Chapter 3 considers two classic, yet opposing, philosophies contained in Canadian law: "doing good" (inclusion) and "doing justice" (exclusion). In "Doing Good or Doing Justice: The Juvenile Delinquents Act and the Young Offenders Act," Anna Leslie expertly compares and contrasts these two different approaches to judicial organization with the JDA and the YOA, by incorporating elements of both a social control and a conflict theoretical perspective.

CHAPTER 1

Adolescent Life-Worlds and Deviant Involvements:[1]
A Research Agenda for Studying Adolescence as Lived Experience[2]

Robert Prus
University of Waterloo

Thinking is a process of conversation with one's self when the individual takes the attitude of the other, especially when he takes the common attitude of the whole group, when the symbol that he uses is a common symbol, so that it has a meaning common to the entire group, to everyone who is in it and anyone who might be in it. It is a process of communication with participation in the experience of other people.
[Mead 1936:380–381]

Some people tend to shroud adolescent life-worlds and deviance involvements in mystique. In contrast, in this chapter I set out a research agenda that builds on studies of human lived experience in other arenas of community life, and show how the study of adolescent and deviant life-worlds can contribute to a more thorough understanding of community life.

Working from a symbolic interactionist perspective (Mead 1934; Blumer 1969), I will draw attention to the need for examining adolescent involvements and activities (a) within the community contexts in which they occur, (b) in ways that consider the meanings the participants have for the activities at hand, and (c) with respect to the processes by which human action and interchange take place.

The term "adolescent" is used here more or less synonymously with the term "teenager" to denote that interim time of life when one is no longer seen as a high-dependency, childlike being but has not yet been accorded the full rights and obligations associated with adulthood.[3] "Deviance" is in many respects the more important term here, since it more clearly conjures up notions of morality—disrespectability on the one hand and trouble and community reaction on the other.

The term "deviance," as used here, refers to any human activity, appearance, or thoughts that some audience (self and/or others) perceives as negative. Negative qualities could be assigned to any other objects (i.e., spirits, animals, inanimate objects), but we are concerned primarily with those attributed to particular people or sets of people. Considerable differences regarding what constitutes "deviance" or "real deviance" may exist between communities and among people within particular communities; it should also be recognized that the same people may dramatically alter their notions of deviance over time. Likewise, people may ascribe mixed definitions (deviant and otherwise; e.g., dangerous, but exciting) to particular targets, as well as invoke all sorts of qualifications that intensify or diminish what they envision as the deviant features of the situations at hand. Noteworthy, too, is that people can and do promote particular definitions of deviance and respectability as well as resist and challenge viewpoints others hold.

In this chapter I do not intend to judge adolescent moralities and wisdoms, nor do I intend to remedy or improve adolescent situations in any manner. Rather, my purpose is to provide researchers with a theoretical approach, a set of concepts, and a methodology for achieving intimate familiarity with adolescent life-worlds. While this material is exceedingly relevant to adolescent "deviance," it is even more applicable to the study of adolescent life-worlds in general. Indeed, the model presented here for studying human behaviour will enable us to better understand people's behaviours in *any* situation across a range of settings.

In what follows, I introduce symbolic interactionism as a theoretical approach to the study of human lived experience. Next, I examine ethnographic research as a method for studying the human condition. I then discuss subcultures and the particular relevance of subcultural life-worlds for the study of adolescent experiences and activities. In the last part of the chapter, I present a process-oriented research agenda for examining the life-worlds (deviant and otherwise) in which adolescents find themselves involved. Since all of these themes merit much more attention than I can pay them here, I must caution readers about the necessarily cryptic or truncated nature of this discussion. That being said, I hope that this overview will enable readers to appreciate the need to consider adolescent life-worlds and deviant involvements as instances of human lived experience that can be understood only within the context of ongoing community life.

✱ Symbolic Interaction and the Study of Human Lived Experience

> Symbolic interaction rests in the last analysis on three simple premises. The first premise is that human beings act toward things on the basis of the meanings they have for them ... The second premise is that the meaning of such things is derived from, or arises out of, the social interaction that one has with one's fellows. The third premise is that these meanings are handled in, and modified through, an interpretative process used by the person in dealing with the things he encounters. [Blumer 1969:2]

Although the points that Herbert Blumer (1900–1984) outlines in the preceding quotation seem both simple and basic to everyday understandings of human group life, they have profound implications for the questions of what constitutes "social science" and how one is to approach the study of human life-worlds, such as those of the adolescence experience. Symbolic interactionism is the study of how people make sense of their life situations and how they go about their activities, in conjunction with others, on a day-to-day basis. It is very much a down-to-earth approach; its notions of how human group life is accomplished are firmly grounded in the day-to-day practices and experiences of the people whose lives one purports to study.

Symbolic interactionism was developed mainly by George Herbert Mead (1934) and Herbert George Blumer (1969).[4] These two men were inspired mainly by the hermeneutics (interpretive understanding) of Wilhelm Dilthey, and by American pragmatism, which emphasized the practical accomplishment of human activity. As well, interactionism has been informed by Cooley's (1909) method of "sympathetic introspection" (more commonly known as ethnographic research or field research), which requires that researchers immerse themselves in the life-worlds of those they study and attempt to appreciate how people make sense of the world as they know it.

Central to the interactionist approach is the notion that human life is *community* life; that *human life is thoroughly intersubjective in its essence*. This approach recognizes that human behaviour cannot be understood in isolation from the community. Humans derive their (social) essences from the communities in which they are located, and human communities are built on shared (or intersubjectively acknowledged) symbols or languages. In sum, there can be no self without the (community) other.

While people may be born with physiological capacities of sorts, an individual awareness of the world (i.e., ability to learn, think, and create) depends on the acquisition of a (community-based) language. It is only through language (and interacting with others) that humans can acquire a "stock of knowledge" or develop a mind. Only through language can individuals distinguish and make sense of the objects (including themselves) that constitute their worlds.

In the course of learning the language of a community, people begin to acquire rudimentary understandings or perspectives on human life-worlds. Only after they develop rudimentary understandings of "the world" do they begin to exhibit some sort of reflectivity and meaningful human agency. Only after acquiring a language-based set of understandings can people take themselves into account in developing and pursuing particular lines of action. As Mead observes, it is language that makes the possession of a "self" possible:

> The language process is essential for the development of the self. The self has a character which is different from that of the physiological organism proper. The self is something which has a development; it is not initially there at birth, but arises in the process of social experience and activity, that is, arises in the process of social experience and activity. [Mead 1934:135]

Language acquisition and use, therefore, is at the core of human intersubjectivity. Only when people share sets of symbols can they communicate with one another, and show awareness of the viewpoints of others. People who share common language do not automatically act rationally or cooperatively. However, language provides the basis for people to establish common (community) understandings; and it is through ongoing (symbolic) interaction with the other that one may establish more precise levels of intersubjectivity or more comprehensive understandings of the perspectives of the other, as well as more intricate senses of self.

While human worlds are symbolically or linguistically constructed (i.e., effectively denoting multiple symbolic realities), *the human world is also a world of activity*. Thus, just as one cannot reduce the study of human behaviour to the study of individual qualities, similarly one cannot reduce human behaviour to symbolic or linguistic realities, even though people's activities are meaningful only within the symbolic frameworks that humans collectively develop in the course of their existence.[5] Some human activity is directly predicated on the struggle for existence in an environment that is often physically hostile; but human behaviour has many other bases besides this one. In fact, humans may direct their attention to an infinite number of areas. Indeed, because of the diverse meanings that people are able to attach to any objects of their awareness, researchers must be especially attentive to the ways that people assign (and alter) those meanings, and to the ways that they distinguish, define, and act toward these experiential essences.

People do not merely act toward objects. As self-reflective, interacting beings, people direct, monitor, assess, and adjust their own behaviours toward objects (which include other people and the self). This has profound implications for the study of human behaviour.

People are capable of learning through "object association" or conditioning; however, because of the intersubjective nature of the human condition, humans can greatly transcend the modes of learning associated with other mammal species. The human capacity for intersubjectivity, as indicated by language and cultural development, meaningful interaction, self-reflectivity, and minded behaviour, introduces complexities that require a theoretical and methodological approach that is entirely different from those which may be appropriate for studying other animals (including the most sophisticated nonhuman mammals).

Likewise, it is not enough to ask about people's attitudes or backgrounds and to try to correlate these in some manner with people's behaviours (or the consequences of their behaviours). People are not like billiard balls; their direction and movements are not mindlessly determined by external forces.[6] Nor, as Blumer (1969) correctly argues, are people simply mediums through which various forces or variables may find expression. People *think;* they interpret, they define, they locate themselves in the setting, they anticipate, they act, they interact, they assess, and they adjust, mindfully. Although people need not act "wisely" or "sensibly," one clearly cannot study the human condition without carefully considering the very features that are distinctively human. Any "science of human behaviour" should respect, both conceptually and methodologically, the intersubjective features of the human condition.

Mindful of these concerns as they pertain to field research, it may be instructive to specify a set of assumptions that people working within an interactionist/interpretive tradition normally make (sometimes explicitly, sometimes implicitly) when they study human lived experience. These assumptions are expressed in the following points:

1. *Human group life is intersubjective.* Human group life reflects a shared linguistic or symbolic reality that takes its shape as people interact with one another. Human group life is community life and cannot be reduced to individual properties. All meaningful essences, including the more solitary experiences and activities of (linguistic) members of human groups, derive from or are built on comprehensions of "the reality of the other."

2. *Human group life is (multi)perspectival.* There is no singular or objective reality that people experience in some uniform manner. Rather, it is recognized that people distinguish and develop meanings for [objects] as they interact with one another and develop styles of relating to those objects. This process is known as symbolization.[7] When groups of people arrive at a consensus as to the existence and meanings of particular objects, they tend to envision their definitions of situations as "real" or "objective."[8] To understand a particular group of people, one must carefully consider what these groups consider "real." It is these paramount "realities" that provide a means for us to understand people's participation in the situations at hand. People operate in versions of (multiple) realities, which they share (albeit imperfectly) with others at an "intersubjective" level.

3. *Human group life is reflective.* Through interaction with others, and by taking the viewpoint of the other with respect to oneself, people develop the capacity to become objects of their own awareness. Through what Mead (1934) terms "role-taking," people can attribute meanings to their own "essences" and develop lines of action that take themselves (and other objects) into account. When people can see themselves from the standpoint of the other, and when they can "converse with themselves," meaningful initiative (i.e., human agency, enterprise, intentionality) is fostered; people learn to act in ways that take themselves into account. As reflective entities, people may pursue activities on their own as well as resist activities imposed on them by others. (It is not assumed that people will act "wisely" or will be successful in their undertakings.)

4. *Human group life is activity based.* Human behaviour is meaningful only within intersubjectively mediated contexts; this implies an ongoing interpretive process with respect to both solitary and collective behaviours. Human group life is organized around the doing, constructing, creating, building, forging, coordinating, and adjusting of behaviour. Activity draws our attention to the matter of ongoing enterprise, to the constituent notions of defining, anticipating, invoking, encountering resistance, accomplishing, experiencing failure, reassessing, and adjusting—on both interactive as well as more solitary behavioural levels.

5. *Human group life is negotiable.* This assumption further acknowledges that people can and do influence and resist the influences of others, but makes the interactive dimension of human reflectivity more explicit. Thus, notions of cooperation, competition, conflict, and compromise are central to human interaction. Although all matters of interaction may be quite uneven, some element of mutuality, sharedness, or intersubjectivity is evident whenever people respond to or try to shape the behaviours of others.

6. *Human group life is relational.* People do not associate with one another in a random or undifferentiated manner; rather, they tend to associate somewhat selectively with others as they bond with the community. This acknowledges the differing identities (i.e., self and other definitions) that people attach to one another, as well as the loyalties, disaffections, and other interactional styles that emerge between people in the course of human interaction. Many of the activities in which people engage are made particularly meaningful and shaped in certain ways because of people's attentiveness to specific others in the setting. Thus, ensuing definitions and negotiations of reality (including language), depend centrally on people's involvements and embeddedness in particular groups or affiliational networks within the broader community of others.

7. *Human group life is processual.* Human lived experiences are viewed as emergent or ongoing social constructions or productions. The emphasis is on how human group life is shaped by people as they work out their activities in conjunction with others at this, that, and other points in time. While intersubjectivity, particular world views, reflectivity, negotiated interchange, and relationships are all central to the interactionist approach to the study of human lived experience, so is the matter of process.

Process is basic to an understanding of these other themes. Intersubjectivity (and the sharing of symbolic realities) is an ongoing process. Perspectives are also best approached in process terms, as the meanings that people attach to objects are developed, acted upon, and changed over time. Likewise, reflectivity is not only a product of ongoing association, but assumes its significance as "human agency" when people go about their activities. Reflectivity becomes expressed as people engage in instances of definition, interpretation, intentionality, assessment, and minded adjustments over time. Activity is most appropriately examined in process terms: people define situations, make indications to themselves regarding future states, and monitor and readjust their behaviours as they work their way through situations both on a solitary basis and in conjunction with others. Negotiation or interchange also assumes a processual dimension as people endeavour to shape their relations with others. Matters of influence and resistance not only imply the pursuit of particular interests but draw attention to people's capacities to assume roles as both targets and tacticians in their encounters with others. Relationships, as well, are most effectively examined in processual terms (or as having natural histories) with respect to their emergence, intensification, dissipation, and possible reconstitution, as people define themselves and attempt to deal with those with whom they associate over time. The conceptual and methodological implication is this: since all aspects of group life take place in process terms or take their shape over time, it is essential that the human condition be studied in ways that are acutely mindful of the emergent nature of human lived experience.

✸ Doing Ethnographic Research: The Quest for Intimate Familiarity[9]

Sympathetic introspection, putting himself in intimate contact with various sorts of persons and allowing them to awake in himself a life similar to their own, which he afterwards to the best of his ability, recalls and describes. In this way he is more or less able to understand—always by introspection—children, idiots, criminals, rich and poor, conservative and radical—any phase of human nature not wholly alien to his own. [Cooley 1909:7]

Since people differ from other objects of study by virtue of their interpretive (and interactive) capacities, those embarking on studies of the human condition need to be sensitive to the "double hermeneutic" (i.e., the task of interpreting entities that themselves interpret the worlds they experience).[10] The "objects" (people and their activities) that social scientists study not only interpret other aspects of their worlds, but they also disclose (and recast) their interpretations as they interact with others and reflect upon their experiences in the course of their daily routines. Further, not only may people attempt to make sense of researchers' attempts to study them, but as skilled interactants in their own right, they may act back on the researchers. They can help researchers by openly sharing aspects of their worlds. They can also withhold cooperation, engage in purposive deception, and embark on other types of evasive and concealing activity. The message is clear: social scientists require a methodology that is thoroughly sensitive to the human capacity for "symbolic interaction."

Human behaviour is a socially contextualized, ongoing interactive process. To ignore any of the features of group life discussed earlier (intersubjectivity, multiple perspectives, reflectivity, activity, negotiability, relationships, and processes) is to violate central qualities of our subject matter. If we are to be true to our subject matter (i.e., human group life), we should be attentive to all of these aspects of human association.

The research implications of these assumptions are profound. People studying people should consider (a) the intersubjective nature of human behaviour; (b) the viewpoints of those whose worlds they examine; (c) the interpretations or meanings that people attach to themselves, to other people, and to other objects of their experience; (d) the ways that people accomplish their activities on a "here and now" basis; (e) the attempts that people make to influence (as well as accommodate and resist) the inputs and behaviours of others; (f) the bonds that people develop with others over time, and the ways in which they attend to these relationships; and (g) the processes, natural histories or sequences of encounters, exchanges, and events that people develop and experience.

While every ethnography (interactive study of the way of life of a group of people) will establish its own emphases, ethnographers generally rely on three main sources of data: observation, participant observation, and interviews.

Observation encompasses not only those things that one directly sees and hears, but also any documents, diaries, records, and the like that one may find in a particular setting. These materials can be valuable, but one must recognize that the worth of any observation or artifact depends on the researcher's clear understanding of how it was experienced and constructed by those being studied. On its own, observational material cannot provide enough material for an ethnographic study, because the researcher would have to make extensive inferences regarding people's meanings and intentions. However, observational materials can be very valuable in helping researchers formulate questions to be pursued in interviews; they can also provide a means of assessing and contextualizing the information obtained through interviews and participant observation.

Participant observation adds an entirely different and vital dimension to the notion of observation. Although this practice has often been dismissed as "biased" or "subjective" by those who think that researchers should distance themselves from their subjects, the participant observer role allows the researcher to get infinitely closer to the lived experiences of the participants. Still, while their own experiences may afford researchers invaluable vantage points for appreciating certain aspects of this or that life-world, and may also enable them to access the experiences of others in the setting in a much more meaningful fashion (i.e., than through questionnaires or experiments), researcher participants in the field should strive for as much balance as possible by attending openly to the experiences of all of those who constitute the setting under consideration.

Like those doing straight observation, researchers engaged in participant observation normally try to remain fairly unobtrusive or nondisruptive in the setting being studied. However, this strategy requires a more active (and interactive) role as researchers attempt to fit into the settings at hand. Insofar as participant observation allows researchers to experience first-hand some aspects of the life-world of the other, it offers a rather unique and instructive form of data. Also, since it typically puts researchers in close, sustained contact with others, it allows one to gain insights through ongoing commentary and other interactions. Participant observation thus provides a doubly privileged form of contact.

Interviews represent the third major method of gathering ethnographic data. In some circumstances they may be the primary source of data for field researchers. By inquiring extensively into the experiences of others, interviewers may learn a great deal about the life-worlds of others. Interviews should not be seen as substitutes for more extensive involvement; however, when researchers are able to establish a good working rapport with others and can inspire trust and openness, they may obtain much insight into the life situations of these other people.

Ethnographers sometimes develop fairly extensive interview formats, but these are best allowed to take shape in the field as researchers learn more about the situations and the participants involved. The ethnographic interview is characterized by careful and receptive listening, open-ended queries, and extensive probing. It reflects a generalized curiosity about the situation of the other. Sets of questions are developed as the researcher spends more time in the setting and the company of the other. Researchers in the field vary greatly in how they approach interviews; generally, however, greater receptivity and a willingness to let the other "talk back" is fundamental to the interview "relationship."

Unless the effort is made to uncover, ascertain, and qualify the meanings that others hold for objects in their life-worlds, and to learn how people go about their daily lives, it makes little sense to talk about studying human lived experience. While each research setting is somewhat different from the next (as is each encounter with the same person), one generally gets better data, and more data, by spending more time in the setting and by more fully participating in the life-world of the other. When researchers can gather observational, participant observation, and interview data more or less at the same time, this generally leads to a more complete understanding of the other. Researchers who immerse themselves in the setting are not only more likely to be exposed to a wider and deeper range of materials; they are typically much better situated to inquire about, pursue, and assess incoming information gleaned through all of these techniques.

✳ The Human Community and Subcultural Involvements

> Every gang tends to develop its own code of conduct, of which its members
> are more or less aware and which may be more or less rigidly enforced upon
> them [200] ... While the nature of the gang code varies in different groups,
> depending on differences in social environment and experiences, it tends to
> include in every case some form of expression of primary-group virtues, or
> moral attitudes which focus about the group rather than the welfare of its
> individual members. [202] ... *To understand the gang boy one must enter into*
> *his world with a comprehension, on the one hand, of this seriousness behind*
> *his mask of flippancy or bravado, and on the other, of the role of the roman-*
> *tic in his activities and in his interpretation of the larger world of reality.* [96]
> [Thrasher 1927 (1963)]

As implied in the discussion of multiple realities, every human community and
every group within a particular human community may adopt different orientations toward the world. Without discussing these diversities in great detail,
it may be useful to note that communities typically consist of networks upon
networks of people associating with one another. Each group in the larger
community may share features with others in that setting, but each group also
develops its own set of understandings and practices over time. While considerable overlap may characterize certain groups in the broader community, it is
most instructive to consider how each subcommunity, subculture, or group
within the broader community may be distinguished with respect to five
dimensions—perspectives, activities, identities, relationships, and commitments. These dimensions are central to the study of life-worlds generally; they
may be especially valuable in the study of adolescent life-worlds and deviant
involvements, since a great deal of adolescent lived experience is situated
within particular subcultural contexts. Thus, I will discuss these five dimensions briefly before considering adolescent life-worlds more specifically.

Subcultures are characterized by interaction, a sense of identity (distinctiveness), and some continuity over time.[11] They are a central theme in the
study of adolescent life-worlds more generally and deviance specifically.[12] As
sites where it "all comes together," subcultures often represent the focal points
of a great deal of activity ("deviant" and otherwise).

Some subcultural themes are very widespread and diffuse (e.g., the notions
of "youth," "sports," or "drug" subcultures; however, for most purposes,
subcultures are defined by their more immediate networks of associations and
their more situated activities. People involved in more general subcultural
movements may share certain viewpoints, engage in somewhat parallel practices,

follow some common celebrities (e.g., in the media), and so on. They may also be involved with others in somewhat similar themes on a national or international level (e.g., consider music, fashion, and religious subcultures), and they may from time to time interact with people from other communities. However, most people's subcultural involvements are largely defined by the more immediate groupings to which they belong on a here-and-now basis.

Likewise, we should consider the much smaller subcultures or group affiliations that people develop on a very local or immediate level. These local subcultures, as represented by groups, cliques, associations, clubs, gangs, and ongoing friendships, may not be very elaborate, but they are likely to be the focus of some very central adolescent experiences.[13] These local groups may involve only two or three people; because of their situated relevance on a day-to-day, moment-to-moment basis, they can be particularly important in defining and shaping adolescent life experiences. Even so, one must appreciate that these smaller subcultures are embedded within larger adolescent subcultural contexts; thus we may expect some movement across subgroups within these larger subcultural settings. We may also expect a variety of monitoring and adjustive practices as members of smaller groups attend to broader sets of others in various ways (admire, reject, cooperate, compete, conflict) as life in the larger theatre unfolds, and as the lives and experiences of others intersect with their own in this and that manner.

People are much more likely to join subcultures when they know others who already belong; subcultures tend to be much looser, less well organized, and less distinct than is commonly portrayed in the media (Simmons 1969:88–92). People involved in subcultures typically are subject to considerable ambivalence relating to belongingness, identity, perspectives, and loyalty. They are also exposed to possible rejection, internal factions, conflicts, and animosities.[14] Individual involvements thus reflect ongoing assessments, dilemmas, and negotiations as those participating in particular contexts attempt to work out their lives in conjunction with others. Mindful of these qualifications, in the next few pages I will consider relationships, perspectives, activities, identities, and commitments associated with subcultural involvements. These themes are interconnected in various ways, so that a discussion of one almost inevitably requires consideration of the others.

Developing Relationships

For those who become involved in subcultural contexts, "fitting in," or developing viable working and personal associations with the other participants, is a key consideration.[15] Although people sometimes achieve some acceptance in particular groups by virtue of their presence in these settings for extended periods of time, people are generally most readily accepted by the other participants when they (a) are introduced into the setting by existing participants, and (b) are seen to represent opportunities or resources by which other participants may realize desired ends. Also, newcomers are more likely to feel comfortable in subcultural contexts when (c) others take an active interest in ensuring their fuller participation. In the short run, this involves someone introducing newcomers to others, informing them of prevailing practices, and providing some encouragement in the face of immediate anxiety or adversity. In the long run, these relationships, and those that people may later develop, are critical to success (and continuity) within particular subcultural contexts, for subcultural involvements involve ongoing associations with others. Conversely, the development of factions and animosities among insiders may be a key factor in people's decisions to disengage themselves from particular subcultural groupings.

Acquiring Perspectives

A second facet of subcultural involvement has to do with newcomers accepting and later helping to perpetuate group perspectives or world views. Those with associates (e.g., friends, relatives) already involved in the setting are more likely to accept group perspectives that jar with their earlier viewpoints. This is because people tend to trust their associates, and because people tend to enjoy the role of tutor or facilitator. Still, note that even before contact with the group, the newcomer may have held a viewpoint that was similar to the group's.[16]

Even when group perspectives are not well articulated, or are only partially accepted by the participants, the rationales generated in subcultural contexts may still advantage group members over their solitary counterparts, who have to work things out more entirely on their own. To the extent that group perspectives suggest a shared or seemingly "objective" reality—what Schutz (1962) termed "intersubjective consensus"—subcultural perspectives allow participants to normalize if not positively emphasize activities and actors that may be considered "deviant" by others (see also Goffman 1963; Higgins 1979; Evans and Falk 1986; Sanders 1991; and Wolf 1991).

Doing Activities

The third major component of subcultural involvements revolves around the "activities" particular involvements entail. Subcultures represent "apprenticeship forums." They are places to learn certain kinds of skills, often with the encouragement and tutelage of others.

In formulating the theory of "differential association," Sutherland (1939) observed that both the *orientations* (perspectives) that people developed toward crime and the *techniques* they acquired for engaging in criminal activities were learned mainly through intimate association with particular sets of others. People's involvements in deviant activities are centrally related to the pursuits of their associates. Although people may not accept these life-worlds as their own, their (subculturally involved) associates may encourage their involvement in some very noteworthy respects. As Becker (1963) observed in his study of marijuana users, subculturally involved associates may not only provide newcomers with justification for activities; but they also may teach newcomers techniques for engaging in activities, selectively define and focus their attention on the "enjoyable" aspects of these experiences, and help neutralize any discomforting aspects of the experience.

Sutherland's and Becker's ideas have been substantiated by a great deal of ethnographic research on deviance and on nondeviant involvements.[17] People's ongoing (subcultural) activities may be greatly facilitated by the networks that participants develop between themselves and their "supporting others" (e.g., partners, suppliers, clients, assistants). To the extent that their activities are group events, the participants typically enjoy an advantage over solitary actors in regard to the planning, implementation, and aftermath of any activities in which they participate. Newcomers are less likely to experience "stage fright" (Lyman and Scott 1970:159–188) as a consequence of group encouragement; and besides obtaining the assistance of others in conducting the focal activity, participants are also more likely to receive support in resolving many of the difficulties that emerge in the entire course of their involvement.[18]

Achieving Identity

Subcultural affiliations also help participants sharpen and sustain "identities" (i.e., self and collectively developed images of self) and reputations as certain kinds of people. Those participating in groups find it easier to develop terms (identities) to refer to styles and variations of membership participation.

Some subcultures involve more "identifiers" (e.g., practices and modes of expression) that are readily visible to both insiders and outsiders (Klapp 1969). These group "markers" set participants apart from others in the community (e.g., outlaw bikers' paraphernalia—Wolf 1991; tattoos—Sanders 1991). By becoming known as "certain kinds of people," members of subcultures may become subject to various inclusions and exclusions that make them more likely to continue their participation in the subculture. People identified as particularly strong members of the group are likely to receive encouragement from within the group to stay involved.[19] At the same time, people acquiring an image associated with a group that outsiders dislike are likely to find that outsiders are not especially willing to accept them when they desire to "go straight."[20] In general, whether the identities in question are considered positive or negative, or whether the actors in question do or do not like the identities imputed to them, the labels and reputations that people acquire can have a profound impact on how people (insiders and outsiders) act toward subculturally affiliated individuals and on the likelihood that those so identified will stay involved in those subcultural settings.

Making Commitments

The fifth feature of subcultural involvements, "making commitments," takes two major forms: "activity commitments" and "continuance commitments." Activity commitments reflect the investments (money, time, energy, options forgone) people make in facilitating their involvements. Continuance commitments (Stebbins 1970, 1971; Hearn and Stoll 1975) reflect the losses people anticipate they would experience if they were to leave this setting (i.e., a sense of closure or obligation to remain). While people may make commitments to situations on either a solitary or a subcultural basis, subcultural commitments are often more complicated and extensive than those pertaining to solitary pursuits. In particular, since one's subcultural investments are more likely to be intertwined with those of other people, group participants become more vulnerable to the ongoing recruitment efforts of these others. Finally, since they are more tightly bound in a network of others, subcultural participants often have more to lose (via continuance commitments; e.g., relationships, identity, outcomes) should they try to become disentangled from these situations (Sutherland 1937; Lofland 1966; Prus and Irini 1980; Steffensmeier 1986; Prus and Sharper 1991; Wolf 1991).

Overall, these five elements—relationships, perspectives, activities, identities, and commitments—define the roles of those involved in subcultural contexts. Each should be recognized if we are to arrive at a more complete understanding of people's participation in particular lifestyles. Researchers are urged to pay more attention to how people "work out" their involvements in subcultural settings, whether these are defined as "deviant" or "respectable" within the broader community.

✹ Experiencing Adolescence: A Research Agenda

> No theorizing, however ingenious, and no observance of scientific protocol, however meticulous, are substitutes for developing a familiarity with what is actually going on in the sphere of life under study. [Blumer 1969:39]

Adolescence has been the focus of a great deal of attention in the popular media and in academia because of the ambiguity and turbulence associated with this time of life; yet surprisingly little has been done either to depict the life-worlds that adolescents actually experience or to analyze adolescent experiences from the perspective of teenagers themselves. When not condemning adolescent activities on moral grounds, the media have often exploited adolescence as an entertainment theme. Social scientists have largely focused on the possible reasons why adolescents act in certain ways, or they have portrayed adolescent troubles as symptomatic of underlying social change and various "social problems" (revolving around poverty, slums, disrupted family situations, and the like). Rarely have those discussing adolescence spent much time talking to teenagers about their strategies for dealing with the world around them.

This section of the chapter outlines a *research agenda* that could shed considerable insight into the life-worlds, practices, and experiences of both adolescents and the people they deal with on a day-to-day basis.

I began this chapter with the intention of enhancing understandings of adolescent involvements in deviance; however, it quickly became apparent that we cannot consider adolescents' involvements in deviance in isolation from their involvements in other activities. In the same way, we cannot fully understand adolescent life-worlds (and involvements in deviance) without considering adolescents' relationships with others, such as parents, teachers, employers, and religious leaders—nonadolescents with whom adolescents may have considerable contact. I mean this chapter to be a device that will allow researchers to examine a great many facets of the adolescent life-world, and of community life generally.

Readers are cautioned that this chapter represents a tentative working statement—one that should be expanded, qualified, and altered along the way so that it better reflects people's actual experiences. At the same time, however, this chapter provides a focused and relatively coherent point of departure and synthesis. Because this material (a) has been developed from an interactionist perspective, (b) encourages an ethnographic methodology, and (c) attends rigorously to people's lived experiences, it offers exceptional theoretical and methodological consistency, especially when compared to many of the highly fractured (mixed-theoretical, mixed-methodological) approaches used in studies of adolescence.

This chapter provides a conceptual grid that can be used (and revised) as an analytical reference point. It represents a medium of sorts for building and assessing materials that relate to the lived experiences of young people in the community. Insofar as the central objective is to understand (rather than remedy) people's situations, the interactionist perspective is nonpartisan and nonmoralistic. Thus, for instance, terms such as "deviant," "good," and "conventional morality" are seen as reflecting the viewpoints of various audiences. Instead of trying to reform or change adolescents, the model presented here concentrates on how young people attempt to come to terms with one another and with other members of the community on a day-to-day basis. Finally, in addition to outlining a number of situations (activities) that seem central to appreciating the adolescent life-world, this model makes references to sets of *processes* that locate the activities of adolescents within the more generic practices of the human community.

Focusing on Activities

Rather than ask people's opinions on things or rely on rates of delinquency and the like, this approach focuses on people's activities—on the things that adolescents do as they work their way through situations on a day-to-day, moment-to-moment basis. This is not to suggest that people's attitudes or views on things are unimportant, but rather to emphasize that action is central to any comprehension of the human condition.

Humans are active beings, and in studying how people go about doing, accomplishing, generating, assembling, forging, creating, or constructing their behaviours, we will become especially appreciative of the meanings people have for things and how these meanings change as people act toward one another and other objects of their awareness on a situated, "here and now" basis.

The approach taken here also suggests that we do not need a special theory for adolescents, just as we do not need separate theories for deviants and normals, the rich and the poor, children and old people, males and females, the tall and the small, and so on. While researchers must consider how humans define (social) contexts and how they act within those contexts, the emphasis is on developing a theory and a methodology that is thoroughly attentive to the human condition, in all its manifestations.

For our immediate purposes, this means that while adolescents may be younger or older than others in the community, have more or less money to work with, assume this or that physical appearance, prefer these or those types of music, attire, and adornments, and so on, they are not especially different from people in most other stages of life. Only some things that adolescents do are age-demarcated. While it is important to attend to these things, to concentrate on "age-demarcated" matters would result in a distorted image of the adolescent experience.

Thus, one can learn about adolescent life by examining the life-worlds of others (and their relationships, subcultural involvements, and the like); in the same way, by examining the life-worlds of adolescents in great detail, social scientists may learn much about the situations people find themselves in more generally. While some content variations between adolescent life-worlds and the community at large seem inevitable, the processes (developing perspectives, acquiring identity, doing activity, developing relationships, making commitments) involved in the adolescent "struggle for existence" are exceedingly parallel to those characterizing other people in other settings. Just like people of other ages and circumstances, adolescents must manage ambiguity, "be someone," perform activities, make and keep friends, hedge bets, and so on.[21]

This approach focuses mainly on adolescent viewpoints (as opposed to those of outsiders). However, it is also recognized here that adolescence is *not* a homogeneous state of affairs. Thus, researchers must consider carefully the diversity of adolescent approaches to situations. We must also recognize that the same people may assign multiple meanings to the same situations (e.g., fun, but dangerous, costly, challenging) at particular points in time, and that people's definitions of situations may shift (sometimes abruptly) over time.

This means that attempts to establish generalized "adolescent attitudes" are apt to be of little use in understanding adolescent behaviour. While certain things may "be typically adolescent"—such as general inclinations to disidentify with children—researchers are obligated to consider how adolescents make sense of, and develop lines of action toward, situations on a much more immediate or focused basis than general sorts of attitudes or orientations may suggest.

Listed below are what seem to be the central activities around which the adolescent life-world revolves. In the absence of sustained interactionist/ethnographic research on adolescence, both this listing and the later elaborations of it should be seen only as tentative guidelines. Note as well that the last item (epilogue) in this list is somewhat at variance from the others, in that it focuses on those with whom adolescents commonly interact rather than on adolescents themselves.

- Acquiring perspectives: encountering and considering world views
- Developing peer relationships: managing intimacy and distancing
- Establishing and maintaining identities in the adolescent community
- Getting involved and involving others in deviance and respectability
- Doing things: experiencing adolescence in the here and now
- Encountering the conventional morality of the broader community
- Forming associations: deviance, respectability, and the ganging process
- Anticipating the future: the problem of fitting into the broader community
- Epilogue: dealing with adolescents—other people's relationships and experiences

Acquiring Perspectives: Encountering and Considering World Views

> I want to be sure that we see that the content put into the mind is only a development and product of social interaction. It is a development which is of enormous importance, and which leads to complexities and complications of society which go almost beyond our power to trace, but originally it is nothing but the taking over of the attitude of the other. [Mead 1934:191]

The notion of "acquiring perspectives" (viewpoints, realities, frames of reference, interpretive frames, ideologies) draws attention to both the ambiguity that characterizes adolescence and the extensive opportunities that this set of years provides for people to attain and sort out varying "stocks of knowledge." As they encounter vast realms of ambiguity, and as they grow painfully aware of various contradictions in the human condition and of their own personal limitations, adolescents (in varying degrees of reflectivity) may expend considerable effort "puzzling through things" or "attempting to make sense of things." This should not surprise anyone. Most adolescents are more adept than most children at dealing with "multiple realities" in cognitively sophisticated ways. As well, adolescents are apt to be challenged—by the formal educational system, their parents, other adults, and (perhaps even more directly) by their peers, to move beyond the "taken for granted" (Schutz 1962) notions of reality that characterize "children at school or play."

Adolescents have difficulty attaining conceptual coherence in their world views partly because people's perspectives tend to be much more diverse and situated than might be commonly supposed. In order to talk fruitfully of perspectives as analytical features of the adolescent life-world, we must examine these perspectives within particular situations. Adolescents thus may be seen to develop multiple (and often conflicting) perspectives on school, dating, religion, smoking, drinking, drug use, work, possessions, athletics, and the like. Similarly, through both (a) direct association with parents, siblings, teachers, and an assortment of peers and (b) the definitions of reality that they may encounter through any number of media sources, adolescents are likely to encounter a variety of others promoting similar and different viewpoints. Further, while we may normally think of adolescents as being exposed somewhat involuntarily to these other definitions, it is important to appreciate that they may actively pursue particular types of information on their own and may be very active in encouraging other adolescents to entertain viewpoints similar to those they currently hold.[22]

With the caution that one should be particularly cognizant of the (sometimes highly) situated nature of these viewpoints, researchers wishing to examine how adolescents acquire perspectives on their life-worlds may find it useful to consider processes such as the following:

- Encountering perspectives (definitions of reality) from others
- Assessing (new, incoming) perspectives and resisting unwanted viewpoints
- Developing images of objects (including images of other people and oneself)
- Learning (cultural) patterns of objects (e.g., rules of thumb, norms, fashions)
- Defining situations (i.e., applying perspectives to the "cases at hand")
- Dealing with ambiguity (lapses and limitations in existing explanations)
- Resolving contradictions (dilemmas within and across paradigms)
- Extending or improvising on existing perspectives
- Promoting (and defending) perspectives to others
- Rejecting formerly held viewpoints
- Adopting new viewpoints[23]

Developing Peer Relationships: Managing Intimacy and Distancing

The principle which I have suggested as basic to human social organization is that of communication involving participation in the other. This requires the appearance of the other in the self, the identification of the other with the self, the reaching of self-consciousness through the other. [Mead 1934:253]

A great deal of adolescent life revolves around the relationships teens have with one another. However, adolescents often have much more recreational time than adults and enjoy many more contact occasions for pursuing associations with others. Adolescence is a time to learn more about the nature of human relationships and the ways that one may feasibly deal with others in the community. Adolescence thus is a period characterized by considerable openness, but it is also a time when many people find themselves tested more or less constantly by others. Further, many of these tests occur spontaneously in "live theatres" in which wide ranges of praise, tolerance, or ridicule may be encountered. Even the smallest things may become sources of unexpected denigration and embarrassment.

For adolescents, "developing relationships" generally involves making friends and enemies, dealing with smaller peer groups or cliques, and becoming involved in dating and/or sexual relationships. While the associations in which adolescents are involved may overlap extensively, each realm provides a means for researchers to gain a fuller sense of the multifaceted nature of adolescent relationships.

Making Friends
    Meeting Others/Making Contacts with Others
    Attractions/Reservations/Neutralizations
    Being Pursued/Pursuing Others
    Losing Friends
    Distancing Oneself from Others/Dropping and Rejecting Friends

Being Best Friends[24]
    Defining Best Friends
    Selecting and Competing for Best Friends
    Sharing and Defining Experiences
    Developing Strategies for Dealing with Outsiders (parents, other peers)
    Exhibiting and Disregarding Loyalty to Best Friends
    Becoming Disaffected with Best Friends
    Breaking Up with Best Friends
    Resuming Friendships

Having Enemies
    Being Disliked/Disliking Others
    Becoming Indignant about Others' Treatment of Self

Hassling Disliked Others
Embittered Encounters
Escalating Confrontations[25]

Dealing with Groups/Subcultures/Cliques/Gangs
Forming Associations with Several Others
    Having "Buddies" (cliques) within Groups
    Getting Support from Others
    Including and Excluding Others
    Managing Intimacy and Distancing Oneself in Group Settings
Dealing with Rival Groups

Dating Relationships
Learning about Dating
Daydreaming about and Anticipating Encounters
Dealing with Stage Fright
Making Dates
Anticipating and Getting Ready for Dates
Going Out on Dates
Doing Things on Dates
Managing Intimacy and Distancing Oneself in Dating Situations
Assessing Experiences on One's Own and with Others
Sustaining Relationships and Playing the Field
Dealing with Disenchantments and Setbacks
Breaking Up
Becoming Reinvolved

Experiencing Sexuality[26]
Getting Exposure to Sexuality—Friends, Family, Other Associates, Media
Learning to Conceptualize (think about, talk about, learn about) Sexuality
Experimenting with Sexuality
Dealing with Bodily Changes
Stage Fright, Imaginations, and Anticipations
Ambiguities, Predicaments, Dilemmas, Contradictions
Actual Encounters with Others
Assessing Experiences on One's Own and with Others
Continuity, Disinvolvements, Reinvolvements
Dealing with Disenchantments, Problems, Disasters

Although the processes following were developed with respect to people's relationships more generally, readers may find in this listing matters that may enable them to more fully appreciate aspects of the relationships adolescents have with one another in the manners discussed in the preceding topics:

- Getting prepared for generalized encounters
- Defining self as available for association
- Defining (specific) others as desirable associates
- Making approaches/receiving openings from others
- Encountering (and indicating) rejection/acceptance
- Assessing self and other for "goodness of fit"
- Developing interactional styles (in each relationship)
- Managing openness and secrecy
- Developing understandings, preferences, loyalty
- Managing distractions (and outside commitments)
- Juggling (multiple) relationships
- Severing relationships (disentanglement)
- Renewing relationships[27]

Establishing and Maintaining Identities in the Adolescent Community

> A social self of this sort might be called the reflective or looking-glass self:
>   "Each to each a looking-glass
>   Reflects the other that doth pass." [Cooley 1922:184]

> [The looking-glass self] seems to have three principal elements: the imagination of our appearances to the other person; the imagination of his judgement of that appearance; and some sort of self-feeling, such as pride or mortification. [Cooley 1922:184]

As Charles Horton Cooley (1864–1924) observed, we live in a world of images. People may find it advantageous to be seen in particular ways, and they sometimes extensively engage in *impression management* or the selective *presentation of self* (Goffman 1959, 1963) in attempts to both *acquire* more desired images in the community of others and *resist* unwanted identities and reputations that others may assign. Most adolescents are well aware that the labels, nicknames, and reputations they acquire in the community of others can greatly affect their ability to experience the world in a desirable way.

The material in this section focuses on the emergent, relatively fragile, and profoundly social images that people may acquire as adolescents, and on their attempts (successful and otherwise) to shape (promote and resist) these images in the arenas in which they operate on a day-to-day basis.

Being Somebody
    Achieving Popularity
        Striving for Celebrity Status
        Attaining Esteem among One's Peers
    Being Cool
        Impressing Others
        Maintaining Composure
    Proving Oneself to Others
        Displaying Success
        Dealing with Failure
    Being Unique
        Getting Ideas for Expressing Oneself
        Encountering Reactions
        Making Adjustments

Being Acceptable
    Blending in/Fitting in (with those at hand)
    Being Okay (to hang around with)

Experiencing Negativity
    Encountering Personal Denigrations, Disrespectability, Stigma, Embarrassment, Shame
    Feeling Alone
    Dealing with Rejection
    Resisting Denigrations
    Putting Others Down
    Using Stigma as an Excuse for Other Personal Shortcomings
    Trying to Make the Scene (in spite of image problems)
    Finding Alternative Associates
    Living through It[28]

Insofar as it may shed further light on adolescent image concerns of the sort just outlined, readers may find it useful to consider how people do "identity work" at a more generic level:

- Encountering definitions of self from others
- Attributing qualities to self (self-definitions)

- Comparing incoming and self-assigned definitions of self
- Resisting unwanted identity imputations
- Selectively conveying information about self to others
- Gleaning information about others
- Assigning identities to others
- Promoting specific definitions of others
- Encountering resistance from others
- Reassessing identities imputed to others[29]

Getting Involved and Involving Others in Deviance and Respectability

> In short, what was once frightening and distasteful becomes, after a taste for it is built up, pleasant, desired, and sought after. Enjoyment is introduced by favorable definitions of the experience that one acquires from others. Without this, use will not continue, for marijuana will not be for the user an object he can use for pleasure. [Becker 1963:56]

The specific activities in which people become participants may vary greatly, but an important aspect of adolescent involvement revolves around matters of "deviance and respectability," as these are envisioned within immediate peer group settings, within the broader adolescent subculture, and within the community at large. Here, we start to appreciate the intertwining of involvements and reputations, and the sometimes intricate and devious juggling acts that may be involved in people's attempts to "look respectable" when faced with multiple audiences with potentially diverse notions of morality.

When discussing people's involvements in "doing good or bad" by conventional standards, there are two major processes to be taken into account. One relates to how people become involved in particular situations. The other relates to how people may encourage others to get involved. The two subprocesses are interrelated, but differentially emphasize people's roles as both *participants* and *recruiting agents*. Since both processes involve several stages, these will be discussed at a more generic level before we focus more specifically on the adolescent situation.

Getting Involved in Situations[30] "Being involved" relates to the sequencing of people's participation in settings. The "how" (vs. why) of involvements is emphasized, and consideration is given to the history of people's participation in particular situations (Becker 1963; Prus 1994, 1996). Each individual involvement is best envisioned against a backdrop of multiple, shifting, and potentially incompatible involvements that people may have in other settings.

Four subprocesses of involvement may be delineated with respect to people's participation in situations: (a) initial involvements, (b) continuities, (c) disinvolvements, and (d) reinvolvements.[31]

A. Getting Started (initial involvements). There are three major ways in which people become involved in situations: seekership, recruitment, and closure. People sometimes become involved in situations accidentally or unwittingly, but most involvements reflect the first three routings. *Seekership* refers to instances in which people pursue self-defined interests or fascinations through particular involvements. *Recruitment* refers to efforts by others to involve people in particular situations. *Closure* refers to situations in which people feel obliged or pressured to pursue a particular line of action even though this may not be a desired form of activity. Any one of these three common routings may result in participation in particular settings; however, they usually work in some combination.

Often, people will be reluctant to get involved in an activity. At times like this, they must find a way to overcome their reluctance, or others must overcome it for them.[32] The following themes are pertinent to understanding how people become participants in the situations in which they find themselves:

- Engaging in "seekership" (pursuing self-attributed interests)
- Being recruited (others attempt to foster interest, encourage participation)[33]
- Experiencing "closure" (perceiving pressing obligations, limited choices)
- Managing reservations (overcoming doubts, stigma, risks)[34]

B. Sustaining and Intensifying Involvements (continuities). People's initial routings into situations may be factors in their willingness to continue particular ventures; however, once they have become involved, other aspects of their situations may become *more* important. Overall, the ethnographic literature suggests that people are more likely to maintain particular involvements as they more thoroughly:

- Internalize perspectives (viewpoints consistent with particular involvements)
- Achieve identities (self and other definitions consistent with particular involvements)
- Accomplish activities (competence and composure in the focal setting)
- Make commitments (make investments, develop dependencies in the setting)
- Develop relationships (experience positive bonds with others in the setting)
- Forgo alternative involvements (neglect outside options, "bridge-burning")

These subcultural themes (perspectives, identities, etc.), which were discussed earlier, are exceedingly consequential for continuity. People doing things more exclusively on their own lack many of the supports for continuity available to subcultural participants; as a result they are less likely to continue particular pursuits. People's participation in subcultures may be quite uneven, but the more fully people organize their routines along these lines, the more likely they are to continue as participants. Continuity may be fostered along all of these matters, as people become more entrenched in the subculture.

C. Becoming Disinvolved. Insofar as it is unlikely that people would be uniformly highly involved in all dimensions of the situation at hand, continuity and discontinuity are more closely intertwined than might at first seem. Indeed, not only are people's involvements in many situations likely to be partial with respect to one or more of these dimensions, but we would also expect that people could question the viability of their involvements along any of these dimensions at any point in time. It should not be assumed that dissatisfaction on any one realm would necessitate disinvolvement (i.e., consider the problems of simultaneous disentanglement on all of these dimensions), but disinvolvement is more likely when people begin to:

- Question the viability of perspectives (facing obstacles, dilemmas) central to the situation
- Reassess their identities (consistent with desired images of self?) in the setting
- Find focal activities troublesome (boring, unpleasant, cumbersome, unproductive)
- Find themselves freed up from existing commitments (free to "relocate")
- Sever relationships (through conflict, animosity, exclusion) with the other participants
- Encounter opportunities for alternative involvements[35]

D. Becoming Reinvolved. When people's involvements in later settings are unsatisfactory (vis-à-vis perspectives, identities, activities, commitments, relationships), then reinvolvements in earlier situations are more likely. This seems more common as people begin to:

- Define opportunities for reinvolvements in former situations as more feasible
- Envision greater changes to self or former situations that would justify reinvolvement (e.g., face-saving, reassessments)
- Find that they have less extensively organized their routines around their present involvements (i.e., disentanglement from the immediate situation is more easily accomplished)[36]

Involving Others (doing influence work) The influence or persuasion process reflects attempts on the part of people to recruit or "gain the participation, cooperation, or commitments of others" in certain situations. Pitches may be made on a "one to one" basis or to a more diversified audience (e.g., as in a classroom, assembly, or in the media). With larger groups of people, complexity and ambiguity typically become more important factors, and there is a greater likelihood of distractions and challenges, and levels of personal accountability are reduced. As well, opportunities for role-taking and selective adjustment are lessened when one faces the task of "pitching" to more generalized audiences as opposed to interpersonal others. This may involve some additional frustration and result in the creation of some unique group-directed tactics, but otherwise the same basic processes appear to hold for these instances as well. Influence work, or matters pertaining to how people "get their own way" in dealing with others (and encouraging others to do things), is relevant to most if not all realms of the adolescent life-world. While some instances of influence work are much more fully developed than others, a more encompassing model would acknowledge the following subprocesses:

- Formulating (preliminary) plans
- Role-taking (inferring/uncovering the perspectives of the other)
- Promoting interest in one's objectives
- Generating trust
- Proposing specific lines of action
- Encountering resistance
- Neutralizing obstacles
- Seeking and making concessions
- Confirming agreements
- Assessing "failures" and recasting plans[37]

In the adolescent situation, almost all peer influence involves person-to-person communication, but this influence work is very much grounded (directly and indirectly) within a larger peer community. A great deal of adolescent activity takes place in school settings and other contexts in which groups of others are commonly present or could easily learn of someone's activities from those closer to the participants in this or that setting. This means that much adolescent activity takes place in quasi-public arenas or at least could be subject to later assessment by others in the larger peer community.

Although adolescents need not be continually or explicitly concerned about this quasi-public feature of their circumstances, this situation does foster an attentiveness to "the generalized other" (Mead 1934) connoted by the larger peer group. While much of the influence work to which adolescents are subjected by their peers may be relatively crude or pointed, both the potential awareness of, and accountability to, a larger peer community provides a convenient and potentially powerful resource for those adolescents wishing to influence their associates. Despite multiple variations of morality and respectability within the larger adolescent community, teens may be able to influence one another by invoking standards and evaluations (praise, ridicule, rejection) relevant to particular group contexts. Acknowledging these situated reference points may not only serve to neutralize adolescents' reservations about doing certain kinds of things; it may also enable them to fit in with this community of people on a day-to-day and moment-to-moment basis.

When we apply the concepts of *involvement* (of self) and *influence* (of others) to adolescent life-worlds, we are able to more thoroughly explore the interaction dynamics and reflective considerations undergirding people's subcultural involvements. The themes of *getting involved* and *involving others* enable researchers to trace the careers of particular people in subcultural settings over time; they also draw attention to the interconnectedness (and interdependencies) of people's involvements as co-participants within and across particular settings. Some close friends, for instance, may not merely encourage and discourage one another's participation in particular settings on a here-and-now basis; they may also become jointly involved in several subcultural contexts over a period of time.

We will soon consider a number of more specific activities in which adolescents may become involved. First, it would be useful to consider adolescents' involvements in deviance and respectability on a preliminary but general sense since these notions cut across so many realms of adolescent activity. As with other subcultures, multiple views of deviance (and undesired practices) are evident in the adolescent community. Adolescents, and others involved in subcultural pursuits of various kinds, often juggle moralities and images of self as they attempt to achieve realms of respectability and freedom while pursuing interests, associations, and activities that differ from those that are acceptable in the broader community. Indeed, they may achieve degrees of prestige in certain groups by more extensively ignoring or even flaunting the morality associated with the larger community (e.g., see Becker 1963:79–119; Sanders 1991; Wolf 1991).

Without commenting on the viability of prevailing community moralities or the variants developed and exercised by participants in particular subcultures, it should be noted that adolescents generally are aware of prevailing notions of morality. Whether they accept these notions or not, they realize that others tend to use them as a standard for judging their activities, and their associates. Thus, in valuing certain activities, lifestyles, and companions, adolescents may begin to reference themselves as "bad," "good," or "mischievous" with respect to the prevailing morality of the broader community.

The notions of "being bad," "being good," and "being mischievous" do not refer to types of people; rather, they connote definitions that people may assign to themselves and others who are involved in specific situations. Although people may begin to more routinely envision themselves as good, bad, or mischievous, it is important to recognize the differing opportunities and willingness of adolescents to become involved in situations they envision others defining as bad, good, and mischievous.

A. Being Bad. Whether they develop mystiques about "being bad" and actively pursue situations that seem at variance from conventional moralities, or whether they find themselves defined as "bad," "deviant," "trouble-makers," and such against their preferences, some adolescents openly acknowledge involvements in activities and lifestyles considered disrespectable within the larger community (see Thrasher 1927; Jankowski 1991; Padilla 1992, for some more extreme instances).

In a more comprehensive sense, "being bad" may involve (a) hanging around characters deemed "bad" or "unsavory" in certain respects by more conventional citizens; (b) engaging in activities thought disrespectable or prohibited in more conventional circles; and (c) encouraging others to become involved in these situations.[38] In the adolescent world, this often implies using substances such as alcohol, tobacco, and drugs that are conventionally prohibited for adolescents, as well as engaging in practices involving violence, theft, and truancy. Some of these involvements entail violations of the criminal, municipal, or juvenile codes, but others, such as adolescent involvements in certain kinds of music or levels of sexuality, may be deemed dangerous, immoral, or simply "undesirable."

While people are often "implicated by association," with undesirable companions, those seen as engaging in disreputable practices, and especially those thought to encourage others to become thusly involved, are apt to be defined as "bad" or culpable. These involvements are often interrelated, but it may be useful to differentiate between involvements in particular relationships and settings on the one hand, and involvements in particular activities on the other. In some cases the two sets of involvements are virtually synonymous and people's activities may be largely limited to practices conducted in the presence of particular others. In other instances, however, the activities (e.g., theft, drinking) may involve a variety of associates, with people moving from one setting to the next, actively seeking out (different) other people with whom to engage in what are now established practices. In both instances, analysts should consider not only people's own involvements in associations and activities, but also the efforts they make to encourage the involvements and fuller participation of others. Only in this way can researchers hope to move past vague and relatively unproductive notions of "peer pressure." Required are highly detailed and sustained examinations of adolescents' involvements in the life-worlds of the other:

Getting Involved with Disreputable Characters and Lifestyles
Making Contact with Disreputable Others (seekership, recruitment, closure, reservations)
Developing Mutual Interests
Intensifying Association
Encountering Difficulties with Disreputable Associates
Fading Away from, or Dropping Out of, Disreputable Circles of People
Getting Back into Disreputable Situations
Encouraging Others' Involvements in Disreputable Situations

Engaging in Disreputable Practices
Becoming Initially Involved (seekership, recruitment, closure, reservations)
Continuing and Intensifying Use
Discontinuing Use
Becoming Reinvolved
Encouraging Others to Use Prohibited Substances[39]

B. Being Good. Adolescents who attempt to "be good" are likely to find that the pursuit of conventional morality is often more challenging than they expect. Although people endeavouring to be "good citizens" need not see themselves as particularly "good," they tend to be concerned about maintaining a lifestyle that they consider morally appropriate and that reflects the essential morality of some broader community. This should not be taken to imply that the people "trying to be good" or "doing good" in more conventional terms may not admire those they deem bad or mischievous in certain respects. They may very well engage in behaviours that they deem mischievous more often than they would like. At the same time, however, they are concerned about being good citizens of sorts. Here, the task seems to be one of trying to live up to the expectations they've come to associate with "being good" on the one hand while trying to "avoid trouble" on the other and maintaining a degree of respectability or peer acceptance (see the earlier discussion of identities and relationships) on still another front:

Living Up to Broader Community Expectations
Self-Imposed Standards, Goals, and Objectives
Attending to the Expectations of Parents, Teachers, and Others
Encouraging One's Peers to Be Good, Too[40]

Avoiding Trouble
Avoiding Disrespectable People and Situations
Experiencing Reservations
Developing Rationales
Invoking Justifications for Avoiding Trouble
Risking Ridicule
Encouraging Peers to Avoid Trouble

C. Being Mischievous/Being Illusive. Insofar as they've not been extensively branded or self-identified as "bad," yet find aspects of unconventional lifestyles and practices intriguing in certain respects, people adopting more mischievous or illusive postures may show the greatest vacillations between "being bad" and "being good." Some of these involvements are viewed as playful, prankish, or impish in thrust (i.e., enough to get one into trouble, but presumably not enough to violate basic moral codes of the broader community); other activities may be pursued covertly by adolescents who are fully aware that these activities are deemed severely morally reprehensible in the broader community. Typically, however, and in contrast to those already branded as bad or more fully involved in deviant lifestyles, these individuals tend to see themselves as basically respectable people whose situated involvements have a deviant or disreputable quality associated with them.

As actors who are more or less simultaneously attentive to (a) the advantages of achieving peer respect for their independence, (b) the satisfactions they associate with the pursuit of particular interests, and (c) the advantages of maintaining an acceptable image with respect to those in the broader community who may be able to affect their situation (both for good and for ill), these adolescents live, in varying degrees, on the margins of (dis)respectability. While many of these involvements are highly transitory, people who participate more extensively in a variety of deviant activities or who have become somewhat more involved in certain deviant lifestyles often become rather adept at invoking the deceptions essential to managing what Goffman (1963) terms "double lives."

Should more conventional segments of the community (parents, teachers, police officers) learn of these involvements, a set of processes may come into play that could result in "mischievous" characters being labelled as deviants or troublemakers (see Tannenbaum 1938; Lemert 1951, 1967; Becker 1963; Prus 1975a, b; Snyder 1994b). Some people may be labelled as deviants much more quickly and on much less substantive grounds than others, but once adolescents are more openly and broadly alleged to be disreputable, they are apt to find their lives more complicated and frustrating as a consequence. Most adolescents will likely be given several chances and many never actually move beyond mischief-like designations; others may find that the boundaries between respectability and deviance can collapse with devastating quickness when some members of the more conventional community begin to equate their mischief with serious trouble. There is much to be learned about adolescent "flirtations with deviance," but the following processes seem central:

Assuming a Cloak of Daring or Bravado[41]
    Expressing Peer-Directed Bravado
    Pursuing Their Own Fascinations
    Maintaining Images as Conventionally Respectable
    Lying, Deceiving, Concealing
    Getting Caught and Living with the Consequences
    Encouraging Others to Be Mischievous/Bad[42]

Doing Things: Experiencing Adolescence in the Here and Now

> Action is built up in coping with the world instead of merely being released from a pre-existing psychological structure by factors playing on that structure. By making indications to himself and by interpreting what he indicates, the human being has to forge or piece together a line of action ... The fact that the human act is self-directed or built up means in no sense that the actor necessarily exercises excellence in its construction. Indeed, he may do a very poor job in constructing his act ... Such deficiencies in the construction of his acts do not belie the fact that his acts are still constructed by him out of what he takes into account. [Blumer 1966:536–537]

The preceding materials addressed a number of matters central to an appreciation of adolescent experiences; the following themes draw more precise attention to additional "free-time" pursuits and some of the other dilemmas characterizing adolescent lifestyles. These themes overlap to some extent both with the earlier materials and with each other, but each denotes a realm of activity worth further consideration on its own. Given the number of topics pertinent to adolescent life-worlds, only a rudimentary listing is provided for each:

Experiencing and Avoiding Boredom
    Noticing Boredom
        On One's Own
        Attending to Others' Definitions of One's Situation
    Doing Things at Home
    Having Homework
    Being Involved in Extracurricular Activities at School
    Pursuing Outside Activities (hobbies, sports, volunteer work, paying jobs)
    Having (and relating to) Friends (teens, adults, children)

Getting Entertainment
    Having Fun on One's Own
        Developing Fascinations/Challenges
        Getting into Trouble
    Hanging Around Friends
        Defining Fun
        Negotiating Activities
        Coordinating Activities
        Assessing Activities
        Sustaining Activities
        Encountering Distractions
        Getting into Trouble
    Hanging Around Other Adolescents
        Making the Scene
        Partying
        Experiencing the Ultimate (sensation, high) Adventure
        Getting into Trouble

Getting Things
    Developing Fascinations with Particular Objects
    Being Fashionable
    Shopping and Spending Practices
    Saving Money (short term/long run)
    Working Parents for Things
    Borrowing and Trading
    Stealing

Getting Money
    Getting Allowances
    Getting Other Money from Home

Getting a Job
Managing Money
Borrowing and Repaying Money
Selling One's Possessions
Gambling
Engaging in Illegal Activities for Financial Gain

Getting a Job
Searching for Work
Dealing with Rejection
Finding Work
Dealing with the Boss
Relating to Co-workers
Dealing with Customers/Others
Making Adjustments at Home
Juggling Work, School, and Recreational Interests
Making and Managing Money

Being Free (Unencumbered) from Conventional Restraints
Avoiding Accountability/Responsibility
Seeking and Negotiating Independence
At School
At Home

Getting and Managing Wheels
Learning to Drive
Borrowing
Owning
Getting Around
Impressing Others
Covering Expenses
Encountering Driving-Related Troubles

Running Away
Becoming Disenchanted
Attractions Elsewhere
Finding Companions
Locating a Place
Obtaining Food
Getting Money
Going Back

Dealing with Subsequent Adjustments and Conflicts
Leaving Again

As suggested in the themes just outlined, the *performance* or *doing* of activity highlights the "problematics of accomplishment." It should be noted that no assumption is made about people acting "wisely" or "rationally" in any objective sense. Wisdom and rationality are not merely matters of definition; these notions remain to be worked out in process (see Prus 1989b, especially 139–142). Further, even when people explicitly try to act in ways they deem wise, rational, and the like, reality is not theirs alone to determine. Indeed, matters of ambiguity, uncertainty, and resistance on the part of others can make human endeavour particularly problematic. Thus, one may apply the following subprocesses to any of the activities just discussed. Whether one is discussing "getting a job," "getting entertainment," "getting and managing wheels," or even "running away," despite the commonplace "good intentions" that accompany many adolescent ventures, performance often becomes a matter of situated adjustments that may take one some direction from that suggested by one's initial plans:

- Making (preliminary) plans
- Getting prepared
- Managing stage fright (reservations, if any)
- Developing competence (stock of knowledge, tactics, applications)
- Coordinating events with others (team members and others)
- Dealing with ambiguity, obstacles, resistances, and distractions
- Conveying images of competence (displaying ability, composure)
- Encountering competition
- Making ongoing assessments and adjustments[43]

Each realm of adolescent involvement brings with it a set of contextual features that help define it as a unique configuration. At the same time, however, by attending to processes of the sort just outlined, researchers may develop a stock of knowledge that enables them to more fully appreciate adolescent behaviour across a range of settings.

Encountering the Conventional Morality of the Broader Community

Self-criticism is essentially social criticism, and behaviour controlled by self-criticism is essentially behaviour controlled socially ... Hence, social control, so far from tending to crush out the human individual or to obliterate his self-conscious individuality, is, on the contrary, actually constitutive of and inextricably associated with that individuality; for the individual is what he is, as a conscious and individual personality, just in as far as he is a member of society, involved in the social process of experience and activity and thereby socially controlled in his conduct. [Mead 1934:255]

Although the adolescent life-world has its own sets of moralities, monitoring practices, and sanctions, adolescents must also deal with representatives of a broader community whose interests may be quite at variance from those of their peers. Thus, while matters of morality represent concerns for people more generally, they may seem of greatest concern for adolescents, who find themselves expected to learn and juggle potentially diverse moralities. As well, whether they realize it or not, in developing orientations toward morality and working out their own activities, adolescents may also be establishing patterns that remain with them in much of their later life.

The earlier, more generic statements on people's involvements and the recruitment of others into "deviance and respectability" are pertinent across the range of contexts considered here. However, more focused examinations of each of the settings outlined here are essential. Such examination enables one to locate deviance and respectability within the activities (and associated meanings) relating to these realms of adolescent endeavour; it also allows one to see how adolescents come to terms with community life on a more comprehensive basis. Research in these areas could not only indicate how adolescents interact with nonadolescent others in a variety of contexts, but could also provide valuable statements on how schools, families, religions, control agencies, and the like operate in practice and are experienced by a central set of participants. Close examinations of adolescents (troublesome and otherwise) can shed considerable light on what "school," "family," and "church" life involves on a day-to-day basis:

Managing School Routines[44]
    Getting to School
    Attending Classes
    Avoiding School/Classes
    Trying to Have Fun in Class
    Relating to Teachers
    Dealing with Recesses/Breaks
    Socializing with Friends
    Dealing with Peers after School
    Doing/Avoiding Assignments
    Preparing For and Taking Tests

Coping with Outside Involvements and Events
Making the Grade
Managing Disappointment
Facing Failure
Leaving School Prematurely
Graduating

Dealing with Families

Experiencing Easy and Difficult Times in Family Situations
Dealing with Parents
Managing Relations with Siblings
Trying to Normalize Family Routines
Trying to Educate the Family
Being Embarrassed by the Family
Trying to Maintain Respectability in the Family
Trying to Live Up to Family Expectations for Oneself
Getting One's Own Way in the Family
Doing and Avoiding Family Duties
Getting into Trouble in the Family

Experiencing Religiosity

Being Involved in a Religious Community[45]
Reconciling Religious Dilemmas and Doubts
Maintaining a Religious Sense of Self
Making Adjustments to Adolescents
Managing Contacts with Religious Leaders
Encountering Religious Communications from Others (e.g., family, friends)
Getting into and Managing Trouble in the Religious Community
Dating Within and Across Religious Lines

Encountering Control Agents

Dealing with the Police, Courts, Agencies
Finding Supportive Others
Maintaining Peer Relationships While in Trouble
Acquiring a Reputation for Trouble
Dealing with Restrictions

Forming Associations: Deviance, Respectability, and the Ganging Process

The majority of gangs develop from the spontaneous play-group ... In the course of business or pleasure, a crowd, in the sense of a mere gathering of persons, is formed [25] ... On this basis of interests and aptitudes, a play-group emerges ... Such a play-group may acquire a real organization. Natural leaders emerge, a relative standing is assigned to various members and traditions develop. *It does not become a gang, however, until it begins to excite disapproval and opposition, and thus acquires a more definite group consciousness.* [26] ... This is the real beginning of the gang, for now it starts to draw itself more closely together. It becomes a conflict group. [27] [Thrasher 1927 (1963)]

The ganging process is a continuous flux and flow, and there is little permanence in most of the groups. New nuclei are constantly appearing and the business of coalescing and recoalescing is going on everywhere in the congested areas. Both conflict and competition threaten the embryonic gangs with disintegration ... Some new activity of settlement, playground or club frequently depletes its membership. [Thrasher 1927(1963:31)]

The material introduced here presupposes familiarity with the earlier material dealing with perspectives, relationships, identities, and involvements (and the influence process), as well as with adolescent activity-related themes and concerns with conventional morality. However, it considers more directly the processes by which associations (most particularly primary groups; Cooley 1909) are formed and sustained within adolescent life-worlds.

While I am writing this chapter with the *gang phenomenon* in mind, the reader must recognize that (a) primary group associations are fundamental to all human lived experiences as we know them; (b) notions of morality (however diverse) and deviance seem generic to all associations; and (c) although only some adolescent groups become defined as gangs, mobs, and the like, even those that are so defined are best approached and understood, not as bizarre life-forms, but as fundamental instances of primary group association.

Unfortunately, despite a great deal of talk about adolescent groupings, we know little about the processes by which these associations are formed, sustained, or ended. Little work on adolescent life, delinquency, or gangs has been ethnographic in thrust, and most of the work that has an ethnographic cast has failed to consider the social processes characterizing group development. In this respect, our knowledge of adolescent groupings and gangs has not advanced significantly since Thrasher's (1927) depiction of "gangland" in Chicago and Shaw's (1930; 1931) ethnographic statements on "street delinquency."[46]

Some of the lack of progress reflects the longstanding concern in the community at large about "resolving problems" related to the juvenile condition. This has meant an emphasis on the search for "quick fixes" in control, remedial responses, and policy formation as opposed to concerns with examining and understanding the life-worlds of adolescents more generally. For their part, social scientists have contributed surprisingly little to an understanding of adolescent group life. Catering somewhat to the interests of control agents, policy makers, and funding sources, social scientists have spent a great deal of time chasing "factors" (such as social class, gender, race, personality typifications, attitudes, and self-concepts) that they suppose might somehow "cause" crime and delinquency. Many considerations of adolescence in the social sciences also have been subjected to a variety of "grand theories" (Freudianism, personality theories, functionalism, Marxism) that, quite simply, lack intimate familiarity with adolescent (and other human) lived experiences. The end result in all of these instances has been an extended inattention on the part of social scientists, policy makers, and others generally to both the life-worlds experienced by those very people whose behaviour is seen as problematic and to the actual processes by which human group life takes its shape.[47]

Not only have those discussing adolescence and deviance generally failed to consider the intersubjective nature of human experience, but they have also failed to consider social processes in other realms of community life that parallel adolescent group life. Consequently, most social inquiries (data) and analyses dealing with adolescence are distant from their purported subject matter and conceptually ill-informed as well. There is little in this (rather massive) literature that is genuinely instructive for developing a viable understanding of adolescent life-worlds.

Recently, we have begun to see something of a renewed emphasis on ethnographic examinations of the adolescent situation. So far, though, this work has been rather limited and tentative. It also has remained significantly shrouded in the "deviant mystique." While agreeing with Hagedorn (1990), who argues for the fundamental need for researchers to go into the field to establish greater familiarity with their subject matter, one might observe that even the best, recently published, ethnographic material in this area (e.g., Campbell 1984; Jankowski 1991; Padilla 1992) has suffered from (a) relatively obscure and mixed theoretical viewpoints, (b) tendencies to mystify gangs, violence, gender, and characters ("personalities"), and (c) a relative disregard of fundamental social processes. Thus, despite the immense effort and personal courage that underlie some of these ventures, they have not been especially instructive overall.

Not having conducted a sustained ethnographic examination of the adolescent life-world, I also lack data of a direct substantive sort to offer. However, in drawing upon a series of Chicago-style ethnographies that have examined a great many different subcultural and interpersonal contexts in intimate detail—including my own studies of the activities, associations, and life-worlds of hustlers and thieves (Prus and Sharper 1977; Prus and Irini 1980)—I would suggest that researchers interested in the formation and maintenance of grouping and gangs in the adolescent life-world might find it valuable to consider the processes of group association outlined more generally here. Not only may these notions offer particularly important vantage points from which to consider adolescent involvements in groups and gangs of all sorts, but focused examinations of these processes would also provide researchers with a basis on which to compare and contrast their findings with others who are involved in research on associations in other human (adolescent and other) contexts.

The forming and sustaining of associations with others depends on people finding advantages to incorporating others into their routines. Regardless of the size, duration, and formality of these associations, these groupings (however tentative) enable people to pursue activities and ventures that they may be unwilling or unable to accomplish on their own.

The formation of an association of some sort does not ensure any particular degree of individual or collective success; nor need associations be pursued or experienced so explicitly. Thus, "hanging around" particular others may be deemed (merely) interesting, fun, stimulating, or better than being by oneself. Should the participants come to define a group or gathering as having some mutual interest, they may begin to assume some initiative in developing and sustaining its integrity. Although many associations or gatherings are quite fleeting in nature, three subprocesses seem relevant in a great many cases. These are establishing associations; objectifying associations; and encountering outsiders.[48]

Establishing Associations

> They liked brawls and fights, and the gang helped to satisfy these wants with less personal discomfort than might occur if one fellow alone started hostilities or tried to steal something. [former gang associate—Thrasher 1927 (1963:37)]

While people involved in more fleeting alignments may circumvent or truncate some of the following processes, those involved in longer-term associations (especially those defining themselves as a group, team, side, gang, crew, mob, band, or tribe) seem likely to pursue activities of this sort:

- Anticipating the Value of Collective Enterprise
- Involving Others in the Venture (recruitment, screening, minimizing reservations)
- Justifying the Group (developing perspectives, moral viewpoints)
- Celebrating the Venture (witnessing, recognizing, emphasizing—within the group)
- Defining the Team (membership criteria, positions, responsibilities)
- Establishing Communication Forums (interpersonal, media)
- Pursuing Resources for the Group
- Arranging Member Assemblies (encounters, practices)
- Providing Instruction for Members (perspectives, techniques)
- Monitoring Members
- Assessing Member Performances
- Motivating and Disciplining Members
- Rejecting and Reinstating Members
- Facing Internal Upheaval (splintering, factions, challenges from within)
- Facing Generalized Loss of Interest
- Dealing with Dissolution
- Attempting to Revitalize Cooperative Ventures[49]

Objectifying Associations Sometimes the participants in particular groups wish to remain unnoticed by outsiders; very often, however, they want to be highly visible in the broader community. Groups that want the community to objectify them may resort to recruitment drives, public rallies, and the like, as well as embrace a striking physical appearance. Groups that want to remain "undercover" are still likely to adopt certain practices (e.g., codes, oaths, secretive assemblies, insider symbols, and jargon) to make their existence appear "more real" to their members:

- Developing a group identity (name, logo, flag)
- Stipulating justifications for existence and operations
- Creating identity markers for members (uniforms, appearances, signs)
- Defining exclusiveness (selectivity, oaths, codes, jargon)
- Establishing a public presence (announcements, advertising, rallies, protests)
- Legitimating the group publicly (endorsements, credentials, charters, licences)
- Demarcating territories and jurisdictions (buildings, places, locations)[50]

The objectification process intensifies when *outsiders* (intentionally or otherwise) engage in "identity work" pertaining to particular associations.

Whatever their reasons for performing this identity work (curiosity, fascination, entertainment, knowledge, fear, condemnation, control, elimination), insofar as they serve to identify, talk about, and act toward particular associations as if they were unique, prominent, important, and so on, outsiders contribute to the "realism" of particular subcultural essences. Outsider activities of the following sort are particularly noteworthy in generating a public profile for particular (subcultural) associations:

- Defining a set of people as constituting a group or interactive entity within the community
- Associating (assigning, acknowledging) specific names (and other identity markers) with the group
- Attributing particular properties (qualities and evaluations) to the group
- Discussing (talk, rumour, media messages) the group with others in the community
- Making more concerted efforts (i.e., condemning, controlling) to attend to or deal with the group as an entity within the broader community

Encountering Outsiders Once established, groups often face the task of dealing with an assortment of individuals and groups within the larger community of operations. They may seek out particular individuals and groups as a result of their collective interests (targets, suckers, marks); other outsiders may be seen as adversaries or obstacles to their undertakings. The group's interest in particular (outsider) individuals and groups can be quite wide-ranging, but the following matters tend to be noteworthy more generally:

- Representing the organization's interests
- Making contact with others (establishing co-presence, making the scene)
- Defining the theatre of operation (places, objectives, strategies)
- Identifying others (targets, cooperators, adversaries, witnesses, nobodies)
- Pursuing organizational objectives through the others (cooperation, influence work)
- Confronting others (challenges, competitions, conflicts)
- Protecting (sometimes concealing) the organization from the others
- Readjusting group routines to more effectively deal with the others[51]

While I can do little more here than sketch out some processes that appear important to the development of adolescent groupings (and gangs), sustained research activity along these lines would generate a much fuller and more vital understanding of this life-world. As well, since processes like these characterize people's associations throughout the community at large, this literature could make a valuable contribution to the understanding of group formation processes more generally.

Anticipating the Future: The Problem of Fitting into the Broader Community

Adolescent concerns with the future are far from uniform, but most teens seem to experience at least a vague sense of anxiety from time to time regarding their place in the future. These apprehensions seem likely to become more acute as teens anticipate completing high school, but even here some people's concerns are exceedingly fleeting and reluctant at best. In contrast, some adolescents (typically with the encouragement and support of their families) may develop a particularly clear direction regarding future lifestyles and specific careers. It is against this backdrop of vague anxieties, sporadic concerns, tentative plans, and occasional instances of resolute direction that the following list has been developed:

Developing Casual Career Interests and More Intense Fascinations
> Daydreaming about Desired Situations
> Maintaining Optimism
> Pursuing Focused Agendas

Encountering Occupational Exposures, Encouragements, and Skills
> Receiving Family Encouragements, Supports, and Financial Support
> Getting Exposure to Family Businesses
> Picking Up Part-time and Summer Work
> Observing Family Careers and Work Patterns
> Engaging in Volunteer Activities

Achieving and Maintaining Grades
> Encountering Encouragements and Discouragements
> Keeping Options Open
> Avoiding Distractions and Diversions
> Dropping Out of School
> Going Back to School

Disattending to the Future
> Kicking Around
> Default Options
> Extending Adolescent Ventures into Later Life

Epilogue: Dealing with Adolescents—Other People's Relationships and Experiences

Breaking windows, annoying people, running around porches, climbing over roofs, stealing from pushcarts, playing truant—all are items of play, adventure, excitement. To the community, however, these activities may and often do take on the form of a nuisance, evil, delinquency, with the demand for control, admonition, chastisement, punishment, police, court. [Tannenbaum 1938:17]

To more fully understand the phenomenon of adolescence, it is instructive to consider how other people experience adolescents. These "others" include parents, teachers, neighbours, relatives, friends of the family, employers, activity directors, religious leaders, and (in some cases) police officers and other control agents. While other adults sometimes become very central to the experiences of particular adolescents, parents and teachers tend to be especially important because it is with these adults that adolescents most often deal on a daily basis.

Adult encounters with adolescents are sometimes voluntary and fleeting in nature; however, in the case of parents and teachers, such encounters typically are more constraining, imply heightened degrees of obligation, and are relatively enduring over some period of time. These relationships are usually meant to be benign, instructive, and otherwise helpful to the adolescents in question, but this assumes relatively high levels of cooperation on the part of adolescents. Thus, while a considerable amount of influence work may be implied on the part of parents and teachers, these same people may be subject to considerable resistance *and* influence work from those very same adolescents. Both parties may thus assume roles as tacticians and targets in their dealings with one another.

As well, while people's means of relating to adolescents may imply certain role expectations, the implementation of these roles may be very uneven from case to case. Thus, for example, "parents" may differ greatly in the interest that they take in various aspects of the parenting role and some may have little or no involvement with their offspring on a day-to-day, month-to-month, or even year-to-year basis. Even when adolescents have daily contact with one or both parents, researchers should try to ascertain just what it means, in actual practice, when parents say they are "concerned about" or "monitor" their adolescent's activities or that they "screen" their companions, for instance.

Although one could develop listings somewhat parallel to those presented here for other adults (e.g., neighbours, other relatives, religious leaders, employers), it is anticipated that research that examines practices of the sort indicated on the part of parents, teachers, and control agencies will significantly add to our overall understanding of the adolescent situation.

Parent Experiences with Adolescent(s)
- Making Commitments, Assuming Responsibility for (the child) Adolescent
    - Educating/Providing Perspectives/Helping Develop a Stock of Knowledge
    - Shaping Characters and Establishing Morality
- Providing Financial Support
    - Providing Money for Adolescent
    - Purchasing Goods for Adolescent
    - Shopping with Adolescent
- Providing Transportation
    - Busing/Taxiing/Chauffeuring (by parent) Adolescent Around
    - Lending/Buying Vehicles for Adolescent
- Experiencing Companionship (and friendship) from Adolescent
    - Appreciating Friendship/Affection
    - Getting Help/Assistance from Adolescent
    - Identifying with Adolescent
    - Living Vicariously through Adolescent
    - Dealing with Adolescent Upsets
    - Having Disputes with Adolescent
    - Managing Relations with Adolescent and One's Spouse
    - Managing Relations with Adolescent and His/Her Siblings
    - Dealing with Adolescent's Friends and Associates
    - Being Disappointed with Adolescent Companionship
- Preventing and Dealing with Trouble
    - Monitoring Adolescent
    - Sanctioning Adolescent
    - Providing/Screening Entertainment
    - Screening Adolescent's Companions
    - Deterring/Preventing Troublesome Involvements with People/Activities
    - Dealing with Adolescent Troubles (family, neighbours, school, police, other)
    - Encountering Adolescent Pregnancies (and grandchildren)
- Anticipating and Experiencing Post-Adolescence
    - Planning for Adolescent's Future
    - Making Sacrifices for Adolescent's Future
    - Helping Adolescents Anticipate the Future
    - Helping Adolescents and Post-Adolescents Adjust to Higher Education, Careers, Adulthood, Housing, Marriage, and Children
    - Maintaining Contact with Post-Adolescents (and their families)

Teacher Experiences with Adolescents

    Dealing with Adolescents as the Generalized Other

        Getting Teaching and Class Assignments

        Setting Class Agendas

        Developing Secondary Agendas (e.g., morality, citizenship)

        Meeting and Conducting Classes

        Attempting to Generate Congenial Working Environments

        Giving, Grading, and Returning Assignments

    Making Personalized Adjustments

        Becoming Acquainted with Students More Individually

        Typifying/Categorizing Students

        Providing Extended Academic Assistance

        Providing Personal and Vocational Counselling and Assistance

        Dealing with Cooperation Problems

        Protecting Students from Each Other

    Dealing with Trouble[52]

        Developing Personal Rules of Thumb

        Making Rules Explicit to the Class

        Keeping Order

        Encountering Perplexing Situations

        Dealing with Individuals versus Groups

        Involving Third Parties (referrals, consultants)

        Dealing with Parents

        Discussing Adolescent Situations with Other Teachers

        Assessing One's Work Role/Teaching Career

        Making Adjustments

Control Agent Encounters with Adolescents[53]

    (Police, probation and parole officers, social workers, therapists, rehabilitation workers)

    Making Contact

        Third-Party Referrals, Agency-Initiated Contact, Adolescent Self-Referrals

    Typifying/Categorizing Adolescents with Respect to Trouble

        Ascertaining Trouble in the Situation

        Defining Individual (and group) Culpability and Responsibility

    Providing Protection

        For the Community at Large

        For Specific Targets of Adolescent Ventures

        For Adolescents in Trouble (from Others/from Self)

Attempting to Influence Troublesome (and potentially troublesome) Adolescents
    Dealing with Adolescents Individually and in Groups
    Striving for Control, Containment, and Elimination of Trouble
    Providing "Treatment" for Troublesome Cases
    Referring Troublesome Cases to Other Agents, Outside Agencies
Portraying Competence (as a control agent)
    Maintaining Organizational (agency) Integrity and Images
    Providing "Evidence" of Effectiveness
    Dealing with Individual Cases
    Attending to the Larger Mandate
    Maintaining Order in the Situations at Hand
Managing Accountability
    Working with (a potentially manipulative, volatile, yet presumed "vulnerable") Clientele
    Relating to Supervisors and (other) Staff
    Dealing with Parents and Those That Parents Have Mobilized
    Contending with Other Control Agencies
    Encountering Obstacles with Outside Agencies
    Negotiating Cases with Outside Agencies
    Consulting with Others regarding Cases at Hand
    Maintaining Documentation

✹ Conclusion

The empirical social world consists of ongoing group life and one has to get close to this life to know what is going on in it. If one is going to respect the social world, one's problems, guiding conceptions, data, schemes of relationship, and ideas of interpretation have to be faithful to that empirical world. This is especially true in the case of human group life because of the persistent tendency of human beings in their collective life to build up separate worlds, marked by an operating milieu of different life situations and by the possession of different beliefs and conceptions for handling these situations. [Blumer 1969:38]

I hope that by writing this chapter I will have helped generate a body of ethnographic inquiry that will add to our understanding not only of adolescence but also of the human condition more generally. Although certain experiences (and ambiguities) may seem particularly acute during adolescence, this time of life is one of great curiosity, learning, testing, and interpersonal manoeuvring.

Whether they wish to be the focus of attention or not, adolescents often find themselves on centre stage, in live theatre, performing amid diverse and uneven "supporting casts" before sets of audiences that often seem very critical, if not contradictory, in their appraisals and reactions. Adolescence thus represents a time of considerable dramatic realization. It can be an exciting, fun, carefree time, but it can also be a boring, confusing, frustrating, sensitive, and frightening time.

Ethnographic research along the lines outlined here can generate a great deal of substantively informed insight into the adolescent situation. This research must be done if social scientists and others are to begin to understand the adolescent life-world. This research is even more worth doing when you consider that the adolescent life-world does not exist unto itself but spills into, and intersects with, and shapes in various ways, the life experiences of a great many people in the community. Finally, since adolescent life-worlds are prototypes of subcultural pursuits more generally, this material can be used to foster generic appreciations of people's lived experiences in a great many contexts, especially those characterized by some sense of diversity within the broader community.

In closing, I must introduce one further caution. This pertains to the matter of *respecting the ethnographic other*. Not only must researchers attempt to convey the lived experiences of adolescents (or others being studied) to prospective readers in an open, careful, thorough manner, but the data gathered in the field must retain primacy over researchers' pre-existing conceptualizations of the adolescent experience. This means that researchers must put aside any moral or ideological agendas and personal disaffections they might hold regarding adolescence in general or certain adolescents in particular, and that they must use the material they gather in the field as the essential means of assessing (and reconstructing where necessary) any theoretical formulations (including the one presented here). Only in this way, by establishing an ongoing dialogue between working concepts and ongoing field research—by encouraging adolescents and others "to talk back to us"—may we develop a social science that is genuinely attentive to human lived experience and the interrelated practical accomplishment of human group life.

Notes

1. This paper is dedicated to all those adults who think they would be able to deal with adolescence a whole lot better the second time around, and to all those adolescents who think they can handle adulthood a whole lot better than any adult could.

2. I would very much like to thank Frank Fasick, Lorraine Prus, and Keith Warriner for their thoughtful comments on earlier drafts of this paper and for sharing their observations regarding their own adolescent experiences and those of others with whom they are familiar. In working through this article, I also found myself indebted to all of those who were part of my own experiences as an adolescent. This paper is very much a reflection of those experiences and of those of others I've observed over the years.

3. Frank Fasick (1994) provides a thoughtful account of "the *invention* of adolescence" as a rather uniquely institutionalized stage of human development in Western society. In particular, Fasick indicates how people in Western society responded to changes in population growth and other matters such as industrialization, urbanization, education, and commercialization to "objectify" (define, legitimate, stabilize, and emphasize) what might otherwise remain a relatively nebulous or indistinct aspect or stage of human development. For a somewhat parallel historical statement on the emergence (or discovery) of juvenile delinquency (as concept, a legal category, an institutionalized mode of response), see Platt (1969).

4. For a more detailed account of both the roots of symbolic interactionism and the varieties of interpretive approaches to the study of human group life, see Prus (1996). For other statements on symbolic interactionism, see Mead (1934) and especially Blumer (1969), but also Shibutani (1961), Lauer and Handel (1977), Karp and Yoels (1979), and Strauss (1993).

5. This attentiveness to the human production of action represents a vital point of divergence between interactionist and postmodernist approaches to the human condition (Dawson and Prus 1993a,b; 1994; Prus 1996).

6. Attentiveness to the necessity of developing a social science that adequately respects the intersubjective nature of the human group is very much rooted in the hermeneutics of Wilhelm Dilthey (1833–1911) [see Ermarth 1978]. This idea has been pursued very centrally by Mead (1934) and Blumer (1969). For an extended consideration of positivist and interpretive approaches to the study of human behaviour and the ensuing debates, see Prus (1996).

7. Mead (1934:78) observes, "[Things] become 'objects' or are brought into existence through a process of symbolization: *Symbolization constitutes objects not*

constituted before, objects that would not exist except for the context of social relationships wherein symbolization occurs. Language does not simply symbolize a situation or object that is already there in advance; it makes possible the existence or appearance of that situation or object, for it is a part of the mechanism whereby that situation or object is created."

8. See Schutz (1962) and Berger and Luckmann (1966) for elaborations of the "objectification" (and typification) process as this pertains to people's sense of reality and their "stocks of knowledge."

9. For an account of the development of ethnographic research in anthropology and sociology (especially, symbolic interaction), see Prus (1996). For other materials dealing with ethnographic research, see Paul (1953), Becker (1970), Wax (1971), Bogdan and Taylor (1975), Lofland and Lofland (1984), Jorgensen (1989), and Shaffir and Stebbins (1991).

10. See Dilthey (Ermarth 1978), Mead (1934), Blumer (1969), Giddens (1976, 1984), and Prus (1996) for elaborations of these notions as they apply to the social sciences. Although Giddens appears to have been the first person to use the term "double hermeneutic," it was Dilthey who first made the case for a social science that considered the uniquely hermeneutic or intersubjectivist nature of the human condition.

11. These notions of subculture were first developed in Prus and Irini's (1980) study of the "hotel community." Readers will observe that the hotel community takes its essence from the presence of several interrelated subcultures.

12. The terms *subcultural deviance* and *group-based deviance* are used interchangeably here. This is with the recognition that "subcultures" (and other reasonable facsimiles) can vary greatly in size, proportions of the general population, duration, articulation, and extensiveness of perspectives and activities, and distinctiveness. Likewise, the participants may enter, remain, and depart from these groups with very different types and levels of interests, expectations, and participation. Unruh (1979) and Prus and Irini (1980) speak specifically to these latter levels of participation.

13. It also may be highly instructive to consider "families as subcultures." This recognition may provide a valuable departure point for both studies of the social construction (and maintenance) of family life-worlds and adolescent lived experiences.

14. These notions are supported by research on delinquents, thieves, and hustlers (Shaw 1930; Sutherland 1937; Prus and Sharper 1977; Prus and Irini 1980), drug users (Ray 1961; Adler and Adler 1983a,b), the police (Skolnick 1966; Rubinstein 1973), gamblers (Lesieur 1977), outlaw bikers (Wolf 1991), and rock musicians (O'Bireck 1993).

15. For more material on the role that relationships play in continuities in deviance, see Shaw (1930), Cressey (1932), Sutherland (1937), Becker (1963:59–119),

Lofland (1966), Lesieur (1977), Prus and Sharper (1977), Prus and Irini (1980), Adler and Adler (1983a,b), Steffensmeier (1986), and Wolf (1991).

16. For depictions of pre-existing viewpoints and interests that foster involvements in particular subcultures (via seekership and neutralized familiarity), see Festinger et al. (1956), Lofland (1966), Prus and Sharper (1977), Prus and Irini (1980), and Wolf (1991).

17. See, for instance, research on delinquents (Shaw 1930), taxi-dancers (Cressey 1932), professional thieves (Sutherland 1937), marijuana users (Becker 1963), hustlers (Reiss 1961; Prus and Sharper 1977; Prus and Irini 1980), drug dealers (Adler and Adler 1983a), fences (Steffensmeier 1986), and bikers (Wolf 1991). Highly parallel themes are evident in studies of magic (Prus and Sharper 1991), ballet (Dietz 1994), shuffleboard (Snyder 1994a), and feminism (Wolf 1994); this suggests that people's involvements in particular networks are central to their subsequent viewpoints and activities.

18. These latter themes are particularly evident in Sutherland (1937), Reiss (1961), Lesieur (1977), Prus and Sharper (1977), Prus and Irini (1980), and Wolf (1991).

19. For instances of insider encouragement to continue one's subcultural involvements, see Shaw (1930), Sutherland (1937), Becker (1963:41–119), Lofland (1966), Prus and Irini (1980), Adler and Adler (1983a,b) Steffensmeier (1986), Ebaugh (1988), Prus and Sharper (1991), Sanders (1991), Wolf (1991), and O'Bireck (1993).

20. Tannenbaum (1938) and Lemert (1951; 1967) provide the classic statements on both the exclusionary practices of the moral community and the tendency for the targets of those exclusionary practices to become "secondary deviants." For instances of these practices at work, see Ray (1961), Lemert (1962), Wiseman (1970), and Prus and Irini (1980).

21. For a fuller statement on "generic social processes," see Prus (1994, 1996).

22. Blumer's (1933) and Blumer and Hauser's (1933) studies of adolescent experiences with the media are especially revealing (and relevant) with respect to the ways in which young people may seek out and use the media in attempts to come to terms with their life situations.

23. This listing of subprocesses on "acquiring perspectives" is taken from Prus (1994:396–397). Most ethnographies nicely illustrate themes pertaining to "the acquisition of perspectives" and almost inevitably address notions of identities, involvements, activities, and relationships as well, for these elements are very much interrelated in subcultural lifestyles. Some book-length ethnographies that do a particularly effective job of conveying the ways people become exposed to, and familiar with, particular world views include Anderson (1923), Shaw (1930), Blumer (1933), Blumer and Hauser (1933), Sutherland (1937), Becker et al., (1961, 1968), Goffman (1961), Lofland (1966), Edgerton (1967), Scott (1968), Bartell (1971), Dietz (1983), Fine (1983), Kleinman (1984), Evans and Falk

(1986), Stebbins (1990), Charmaz (1991), and Wolf (1991). Becker (1963) provides a highly instructive account of the ways that people acquire a set of perspectives on marijuana use. Similar definitional processes would seem operative not only with respect to adolescent experiences with cigarettes and alcohol, but also with respect to music, sexuality, dating, driving, eating habits, fashion involvements, and the like.

24. Whether people's experiences with "best" or "close" friends are more fleeting or more enduring, these relationships can be exceptionally consequential in a "here and now" sense. These relationships establish arenas in which adolescents commonly share (and mutually assess) their most intimate and exciting experiences as well as their most perplexing and distressing experiences. As well, even on a shorter-term basis, these same people are apt to accompany one another across a range of contexts and activities. Thus, they are likely to have access to all sorts of privileged information about the other. Likewise, because of this closeness, they are in a particularly viable position in which to influence one another (high levels of trust and affinity, greater awareness of particular interests and vulnerabilities, and so forth).

25. For interactionist materials dealing with interpersonal confrontations, see Emerson and Messinger (1977), Prus (1978), Athens (1980), Prus and Irini (1980), and Wolf (1991). In contrast to those who may be inclined to reduce interpersonal conflicts to matters of factors or personalities, those assuming a more consistent interactionist viewpoint tend to be particularly concerned with people's definitions of the situation (and senses of self) as well as the emergent or processual nature of human interchanges.

26. Although dating and sexuality often overlap, there are substantial advantages to separating the two both for purposes of inquiry and analysis. The two need not be synonymous in their directions, contexts, opportunities, pursuits, or accomplishments. Researchers working in this area would also want to be attentive to what people envision as "sexuality" at this and that point in their lives.

27. This material on developing relationships is derived from Prus (1994:408–409). The development, maintenance, and severance of relationships is given more explicit attention in the following monographs: Shaw (1930), Waller (1930), Hunt (1966), Lofland (1966), Wiseman (1970), Bartell (1971), Lesieur (1977), Prus and Irini (1980), Fine (1983), Adler (1985), Steffensmeier (1986), Vaughan (1986), Prus (1989a), Prus and Sharper (1991), and Wolf (1991). Lemert's (1962) analysis of "paranoia and the dynamics of exclusion" deserves special recognition as one of the most insightful accounts of interpersonal relationships.

28. The contemplation of ending one's life is a very real prospect when people encounter what they envision as extensive and unavoidable negativity or meaninglessness. Here as well, one may begin to examine this phenomenon in process terms. Although it is impossible to interview those who have actually taken their

own lives, one may still ask others about times in which they may have considered ending their own lives and the circumstances surrounding these occasions, being particularly mindful of people's definitions of their situations (and selves) and their interchanges with others over time. While much interactionist/ethnographic work could be done along these lines, readers may like to consider the tentative efforts of Douglas (1967), Jacobs (1967), and Henslin (1970).

29. This listing of processes pertaining to identity work is from Prus (1994: 397–399). Ethnographic monographs that are particularly attentive to identity work and self images include Edgerton (1967), Bartell (1971), Dietz (1983), Evans and Falk (1986), Haas and Shaffir (1987), Charmaz (1991), Sanders (1991), and Wolf (1991). For reviews of the literature on "identity work" as this pertains to type-casting, public designations, and resisting unwanted imputations, see Prus (1975a,b, 1983). These reviews build centrally on the conceptual work of Goffman (1959, 1963) and Klapp (1964, 1969, 1971), among others.

30. This statement on involvements or career contingencies is taken from Prus (1994:400–403), but was very much developed from research on the clergy (Prus 1976), card and dice hustlers (Prus and Sharper 1977), and an assortment of participants in the hotel community (Prus and Irini 1980).

31. Among the monographs that more explicitly address involvements or career contingencies in ethnographic inquiries are Shaw (1930), Cressey (1932), Sutherland (1937), Becker et al. (1961), Lofland (1966), Bartell (1971), Ditton (1977), Lesieur (1977), Prus and Irini (1980), Dietz (1983), Fine (1983), Haas and Shaffir (1987), Prus and Sharper (1991), Sanders (1991), and Wolf (1991).

32. Although other sources have been consequential as well, central inspiration for these involvement routings was derived from Lofland (1966; seekership, recruitment), Lemert (1953; closure), Becker (1963; recruitment, reduced reservations), Matza (1964; drift or reduced reservations), and Klapp (1969; seekership). Much of the work I have done has in various ways focused on the involvement process and has benefitted extensively from examinations of these notions (Prus 1976; Prus and Irini 1980; Prus 1989a,b; Prus and Frisby 1990; and Prus and Sharper 1991).

33. For a further elaboration of recruitment practices, see the subsequent discussion of "influencing others." See Prus (1989a) for a detailed ethnographic examination of the recruitment practices of salespeople engaged in "eye to eye, belly to belly" selling. Many adolescents may disidentify with the sales role, but overall they tend to be fairly effective "salespeople" when dealing with their peers (i.e., promoting their involvements in situations) and their parents. They may be especially effective with their friends, among whom may exist much pre-established trust as well as more extensive situational identifications and interests.

34. The matter of initial involvements is given particular attention in Shaw (1930), Cressey (1932), Sutherland (1937), Becker et al. (1961), Lofland (1966), Bartell (1971), Ditton (1977), Lesieur (1977), Prus and Irini (1980), Fine (1983), Haas and Shaffir (1987), Prus and Sharper (1991), Sanders (1991), and Wolf (1991).

35. See Ebaugh (1988) for a review of the literature on "Becoming an Ex," as well as an instructive attempt to formulate the generic social processes constituting disinvolvement. As with continuity and disinvolvement, it seems instructive to be attentive to the interlinkages of disinvolvement and reinvolvement processes. The implication is that all of these notions are much more fluid, partial, and ambiguous than seems commonly supposed.

36. Only a few studies have addressed the reinvolvement process in a substantial manner. See Ray (1961), Wiseman (1970), Lesieur (1977), Prus and Sharper (1977), and Prus and Irini (1980). Taken together, these studies suggest that considerable vacillation (disinvolvement and reinvolvement) may represent commonplace experiences for people involved in, and attempting to disentangle themselves from, many situations.

37. Notions of persuasion (influence and negotiation processes) are especially evident in the following monographs: Shaw (1930), Sutherland (1937), Festinger (1956), Lofland (1966), Emerson (1969), Wiseman (1970), Bartell (1971), Prus and Irini (1980), Ross (1980), Fine (1983), and Prus and Sharper (1991). The subprocesses outlined here are most extensively detailed in an analysis of interpersonal selling activity (Prus 1989a).

38. Sometimes, too, people's moral characters may be cast into doubt when they are seen as sympathetic with those deemed disrespectable, even though it is not apparent that they have any active contact with, or any interest in pursuing contact with, these others. Scholars doing research on deviance also tend to become "implicated by association" or become stigmatized as a consequence of doing research that involves disrespectable others (Henslin 1972).

39. While all of the material on influencing or recruiting others is pertinent here, Becker's (1963) account of marijuana users and Prus's (1983) study of drinking are particularly relevant.

40. As suggested in Prus's (1983) study of drinking activity, considerable stigma may be associated with those who try to discourage companions from pursuing more adventurous lines of action, particularly in settings in which the activities in question are endorsed by some participants. It may be very worthwhile to pursue this theme in other ethnographic studies.

41. While Goffman's (1959, 1963) work on impression management is central to "cloaking practices," readers may refer to studies of developmentally impaired persons (Edgerton 1967), medical students (Haas and Shaffir 1987), hustlers and

magicians (Prus and Sharper 1991), and university students (Albas and Albas 1994) for other instances of deception and concealment in people's attempts to selectively maintain an image.

42. It should not be assumed that equal concern is given to the management of respectable identities for oneself and one's peers or companions. Indeed, in another variant of "being mischievous," people sometimes delight in creating and directing dramas in which friends and other associates become "caught in the act of 'being bad.'"

43. This listing of the subprocesses subsumed by "performing activities" is from Prus (1994:404). The following book-length monographs provide some of the more focused materials on how people accomplish activities: Anderson (1923), Shaw (1930), Emerson (1969), Bartell (1971), Letkemann (1973), Hargreaves et al. (1975), Ditton (1977), Lesieur (1977), Prus and Irini (1980), Ross (1980), Dietz (1983), Fine (1983), Mitchell (1983), Albas and Albas (1994), Steffensmeier (1986), Prus (1989a,b), Charmaz (1991), Prus and Sharper (1991), and Wolf (1991).

44. While addressing people's educational experiences more generally, readers may benefit from examining the ethnographic studies of Becker et al. (1961, 1968), Hargreaves et al. (1975), Albas and Albas (1994), Haas and Shaffir (1987), and Adler and Adler (1991).

45. Although not all adolescents come from "religious backgrounds," this does not negate the importance of religious involvements for many people's experiences as adolescents. Indeed, those more extensively involved in religious communities may find adolescence a particularly difficult time as a consequence of the cross-pressures they experience from scripture, religious leaders, and members of their family (and the religious community at large). In addition to their own self-monitoring practices, self-appraisals, and doubts, adolescents are likely to find that these other people may be very reluctant to see adolescence as a justification for neglecting the faith.

46. Shaw's work (1930, 1931) consists mainly of case-study ethnographies. The Thrasher (1927) volume is much more difficult to describe in conventional methodological terms. Insofar as it represents a survey of over 1,300 gangs, it represents a mammoth undertaking. However, instead of relying on a question-naire of some sort, the volume is more on the nature of an ethnographic collage or potpourri that draws unevenly on a great many diverse sources and materials from gang members, control agencies, and the media. As Thrasher indicates, it is an exploratory venture and is to be viewed as a suggestive rather than a definitive document.

47. For more extended discussions of the inadequacies of "positivist/structuralist" social science for studying the human condition, see Blumer (1969), Gergen (1982), and Prus (1996).

48. These discussions (particularly the listings of the subprocesses involved) are taken from Prus (1996).

49. The following materials ethnographically depict the ways in which people attempt to establish groups or associations of sorts: Sutherland's (1937) professional thieves; Karsh et al.'s (1954) union organizers; Lofland's (1966) doomsday cult; Rubington's (1968) bottle-gangs; Prus and Sharper's (1977) road hustlers; Adler's (1985) drug dealers; Prus and Frisby's (1990) party plans; and Wolf's (1991) outlaw bikers. Although conceptually more disparate, readers will find aspects of these processes discussed with specific reference to juvenile gangs in Thrasher (1927), Shaw (1930, 1931), Jankowski (1991), and Padilla (1992).

50. For instances of "objectification" practices of groups wishing to become known in the community at large, see Goffman (1961), Wiseman (1970), Gusfield (1981, 1989), and Prus (1989a,b). For examples of internal objectification practices among those wishing to remain unnoticed in the larger community, see Sutherland (1937) and Prus and Sharper (1977). Still other groups may desire or flirt with a semipublic recognition—e.g., taxi-dance hall operators (Cressey 1932), drug dealers (Adler 1985), fences (Steffensmeier 1986), and outlaw bikers (Wolf 1991). For depictions of some of these processes as they pertain to juvenile gangs, see Thrasher (1927), Jankowski (1991), and Padilla (1992).

51. Those interested in how groups (organizations) make contact with and deal with outside parties (e.g., targets, clients, suspects) may wish to examine Cressey (1932), Sutherland (1937), Goffman (1961), Lofland (1966), Emerson (1969), Wiseman (1970), Prus and Sharper (1977), Prus and Irini (1980), Ross (1980), Haas and Shaffir (1987), Prus (1989b), and Wolf (1991). Focusing on juvenile gangs more specifically, Thrasher (1927), Shaw (1930, 1931), Jankowski (1991), and Padilla (1992) provide some illustrations of these notions in those settings.

52. For a particularly insightful discussion of the ways in which teachers handle "deviance in the classroom," see Hargreaves et al. (1975).

53. For some ethnographic literature that focuses more specifically on the processing of juveniles by control agencies, see Cicourel (1968), Emerson (1969), and Meehan (1992). See Prus (1992) for a conceptual statement on influence work in human services settings.

References

Adler, Patricia. 1985. *Wheeling and Dealing*. New York: Columbia University Press.

Adler, Patricia, and Peter Adler. 1983a. "Relationships Between Dealers: The Social Organization of Illicit Drug Transactions." *Sociology and Social Research* 67:260–278.

———. 1983b. "Shifts and Oscillation in Deviant Careers: The Case of Upper-Level Dealers and Smugglers." *Social Problems* 31:195–207.

———. 1987. *Membership Roles in Field Research*. Newbury Park, CA: Sage.

———. 1991. *Backboards and Blackboards: College Athletes and Role Engulfment*. New York: Columbia University Press.

Albas, Daniel C., and Cheryl Mills Albas. 1994. "Studying Students Studying." Pp. 273–289 in Mary Lorenz Dietz, Robert Prus, and William Shaffir (eds.), *Doing Everyday Life: Ethnography as Human Lived Experience*. Toronto: Copp Clark Longman.

Anderson, Nels. 1923. *The Hobo*. Chicago: University of Chicago Press.

Athens, Lonnie. 1980. *Violent Criminal Acts and Actors: A Symbolic Interactionist Study*. Boston: Oxford University Press.

Bartell, Gilbert. 1971. *Group Sex*. New York: Signet.

Becker, Howard S. 1963. *Outsiders*. New York: Free Press.

———. 1970. *Sociological Work: Method and Substance*. Chicago: Aldine.

Becker, Howard, Everett Hughes, and Blanche Geer. 1968. *Making the Grade: The Academic Side of Student Life*. New York: Wiley.

Becker, Howard, Everett Hughes, Blanche Geer, and Anselm Strauss. 1961. *The Boys in White*. Chicago: University of Chicago Press.

Berger, Peter, and Thomas Luckmann. 1966. *The Social Construction of Reality*. New York: Anchor.

Blumer, Herbert. 1933. *Movies and Conduct*. New York: Macmillan (Reprinted 1970. New York: Arno Press).

———. 1966. "Sociological Implications of the Thought of George Herbert Mead." *American Journal of Sociology* 71:535–548.

———. 1969. *Symbolic Interaction*. Berkeley, CA: University of California Press.

Blumer, Herbert, and Hauser, Philip. 1933. *Movies, Delinquency and Crime*. New York: Macmillan (Reprinted 1970. New York: Arno Press).

Bogdan, Robert, and Steven J. Taylor. 1975. *Introduction to Qualitative Research Methods: A Phenomenological Approach to the Social Sciences*. New York: Wiley Interscience.

Campbell, Anne. 1984. *The Girls in the Gang: A Report from New York City*. New York: Basil Blackwell.

Cameron, Mary O. 1964. *The Booster and the Snitch*. Glencoe, IL: Free Press.

Charmaz, Kathy. 1991. *Good Days and Bad Days: The Self in Chronic Illness*. New Brunswick, NJ: Rutgers University Press.

Cicourel, Aaron V. 1968. *The Social Organization of Juvenile Justice*. London: Heinemann (1976).

Cooley, Charles Horton. 1909. *Social Organization: A Study of the Larger Mind*. New York: Schocken.

———. 1922. *Human Nature and the Social Order* (1902). New York: Schocken.

Cressey, Donald. 1953. *Other People's Money: A Study in the Social Psychology of Embezzlement.* Glencoe, IL: Free Press.

Cressey, Paul G. 1932. *The Taxi-Dance Hall.* Chicago: University of Chicago Press.

Cummings, Scott, and Daniel K. Monti. 1993. *Gangs: The Origins and Impact of Contemporary Youth Gangs in the United States.* Albany, NY: State University of New York Press.

Dietz, Mary Lorenz. 1983. *Killing for Profit: The Social Organization of Felony Homicide.* Chicago: Nelson-Hall.

Dietz, Mary Lorenz, Robert Prus, and William Shaffir. 1994. "On Your Toes: Dancing Your Way into the Ballet World." Pp. 66–84 in Mary Lorenz Dietz, Robert Prus, and William Shaffir (eds.), *Doing Everyday Life: Ethnography as Human Lived Experience.* Toronto: Copp Clark Longman.

Ditton, James. 1977. *Part-Time Crime: An Ethnography of Fiddling and Pilferage.* London: Macmillan.

Douglas, Jack D. 1967. *The Social Meanings of Suicide.* Princeton, NJ: Princeton University Press.

Ebaugh, Helen Rose Fuchs. 1988. *Becoming an Ex.* Chicago: University of Chicago Press.

Edgerton, Robert. 1967. *The Cloak of Competence: Stigma in the Lives of the Mentally Retarded.* Berkeley, CA: University of California Press.

Emerson, Robert M. 1969. *Judging Delinquents.* Chicago: Aldine.

Emerson, Robert M., and Sheldon L. Messinger. 1977. "The Micro-Politics of Trouble." *Social Problems* 25:121–134.

Ermarth, Michael. 1978. *Wilhelm Dilthey: The Critique of Historical Reason.* Chicago: University of Chicago Press.

Evans, A. Donald, and W.W. Falk. 1986. *Learning to Be Deaf.* Berlin: Mouton.

Fasick, Frank. 1994. "On the Invention of Adolescence." *Journal of Early Adolescence* 14:6–23.

Festinger, Leon, Henry Riecken, and Stanley Schacter. 1956. *When Prophecy Fails.* New York: Harper and Row.

Fine, Gary A. 1983. *Shared Fantasy: Role Playing Games as Social Worlds.* Chicago: University of Chicago Press.

Gergen, Kenneth. 1982. *Toward Transformation in Social Knowledge.* New York: Springer-Verlag.

Giddens, Anthony. 1976. *New Rule of the Sociological Method.* London: Hutchinson.

———. 1984. *The Constitution of Society.* Cambridge: Polity.

Goffman, Erving. 1959. *The Presentation of Self in Everyday Life.* New York: Anchor.

———. 1961. *Asylums.* New York: Anchor.

———. 1963. *Stigma.* Englewood Cliffs, NJ: Spectrum.

Haas, Jack, and William Shaffir. 1987. *Becoming Doctors: The Adaption of a Cloak of Competence.* Greenwich, CT: Jai.

Hagedorn, John M. 1990. "Back in the Field Again: Gang Research in the Nineties." Pp. 240–259 in Ronald Huff (ed.), *Gangs in America*. Newbury Park, CA: Sage.

Hargreaves, David, Stephen Hester, and Frank Melor. 1975. *Deviance in Classrooms*. London: Routledge and Kegan Paul.

Hearn, H.L., and Patricia Stoll. 1975. "Continuance Commitments in Low-Status Occupations: The Cocktail Waitress." *Sociological Quarterly* 16:105–114.

Henslin, James. 1970. "Guilt and Guilt Neutralization: Responses and Adjustment to Suicide." Pp. 192–228 in Jack Douglas (ed.), *Deviance and Respectability*. New York: Basic.

———. 1972. "Studying Deviance in Four Settings: Researcher Experiences with Cabbies, Suicidees, Drug Users, and Abortionees." Pp. 35–70 in Jack D. Douglas (ed.), *Research on Deviance*. New York: Random House.

Higgins, Paul. 1979. "Outsiders in a Hearing World: The Deaf Community." *Urban Life* 8:3–22.

Hunt, Morton. 1966. *The World of the Formerly Married*. New York: McGraw-Hill.

Jacobs, Jerry. 1967. "A Phenomenological Study of Suicide Notes." *Social Problems* 15:62–72.

Jankowski, Martin Sanchez. 1991. *Islands in the Street: Gangs and American Urban Culture*. Berkeley, CA: University of California Press.

Jorgensen, Danny. 1989. *Participant Observation*. Newbury Park, CA: Sage.

Karp, David A., and William Yoels. 1979. *Symbols, Selves, and Society: Understanding Interaction*. New York: Lippincott/Harper & Row.

Klapp, Orrin. 1964. *Symbolic Leaders*. London: Minerva.

———. 1969. *The Collective Search for Identity*. New York: Holt.

———. 1971. *Social Types: Process, Structure and Ethos*. San Diego, CA: Aegis.

Kleinman, Sherryl. 1984. *Equals before God: Seminarians as Humanistic Professionals*. Chicago: University of Chicago Press.

Lauer, Robert H., and Warren H. Handel. 1977. *The Theory and Application of Symbolic Interaction*. Boston: Houghton-Mifflin.

Lemert, Edwin. 1951. *Social Pathology*. New York: McGraw-Hill.

———. 1953. "An Isolation and Closure Theory of Naive Check Forgery." *Journal of Criminal Law, Criminology and Police Science* 44:296–307.

———. 1962. "Paranoia and the Dynamics of Exclusion." *Sociometry* 25:2–25.

———. 1967. *Human Deviance, Social Problems and Social Control*. Englewood Cliffs, NJ: Prentice-Hall.

Lesieur, Henry. 1977. *The Chase*. New York: Anchor.

Letkemann, Peter. 1973. *Crime as Work*. Englewood Cliffs, NJ: Prentice-Hall.

Lofland, John. 1966. *The Doomsday Cult*. Englewood Cliffs, NJ: Prentice-Hall.

Lofland, John, and Lyn Lofland. 1984. *Analyzing Social Settings*. Belmont, CA: Wadsworth.

Lyman, Stanford, and Marvin Scott. 1970. *Sociology of the Absurd.* New York: Appleton-Century-Crofts.

Matza, David. 1964. *Delinquency and Drift.* New York: Wiley.

Mead, George H. 1934. *Mind, Self and Society,* Charles W. Morris (ed.). Chicago: University of Chicago Press.

———. 1936. *Movements of Thought in the Nineteenth Century,* Merritt A. Moore (ed). Chicago: University of Chicago Press.

Meehan, Albert J. 1992. "'I Don't Prevent Crime, I Prevent Calls': Policing as a Negotiated Order." *Symbolic Interaction* 15:455–480.

Mitchell, Richard G., Jr. 1983. *Mountain Experience.* Chicago: University of Chicago Press.

O'Bireck, Gary. 1993. *Gettin' Tall: Cocaine Use within a Subculture of Canadian Professional Music.* Toronto: Canadian Scholars' Press.

Padilla, Felix. 1992. *The Gang as an American Enterprise.* New Brunswick, NJ: Rutgers University Press.

Paul, Benjamin. 1953. "Interview Techniques and Field Relationships." Pp. 430–451 in Alfred L. Kroeber (ed.), *Anthropology Today: An Encyclopedia Inventory.* Chicago: University of Chicago Press.

Platt, Anthony. 1969. *The Child Savers.* Chicago: University of Chicago Press.

Prus, Robert. 1975a. "Labeling Theory: A Reconceptualization and a Propositional Statement on Typing." *Sociological Focus* 8(1):79–96.

———. 1975b. "Resisting Designations: An Extension of Attribution Theory into a Negotiated Context." *Sociological Inquiry* 45(1):3–14.

———. 1976. "Religious Recruitment and the Management of Dissonance: A Sociological Perspective." *Sociological Inquiry* 46:127–134.

———. 1978. "From Barrooms to Bedrooms: Towards a Theory of Interpersonal Violence." Pp. 51–73 in M.A.B. Gammon (ed.), *Violence in Canada.* Toronto: Methuen.

———. 1983. "Drinking as Activity: An Interactionist Analysis." *Journal of Studies on Alcohol* 44 (3):460–475.

———. 1989a. *Making Sales: Influence as Interpersonal Accomplishment.* Newbury Park, CA: Sage.

———. 1989b. *Pursuing Customers: An Ethnography of Marketing Activities.* Newbury Park, CA: Sage.

———. 1992. "Influence Work in Human Services Settings." *Current Research on Occupations and Professions* 7:41–56.

———. 1994. "Generic Social Processes: Intersubjectivity and Transcontextuality in the Social Sciences." Pp. 393–412 in Mary Lorenz Dietz, Robert Prus, and William Shaffir (eds.), *Doing Everyday Life: Ethnography as Human Lived Experience.* Toronto: Copp Clark Longman.

————. 1996. *Symbolic Interaction and Ethnographic Research: Intersubjectivity and the Study of Human Lived Experience*. Albany, NY: State University of New York Press.

Prus, Robert, and Wendy Frisby. 1990. "Persuasion as Practical Accomplishment: Tactical Maneuverings at Home Party Plans." Pp. 133–162 in Helena Znaniecki Lopata (ed.), *Current Research on Occupations and Professions: Societal Influences*. Greenwich, CT: Jai Press.

Prus, Robert, and Styllianoss Irini. 1980. *Hookers, Rounders, and Desk Clerks: The Social Organization of the Hotel Community*. Salem, WI: Sheffield.

Prus, Robert, and C.R.D. Sharper. 1977. *Road Hustler: The Career Contingencies of Professional Card and Dice Hustlers*. Lexington, MA: Lexington.

————. 1991. *Road Hustler: Hustlers, Magic and the Thief Subculture*. New York: Kaufman and Greenberg.

Ray, Marsh. 1961. "The Cycle of Abstinence and Relapse among Heroin Addicts." *Social Problems* 9:132–140.

Reiss, Albert J., Jr. 1961. "The Social Integration of Queers and Peers." *Social Problems* 9:102–120.

Ross, H. Lawrence. 1980. *Settled Out of Court*. New York: Aldine.

Rubinstein, Jonathan. 1973. *City Police*. New York: Ballantine.

Sanders, Clinton. 1991. *Customizing the Body: The Art and Culture of Tattooing*. Philadelphia: Temple University Press.

Schutz, Alfred. 1962. *Collected Papers I: The Problem of Social Reality*. The Hague: Martinus Nijhoff.

————. 1964. *Collected Papers II: Studies in Social Theory*. The Hague: Martinus Nijhoff.

Scott, Marvin. 1968. *The Racing Game*. Chicago: Aldine.

Shaw, Clifford. 1930. *The Jack-Roller: The Natural History of a Delinquent Career*. Chicago: University of Chicago Press.

————. 1931. *The Natural History of a Delinquent Career*. Chicago: University of Chicago Press.

Shibutani, Tamotsu. 1961. *Society and Personality*. Englewood Cliffs, NJ: Prentice-Hall.

Skolnick, Jerome. 1966. *Justice without Trial*. New York: Wiley.

Snyder, Eldon. 1994a. "Getting Involved in the Shuffleboard World." Pp. 85–108 in Mary Lorenz Dietz, Robert Prus, and William Shaffir (eds.), *Doing Everday Life: Ethnography as Human Lived Experience*. Toronto: Copp Clark Longman.

————. 1994b. "Interpretations and Explanations of Deviance among College Athletes: A Case Study." *Sociology of Sport Journal* 11:231–248.

Stebbins, Robert. 1970. "On Misunderstanding the Concept of Commitment." *Social Forces* 48:526–529.

———. 1971. *Commitment to Deviance: The Nonprofessional Criminal in the Community*. Westport, CT: Greenwood Press.

———. 1990. *The Laugh-Makers*. Montreal: McGill-Queen's University Press.

Steffensmeier, Darrell J. 1986. *The Fence: In the Shadow of Two Worlds*. Totowa, NJ: Rowman and Littlefield.

Strauss, Anselm. 1993. *Continual Permutations of Action*. New York: Aldine de Gruyter.

Sutherland, Edwin. 1937. *The Professional Thief*. Chicago: University of Chicago Press.

———. 1939. *Principles of Criminology* (3rd edition). Philadelphia: Lippincott.

Tannenbaum, Frank. 1938. *Crime and the Community*. New York: Columbia University Press.

Thrasher, Frederic M. 1927. *The Gang: A Study of 1,313 Gangs in Chicago* [1963 abridged edition]. Chicago: University of Chicago Press.

Unruh, David. 1979. "Characteristics and Types of Participation in Social Worlds." *Symbolic Interaction* 2:115–129.

Vaughan, Diane. 1986. *Uncoupling: Turning Points in Intimate Relationships*. New York: Oxford University Press.

Waller, Willard. 1930. *The Old Love and the New*. Carbondale, IL: Southern Illinois University Press (1967).

———. 1932. *The Sociology of Teaching*. New York: Russel and Russel (1961).

Wax, Rosalie. 1971. *Doing Fieldwork*. Chicago: University of Chicago Press.

Wiseman, Jacqueline. 1970. *Stations of the Lost: The Treatment of Skid Row Alcoholics*. Englewood Cliffs, NJ: Prentice-Hall.

Wolf, Charlotte. 1994. "Conversion into Feminism." Pp. 143–157 in Mary Lorenz Dietz, Robert Prus, and William Shaffir (eds.), *Doing Everyday Life: Ethnography as Human Lived Experience*. Toronto: Copp Clark Longman.

Wolf, Daniel. 1991. *The Rebels: A Brotherhood of Outlaw Bikers*. Toronto: University of Toronto Press.

CHAPTER 2

What Do 'They' Know? Delinquency as Mediated Texts

L.A. Visano

York University

The old-fashioned respect for the young is fast dying out.
Oscar Wilde

✸ Delinquency, Discipline, and Distance

A critical analysis of delinquency, as it is officially constructed by statistics and routinely projected by the media, provides a long-overlooked appreciation of the relationship between youth and law. Simply, juvenile delinquency is a text constituted according to numbing numbers, bureaucratic babble, and legal traditions. This paper highlights the cultural bases of conflict directed at youths. There are discrepancies between the familiar *images* about youths and the alien *realities* of youth. Within the phenomenology of youth the concept of "distance" provides a compelling coherence. Within this relational perspective of "law and society," delinquency is not solely confined to individual or institutional constructions; rather, delinquency is a consequence of complex configurations within culture, law, and the political economy. In short, delinquency (the text) constitutes and is constituted by relations of power (subtext) that are mediated by cultural forms of the media (intertexts). There is no integrated text of delinquency—only fragmented narratives that distance youth. The criminological canons depict delinquency as a text located in the body of the juvenile. Laws, practices, and policies respond to trouble as an autonomous object with a system of propositions.

The culture of juvenile justice, filtered through stunning statistics and enslaving images, privileges the ideology of individualism, corporate power, and the authority of the state. Moreover, delinquency is constructed within a framework of sophisticated surveillance that is characteristic of industrial and post-industrial societies. This ubiquitous moral regulation is legitimated by institutions of the law, media, work, and education that articulate the sanctity of discipline. The prevailing legal–materialist values based on the sovereignty of individualism destroy the dignity of those individuals, organizations, and communities deviantized as the "others"—youths. The "official" versions of delinquency are manipulated by the numerous stakeholders for self-serving reasons. The processes and structures of delinquency are indistinguishable from forms of representation of youth. In the production of these texts, the concept of youth disappears or is reduced to the presentation of trouble.

✸ Stupefying Statistics as Technocratic Talk

In Canada, juveniles account for 14 percent of all those charged with violent crimes (Department of Justice 1993:3). In 1991, Canadian police laid 18,769 charges against youths for violent offences; in 1986, they laid only 9,275—less than half as many (*Toronto Star*, May 6, 1993:A21). This was despite the fact that the population of youths *decreased* between 1986 and 1991. Statistics Canada reported that the number of youth court cases involving violence increased by 9 percent between 1991–92 and 1992–93. In 1993–94, there were 116,000 cases, representing 213,000 charges, processed in youth courts in Canada (Canadian Criminal Justice Association 1995:12). In 1986, there were 17 murders and 4 manslaughter cases involving young offenders; in 1991, the numbers were 32 and 12 (Statistics Canada 1992a:5). The murder rate for youths remained the same between 1986 and 1991. Between 1986 and 1992, an average number of 45 youths were charged with homicide (murder, manslaughter, infanticide) each year (Department of Justice 1993:3). In 1992–93, youth courts heard 42 murder cases; 74 attempted cases; 10 manslaughter cases; and 5 aggravated sexual assault and 311 aggravated assault cases (Department of Justice 1994).

Most charges laid against youths are for property offences such as theft. In 1992, the number of youths aged 12 to 17 arrested for *all crimes* fell by almost 5 percent from the previous year; arrests for violent crimes increased by 6 percent (Canadian Criminal Justice Association 1994:11). There were 94 cases transferred to adult court (ibid). In 1992, 140,000 youths were charged with Criminal Code and other federal statute offences—an increase of 25 percent in seven years. Of the 115,000 cases heard by youth courts in 1992–93, 66 percent resulted in findings of guilt. One-third of those found guilty were given a custody sentence. On an average day, 4,734 youths were in correctional facilities; of these, one-third were in secure custody facilities (Department of Justice 1994).

Canada's justice system, from policing to corrections, costs $150 million every week (Canadian Criminal Justice Association 1994:12). It costs up to $128,000 a year to keep a young offender in secure custody (ibid:4). Specifically, it costs the province $200 to $300 a day to jail a young offender (*Ottawa Citizen*, December 10, 1994:A2).

The 1992 American National Crime Survey reports that 3 million crimes occur in or near American schools every year—one every ten seconds. In 1990, 3,398 youths aged 10 to 19 were murdered. In the 1980s, 19,346 teenagers were murdered. The teenage murder rate in the 1990s is roughly twice that of the turbulent 1960s (Foster 1993:56). Homicide arrests of youths aged 10 to 14 rose from 194 to 301 between 1988 and 1992 (Lacayo 1994:21). During the three-year period 1991 to 1994 in Los Angeles, 460 homicides were committed by people under 18 (ibid). Homicide is the third-leading cause of death in the United States for elementary and middle school children. For instance, Milwaukee, a city of 630,000, recorded six juvenile arrests for homicide in 1983, compared to 82 in 1992 (*Time*, December 20, 1993:25).

In the United States, young people (12 to 17 years old) are more likely than anyone else to be the victim of violent crime. The U.S. Department of Justice reports that members of this age group are robbed, raped, or assaulted at five times the rate suffered by adults 35 or older (74.2 cases per 1,000 compared to 13.9 per 1,000; *The Globe and Mail*, July 18, 1994:A7). One in 13 juveniles was a victim of a violent crime in 1992; in 1987, the figure was one in 17. In 1992, there were 6.6 million violent crimes in the United States and about 23 percent of the victims were juveniles (ibid). The same U.S. Department of Justice report also noted the following: 1.5 million violent crimes were committed against juveniles (Bureau of Justice Statistics Update 1991:3); two-thirds of the victims were attacked by someone aged 12 to 20; 83 percent of crimes were assaults; 56 percent did not involve weapons or serious injury, while 27 percent involved serious injury. For serious juvenile court cases (BJS, July 24, 1994), the juvenile court case load in the United States grew 26 percent between 1987 and 1992, although cases involving drug offences fell 12 percent. Males were involved in 81 percent of all delinquency cases. White juveniles were the offenders 65 percent of the time, black juveniles 31 percent of the time. In 20 percent of the cases the juvenile was held in a detention facility for at least part of the process. Of the almost 1.5 million juvenile court cases handled during 1992, about 11,700 were transferred to an adult criminal court. Between 1988 and 1992 the number of juvenile court cases involving crimes against people grew 56 percent; for property crimes the increase was 23 percent; for public order offences it was 21 percent. (Table 2.1 shows the breakdown.)

John Wilson, Acting Administrator of the U.S. Justice Department's Office of Juvenile Justice and Delinquency Prevention, states: "The trend is sharply up and this is greatly troubling." The American courts handled about 118,600 murders, rapes, robberies, and aggravated assaults in 1992—a 68 percent increase over 1988. According to Wilson, "such a substantial increase in serious violent crimes committed by young people is a telling indicator of the

Table 2.1

American Juvenile Justice Cases (processed) for 1992

Crimes against people	301,000
Criminal homicide	2,500
Forcible rape	5,400
Robbery	32,900
Aggravated assault	77,900
Simple assault	152,800
Other violent sex offences	9,900
Other crimes against people	19,800
Property crimes	842,200
Burglary	156,400
Larceny-theft	361,600
Motor vehicle theft	73,000
Arson	8,300
Vandalism	121,700
Trespassing	58,500
Stolen property offences	28,900
Other property offences	33,700
Drug law violations	72,100
Public order offences	255,900
Obstruction of justice	87,100
Disorderly conduct	69,300
Weapons offences	41,000
Liquor law violations	12,500
Non-violent sex offences	12,900
Other public order offences	33,000

Source: BJS, July 24, 1994.

enormity of the problems we face." Likewise, New York's Democrat representative Charles Schumer warned, in *USA Today*:

> Disturbing figures about violence in America are released so often we treat them as if they were a box score from yesterday's baseball game. Our country has to take radical action to counter this trend of violence. [July 18, 1994]

In the United States the character of juvenile delinquency has become increasingly shaped by firearms. Young people between 16 and 19 are the most frequent victims of firearm violence. In 1992, this group was victimized by firearms 21 percent more often than those 20 to 24 years old and three times more often than those aged 35 to 49 (BJS 1994c). Gunshots now cause one-quarter of all deaths among American teenagers, according to the National Center for Health. Bullets killed 4,200 American teenagers in 1990, up from 2,500 in 1985. Fifty thousand children were killed by guns between 1979 and 1991—a figure equivalent to the number of Americans killed in the Vietnam War (*Toronto Star*, January 23, 1994:E5). About 15 American children are killed every two days by firearms. Another 30 are wounded. An American child is 15 times more likely to die by gunfire than a child in Northern Ireland. According to the Atlanta-based Centers for Disease Control, one American student in 5 carries a weapon of some kind to school, and one in 20 carries a gun; firearms have replaced traffic accidents as the leading cause of injury-related death among young Americans.

Young black males are the most vulnerable to handgun crime. Among males 16 to 19, the victimization rate for blacks was four times the victimization rate for whites. (Table 2.2 gives the breakdown for this statistic.) Black

Table 2.2

Non-Fatal Crimes Committed with Handguns per 1,000 Persons, 1987–92

Victim's age	Males		Females	
	White	Black	White	Black
12–15	3.1	14.1	2.1	4.7
16–19	9.5	39.7	3.6	13.4
20–24	9.2	29.4	3.5	9.1
25–34	4.9	12.3	2.1	9.0
35–49	2.7	8.7	1.4	3.3
50–64	1.2	3.5	0.7	1.6
65 or older	0.6	3.7	0.2	2.3

Source: Bureau of Justice Statistics 1994b; Visano 1993.

male teenagers are more likely to be violent crime victims than any other group of Americans. Their average annual victimization rate is 113 per 1,000 residents, or about one in 9. For white male teenagers the rate is 90 per 1,000, or about one in 11. About one in 32 urban black males from 16 through 24 years old is a handgun victim every year (BJS, Nov. 21, 1993). The number of murders with a handgun totalled 13,200 in 1992, a 24% jump from the five-year average. Blacks were three times as likely as whites to be victims of handgun crimes; young black males were the most vulnerable group to handgun crimes.

✹ Legal Layers and Cultural Codes of the Young Offenders Act

Canadian statistics show that charges against young offenders and incidents of youth violence have levelled off over the past decade. Yet public concern remains high. How we deal with young offenders says a great deal about our values as a society and will have an impact on the caseload that our justice system will have to bear in the future (Canadian Teachers' Federation 1995). A 1993 discussion paper issued by the federal Department of Justice states that the crime rate among Canadian youths has remained more or less constant over the past five to ten years. Yet "Canadians are more concerned about youth crime now than we have been at times in the past"(ibid). According to 1992 figures, youths 12 to 17 were responsible for less than one-quarter of Criminal Code charges and for only 14 percent of violent crimes. Most of the charges against youths in 1992 were for property offences, ranging from theft under $1,000 to more serious crimes such as break and enter. Almost half of all charges for violent offences consisted of "minor" assaults like slaps and punches. The number of minor assault charges increased between 1986 and 1992, the federal paper stated. It is not known whether this increase reflects police officers' greater willingness to lay charges for more minor assaults, or whether such incidents are merely being reported to police more often than before. As noted earlier, between 1986 and 1992 an average of 45 young people were charged with homicide each year. One in five charges for violent offences involved assault with a weapon, and one in ten involved sexual assault. In 1992–93, statistics on youth crime from the Canadian Centre for Justice Statistics showed a 7 percent decrease in property crime and a 9 percent increase in violent crime over the previous year. A careful scrutiny indicates that two-thirds of the latter increase was due to greater reporting of minor assaults, such as fights and scuffles (*Ottawa Citizen*, December 10, 1994:A1). According to the Canadian Centre for Justice Statistics, between 1986 and 1993 the youth court caseload in Canada increased 27 percent, mainly because of a rise in administrative offences such as failure to comply with a disposition and failure to appear in court (ibid, December 12, 1994:A2).

In 1994, in response to a "public panic" and the concomitant pressures to crack down on violent youth crime, Canada's justice minister, Allan Rock, tabled Bill C-37 to amend the Young Offenders Act (YOA) to move 16 and 17 year olds to adult court to face adult punishment if they are charged with serious criminal acts. The new law will lower the age limit from 18 to 16 for young offenders who have committed one or more of the six most serious crimes in the Criminal Code: first-degree murder, manslaughter, kidnapping, armed robbery, rape, and aggravated sexual assault. Youth court sentences will be increased to a maximum of ten years from five years for those convicted of first-degree murder; and second-degree murder will move to seven years maximum. Young offenders charged with the above offences will have the option of a trial by judge alone or by judge and jury, as is required under the Charter of Rights and Freedoms. Changes to parole eligibility will ensure that youths sentenced in the adult system will serve longer periods in custody. They will, however, be segregated from hardened adult inmates. Also, there will be no prosecution of those under 10 years of age. The proposed amendments are designed to provide strategic approaches to reform young offender laws and systems. The declaration of principles in the YOA will be changed to indicate that the primary objective of the youth system is the protection of society, which is best served by the rehabilitation of young offenders wherever possible (Department of Justice 1994:3). Under the new law, the onus will be on the 16 and 17 year olds charged with murder to show that they should be tried in youth court rather than adult court, where the penalty is life imprisonment instead of ten years.

For many years the YOA and its predecessor, the Juvenile Delinquents Act (JDA), have been scapegoats for Canada's social problems. As noted by the Canadian Criminal Justice Association, current changes to the YOA are hasty piecemeal proposals; their solutions are a short-term response to the ill-founded perception that youth crime is increasing (Canadian Criminal Justice Association 1994). Despite their obvious quick-fix appeal, the above changes will not solve the problem of youth violence. Why replicate and model the juvenile justice system after the adult criminal justice system, which has not deterred violent crime? Moreover, juvenile laws were historically designed to intervene and redirect youths in trouble within a "child saving" protectionism. Since its inception, the YOA has been a punitive measure, contradicting the principles of "doing good." Juvenile laws have had difficulties balancing "doing justice" with "doing good." Getting tough has been costly and has had limited results. This money could be better spent on prevention and rehabilitation, for example on the development of a wider range of community alternatives and programs such as specialized foster care, intensive tracking, day centres, and so on (ibid). For instance, the pressure to "fix" the problem of violence in schools (especially as it relates to weapons) is typically placed on the police and the schools. These very narrow solutions include hiring more security personnel, increasing discipline, hiring better teachers, teaching more relevant courses, applying zero tolerance, and offering smaller classes. These responses tend to decontextualize violence in the wider community (Solicitor General 1994:1). A zero tolerance policy will inflate crime statistics given that all violence, including minor cases, will be reported.

Interestingly, the levels of analysis evident in the above changes to the YOA remain confined to "manageable" remedies at the interpersonal and organizational level. To illustrate, the following factors are continually recycled: family problems, including conflicts at home, abuse in its varying forms, or parents' involvement in criminal activity; school problems, including truancy, learning disabilities, failing grades, or conflict with teachers; a history of antisocial behaviour; drug or alcohol abuse; peer influences; membership in a gang (Canadian Teachers' Federation 1995). The text of juvenile delinquency as measured by official numbers and articulated juridically has always been shaped by political expedience in interpreting public sentiments, by a flurry of proposals from an endless parade of self-serving consultants, by bureaucratic pressures, and by powerful moral entrepreneurs, from the police to child welfare advocates. Consequently, juvenile offenders and their respective reactors have become the foci while the following remain untouched: inequality, the equivocation of law, the institutions of authority like the family, the nature of the educational system, the sensationalizing media, the lack of political will in seeking genuine remedies, unemployment and underemployment, unequal opportunities, the underfunding of social services, the manufacture and proliferation of both drugs and weapons, the overrepresentation of minorities, and the pervasive culture of violence. Despite the YOA's lofty pronouncements of neutrality, its spirit, content, and applications have been and will continue to be unresponsive to social injustices (Fitzpatrick 1990:259).

By providing "universalistic" protections, the YOA seeks to transcend material conditions. The liberal–legal appeal of "equality" and the cultural talk of freedom are powerful ideological tools. Legal slogans, mythologies, and rhetoric are empty; as Gates (1990:328) aptly puts it, "cultural nominalism tyrannizes through tautology." The YOA amendments are attractive legal palliatives and a bonanza for legal businesses, replete with convenient mythologies. The YOA is a dogmatic and single-minded collection of liberal narratives that are inherently contradictory. Note the false oppositions regarding the responsibility of the community to the offender and the responsibility of the offender to the community (Platt 1989:9). The act seeks to balance the interests of society with those of young persons; "doing good" and "doing justice"; conscience and convenience; accountability and due process. Witness, for example, the ambiguity, equivocation, and double-talk of the following sections:

3(1)(c): young persons who commit offences require supervision, discipline and control, but because of their state of dependency and level of development and maturity, they also have special needs and require guidance and assistance;

3(1)(f): in the application of this Act, the rights and freedoms of young persons include a right to the least possible interference with freedom that is consistent with the protection of society, having regard to the needs of young persons and the interests of their families.

3(1)(b): society must, although it has the responsibility to take reasonable measures to prevent criminal conduct by young persons, be afforded the necessary protection from illegal behaviour.

3(1)(e): young persons have rights and freedoms in their own right, including those stated in the Canadian Charter of Rights and Freedoms ...

These exaggerated oppositional claims are further exacerbated when the principle of law is contrasted with the discretionary practices of legal agents. An examination of the actual provisions of fundamental rights, or of the behaviour of law, will challenge prevailing myths about juvenile justice. For example, in the YOA or its amendments there is little evidence of organizational changes designed to remove direct obstacles to equality. Likewise, the Charter of Rights and Freedoms—the supreme law of the land—has failed miserably in extending to young people the most basic entitlements of citizenship as they relate to health, education, employment, and social services.

The social data overwhelmingly demonstrate that law is unresponsive to current societal concerns. Law, as a "disembodied spectacle" (O'Neill 1985) is largely divorced from its larger social foundations—the people. As Foucault admonished: "One should start with popular justice, with acts of justice by the people, and go on to ask what place a court could have within this" (1980:1). Fundamental ideological disputes characterize the relationship between law and society. Everyday life is so legally constructed that the social actor has become a "juridic" agent ever bearing in mind the universal backdrop of law.

Law has become the language of official authority. Within the lexicon of law, the basic idea of juvenile justice is too relativistic. Turgid case law, incomprehensible legalese, and abstract principles do not fit well with principles of justice. Law is both remedial and coercive: a blessing for some and a curse for others. Law protects and punishes, imprisons and liberates. The laurels of law can easily become its wreaths. Does the law, therefore, appropriately reflect the dynamics, dialectics, and diversity of Canada's youth? The YOA cannot on its own facilitate the resolution of social disputes. In fact, law is essentially a system of restraints that is inimical to freedoms (Friedenberg 1971:45). Too much reliance on the judiciary as a forum for the provision of justice invites difficulties. Legal discourses on equality limit the scope for social change by justifying pre-existing distributions of opportunities (ibid).

Just as society is legally constituted, law is "linguistically constructed" (Leyh 1992:285). Accordingly, the YOA must be understood in terms of the contemporary contexts of meaning (ibid:284). This means that our under-standing of the text of juvenile delinquency and its attendant laws is culturally contingent. There is no unmediated relationship to the world of phenomena. Conceptually, delinquency per se lacks essentialism or foundationalism. Rather, delinquency as a cultural construction is historically situated. History and its legal traditions are overshadowed by what prevailing ideologies present as pressing.

The North American juvenile justice system was designed 100 years ago to reform youths found guilty of minor crimes. Increasingly, the system has become overwhelmed by teen violence. As of September 1994, three American states—California, Arkansas, and Georgia—had enacted laws reducing the "age of adult crime" to 14. Youths 14 to 17 charged with certain crimes are automatically tried as adults.

> The behaviour of young offenders, especially when their actions are violent, challenges some of our most basic assumptions about the education system. When even a small number of teenagers break the law or commit violent acts, their aggression raises questions about the ability of society to transmit the values of caring, responsible citizenship. [Canadian Teachers' Federation 1995: Issue Sheet No. 10]

The above passage assumes a fundamental consensus, a taken-for-granted common sense about the authority of institutions and the troubling character of youth. In the following section we examine how the above text of delin-quency is preserved and promoted.

✹ Mediated Messages: Commercial Contexts of Truths

From popular and seemingly innocuous televised cartoons to more sober news-casts in the mainstream media, certain versions of the truth are learned. All aspects of the dominant Canadian culture project a complex set of "shared" understandings, beliefs, and customs that in turn frame conventional thinking. Everyday practices are replete with significant ceremonies, signs, symbols, cues, and clues, which pattern gestures, rituals, and performances, which in turn stage degrees of cultural affiliations. Thus, social membership or a bind-ing way of life constitutes and is constituted by the interplay between specific behavioural circumstances and powerful ideologies that structure society. Institutionalized behaviour, identity, and thought have become "naturalized" to the extent that deviance has become framed according to very familiar commonsense notions. But how is this sense of knowing something about delinquency acquired?

Conceptually, delinquency exists in reference to well-established (if poorly understood) impressions grounded in the canons of orthodox ideas and "common" experiences. Within all societies "coated" images and coded repre-sentations of knowledge, personified categories, and empirically verifiable "facts" of deviance are always circulated. These interpretations, respected as self-evident truths, discipline understanding by compelling comfortable if not convenient compliance. Specifically, now, how does the dominant culture control the definition of delinquency? How do individual and collective insights that moralize, pathologize, and criminalize emerge?

In this section we will examine the role of moral entrepreneurs who are obsessed with regulating differences and punishing defiance. One of the most powerful of these is the media, who conceal as much as they reveal about delinquency. Because of the pervasive influence of the media, the general public feels competent to talk about crime generally and juvenile delinquency specifically. This general public is encouraged to cite trite truths or glib gospels according to newspapers and television and radio accounts, and to participate as crime experts well nourished by media illusions, deceptive bits, and biased fragments. Yet this public rarely questions the sources of its knowledge. Media crime talk satisfies basic consumption needs (O'Neill 1985:91–117). What, then, is the image of the delinquent in the public eye?

By manufacturing morality plays, the media reduce deviance to a juridic and analgesic chatter of crime news. This convenient obsession with crime news by the corporate media (who have become the new social philosophers, engineers, and theologians) alludes to customary meanings of morality. But crime news as a discourse actually obstructs meaningful explanations. Typically, delinquency as an extreme expression of disturbance is celebrated opportunistically as a forum for public commentary and as a mechanism for solidifying the approbation of a consensually oriented society. Images of delinquency act as cultural markers mirroring a generic deference to the authority of law and the morality of traditional customs. A more prudent discussion of the presentation and brokerage of crime news, however, summons a critical analysis of the influences of culture, political economy, and history. As will be argued, the dominant order scripts crime as a commodity that is marketable and profitable for those who have a stake in conformity. Crime news, as an exercise of control, is linked to privilege. Accordingly, we ask the following: Who benefits from the reported incidence of delinquency? What does crime news produce and reproduce about existing hegemonic imperatives? What elements of the dominant culture define the appropriateness of conformity? To what extent are "stories" of delinquent youth contextualized culturally, mediated politically, and articulated legally? What cultural capital is gained by these distorted tales, revered myths, and absolutist monologues?

Interestingly, the mainstream print and electronic media disguise themselves as authoritative knowledge brokers, bringing together the collective conscience of a community (a normative moral consensus) by concentrating public attention on "their" definitions of disrepute, deviance, or delinquency. Through processes of exclusion the media purport to explain a view that recreates a "one-dimensional mind" (Marcuse 1964:10). By mythologizing, by publicizing a particular narrative of youth crime, and by promoting moral recipes, the media mediate knowledge and indoctrinate values. Inevitably, electronic colonialism triumphs. The media not only seek to establish dependency relationships but also succeed in socializing thought by inculcating a set of foreign norms, values, and expectations (McPhail 1981:20). Sets of interrelated beliefs for buttressing a particular social order are projected. Symbols are manipulated to control how readers define situations; readers are perceived as ill-informed and analytically lazy. Knowledge is filtered through self-serving organizational lenses that demand deference from an all-too-willing public. The media as a vehicle of cultural incarceration do more than deliver messages; more importantly, they sustain dominant elitist values. Freedom of the press, for example, is nothing more than the freedom to monopolize. As Altheide (1976:173) notes:

Events become news when transformed by the news perspective, and not because of their objective characteristics ... the way newsworkers look at the world was shown to be influenced by commercialism, political influence, technology, and scheduling demands.

Though the media state publicly that their social duty is to inform, their main goal is to generate dividends by increasing circulation and advertising revenues. Of interest to the media are stories that are unusual—that are "eccentricities rather than routine" (Martin 1947:57). In this regard, crime stories about kiddies who kill or are killed are especially attractive and easy to sell. As Skogan and Maxfield (1981:142) contend:

> Media coverage of crime emphasizes violence ... Television in particular devotes a substantial proportion of its total news coverage to crime, while the newspapers report a number of stories of violent crime in every issue ...

Research (Surette 1992; McNeely 1995) has suggested that most people receive most of their knowledge of the juvenile justice system through the media, especially through television entertainment. In fact, the most direct "contact" most Canadians have with the juvenile justice system is through television. Television has become the authority (McNeely 1995; Saney 1986), a very powerful agent of socialization and source of knowledge and information.

Television watching, for instance, is a favourite form of entertainment and pastime. The vast majority of Canadian households (97.5 percent) own at least one colour TV (Statistics Canada 1992b). Canadians watch 24.2 hours per week on average (Statistics Canada 1987) and are subjected to over 25,000 commercials per year (De Rooy 1994:15). Many children spend one-third of their waking hours in front of a television screen. Statistics Canada notes that the average child watches 18 hours of TV a week, or a little more than 2.5 hours a day (Brown 1994:78). The average American household has a TV turned on almost eight hours a day; the average American viewer watches four hours a day (McNeely 1995; Papazian 1988). TV has become the greatest consumer of leisure time (*USA Today*, August 19, 1994:11A).

Television is the most popular medium in the world. The French, for example, spend more time watching TV than working (ibid). There are over 1.2 billion TV sets in the world; in Japanese homes TVs are more common than flush toilets (Parker 1994). TV programs are a major American export, worth $2.3 billion annually. There are more than one billion TV sets worldwide; worldwide spending for TV programming is $65 billion and growing 10 percent annually (Lippman 1992: A21). Cable Network News (CNN), a global TV news channel available in at least 140 countries, is an American cultural enterprise. Annually, the United States exports more than 120,000 hours of TV programs just to Europe. In Canada and the USA 98% of households have televisions (Holmes and Taras 1992). In 1993, Canadians spent an estimated $1.6 billion to rent or buy movies for home video (*Toronto Star*, January 4,

1994: A1). On a per capita basis, the United States has the most TVs, with 815 for every 1,000 people; in Canada, the figure is 641 per 1,000. At the other extreme, China has 31 per 1,000 (*The Globe and Mail,* January 1, 1994:D3).

Given both its accessibility and availability, television infiltrates the every-day lives of Canadians. TV is both a cultural producer and a cultural product. It does more than entertain—it also transforms. Its functions are also social, psychological, and behavioural. TV is not only a source of social information; rather lamentably, it has become the *only* credible and comfortable source of knowledge and truth. Television is an incredible power resource, especially since we are dealing not only with a captive audience but also with programs that are deliberately addictive, reflecting romanticized notions of escape under the guise of entertainment.

Television requires little literacy but much faith. This "new religion" (Gerbner 1978:47; De Rooy 1994:40) cultivates images fitting the structure of social relations. This contrived TV reality shapes moods, dreams, and fantasies. This alleged friend of the family assumes many roles. Television does not merely entertain; it also preaches through programs, newscasts, and adver-tisements. Solemn sermons from distant corporate offices are miraculously delivered instantly in simple, attractive, and (of course) colourful formats. Messages are stacked according to the requisite levels of compliance. Commercials divert attention away from authentic reflexivity and "cultivate" followers (believers) through indoctrination. Commercials—"the spreading of the word," that is, the promotion of the message—are TV's raison d'etre. The spirit of capitalism is embodied in the altars of commercials that hold sacred the blessings of the profits. TV commercials are omnipresent—from the prolif-eration of infomercials, to the celebration of products in films (in the movie *The Paper* the star, Michael Keaton, is constantly clutching his can of Coke, and the Coke dispensing machine is always central), to the more direct and deliberately loud TV commercials that follow us even when we leave the room.

TV sets the apolitical agenda, the mindless recipe for success, and the formulas for fitness according to foreign criteria. As the distinguished analyst and former newscaster Peter Trueman (1980:169) noted, television news is a "stolid acceptance of the status quo." TV mirrors the viewer and establishes intimacy; it then extends its net of control widely. Viewers are besieged with appropriate appetites and personalized products. All aspects of the human condition are inspected, from personal hygiene (on commercials) to horrific atrocities (on sensational talk shows). Personal privacy has been appropriated by corporate greed. The viewer's body has been refashioned, the mind remains idle. The viewer is thus held captive. Television annihilates the present lived moment by enabling viewers to enjoy experiences beyond time and space.

These hostages view images on the screen—often new and improved images of themselves (sanitized, homogenized, and, of course, colonized).

Images of crime create a contagion, an infectious public thirst for even more sensational spectacles which are provided in the pages of newspapers, on the newscasts of culturally well-tailored reporters, and on tabloid TV and radio phone-in shows. More than one-quarter of all prime-time shows from the 1960s to the 1990s have focused on themes of crime or criminal justice. Crime is still the number-one theme on television across all types of programming (McNeely 1995; Surette 1992). Tabloid TV shows, although currently not dominant in prime time, must be taken seriously because of the "information" they present for public consumption (McNeely 1995). The audience is encouraged to focus on slick celebrities, commentators, or crime "experts," all of whom are very mindful of the dazzle of their respective sideshows and commercials. Note the following popular programs: "A Current Affair," "A Current Affair Extra," "Inside Edition," "Inside Edition Weekend," "American Journal," "Hard Copy," "48 Hours," "American Justice," "Dateline NBC," "60 Minutes," "Primetime Live," "Cops," "Real Stories of the Highway Patrol," "Patrol," "Top Cops," "America's Most Wanted," "Unsolved Mysteries," "Court TV," "People's Court," "Geraldo," "Sally Jessy Raphael," "Maury Povich," "Oprah Winfrey," "Shirley," "Ricki Lake," "Rolanda," "Donahue," "Jenny Jones," "Montel Williams," "Jerry Springer." Crime news has become the new circus, a public spectacle parading tragic events as advertised entertainment. In one week (April 17–21, 1995), the following topics were noted in a random sample. Geraldo had Teen and Parents Battle, Young Heroin Users, and Teens and Sex. Sally Jessy Raphael included Girls with Ruined Reputations and Precocious Teenage Girls. Maury Povich had Parents Who Spy on Their Children and People Afraid of Their Teenage Children. Ricki Lake had High School Pals Reunite and Jealous Old Boy Friends (*Starweek*, April 16, 1995).

These news carnivals deliver a cornucopia of delectable images that render readers and/or viewers even more vulnerable to manipulation. People use what they learn in the media to construct an image of the world (Surette 1992). These television portrayals give viewers (and others participating in their production) clues about society; thus, they "socialize" the public to a particular image of the criminal justice system (McNeely 1995).

Readers and viewers have become fixated on the bombastic, crude, and shallow crime stories that plague both the electronic and the printed media. Youth crime, in this context, is "programmed and staged" (McNeely 1995), if only to accommodate commercial requirements. Surette (1992:245–246) argues:

In every category—crimes, criminals, crime fighters, the investigation of crime, arrests, case processing, and case dispositions—the media present a world of crime and justice that is not found in reality.

Items are presented as "real" and are often produced in a format and style associated with documentary or news reporting. (About this, questions of social presentation and accuracy can be posed; Altheide 1985.) Television technology has further accentuated this voyeurism with instant, banal, and simplistic social messages that separate the good from the bad for captivated audiences.

But this amusement is troublesome, given its deliberate inculcation of distorted values. The fascination with crime, the appetite for violence, and the delirium of the moment disguise the ongoing media deceit. This susceptibility to the socialization of media-generated values is not surprising considering the American Psychological Association's finding that the average child watches 8,000 murders and 100,000 other acts of violence on commercial television by the time he or she leaves primary school (Roberts 1992:43; *Toronto Star*, July 1, 1993:C7). According to Miriam Miedzian, author of *Boys Will Be Boys: Breaking the Link Between Masculinity and Violence*, by the time children reach 18, they will have watched 26,000 murders on TV (ibid, March 27, 1993:K2). By the time they complete grade 12, they will have spent between 3,000 and 4,000 hours more in front of the television than in the classroom (Canadian Teachers' Federation 1995). Two to five year olds watch, on average, about 28.5 hours of TV per week (kidmedia@airwaves.chi.il.us; Schneider 1989).

Likewise, popular television programs promote conservative ideologies regarding the "survival of the slickest," laissez-faire vigilantism, seductive technological marvels, fantasies, and so on. This co-optation of popular values diverts attention away from sociopolitical struggles inherent in an unequal society. Resistance and oppositional projects are simply dismissed as deviant and for that reason unprofitable.

The twin products of television—information dissemination and entertainment—are shaped by commercial interests. The main product of TV's fascination with crime is the *audience*, which is then sold to advertisers. Since air time is expensive, advertisers are careful to present commercials that capitalize on their investment. *Commercials* are designed to "attract and persuade" (Schietz and Sprafkin 1978:69). Commercial television and television commercials are in the same business, which is to sell products that will generate profits. Both communicate distorted messages (Denisson and Tobey 1991) that manipulate the insecurities and curiosities of the individual and make the viewer feel incomplete. Advertising requires the communication of a value—consumerism. Because of their insecurity, individuals see products as a requirement for survival and success (Moog 1990). Commercials *produce* the wants that must be satisfied. They reinforce consumption and create new appetites, fetishes, and needs.

This doctrinal system diverts the attention of the "unwashed masses" and reinforces basic social values: consumerism, passivity, submission to authority, the overriding virtues of greed and personal gain, lack of concern for others, fear of real or imagined enemies, and so on. The goal is to make the bewildered masses even more bewildered. They need not trouble themselves with what is actually happening in the world. (In fact, it is better if they don't. If they see too much reality, they may try to change it; ibid:95.) This shared consciousness promotes laziness and silence in the service of the larger social machine (Meyrowitz 1992:230). The news media especially offer disciplinary and normalizing discourses, intextually related to each other and to other disciplinary and normalizing institutions (Ericson, Baranek, and Chan 1992: 235). As noted, the media foster paranoia and a fortress mentality so that the only comfort to be found is in front of the TV set. This market provision of security generates its own paranoid demand (Davis 1992:224).

The popular media generally exploit and manipulate in the interests of power and self-preservation by conveying socially sanctioned messages about the consequences of unacceptable conduct. But this personal prison, incarcerated self, or colonized will is fundamentally related to discursive practices. Structures of conformity are constituted through these disciplines. The media evade the most urgent and essential social issues. Narratives are designed to reproduce control, to confer objectlike realities to deviance. Privilege channels thought within conformist boundaries (Chomsky 1989:vii). As a mode of discourse, the pathocentric script of delinquency objectifies challenges by invoking existing codes. Legal, scientific, and professional discourses dominate the language of control.

A more critical approach (McNeely 1995) assumes that cultural products like the media reflect meanings that are grounded in the social structure in terms of hierarchical relations, interests, and the status quo. The media uphold and extend the societal status quo. Cultural products are social.

The various media discipline by producing consent and by enjoying a virtual monopoly over information. Approximately 95 percent of Canadians learn about crime and the criminal justice system through the media (Simmons 1965; Surette 1989:5). The media are no longer merely social mirrors; they now provide the only "windows" through which constituencies can hope to glimpse events, individuals, or relations designated as deviant. Reiman (1990:117) suggests that the media provide "a distorted carnival mirror." The media, however, project many different kinds of messages (O'Sullivan 1990). Since viewers are less aware of the negative effects of the media, they come to truly believe that reality is being portrayed. Notice, for example, your own reactions to the assumptions implicit in the following headlines, all of which appeared on the front pages of newspapers and magazines:

Newsprint Headlines

Metro Crack Capital of Canada: RCMP
Toronto Star, May 30, 1989

Time's Up for Teen Killers
ibid, June 2, 1994

Concert Security: How Safe Are You?
Rolling Stone, April 15, 1993

Drugs in America
ibid, May 3, 1994

Mourners Grapple with Senseless Act
Toronto Star, April 8, 1995

Armed Police to Patrol High Schools
Toronto Star, January 30, 1995

Boy, 14, Gets Death Sentence in Pakistan
Toronto Star, February 19, 1995

Americans Crack Down on Young Offenders
Ottawa Citizen, December 10, 1994

Youth-Crime Proposals Under Attack
Winnipeg Free Press, December 2, 1994

What conclusions about delinquency are we as readers expected to draw? What images are being manipulated? And how? Viewers are being asked to help fabricate a fantasy. According to Surette (1984:16), the media perpetuate negative stereotypes:

Media images of crime and criminals are contained within numerous formats, including news reporting, documentaries, features, and entertainment programming. The images are often inaccurate and are uniformly fragmentary, providing a distorted mirror reflection of crime within society and an equally distorted image of the criminal justice system's response to such behaviour.

As McNeeley (1995) and Adler (1976) suggest, programs are not created in a vacuum, and it would be misleading to treat them in isolation from society. This constant "crime talk" manufactures impressions. Again, perceptions of delinquency are statistically mediated and mass manipulated. The media claim to provide a catechism of self-evident truths, which are essential parts of an infallible dogma that demands reverence. As embodied moral statements, these caricatured fragments portray crime by acceding to convoluted logic, obfuscating symbols, and mystifying rituals. Unqualified deference is obvious in the media coverage of "official statistics." Historical and cultural features of the political economy are rendered invisible and seldom examined by the media and other socializing influences. The public chatter on crime is limited to news that entertains for the emotional moment, to the quick fix that dazzles, pacifies, or terrifies people into inaction. Within the dominant culture, delinquency is a currency in popular discourse. As a result, there is no longer a place for any serious analysis, especially of fundamental social issues.

To what, then, is the attention of the general public directed? What currency is exchanged in crime talk? The above review of the more salient official statistics, as mediated by the press, is offered as a means to consider both the current incidence of crime and (more importantly) the social implications of official crime trends. What, then, do official statistics reveal and conceal? It is instructive to note that crime statistics fall into several general categories: all crimes (reported and unreported); crimes of violence; crimes causing death; murder rates; crimes with firearms; juvenile crimes; and so on. Interestingly, crimes of the powerful (government and corporate) escape mention, let alone counting.

These distorted views may stem largely from public ignorance or false consciousness, supported by the media. Stories about increasing crime rates sell newspapers (Cohen 1973:28–40). Billions of dollars are to be earned by horrifying and titillating the general public. Violence is a commodity sold to generate attention, secure funding (especially for the juvenile justice system and its armies of consultants), and maximize profits for the film industry. Again, images of violence are *always* manipulated. Violence in the form of killings, drive-by shootings, and street fighting accompanied the premieres of such movies as *Juice, Jungle Fever, New Jack City, Ricochet, Fresh,* and *Trespass.* The popularity of both adventure/action and horror films attests to this fixation. Note, for example, the incredible popularity of violent, vigilante, and macho-avenge films that pretend to portray a sense of popular justice. Employing aggressive heroes such as Segal, Schwarzenegger, Bronson, Eastwood, Norris, Stallone, Van Damme, Willis, and so on, Hollywood recycles, promotes, and delivers themes of violence. Consider the following films (and their sequels): *Die Hard, Death Wish, Terminator, Out for Justice, Lethal Weapon, Double Impact, Rambo, Rocky, True Lies, TimeCop.* Violence is no longer restricted to mindless horror films like *Friday the 13th, Doctor Giggles, Nightmare on Elm Street, Child's Play, Halloween,* or even to the mystery/suspense films like *Cape Fear, Natural Born Killers, Reservoir Dogs, Pulp Fiction,* or the 1991 Academy Award winner *Silence of the Lambs*; violence is now embedded in comedies like *Home Alone* and *Hot Shots*, the latter of which boasts that it contains the most killings of any movie.

Video games now rake in $5.3 billion a year in the United States alone, more than $10 billion around the world (Elmer-Dewitt 1993:42). In 1993, Mortal Kombat was the top-grossing release, yet this "game" featured extremely brutal kick-and-punch violence. In Night Trap, five scantily clad women are stalked by blood-thirsty vampires who like to drill holes in their victims' necks and hang them on meat hooks. On average, children play video machines 1.5 hours a day (ibid:41).

To reiterate, the media influence the public's perception of crime. These perceptions, however, are also the result of the socializing influences of traditional education. Education, as a major site of ideological reproductions (Althusser 1971), does more than shape opinions of crime; it also frames consciousness. Conventional pursuits impose silence and inhibit the development of intellectual curiosities that challenge existing commitments. The morality of everyday life is taken for granted; prevailing moral rules are rarely questioned. Traditional models of teaching and learning continue to judge differences, colonize compliance, and shackle the imagination. As Foucault (1979:304) summarizes:

We are in the society of the teacher-judge, the doctor-judge, the educator-judge, the social-worker-judge; it is on them that the universal reign of the normative is based. This carceral network has been the greatest support, in modern society, of the normalizing of power.

The ideological foundations of the above-noted texts of delinquency marginalize young people as "others." Delinquency as a discourse is an important device for interpreting the culture of control. Delinquency is a constructed knowledge that pathologizes and devalues differences.

The criminal justice system calculates the costs of deviance and the value of appropriate sanctions. Ideological manipulations within the legitimation process make delinquency more credible, and in the process make the label even more adhesive. An "objective" frame of reference is the law. This justification of control provides formal images that distort rather than decode processes of delinquency and the "meaningfulness" of crime statistics, clearance rates, or recidivism. The well-protected values of the privileged classes create illusions that demand deference.

In brief, interpretations of delinquency have been reduced to a technology saturated with distorted images, illusions, and fiction. The media have become the only reality, a new truth, the idea or the source of knowledge. Is this false reality of youth peculiar to youths? What is it about the phenomenon of youth that renders it so susceptible to manipulation? How is youth a fertile life stage for texts of delinquency to emerge? How can one analyze the subtext of power in light of prevailing texts of delinquency (incidence of crime) and their contexts of law and popular culture?

✱ Phenomenology of Youth: Polytextures of Power

The Canadian state secures control over the nature of youth crimes using powerful resources. Delinquency is a text within which reside the subtexts of power. Delinquency, as an expression of defiance, enables the differential exercise of state and corporate power. As noted throughout the previous discussions, to know about delinquency is to think, talk, read, write, and research politics. The intellectual processes inherent in critical literacy require an active engagement in ongoing exercises that link structure and biography—that is, continued confrontations with culture are encouraged. Additionally, we have been concerned with the totality of social relations, various social worlds, and their material conditions. In determining how delinquency is constituted, this paper asks the following basic questions: Who defines deviance? What shapes delinquency? How are responses structured? What really gets negotiated? Essentially, what informs our judgments about delinquency?

Culture is a format that mediates a host of contests. Law conditions and contextualizes control. The larger culture frames legal ideologies. In turn, the normative conception of order is shaped by certain versions of delinquency buttressed by images that determine the reaction of individuals and institutions. Images are socially reinforced and are internalized as common sense, claiming to inform empirically any understanding of trouble. In brief, delinquency and its reaction are sociopolitical accomplishments.

A critical cultural calculus incorporates the manufacture of morality, images of danger, the politics of policing trouble, the political economy of peace, the functions of fiction, and the limitations of law. At the cultural level, ideology masks injustices, manufactures coercion, and colonizes consent. Likewise, delinquency is manipulated to legitimate and generate support for the status quo by bombarding the "public" with a plethora of threatening images. As an ideological text, youth crime also contributes to state forma-tions by exaggerating threats to the body politic. Historically, youth crime has always been a commodity exploited conveniently by the state apparatus and the fictive collective morality. The dominant class continues to exercise control by stimulating seductive images that encourage a deference to authority. Authority relations protect the influence of the powerful and secure the compliance of the powerless. An unquestioned hegemony prevails under which coercion succeeds through reason. But what are the sites of this hegemony? And how do state-sponsored crime ideologies penetrate agency?

The study of meanings is inseparable from the study of culture. As Giddens maintains: "All human beings are knowledgeable agents" (1984:281); "social actors are knowledgeable about the conditions of social production in which their day-to-day activities are enmeshed" (ibid, 1982:29). Giddens seeks to overcome dichotomies that overemphasize human intentions, motivations, and actions in relation to experience ("subjectivism") while overemphasizing insti-tutional organization and systemic and cultural constraints ("objectivism"). Instead, there is a reflexive relationship between discourse and social subjec-tivity; social identity and practical consciousness is organized through a specific articulation of images, objects, and words (Valverde 1990). The subject is both knowing and authoring. The juridic or legal subject is agentic. Admittedly, it is essential to consider the reflexive monitoring of action as well as the location of agency as bound by unacknowledged conditions. As Marx and Engels note ([1947] 1960:7):

As individuals express their life, so they are. What they are, therefore, coin-cides with their production, both with what they produce and with how they produce. The nature of individuals thus depends on the material conditions determining their production.

The multitude of productive forces accessible to men determines the nature of society, hence that the history of humanity must always be studied and treated in relation to the history of industry and exchange. [ibid:18]

For Lemke (1988:158), the structure of a text (delinquency) is created by structured social practices. Processes of interactions shape and are shaped by the nature of structures wherein meanings constitute and are constitutive. Language, as a cultural code, relates to a world of meanings. All knowledge and language are culturally coded. Thus, knowledge or even a consciousness about delinquency is a social product. It is precisely here in the realm of knowledge that ideologies are contested, resisted, or accepted.

Knowledge is coded within a language that obfuscates as well as clarifies. Ideology refers to a complex of linguistic-meaning-making processes that are observable and describable in instances of discourse. Clearly, ideology is constructed through discourse. It is in discourse that every determination of the subject depends, including thought, affect, enjoyment, meaning, and identity. The subject is determined by language (Lacan 1977:298–300); the subject disappears in his or her discourse and becomes embodied in the spoken word. In order to reproduce meaning, certain "master signifiers" represent the subject for another signifier (Lacan 1977:316). Thus, a signified is empty until given form by the use of a signifier. This signifier is the "other," the element that "lacks," the part that was not fully expressed. For instance, for centuries youths were made to feel "lacking" and could only be signified through another signifier—the adult. Youths were always construed to be the property of adults. Youths existed at the pleasure of adults. For de Saussure (1986:100):

> the link between signal and signification is arbitrary. Since we are treating a sign as the combination in which a signal is associated with signification, we can express this more simply as: the linguistic sign is arbitrary.

The language of law (the Young Offenders Act) is the main channel through which meanings and patterns of living are transmitted. Language consists of an enabling discourse that exchanges meanings in interpersonal encounters (Halliday 1978:2). On the one hand, language determines the subject; on the other hand, language is an intersubjective reality.

There is also a discrepancy between the projected image of youth and the multiple realities of delinquency. Typically, the identity of youth is performed in each moment rather than fixed in abstract traditions such as law, official statistics, and the media. The "privileging" of adulthood and the "othering" of youth entail exclusions inscribed in authority discourses. The concept of youth has itself become suspect in recent antiessentialist writings. Derrida (Loy 1993) and Lacan have demonstrated the "subversion of the subject" as a function continually constituted and undermined in the chain of signifiers. Caught up in the labyrinth of images, a disoriented identity of youth emerges. In response, youths develop resistance rituals to express more fully the complexity of their identities, as apparent in their talk, attire, demeanour, relationships, and interests.

Clearly, the concept of youth exists as a discoursal practice that is socially situated. That is, an identity is simultaneously a product and a process linked to situationally relevant contextual codes, namely, culture. Equally, delinquency as a coherent set of ideas articulated in interpersonal encounters does not just exist "out there" as an objective thing; rather, delinquency is constructed through historical and cultural practices at the everyday level.

Delinquency is used to transform the youth's consciousness and to regulate morality. Delinquency is manipulated to link the youth to conventions of appropriateness and the other in order to create the deferential subject, to inculcate both a sense of belongingness and a sense of distance. Thus, all authority relations depersonalize, alienate, or "deindividuate." The media transform control by commodifying youths generally. The media industry "impedes the development of autonomous, independent individuals who judge and decide consciously for themselves" (Adorno 1964:19). For Adorno (ibid: 29), culture collaborates with authority and cannot be understood "in terms of itself ... an independent logic of culture." Later, Adorno and Horkheimer (1989:121) argue that ideology justifies the rubbish produced. Youths are by-products or wastes of a callous economic order. Adorno and Horkheimer (ibid:152) note that "culture has always played its part in taming revolutionary and barbaric instincts." Accordingly, the media do not just manufacture illusions but are the tyrannical embodiments of social relations packaged symbolically. The ideology of youth crime confines the body and soul and reproduces itself (Marcuse 1964:12) through the mass deception of the culture industry.

Likewise, Habermas (1984) highlights the role of dogma in keeping individuals in a state of ignorance and repression. The ideological apparatuses of the state (Althusser 1971:143) condition existence by reproducing both productive forces and existing relations of production. The repressive state apparatuses include the juvenile justice system and the various ideological state apparatus—schools, media, the law, and so on. The latter socializing agencies, controlled by dominant ideological discourses, determine the subject, including thought, affect, enjoyment, meaning, and identity.

Legitimation, or the co-optation of mass loyalty and support, is also crucial for the continued existence of delinquency. The media shield and legitimize state-supported conflicts. An important element of the media relates to the manner in which youths are implicated in manifestations of corporate and state policies. The media's complicity is an important aspect of moral regulation. The media help to control the individual without overt force or domination. The language of delinquency has always been used to silence opposition from youths.

The obvious strengths or weaknesses of recent postmodernist formulations will not be addressed here. Suffice it to note that a number of postmodernist contributions refer to ideology and culture. Interestingly, the logic of postmodernism suggests that youth as the subject is fractured and complexly articulated within a plurality of discourses that are never stable, static, or fixed. The foundationalism of law and order is undermined through practices of deconstruction and reflexivity. There is an "incredulity towards the meta-narratives" (Lyotard 1984); unity of knowledge is rejected in favour of diversity and an overlap of meanings (Manning 1991). The dissolution of grand narratives has sparked interest in more context-based, pragmatic, problem-solving, and reform-minded political efforts. In the metanarrative of traditional law, there is a discursive production of the essential subject. The legal subject is constructed within structural inequalities. With the postmodern interpretation, however, there is no bedrock of ultimate truths or deep structures. But neither is postmodernism simply an empty frame, a free-for-all in which everything goes in defiance of a normative order. Coupled with the above cultural insights, an interrogation of the text (delinquency) allows us to analyze the prevailing essentialist ideologies of privilege—power, the mutually constructing and constraining capacity of structure, and the multiplicity of subject-positions offered by enablement and resistance (subtexts). As Lyotard (1984:15) describes:

> A self does not amount to much, but no self is an island; each exists in the fabric of relations that is now more complex and mobile than ever before. Young or old, man or woman, rich or poor, a person is always located at "nodal points" or specific communication circuits, however tiny these may be. Or better: one is always located at a post through which various kinds of messages pass. No one, not even the least privileged among us, is ever entirely powerless over the messages that traverse and position him [sic] in relation to the sender, addressee, or referent.

Postmodernism nevertheless encourages an interrogation of the character, foundation, and enclosures of Western modernity. By interrogating these structures, one uncovers how modernity and dominant forms institutionally marginalize those designated as "the other"—that is, how delinquency is normalized. In this regard, positive identities are habitually constructed by setting up binary differences and specifying others. Deconstructionism reads the margins (youths) in the centre (law). It decentres and de-essentializes the subject by pointing out that *the subject (youth) is constructed in contradictions.*

In the world of TV productions of children and youth, there are crass contrasts such as Bart Simpson and "90210" or "Saved by the Bell"; "life on the street" (for the disadvantaged young) and the community comforts on "Sesame Street"; "violence in the 'hood" and the safety of "Mr. Rogers' Neighborhood"; and so on. According to postmodern thought, identities are always in the process of becoming—they are transforming and open to repositioning. Identities are relational. We encounter youths by transporting and internalizing fears of some onto others. For example, law superimposes the subject as de-essentialized. In the media, contradictions are played out and different forms of legal inferiorization readily occur. Postmodernism seeks to understand the contradictory and contextual nature of youth identity—that is, ideology and culture as forms of identification. Under this approach, delinquency emerges as a complex issue of cultural authority. In examining the mechanical media reproductions of objects, law provides authority and privilege.

The social organization of any delinquent identity consists of a wide spectrum of differentially constituted activities. Decisions are oriented toward the generation of "some" knowledge. Knowledge, for youths, is not only ideologically situated but also articulated as a legitimate consequence of exclusionary practices.

The subtext of privilege is based on a bias that recognizes as superior only those insights that are generated within the text of delinquency. The text legitimates the subtext by constructing distractions—alternative social realities. This subtext of privilege is authentic but obviously inaccessible, while the text of delinquency is easily accessible but rendered inauthentic. That is, authentic voices of the powerful are only echoed, while the authentic voices of the youth are silenced. Youths at the centre are quickly marginalized; the dominant other translates their experiences as inauthentic and punishes them for resisting. Youths are not encouraged to be aware of themselves as knowing beings. Youths as inauthentic intellectuals are created within the dominant cultural hegemony. The concept of youth as a creative way of relating to and transcending the world is not rooted. The consciousness of youth—beliefs, values, self-concepts, validation, and so on—is constrained by cultural and legal categories that alter the character of youth over time.

Within the commerce of ideas, youths are not only depicted as entertainment in the idiot box but are also transformed into boxed idiots. Youths have become the product of mechanical reproduction, to be bought and always deprecated (Benjamin 1968:211). The structure of thinking is reproduced in the physical layout of the page in which reasoning and text cooperate to produce conceptual effects (Barthes 1987:258). Since youths are perceived as lost, they are forgotten and only respected as sideshow attractions for the media. Delinquency as a text is significant not because of its substance but primarily because of its referential character. In other words, delinquency is an index of the affiliation of youth. Delinquency has become the lens through which youths are interpreted, reinterpreted, validated, and repudiated. Delinquency expresses relational and tentative elements of youth. Accordingly, the standpoint of youth acquires meanings through myths, symbols, and metaphors. Statistics, laws, and the media are absolutists that impose closure on the vulnerable and the different. The above institutions situate youth and insert the "language of the game" (Lyotard 1984). Since youths are considered to be people "disconnecting as children" or as "becoming adults," the self-identity of youths is tentative, fragmented, and unclear. They are confined to the world of play and expected to "act their age." Irrespective of their "turf" in malls, theatres, parks, and the like, youths are suspect and forever under surveillance.

☀ Youth as Offended: From States of Delinquency to a Delinquent State

Throughout history, the image of youths as cultural terrorists (Leong 1992) has dominated. Socializing institutions condemned the challenge, resistance, and defiance of youth, preferring instead docile and deferential cultural puppets. There has also been a reluctance to consider these youths as products of the larger social order. Violence, sex, drug consumption, and escape are viewed as counter-hegemonic and destructive. Typically, youths are marginalized: they are not persons in their own right, nor are they allowed voice, let alone representation. These stereotypic notions homogenize and blur diversities. A critical understanding of the media construction of youth and delinquency requires an evaluation of the types of subjects projected. The media construct identities on the basis of information that does not demand serious attention. Youths are not merely senders and receivers, producers and consumers, rulers and ruled—they have been made in the image of the commercial sandwiched between programs. The virulent and assertive media, informed by official reports, succeeds in transforming the youth into "the other," the foreigner, the stranger. An oppositional filter is constructed that invites attacks against the subject—youth. Clearly, distance characterizes this construct. Authority–youth relationships are mediated by notions of "difference" and "otherness."

Within the narration of distance there is a demand for manipulation and control (i.e., *discipline*). For Foucault, discipline is

> a type of power, a modality for its exercise, comprising a whole set of instruments, techniques, procedures, levels of application, targets; it is a "physics" or an "anatomy" of power, a technology. [1979:206]

The state of delinquency is shaped by a delinquent state. Let us review the evidence of state violence against youth. The United States is a world leader in executing juveniles, according to Human Rights Watch. More young persons are on Death Row in the United States than in any other country. Although 112 member countries of the United Nations prohibit the killing of offenders who were under 18 at the time of arrest, the United States does not—nor does Iran or Iraq. In the United States, 40 juveniles were awaiting execution at the end of 1994. Moreover, such executions are on the rise in the United States. For instance, four out of the nine adolescents executed in the United States in the past 15 years were put to death during the last six months of 1993. Since the 1970s, 137 death sentences have been handed out to American juveniles (*Toronto Star,* March 26, 1995:E9). Closer to home, in Ontario, police have been assigned to schools as part of community policing projects designed to prevent crime and humanize the police force.

One does not witness this magnanimous concern for crime prevention when it comes to policing banks, stock exchanges, or the boardrooms of multinational corporations. Why is there no "zero tolerance" policy for corporate criminals, racists, and institutionalized misogynists? How is it that the great majority of people—*especially* youths—suffer systematic inequality? Remember, after all, that youth consists of interrelated or overlapping relations—economic, class, political, legal, and social.

Despite all the talk of diversity, youths are seen as special colonial subjects. This thinking is reproduced routinely in the experiences of youth. In reference to class inequalities, discipline limits discourse and encourages practices that "bend the minds" and "break the bodies" of those judged to be recalcitrant. This is most visible in the impoverishment of young people and children.

Children make up the single largest category of poor people in Canada. Almost half of those depending on food banks for sustenance are children and youths under 18. Forty percent of all food bank users are children. Statistics Canada reports that one out of every nine children under 18 receives emergency food assistance; also, one-fifth of users of food banks are children under 5. In other words, many Canadian children go to school without breakfast, essentially undernourished. School meal programs with nutritionally balanced breakfasts are virtually nonexistent in Canada. In Toronto, 20 percent of all of the city's children live below the poverty line. More than 300,000 children live in poverty in Ontario. According to Statistics Canada, children under 16 made up 26.5 percent of the poor, up from 24.8 percent in 1989 (*The Globe and Mail*, December 19, 1991). Stated differently, 37.1 percent of children in single-mother households live in poverty in Canada compared with 2 percent in Sweden (McQuaig 1992:A21). In the 1990s, 20 percent of American children live in poverty. One-sixth of Canadian children are growing up in poverty; 37 percent of all poor children live in working-poor families (Agency Workshop on Child Poverty 1990:3). In 1990, two-thirds of children in single-mother households were poor. According to a report of a House of Commons subcommittee, 837,000 Canadian children live below the poverty line, with the highest rates in Manitoba and Saskatchewan. In late 1991, the Social Development Council noted that there were one million poor children in Canada (Social Development Council 1991:9). Canada has the second-highest child poverty rate in the developed world (*Toronto Star*, November 23, 1993:A19). A study of 2,503 Ontario children by the Canadian Medical Association shows that those in homes with annual incomes of less than $10,000 are more susceptible to anxiety, depression, and impulsive behaviour. The authors of this report, Ellen Lipman, David Offord, and Michael Boyle, noted:

> We have found [a] strong and consistent relation ... between low family income and psychiatric disorder, poor school performance and social impairment ... Only changes in policy ... will have the broad-based effect necessary to help these disadvantaged children. [*Toronto Star*, August 15, 1994:A3]

In the United States, the poverty rate among urban blacks was 33.8 percent in 1990, up from 21.2 percent in 1969. The poverty rate for white inner-city residents was 14.3 percent in 1990. Moreover, 34 percent of all black children born in the inner city will remain officially poor for their first ten years of life; this is true of only 3 percent of white children. The child mortality rate among families at the lowest income level is double that of families at the highest income level. Likewise, children from families receiving welfare benefits are one-and-a-half times more likely to have chronic health problems. The United States underinvests in children; in 1991, that country paid $26 billion to build and run prisons and take care of parolees and probationaries. That money was spent on 1.1 million people, most of them men. And yet the United States spent less than $23 billion on the 33.5 million women and children served by its main welfare program, Aid to Families with Dependent Children (*Toronto*

Star, October 3, 1993:B5). Shockingly, in Los Angeles, 200,000 people, many of them children, live in garages (*Toronto Star*, January 13, 1988:A22).

Around the world, about 250,000 children under 5 die every week from diseases of poverty—that is one every seven seconds. According to the United Nations' annual report, *The State of the World's Children*, 40,000 children die *every day* from malnutrition and "diseases of poverty" (*Toronto Star*, December 20, 1988:A18, and December 27,1987:B3). The World Bank estimates that one billion of the world's 5.5 billion people live on less than one dollar a day (*Toronto Star*, July 18, 1992:D6). In Brazil, the *meninos de rua*, or impoverished street kids, are often blamed for that country's high crime rates. About 1,500 are killed every year by police or "hired guns." International human-rights groups have denounced Brazil's military police force as one of the most brutal on earth. In greater Sao Paulo, for instance, the police killed 1,470 people in 1992. Yet almost every time Brazilian police have been tried for brutality, the military tribunals have absolved them of wrongdoing (*Time*, August 9, 1993:26–27). Of Brazil's 152 million people, 32 million are children of families earning less than $30 per person a month. The top 20 percent of Brazil's population earns 26 times as much as the bottom 20 percent (ibid).

In his address to the UN Conference on Environment and Development, Fidel Castro (1992:2) noted:

> In the Third World ... infant mortality reaches levels of 115 deaths for every 1000 live births, ... every year 14 million children die before they reach the age of five, ... more than a billion people do not have access to the most elementary health services, ... life expectancy is less than 63 years, and in the poorest countries less than 52, ... more than 300 million children are deprived of their right to schooling, ... almost a billion adults are illiterate, ... more than 500 million people suffered from hunger in 1990, and ... some 180 million children under the age of five suffer from malnutrition.

In Somalia alone, 300,000 children die annually and another 1.5 million are threatened with starvation (*Toronto Star*, August 22, 1993:A15). Forty thousand children die daily worldwide, one-third of them in Africa, a continent with only 10 percent of the world's population (*Toronto Star*, April 18, 1993:F3). By the end of the century, 37 countries—most of them in Africa— will be unable to feed themselves with their own resources (*Toronto Star*, August 27, 1993:A12). There are 50,000 child prostitutes in Brazil (*Toronto Star*, August 27, 1993:F3). Equally significant, 12 million South Africans are caught up in desperate poverty (ibid).

In reference to another expression of abuse, religion serves to hide the indiscretions of authority figures. For instance, how does one make sense of the behaviour of the Christian Brothers at Mount Cashel in Newfoundland, and the 28 Christian clergy charged with hundreds of counts of sexual abuse at Alfred and Uxbridge in Ontario (*Toronto Star*, December 12, 1992:A3)?

✹ Conclusions: Behind and Beyond the Text

Delinquency as a "text" defines knowledge narrowly. In so doing, it is objectified according to a limited range of self-serving organizational criteria. The range of discourses used to construct the delinquency consists of ideological practices. What is articulated as knowledge of delinquency is open to question, given official and media formulations of truth. Both law talk and media images exclude the authentic representation of youth—the diverse experiences and political struggles. This argument is based on the conceptualization of delinquency as inseparable from the structural components of youth. A more coherent framework is warranted in approaching delinquency as a consequence of power imbalances. When studying delinquency, we must shift our own deeply entrenched beliefs and engage in intellectual cynicism regarding organizational practices that constitute the text. Only by going behind and beyond that which is uniformly masqueraded as truths, only by going beyond what Marx referred to as "fetishism of the commodity," and only by going behind the illusions of the media and the narcissism of the familiar codes of crime can we hope to grapple with what "we" really know. In response to the question "What do they know?"—a concern raised constantly by both youths and authorities—the following is asked: What do they *want* to know? *Why* do they want to know? These answers are located in respective subtexts of violence that have characterized and continue to characterize the nature of "our" society.

> Adults are obsolete children.
> Dr. Seuss

A very special thanks is extended to Anthony and his buddies—Steve, Marcello, Chris, and Angelo for their generous assistance. Derek and Richard clarified a number of concerns from the perspective of older teenagers. Tanya and Lisa were helpful in commenting on the media.

References

Adler, R. 1976. *Television as a Cultural Force*. New York: Facts on File.

Adorno, T. 1964. *Prismen, Kulturkritik and Gesellschaft*. Frankfurt: Suhrkamp.

Adorno, T., and M. Horkheimer. 1989. "Selections from The Culture Industry: Enlightenment as Mass Deception." In R. Gottlieb (ed.), *An Anthology of Western Marxism*. New York: Oxford University Press.

Agency Workshop on Child Poverty, 1990, Toronto.

Altheide, D. 1976. *Creating Reality*. Beverly Hills, CA: Sage.

———. 1985. *Media Power*. Beverly Hills, CA: Sage.

Althusser, L. 1971. "Ideology and Ideological State Apparatuses." In *Lenin and Philosophy and Other Essays*. London: New Left Books.

Barak, G. 1988. "Newsmaking Criminology: Reflections of the Media, Intellectuals, and Crime." *Justice Quarterly* 5:565–587.

Barthes, R. 1975. *Le Plaisir du Texte (The Pleasure of the Text)*. Translated by R. Miller. New York: Hill and Wang.

———. 1987. *Mythologies*. New York: Hill and Wang.

———. 1988. "Photography and Electoral Appeal." *Mythologies*. London: Collins.

Benjamin, W. 1968. *Illuminations*. New York: Schocken.

Brown, L. 1994. "Taming the TV Monster." *Starweek Magazine* (October).

BJS. 1991. Bureau of Justice Statistics Update (July)1:1–10.

———. 1993. "20 Years of Measuring Crime Shows Fewer Offenses Overall, But Increased Violence against Minorities and the Young." 202-307-0784. U.S. Department of Justice, Washington, DC (November 21).

———. 1994a. "Delinquency Cases in Juvenile Court, 1992." OJJDP by the National Center for Juvenile Justice, Rockville, MD (July 24).

———. 1994b. "Record Number of Handgun Crimes—Nears One Million a Year." 202-307-0784. U.S. Department of Justice, Washington, DC (May 15).

———. 1994c. "Selected Highlights on Firearms and Crimes of Violence: Selected Findings from National Statistical Series." NCJ-146844. U.S. Department of Justice, Washington, DC

Canadian Criminal Justice Association. 1994. *Bulletin* (September 15), Ottawa.

———. 1995: *Bulletin* (March 15), Ottawa.

Canadian Teachers' Federation. 1995. *Young Offenders and Youth Violence: National Issues in Education*. Issue Sheet No. 10. Ottawa: Canadian Teachers' Federation (ab167@freenet.carleton.ca).

Castro, F. 1992. Address of Fidel Castro to the United Nations Conference on Environment and Development. *Special Supplement of Gramma International*. (June 28).

Chomsky, N. 1989. *Necessary Illusions*. Toronto: CBC Enterprises.

Cohen, S. 1973. *The Manufacture of News*. London: Anchor.

Cohen, J.M., and M.J. Cohen. 1980. *The Penguin Dictionary of Quotations*. New York: Penguin.

Davis, M. 1992. *City of Quartz*. New York: Vintage.

Denisson, D., and L. Tobey. 1991. *The Advertising Handbook*. Bellington, WA: International Self-Counsel Press, 1991.

Department of Justice. 1993. "Toward Safer Communities: Violent and Repeat Offending by Young People." Ottawa: Young Offenders Project, Department of Justice.

———. 1994. Justice Information Backgrounder: Proposed Young Offenders Act Amendments. Communications and Consultation Branch (June).

De Rooy, E. 1994. "Sexism in Television Commercials: A Comparative Content Analysis and Probe into Subjects' Perceptions." Graduate Program, Psychology, doctoral dissertation, York University.

de Saussure, F. 1986. *Course in General Linguistics* (translation, R. Harris). Illinois: Open Court.

Elmer-Dewitt, P. 1992. "Rich vs. Poor" *Time* (June 1):22.

Ericson, R., P. Baranek, and J. Chan. 1992. "Representing Order." In H. Holmes and D. Taras (eds.), *Seeing Ourselves, Media Power and Policy in Canada*. Toronto: Harcourt Brace Jovanovich.

Fitzpatrick, P. 1990. "Racism and the Innocence of Law." In D. Goldberg (ed.), *Anatomy of Racism*. Minneapolis: University of Minnesota.

Foster, D. 1993. "The Disease is Adolescence." *Rolling Stone* (December 9).

Foucault, M. 1979. *Discipline and Punish: The Birth of the Prison*. New York: Pantheon.

———. 1980. *Power and Knowledge: Selected Interviews and Other Writings 1972–1977*. Edited by C. Gordon. New York: Vintage.

Friedenberg, E. 1971. "The Side Effects of the Legal Process" In R. Wolff (ed.), *The Rule of Law*. New York: Simon and Schuster.

Gates, L.H., Jr. 1990. "Critical Remarks." In D. Goldberg (ed.), *Anatomy of Racism*. Minneapolis: University of Minnesota.

Gerbner, G. 1972. "Violence and Television Drama: Trends and Symbolic Functions." In G.A. Comstock and E.A. Rubinstein (eds.), *Content and Control: Television and Social Behavior, Vol. 1*. Washington, DC: U.S. Government Printing Office.

Gerbner, G. 1978. "The Dynamics of Cultural Resistance." In G. Tuchman, A.K. Daniels, and J. Benet. *Hearth and Home: Images of Women in the Mass Media*. New York: Oxford University Press

Giddens, A. 1981. *A Contemporary Critique of Historical Materialism*. London: Macmillan.

———. 1982. *Profiles and Critiques of Social Theory*. London: Macmillan.

————. 1984. *The Constitution of Society: Outline of Theory of Structuration.* Cambridge, U.K.: Polity Press.

Graber, D. 1980. *Crime News and the Public.* New York: Praeger.

Green, J. 1982. *The Pan Dictionary of Contemporary Quotations.* London: Pan Books.

Habermas, J. 1984. *The Theory of Communication Action: Reason and Realization of Society.* Boston: Heinemann Educational Books.

Halliday, M.A.K. 1978. *Language as Social Semiotic: The Social Interpretation of Language and Meaning.* London: Arnold.

Holmes, H., and D. Taras (eds.). 1992. *Seeing Ourselves, Media Power and Policy in Canada.* Toronto: Harcourt Brace Jovanovich.

Hunt, A. 1993. *Explorations in Law and Society: Toward Constitutive Theory of Law.* New York: Routledge.

kidmedia@airwaves.chi.il.us.

Kristeva, J. 1991. *Strangers to Ourselves.* New York: Columbia University Press.

Lacan, J. 1977. *Ecrits: A Selection.* New York: W.W. Norton.

Lacayo, R. 1994. "When Kids Go Bad." *Time* (September 19).

Lemke, J.L. 1988. "Text Structure and Text Semantics." In E. Steiner and R. Veltman (eds.), *Pragmatics, Discourse and Text.* London: Pinter.

Leong, L. 1992. "Cultural Resistance: The Cultural Terrorism of British Male Working-Class Youth." *Current Perspectives in Social Theory* 12:29–58.

Leyh, G. (ed.). 1992. *Legal Hermeneutics: History, Theory, and Practice.* Berkeley, CA: University of California Press.

Lippman, J. 1992. "How Television Is Shaping World's Culture." *Toronto Star* (December 21):A21.

Loy, D. 1993. "India's Postmodern Net." *Philosophy-East-and-West* 43(3) (July): 481–510.

Lyotard, J.F. 1984. *The Postmodern Condition: A Report on Knowledge.* Minneapolis, MN: University of Minnesota Press.

McCormick, K. 1991. *Technological Intrusions.* Research review paper, York University.

McNeely, C. 1995. "Perceptions of the Criminal Justice System: Television Imagery and Public Knowledge in the United States." *Journal of Criminal Justice and Popular Culture* 3 (February 15).

McPhail, T. 1981. *Electronic Colonialism.* Beverly Hills, CA: Sage Library of Social Research.

McQuaig, L. 1992. "Canada's Social Programs: Under Attack." *Toronto Star* (November 11):A21.

Manning, P. 1991. "Strands in the Postmodern Rope: Ethnographic Themes." *Studies in Symbolic Interactionism* 12.

————. 1992. *Organizational Communication*. New York: Aldine de Gruyter.

Marcuse, H. 1964. *One Dimensional Man*. Boston, MA: Beacon.

Martin, K. 1947. *The Press the Public Wants*. London: Hogarth.

Marx, K., and F. Engels [1947] 1960. *The German Ideology, Parts 1,3* New York: International.

Matibag, E. 1991. "Self-Consuming Fictions: The Dialectics of Cannibalism in Modern Caribbean Narratives." *Postmodern Culture* 1(3) (May).

Meyrowitz, J. 1992. "Television: The Shared Arena." In H. Holmes and D. Taras (eds.), *Seeing Ourselves, Media Power and Policy in Canada*. Toronto: Harcourt Brace Jovanovich.

Moog, C. 1990. *Are They Selling Her Lips: Advertising and Identity*. New York: William Morrow.

Moulthrop, S. 1991. "You Say You Want a Revolution? Hypertext and the Laws of Media." *Postmodern Culture* 1(3) (May 1991).

O'Neill. l985. *Five Bodies*. Ithaca, NY: Cornell University Press.

O'Sullivan, C. 1990. *Television*. San Diego: Greenhaven Press.

Papazian, E. (ed). 1988. *TV Dimensions '88*. New York: Media Dynamics.

Parker, R. 1994. "The Myth of Global News." *New Perspectives Quarterly* 2(Winter)1.

Platt, P. 1989. *Young Offenders Law in Canada*. Toronto: Butterworths.

Reiman, J.H. [1979] 1990. *The Rich Get Richer and the Poor Get Prison—Ideology, Class, and Criminal Justice*. New York: Macmillan.

Roberts, B. 1992. "Buying Time." *Our Times*. (September):42–43.

Saney, P. 1986. *Crime and Culture in America*. Westport, CT: Greenwood Press.

Schietz, S., and J.N. Sprafkin. 1978. "Spot Messages within Saturday Morning Television Programs" In G. Tuchman, A.K. Daniels, and J. Benet (eds.), *Hearth and Home: Images of Women in the Mass Media*. New York: Oxford University Press.

Schneider, C. 1989. "Children's Television: How It Works and Its Influence on Children." Pp. 6–7 in *NTC Business Books*. Lincolnwood, IL.

Skogan, W.G., and M. Maxfield. 1981. *Coping With Crime*. Beverly Hills, CA: Sage.

Simmons, J.L. 1965. "Public Stereotypes of Deviants." *Social Problems* 13:222–232.

Smitherman-Donaldson, G., and Tuen A. Van Dijk (eds.). 1988. *Discourse and Discrimination*. Detroit: Wayne State University Press.

Social Development Council. 1991. "Stay in School Supplement." *Social Development Overview* 1(Fall):7–14.

Solicitor General. 1994. *Weapons Use in Canadian Schools*. (Walker, S. G.) User Report: Responding to Violence and Abuse. No. 1994-05. Ottawa: Supply and Services.

————. 1987. *Culture Statistics: Television Viewing in Canada*. Cat. No. 87-208.

————. 1992a. *Canadian Social Trends* (Autumn). Ottawa: Supply and Services.

————. 1992b. *Household Facilities and Equipment*. Cat. No. 64-202.

Surette, R. 1984. *Justice and the Media*. Springfield, IL: Charles C. Thomas.

————. 1989. "Media Trials." *Journal of Criminal Justice* 17:293–308.

————. 1992. *Media, Crime, and Criminal Justice: Images and Realities*. Pacific Grove, CA: Brooks/Cole.

Trueman, P. 1980. *Smoke and Mirrors*. Toronto: McClelland & Stewart.

Valverde, M. 1990. "The Rhetoric of Reform: Tropes and the Moral Subject." *International Journal of the Sociology of Law* 18.

Visano, L.A. 1993. "Legal Injustices: Framing Inequalities." *Humanist Conference*, New Orleans (November 12).

CHAPTER 3

Doing Good or Doing Justice: Ideology in the Juvenile Delinquents Act and the Young Offenders Act

Anna Leslie
Memorial University of Newfoundland

Social control is a process whereby individuals in society are induced, through either coercion or commitment, to comply with the values and laws of society in order to ensure a stable community. Social control ideology in the legal regulation of youth can be summarized and chronicled as a history based on the concepts of "doing good" (inclusion) and "doing justice" (exclusion) (Cohen 1985).

Doing good, as defined by Cohen (1985:245, 250, 252), emphasizes rehabilitation as the primary aim of punishment and is based on the medical model of reform. Individualized justice is accentuated; the needs of the person take precedence over the needs of society. *Inclusion* incorporates the ideas of integration, tolerance, absorption, incorporation, and keeping individuals in the community. Formal structures should be made less formal, and boundaries of control should blur or disappear. Centralized systems should be decentralized or dispersed; professional power to exclude should be weakened; segregation in closed institutions should make way for integration in the open community; and anything that is stigmatizing should be rendered invisible (p. 224). Inclusion is also defined in this chapter to mean greater incorporation of individuals into the justice system.

On the other hand, *doing justice* as a reason for punishment incorporates the ideals of fairness, openness, and safety from abuse. There is a moral value and sense of rightness in law, and punishment is for the collective good. The ideal of doing justice incorporates personal responsibility, and societal needs dominate the needs of the individual (pp. 246, 250, 251, 252). *Exclusion* incorporates the ideas of stigma, segregation, banishment, separation, classification, and punishment. Exclusionary policies and programs make clear distinctions between those who violate rules and those who do not. They segregate offenders in closed institutions and promote formal structures; the professional power to exclude dominates.

Social control theories are located in assumptions about human nature and social change. As these assumptions change, so do the ideologies of crime control and social control. It is difficult to identify clearly which alternatives have been chosen at any particular time; what *can* be identified, Cohen argues, are "cycles"—reactions and counter-reactions, with changes of emphasis in one direction, which are then abandoned (p. 266).

This chapter examines the role of ideology in law, and the origins and justifications of the two ideologies: *doing good* (inclusion) and *doing justice* (exclusion). Using Cohen's definitions of these concepts, I will analyze two statutes regulating Canadian youth—the Juvenile Delinquents Act (S.C. 1908) and the Young Offenders Act (S.C. 1980–81–82–83)—to determine their ideological perspective, the origins of legal change, and the fit of Cohen's analysis to Canadian data.

The history of the legal regulation of youth has been punctuated by reforms. While the enactment of some statutes suggests a degree of disorganization and fragmentation, there is a pattern to be seen. This pattern is based on ideology. Ideology here is defined as a set of beliefs, interests, ideas, and ideals that justify the interests of those who espouse it.

Emile Durkheim saw law as primarily a reflection of the "collective consciousness," the "norms and values" and customs of a people. Others, following Karl Marx, argued that the law reflects the ideals and interests of those who control the economic and power resources of society.

Richard Quinney (1974) sees some value to both claims but suggests that the law reflects existing ideology, and that ideology is largely a reflection of dominant class interests:

> As long as a capitalist ruling class exists, the prevailing ideology will be capitalist. As long as that ruling class uses the law to maintain its order, the legal ideology will be capitalistic as well. [1974b:138]

Lawrence Friedman (1979) has an eclectic view regarding the relationship between ideology and economic structures; generally, however, he emphasizes the role of consensually held values rather than economic structure. "What makes law, then, is not 'public opinion' in the abstract, but public opinion in the sense of exerted social force" (p. 99). Competing interest groups with different power bases are seen as the moving force behind the creation of laws.

William Chambliss (1986:25) sees law creation as a "process aimed at the resolution of contradictions, conflicts and dilemmas which are inherent in the structure of a particular historical period." In other words, laws act as symptom-solving mechanisms. For Chambliss, law creation is contingent on a host of historically specific factors:" It is ... more accurate, and ... better scientific theory to see the relationship between the larger social, economic and political forces ..." (p. 35). He suggests that some laws are passed for the specific interest of an individual, while others emerge as a result of efforts by lobbying groups representing substantial portions of the population; yet others, perhaps the majority, are no more than expressions of the views and interests of legislative committees (p. 27).

The views presented by Quinney, Freidman, and Chambliss contribute to the current debate over law creation. The model presented by Chambliss puts people or groups in the middle of struggles to resolve contradictions by fighting existing laws. In this process, ideological justifications develop, shift, and change; these ideologies in turn become a force of their own, influencing the development of legal institutions and law.

An examination of ideology in statute analysis is necessary because it reveals the forces that helped to shape law (Friedman 1975:148). A social explanation for the development of law assumes the existence of various interests that generate demands to change the legal system. This explanation of law development presumes that when various interests are involved in effecting legal change, there will be belief systems or ideologies that are specific to each group, and that in many instances the ideologies will be in competition.

Cohen (1985:22) offers another version of the function of ideology in statutes:

> Ideals and ideologies cannot much change the story. Stated intentions are assumed *a priori* to conceal the real interests and motives behind the system. They constitute a facade to make acceptable the exercise of otherwise unacceptable power, domination or class interests...

His concluding comment about ideology is that "ideology is important, then, only insofar as it succeeds at passing off as fair, natural, acceptable or even just and humane, a system which is basically coercive" (p. 23).

Changes in ideology are visible throughout the history of the criminal justice system. Ideological change has been reflected in the question of what causes crime. At various times criminality has been seen as having a genetic basis (Lombroso 1876; Sheldon 1949); a psychological basis (McCord and McCord 1960; Gordon 1967; Hirschi and Hindelang 1977); and a social basis (Merton 1938; Durkheim 1951). Incarceration has also been affected by ideological change; the movement here has been from a belief in a system of strict segregation to a belief in decarceration and community involvement. The ideology of rehabilitation has not been untouched. The rehabilitation ideal once played a key role in the management of inmates, but this view is less popular today.

In a similar manner, legislation regulating youth has also been governed by a variety of ideological perspectives. Children who committed crimes were once seen as "wayward" and "dependent," as bad and needing to be remodelled into something good. Now children are viewed as being responsible and accountable for their behaviour. The history of the legal regulation of youth can be documented as a history centred on the concerns of treatment versus punishment, and on policies and programs based on community inclusion or community exclusion (Cohen 1985:218–222; 245). These ideological trends tend to be "either/or" in nature. Yet the society from which they emerge is dominated by a pluralism that "demands that we tolerate contradictions and inconsistencies" (p. 244). In such a society, a conflict emerges between the social environment and the proposed ideological cure.

In areas of crime control, each ideological offering attempts to replace uncertainties with certainties. Yet ideologically, there can be "no totally valid general solutions; only temporary expedients based on our clearly stated values and our sense of the uniqueness of each historical juncture" (p. 244).

In crime control fashions, the dominant themes have been identified as rehabilitation and justice; needs and rights; determinism and free will; institutions and community; lawyer and psychiatrist (p. 249). In the cycle, the failure of one approach to social control is recognized; another approach is then tried; the original approach is then tried again. It is a cycle of discarding one ideological perspective and resurrecting another.

The first dominant theme in crime control fashions to be considered here is the rehabilitative or *doing good* model. This tradition, which evolved from the Progressive movement, dominated juvenile justice policy until the early 1970s and gave "remarkable primacy to the idea of the state as parent" (Rothman 1978:69). Rothman stated:

> The most distinguishing characteristic of Progressivism was its fundamental trust in the power of the state to do good. The state was not the enemy of liberty, but the friend of equality ... In criminal justice, the issue was not how to protect the offender from the arbitrariness of the state, but how to bring the state more effectively to the aid of the offender. [1980:60]

In the instance of children, those in need were viewed as dependent or delinquent.

The rehabilitative model was based on the assumption that criminal behaviour was caused by factors beyond the offender's control (Cavender 1984:203). In the matter of delinquents and delinquency, it was determined that "rehabilitation, not retributive punishment, should guide the sanctioning process" (Cullen and Gilbert 1982:75). The cause of the offender's problem would be determined by the experts; the offender would then be treated to eliminate the abnormality that gave rise to the criminal tendencies; thus, both the offender and society would be protected from further criminal behaviour. To this end, those responsible for "treating" the offender were given widespread discretionary authority. The "punishment/treatment" was to fit the criminal rather than the crime. These principles were the foundation of a series of measures enacted by the Progressives to prevent and relieve dependency and deviance. These sick and trapped young people needed to be saved for their own good (Platt 1987:171, 177; Armitage 1975:248; Scull 1977:5; Pearson 1979:15; Cohen 1979; Hylton 1981).

Juvenile courts were developed to regulate and "treat" instances of dependency and delinquency. They operated on the doctrine of *parens patriae*. In informal hearings, the best interests of the neglected or delinquent child would be determined. The relationship between the state (through the juvenile court judge) and the delinquent or dependent child was nonadversarial; the protections of due process were removed. Juvenile court judges were accorded wide discretionary powers to investigate cases, and to prescribe measures designed for a particular young person. The remedies available to these judges ranged from community supervision to incarceration in a juvenile reformatory.

The aim of the juvenile court was to help, not to punish, individuals. It followed that it was "unnecessary—in fact it was counter-productive—to limit or to circumscribe officials' discretionary power" (Rothman 1978:77). The power of the state was thus enhanced; the legal rights of individuals encountering the state were negligible.

Open-ended sentencing was favoured by the Progressives to ensure that there would be enough time to "treat" and eventually cure offenders. Juvenile court judges still relied on "institutions of care" (Armstrong and Wilson 1973:67)—training schools and reformatories—to discipline the young. Under the Progressives, the language used changed the direction of the discipline. The intention of discipline was to rehabilitate rather than punish the offender. Thus, the state could be perceived to be *doing good*.

The Progressives and their followers were also pioneers in the concept of community corrections. Delinquents and dependents were affected by the community corrections approach in that probation, as an alternative to imprisonment, was expanded. Rothman (1978:80–81) argues forcefully that probation programs didn't work. He points out that probation officers were poorly trained and carried large caseloads. Probation had been designed as an alternative to incarceration; more often, it served as a supplement to it. "The same numbers still went to institutions; the difference was that cases which had once been dismissed or suspended now came under the supervisory network of probation officers" (p. 80).

The Progressives believed that individualized "treatments" were redemptive rather than coercive, but they were assuming that the state would carry out its redemptive function in good faith. There is no evidence to suggest that the Progressives considered that "this discretion would be corrupted to serve organizational and class interests and not to be used to do good as they had planned" (Cullen and Gilbert 1982:79). The introduction of state-enforced treatment was seen not as potentially abusive but as necessary in order to "save" the criminally deviant.

The Juvenile Delinquents Act (in most provinces) and the Welfare of Children's Act (in Newfoundland) represented the most completely developed statement about the ideals and ideas of the Progressive movement. The enveloping ideology of these acts was *parens patriae*, which originated in English common law and, literally translated, means "parent of the state." The doctrine of *parens patriae* included several significant philosophical elements espoused by the juvenile court movement. These have been summarized by Robert Caldwell (1966:362–363) as follows:

1. The Superior Rights of the State. The State is the "higher or ultimate parent" of all the children within its borders. The rights of the child's own parents are always subject to the control of the state when in the opinion of the court the best interests of the child demand it. If the state has to intervene in the case of any child, it exercises its power of guardianship over the child and provides [that child] with the protection, care and guidance needed.

2. Individualization of Justice ... people are different [and] each must be considered in the light of his own background and personality. The court, therefore, must adapt its actions to the circumstances of the individual case by ascertaining the needs and potentialities of the child and coordinating the knowledge and skills of law, science, and social work for the promotion of the child's welfare.

3. The Status of Delinquency. The state should try to protect the child from the harmful brand of criminality. In order to accomplish this, the law created the status of delinquency, which is something less and is variously defined ...

4. Noncriminal Procedure. By means of an informal procedure the juvenile court functions in such a way as to give primary consideration to the interests of the child. In general, the courts have held that the procedure of the juvenile court is not criminal in nature since its purpose is not to convict a child of a crime, but to protect, aid, and guide him, and that therefore, it is not unconstitutional if it denies him certain rights which are guaranteed to an adult in a criminal trial.

5. Remedial and Preventive Purpose. The action of the juvenile court is to save the child and to prevent further criminality. It seeks to provide about the same care and protection that parents should give.

Gilbert and Cullen (1982:80) note that the "Progressives' therapeutic model received its most complete expression in the measures formulated to control delinquent behaviour." The Progressive movement succeeded in establishing a separate court system for juveniles. The concern of the courts was to rehabilitate the young. To this end, the state, under the doctrine of *parens patriae*, would act as parent to bring about conformity. In keeping with the belief that young offenders could be "saved," the state's power to intervene in the lives of the young was greatly expanded.

In conclusion, the Juvenile Delinquents Act clearly represented the *doing good* ideology, for it emphasized correction, rehabilitation, and prevention. Retribution was discredited; the causes of delinquency were seen as socially produced and therefore curable. The "best interests" of young people, although not clearly defined, were stressed over societal needs for justice. The court was to act as a wise, kind, firm, and stern parent under the doctrine of *parens patriae*. The philosophy of the act was based on paternalistic benevolence and individualized justice.

This act was *inclusionary* in several senses. More individuals were included in the juvenile justice system through the introduction of the broad term "delinquency," which included both offenders and "about to be" offenders. Also, probation was central to the act, and delinquents could remain in the community. But the Juvenile Delinquents Act was also *exclusionary*. Delinquents could be confined to prisons and training schools and kept out of the community. Also, there was a stigma attached to the classification "juvenile delinquent."

The Progressives succeeded in thoroughly overhauling the juvenile justice system. The movement's concurrent themes of individualized justice and rehabilitation dominated corrections policy until recently. Over the last 20 years, the controversy over the liberal ideology of *doing good* has centred on two things: the propriety of rehabilitation programs in prisons, and the legitimacy of rehabilitation as a primary aim of punishment. As a fashion in social control, *doing good* has been losing favour with the public and with control agents. Note also that rehabilitation and punishment are opposing concepts. Imprisonment denotes punishment and coercion; rehabilitation implies treatment and choice. Yet these conflicting mandates have been the hallmark of the juvenile justice system from its inception.

Critics of the *doing good* model questioned "the wisdom and propriety of an ideal of the state as parent" and the dependent as child (Rothman 1978:71). They called for the reinstatement of rights and for the assigning of responsibility to individuals. The Progressives believed so deeply in the paternalism of their model that they failed to recognize "the potential of their programs to be as coercive as they were liberating" (p. 72). Indeed, there now exists an almost universal suspicion about the idea of *doing good* in situations requiring incarceration. In the current ideological fashion of crime control, it is more acceptable to approach social policy as social control, thereby immediately recognizing its coercive elements (Cohen 1985).

The Progressives' blueprint for a criminal justice system dedicated to rehabilitating criminal offenders was never fully realized. It appears that community corrections "did not lessen the use of incarceration but provided a means for increased state surveillance of offenders" who previously would have been set totally free after serving their time—if they were not given an unsupervised suspended sentence (Greenberg 1975:12). Because of inadequate officer training and the heavy caseloads borne by probation officers, few offenders on probation received intensive care.

In the area of juvenile justice, it became apparent that dependent and delinquent young people were being abused by their "kindly parent," the state. Eventually it was deemed necessary to grant these individuals the rights of due process so that they could avoid mistreatment. The suspicion of benevolence appears to be directly linked to a pointed distrust of discretionary authority, and "these developments are part of a ... general decline in the legitimacy of the authority of a whole series of persons and institutions" (Rothman 1978:84). The prevailing attitude in juvenile justice is to question how social policy regulates individuals rather than wonder how it rehabilitates or reforms them.

Doing justice as a correctional model has been fashionable more than once. It arose first within the prisoners' movement in the United States as part of a struggle against the state and against racial oppression. It appeared first in a report prepared by a working party of the American Friends Service Committee (AFSC) under the title *Struggle for Justice* (1971). Willard Gaylin (1983), one of the advocates of the "back to justice" model, suggests that reaffirming justice is based on an "honourable moral value," and not just on something that the law mechanically requires. The essence of the justice model is that sanctioning policies should be grounded in a sense of justice. The endeavour to reaffirm justice addresses the question and practice of placing individual welfare beyond the needs of society.

The purposes of the justice model are to restore the ideal of due process and to end many of the abuses that surfaced within the parameters of the rehabilitative model. The justice model combines denunciation, deterrence, and incapacitation as justifications for imposing the criminal sanction. The foundation of the justice model is *denunciation*—the ideal that if rational people violate the law, they deserve punishment.

This argument is based on social contract theory as presented by Jean-Jacques Rousseau and developed by Baron de Montesquieu and Cesare Beccaria. Essentially, social contract theory says that when rational people create a state, agree to be governed by it, and accept its benefits, they also accept a responsibility to obey its laws. The right to punish violators is an essential part of the social contract between the state and those who are part of it. Justice is served by the punishment of those persons who reject their legal obligations by violating the law.

One mandate of the justice model is to enhance social order by ensuring that the laws of society apply equally to all members regardless of their station. It has been argued that this principle is weakened in the administration of law because society "is characterized by structural inequities that affect the distribution of a variety of social advantages and disadvantages." (Cavender 1984:208). Cavender adds that "given these inequities, law and justice simply do not coincide." Assuming that the law is administered fairly, Cavender argues that it cannot deliver a just society when it is imposed on a situation previously characterized by injustice (p. 208). Those who criticize the justice model for undermining social contract theory, in that laws cannot create equality in a society that is based on inequalities (Paternoster and Bynum 1982), are misinterpreting social contract theory. David Greenberg (1983:326) remarks that social contract theory "never claimed to produce equal benefits for all, only some benefits. The theory works as long as everyone is better off with a government than without."

The justice model emphasizes that the offender must be treated as a responsible person. It moves beyond the idea of "determinism," which posits that criminal behaviour is in some way beyond the individual's control. Behaviour as deterministic is located in psychoanalytic theory and is summarized in two axioms by Willard Gaylin (1983:252): "Every individual act of behaviour is the resultant of a multitude of emotional forces and counterforces *and* these forces and counterforces are shaped by past experiences." For supporters of determinism, these two principles provide a way of accounting for any behaviour. From the perspective of behaviour as deterministic, "all acts—healthy, sick, or not-sure-which—share one property. They are predetermined." Accounting for behaviour in this manner seemingly rejects the possibility of isolated or chance acts and overlooks the notion of free will.

The justice model supports the social concept of behaviour in law that assumes free will. Individuals have a choice in action, and as such the social view of behaviour is based on moral principles. Behaviour is either right or wrong, acceptable or unacceptable, approved or disapproved, sanctioned against or not sanctioned against. By acknowledging individual free will, the justice model contributes to the advancement of respect "for individual dignity that arises when the offender is treated as a responsible person" (Cavender 1984:207).

The justice model is reflected in the Young Offenders Act. Although the act does not contain one single ideology, it contains a declaration of principle that speaks to limited accountability, protection of society, the special needs of young persons, alternative measures, rights and freedoms, minimal interference, and parental involvement.

3.(1) It is hereby recognized and declared that

(a) while young persons should not in all instances be held accountable in the same manner or suffer the same consequences for their behaviour as adults, young persons who commit offenses should nonetheless bear responsibility for their contraventions;

(b) society must, although it has the responsibility to take reasonable measures to prevent criminal conduct by young persons, be afforded the necessary protection of illegal behaviour;

(c) young persons who commit offenses require supervision, discipline and control, but, because of their state of dependency and level of development and maturity, they also have special needs and require guidance and assistance;

(d) where it is not inconsistent with the protection of society, taking no measures or taking measures other than judicial proceedings under this Act should be considered for dealing with young persons who have committed offenses;

(e) young persons have rights and freedoms in their own right, including those stated in the Canadian Charter of Rights and Freedoms or in the Canadian Bill of Rights, and in particular a right to be heard in the course of, and to participate in, the processes that lead to decisions that affect them, and young persons should have special guarantees of their rights and freedoms;

(f) in the application of this Act, the rights and freedoms of young persons include a right to the least possible interference with freedom that is consistent with the protection of society, having regard to the needs of young persons and the interests of their families;

(g) young persons have the right, in every instance where they have rights or freedoms that may be affected by this Act, to be informed as to what those rights and freedoms are; and

(h) parents have responsibility for the care and supervision of their children and, for that reason, young persons should be removed from parental supervision either partly or entirely only when measures that provide for continuing parental supervision are inappropriate.

These principles are reflected in the substantive features of the Young Offenders Act and are summarized and critiqued as follows:

3(1)(a) Limited Accountability. Young persons who commit offences should bear responsibility for their contraventions, although not in all instances should they be held accountable as adults. This principle is most clearly reflected in the maximum dispositions under the YOA, which until recently limited fines to $1,000 and limited custodial terms to five years (as opposed to life for adults).[1] There is evidence to suggest that judges are supporting the accountability provisions in other dispositions. This is most clearly demonstrated in the sevenfold increase in the use of victim reconciliation orders and community service orders under the Young Offenders Act in 1985 (constituting 20 percent of all dispositions) compared to the number of orders made under the Juvenile Delinquents Act (3 percent of all dispositions) (Staples 1986:177–185). Bartollas (1985) has suggested that the use of victim reconciliation and community service orders is popular because such arrangements reconcile the "hard liners," who want a tougher stance taken against youth crime, with officials in the youth justice system who acknowledge the lack of punishment meted out to juveniles who commit property crimes.

3(1)(b) Protection of Society. Society must be protected from illegal behaviour. The protection of society is considered to result from the apprehension and punishment of young offenders under the act. The YOA appears to require courts to give full consideration to the protection of society when sentencing. Paragraphs 3 (1) (a) and (b) suggest that the goal of sentencing is the same as in the adult system. However, Peter J. Harris (1987:6) says that there has been considerable argument as to whether the adult sentencing principle of proportionality (the sentence reflecting the seriousness of the offence) is the relevant dispositional concept with respect to the Young Offenders Act. The question raised is about the appropriateness of imposing longer sentences than the offence calls for, to meet the special needs of the young person.

In 1987 the Ontario Court of Appeal provided a clear statement on the sentencing principle, adopting the adult model of sentencing that emphasizes that punishment is to be proportional to the gravity of the offence. "It is clear from this case that the idea that a lengthy sentence can be imposed solely for treatment purposes on the basis of the needs of the young person has been laid to rest once and for all" (Harris 1987:7).

One provision of the YOA that is intended to protect society is Section 16, which governs the transfer of proceedings into adult court. If a young person is thought to pose a threat to society and the proceedings are transferred to adult court, the young person may be subject to the same sanctions as an adult. For serious crimes, this means the possibility of long sentences. However, this section has not been consistently applied, even for serious offences. Youth court judges in British Columbia, Alberta, and Manitoba are more likely to transfer youths to adult court than are judges in Saskatchewan or Ontario (Department of Justice 1989).

Harris (p. 4) says that the frequency of Crown applications for transfer of youths to adult court pursuant to Section 16 of the Young Offenders Act has diminished to a mere trickle since the 1987 Ontario Court of Appeal decision in R. v Mark Z. It was the opinion of the court that, in view of Section 3 of the act, the interests of society and the needs and interests of the young persons are not to be given greater importance over each other. The court also held that "incarceration in the penitentiary would destroy [Mark] as a potentially useful citizen and both the accused and society would lose out if he were sentenced for a lengthy period of time" (R. v Mark, summarized in 1 W.C.B. (2d) 343 (Ont. C.A.), cited by Harris).

Provincial variations in dispositions and transfers to adult court create an unfortunate situation of inequality under the law. For example, a young person's place of residence can mean the difference between spending five years in secure custody and 25 years in a penitentiary.

Although protection of the public is vital, and young persons are to be held responsible for their criminal conduct, the paternalistic approach that characterized the Juvenile Delinquents Act is not to be fully abandoned. Sentencing will not necessarily be punitive, for the long-term protection of society depends on the successful reintegration of youthful offenders into the community.

Paragraphs 3 (1) (c), (f), and (h) outline the most important principles affecting the treatment concerns involved in sentencing. They were quoted earlier in this chapter. While it appears that the Young Offenders Act is essentially a criminal statute, the Section 3 provisions sanction a treatment approach to sentencing.

3(1)(c) Special Needs. Young persons who commit offences require supervision, discipline, and control, but because of their state of dependency and level of development and maturity, they also have special needs and require guidance and assistance.

The special needs of young people are acknowledged in a number of substantive provisions in the act. For example, Section 38 prohibits the publication of information that might identify a young person who is subject to proceedings under the act. Under Section 39, a youth court judge can also exclude members of the public from the proceedings. Sections 40 to 46 restrict access to records concerning proceedings under the act, and in some cases provide for their destruction. These provisions appear to be addressing the process of social typing (Becker 1963) that can occur if the names of young people who commit crimes become widely known. In addition, these substantive provisions also reflect a desire to limit the accountability of young offenders.

Recognizing young people's special needs, the YOA provides that instead of placing a young offender in a correctional facility, a youth court may order detention for treatment in a psychiatric hospital (paragraph 20(1)(i) and Section 22). This is not a custodial disposition and must be based on a court-ordered medical or psychological report recommending treatment. Reasons for assessment can include consideration of an emotional or psychological disorder, a learning disability, developmental impairment, or other conditions that a judge might consider significant in understanding the needs of a young offender. However, such an order can only be made if the young person and (usually) the parents consent.

3(1)(d) Alternative Measures. Where it is not inconsistent with the protection of society, taking no measures or taking alternative measures should be considered for dealing with young persons who have committed offences. Provisions governing alternative measures are addressed in Section 4. Alternative measures programs must be authorized by the provinces and can only be activated if the young person consents to participate and has accepted responsibility for the alleged offence. It was anticipated that extensive use of alternative measures programs would drastically reduce the number of cases dealt with by the courts. However, the alternative measures have not been applied consistently from one province to another. Different ideologies and financial capabilities have led to major variations in youth justice across the country.

3(1)(e) Rights and Freedoms. Young persons processed under the YOA have all the fundamental legal rights enjoyed by adults. They are also protected by specific provisions of the Charter of Rights and Freedoms and the Canadian Bill of Rights. The YOA provides for special steps to be taken to ensure that young persons understand their legal rights, which include the right to remain silent and to have a lawyer or parent present during police questioning (Section 56). Legal counsel must be provided and paid for by the state if the young person is unable to retain counsel. A young person has the right to retain counsel without delay at any stage of the proceedings, and the right to respect the formal rules of criminal procedure to be applied in court. The presence of Crown and defence counsel ensures the requirement of due process and (generally) eliminates the abuses that flourished under the Juvenile Delinquents Act.

Another example of the special rights of young offenders is the provision (in Section 52) that proceedings are to be based on "summary procedures" designed for dealing with less serious charges. The intention is to handle the proceedings relatively quickly. However, the use of the less formal procedure when processing young offenders has led to the concern that in this area the Young Offenders Act is similar to its predecessor and that in reality young offenders are not afforded the same rights of due process as adults.

3(1)(f) Minimal Interference. The rights and freedoms of young persons include a right to the least possible interference with freedom. This principle is demonstrated in the provisions of the act for alternative measures or diversions programs (Section 4). Community-based dispositions such as restitution, community service orders, or probation are all incorporated in the principle of minimal interference. However, there is provincial variation in the utilization of these measures.

3(1)(g) Informed of Rights. All actors involved in the processing of young offenders must ensure that young persons are aware of their rights, including the right to counsel and the right to remain silent (Sections 11, 12, and 19).

3(1)(h) Parental Involvement. While parents are not held legally accountable for the violations of their children, the parental role is included in several provisions of the YOA. For example, parents are entitled to be present after arrest, to be notified of proceedings, and to be involved in dispositional decisions and supervision of the young person before the trial and after disposition where appropriate (Sections 7, 9, 16, 20, 22, and 56). Also:

> Parents have responsibility for the care and supervision of their children and for that reason, young persons should be removed from parental supervision, either partly or entirely only when measures that provide for continuing supervision are inappropriate [paragraphs 3(1)(g)]

In addition, Section 24 of the act addresses the issue of custodial care in family-like settings and the provision of strong community linkages.

The *doing justice* model is recognized in the Young Offenders Act. Young offenders are entitled to fair hearings and to protection against self-incrimination, and are afforded the rights of due process. At the same time, they must bear responsibility for their contraventions. The act is *exclusionary*, for offences are clearly defined and categorized. Distinctions are made between those who violate rules and those who do not.

In addition to *doing justice*, the Young Offenders Act encompasses the *doing good* model, in that the ideal of rehabilitation has not been abandoned. The rehabilitative ideal is most noticeable in the limited maximum sentences for serious crimes, and in the concept of diminished accountability. Sentencing is based on the idea of successful reintegration into the community. The act stresses the young person's right to the least possible interference with freedom that is consistent with the protection of society.

The act recognizes the special needs of young offenders as these relate to their state of dependency and level of maturity, and their requirement for guidance and assistance. The act emphasizes that young persons should be removed from parental supervision either partly or entirely only when measures that provide for continuing parental supervision are inappropriate. The last three provisions provide for individualized justice and accentuate the rights of the young person over the needs of society.

In addition, the act incorporates the concept of *inclusion*. It incorporates more young people into the justice system by stressing proceduralism and formalism, and by adopting diversion programs. Young offenders are diverted into the system and not out of it. Young offenders are also more included in the community through sentencing options that incorporate alternative measures. Stigma has been removed by blurring the boundaries between corrections and community, and also by the adoption of the term "young offender."

The Young Offenders Act is in many respects an enlightened statute. The inequalities that have been encountered in its administration are jarring, when one considers that the act was drawn up in response to the weaknesses of the Juvenile Delinquents Act. These weaknesses centred on provincial variations in transfers to adult court, provincial variations and interprovincial variations in the implementation of alternative measures and diversion programs, and the emphasis on informality and expediency. The Young Offenders Act stresses proceduralism and formalism, and this has resulted in more young people being diverted into the system, not out of it.

The changes in social control ideology that have been identified in the Canadian regulation of youth are not cyclical nor are they separate and distinct; rather, they reflect a combination of social control concepts.

The Juvenile Delinquents Act was more completely aligned with the ideology of doing good; however, it also emphasized exclusion. Individuals were stigmatized by the label juvenile delinquent, and segregation in training schools and confinement to prisons remained part of sentencing under the act.

The Young Offenders Act represents a continuation of combined social control ideologies. *Doing good* and *inclusion* dominate, and the needs of the young person prevail. There is evidence of *doing justice* in the tougher language of the law in that young persons must bear responsibility for their contraventions; there is a clear distinction between rule violators and nonrule violators, and young offenders are entitled to the rights of due process and to procedural safeguards.

Stanley Cohen's suggestion that the ideologies of *doing good* and *doing justice* in social control are separate and distinct has not been confirmed in the Juvenile Delinquents Act and the Young Offenders Act. What has been identified in the Canadian regulation of youth is that while one ideology may be dominant, the statutes combine with approaches. Also, all the components of *inclusion* and *doing justice* as outlined by Cohen were not fully developed in either of the statutes.

Notes

1. Canada's justice minister, Allan Rock, tabled amendments in 1994 (Bill C-37) to the Young Offenders Act (YOA) that will move 16- and 17-year-old youths to adult court with adult punishments if they are charged with serious criminal acts. The new law will lower the age limit from 18 to 16 for young offenders who have committed six of the most serious crimes in the Criminal Code: first-degree murder; manslaughter, kidnapping; armed robbery; rape; and aggravated sexual assault. Youth court sentences will be increased to a maximum of ten years from five years for those convicted of first-degree murder; second-degree murder will be changed to seven years. Young offenders charged with the above offences will have the option of a trial by judge alone or by judge and jury, as is required under the Charter of Rights and Freedoms. Changes to parole eligibility will ensure that youths sentenced in the adult system will serve longer periods in custody. They will be segregated from adult inmates. Furthermore, there will be no prosecution of those under ten years of age. As of April 25, 1995, Bill C-37 passed the house with

some notable amendments, including an increase in the sentence for murder to ten years maximum and some loosening of provisions for publishing information. The most controversial aspect is a "reverse onus" for serious offenders. Those charged with serious violent crimes will automatically be transferred to adult court unless they initiate an appeal to remain in youth court.

References

Allen, F.A. 1971. "Criminal Justice, Legal Values and the Rehabilitative Ideal." Pp. 317–330 in S.E. Grupp (ed.), *Theories of Punishment*. Bloomington: Indiana University.

———. 1981. *The Decline of the Rehabilitative Ideal: Penal Policy and Social Purpose*. New Haven, CT: Yale University.

American Friends Service Committee. 1971. "Working Party, Struggle for Justice: A Report on Crime and Punishment in America." Hill and Wange.

Archambault, O. 1983. "Young Offenders Act: Philosophy and Principles." *Provincial Judges Journal*.

Armitage, A. 1975. *Social Welfare in Canada: Ideals and Realities*. Toronto: McClelland & Stewart.

Armstrong, G., and Wilson, M. 1973. "City Politics and Deviancy Complication." In I. Taylor and L. Taylor (eds.), *Politics and Deviance*. Harmondsworth: Penguin.

Bala, N. 1985. "The Young Offenders Act: Why a New Era in Juvenile Justice?" Presented at Canadian Psychological Association Annual Meeting, Halifax.

———. 1986. "The Young Offenders Act: A New Era in Juvenile Justice." Barbara Landau (ed.), *Children's Rights in the Practice of Family Law*. Toronto: Carswell.

Bala, N., and D. Cruickshank. "Children and the Charter of Rights." In B. Landau (ed.), *Children's Rights and the Practice of Family Law*.

Bala, N., H. Lilles, and G.N. Thomson. 1982. "Child Saving and Children's Rights." *Canadian Children's Law*, Chapter 6.

Balch, R.W. 1975. "The Medical Model of Delinquency: Theoretical, Practical and Ethical Implications" *Crime and Delinquency* 21:116–129.

Bartollas, C. 1985. *Correctional Treatment: Theory and Practice*. Englewood Cliffs: Prentice Hall.

Becker, Howard. 1963. *Outsiders—Studies in the Sociology of Deviance*. New York: Free Press.

Brickley, Stephen, and Elizabeth Comack (eds.). 1986. *The Social Basis of Law*. Toronto: Garamond.

Caldwell, Robert G. 1966. "The Juvenile Court: Its Development and Some Major Problems." In Rose Giallombardo (ed.), *Juvenile Delinquency: A Book of*

Readings. New York: John Wiley and Sons.

Cavender, Gary. 1984. "Justice Sanctioning and the Justice Model." *Criminology* 22(2):203–213.

Chambliss, William. 1986. "On Lawmaking." Pp. 27–52 in Stephen Brickley and Elizabeth Comack (eds.), *The Social Basis of Law*. Toronto: Garamond Press.

Cohen, Stanley. 1979. "The Punitive City: Notes on the Dispersal of Social Control." *Contemporary Crises* 3:339–363.

———. 1985. *Visions of Social Contract*. Cambridge, MA: Polity Press.

Cohen, Stanley, and Andrew Scull (eds.). 1983–85. *Social Control and the State*. Oxford: Basil Blackwell.

Cullen, Francis T., and Karen E. Gilbert. 1982. *Reaffirming Rehabilitation*. Cincinnati: Anderson.

Department of Justice. 1989. Consultation Document. *The Young Offenders Act*. Proposals for Amendment (June).

———. 1994. Justice Information Backgrounder: Proposed Young Offenders Act Amendments. Communications and Consultation Branch (June).

Donzelot, Jacques. 1979. *The Policing of Families*. Trans. Robert Hurley. New York: Random House.

Durkheim, Emile. 1893 [1933]. *The Division of Labour in Society*. Glencoe, IL: Free.

———. [1951]. *Suicide: A Study in Sociology*. Trans. J.A. Spaulding and G. Simpson. New York: Free Press.

———. [1969]. "Types of Law in Relation to Social Solidarity." *Sociology of Law*, W. Aubert (ed.). Baltimore: Penguin.

Freidman, Lawrence M. 1975. *The Legal System: A Social Science Perspective*. New York: Russell Gage.

———. 1979. *Law and Society: An Introduction*. Englewood Cliffs, NJ: Prentice Hall.

Gaylin, Willard. 1983. *The Killing of Bonnie Garland: A Question of Justice*. New York: Penguin.

Gaylin, Willard, Ira Glasser, Steven Marcus, and David Rothman. 1979. *Doing Good*. New York: Pantheon.

Giallombardo, Rose (ed.). 1966. *Juvenile Delinquency: A Book of Readings*. New York: Wiley.

Glaser, D. 1964. *The Effectiveness of Prison and Parole Systems*. Indianapolis: Bobbs-Merrill.

Gordon, Robert A. 1967. "Social Level, Social Disability and Gang Interaction." *American Journal of Sociology* 73:42–62.

Greenberg, David F. 1973. "Reflections on the Justice Model Debate." *Contemporary Crises* 7:313–327 (November).

———. 1975. "Problems in Community Corrections." *Issues in Criminology* 10 (Spring).

Griffiths, J. 1969. "Ideology in Criminal Procedure or a Third Model of the Criminal Process." *Yale Law Journal* 79.

Harris, Peter J. 1987. *R. v. Mark* in 1 W.C.B. (2d) 343.

Hylton, J. 1981. "Community Corrections and Social Control: The Case of Saskatchewan, Canada." *Contemporary Crisis* 5:193–215.

Hirschi, Travis, and Michael Hindelang. 1977. "Intelligence and Delinquency: A Revisionist Review." *American Sociological Review* 42:571–586.

Ignatieff, Michael. 1978. *A Just Measure of Pain: The Penitentiary in the Industrial Revolution*. New York: Macmillan.

McCord, William, and Joan McCord. 1960. *Origins of Alcoholism*. Stanford: Stanford University Press.

Martinson, R. 1974. "What Works—Questions and Answers about Prison Reform." *The Public Interest* 35:22–54.

Merton, Robert K. 1938. "Social Structure and Anomie." *American Sociological Review* 3:672–682.

Monachesi, Elio. 1972. "Cesare Beccaria." In Hermann Mannheim (ed.), *Pioneers in Criminology*. New Jersey: Patterson Smith.

Paternoster, R., and T. Bynum. 1982. "The Justice Model as Ideology: A Critical Look at the Impetus for Sentencing Reform." *Contemporary Crises* 6:7–24.

Pearson, G. 1979. *The Deviant Imagination*. London: MacMillan.

———. 1982. *Hooligan: A History of Respectable Fears*. London: Macmillan.

Platt, Priscilla. 1987. Getting Help Under The Young Offenders Act—Fact or Fiction. The Law as of August 1987, 1–14. Ontario Bar Admission Course Materials.

Platt, Anthony. 1974. "The Triumph of Benevolence: The Origins of the Juvenile Justice System in the United States." Pp. 356–389 in Richard Quinney (ed.), *Criminal Justice in America: A Critical Understanding*. Boston: Little, Brown.

———. 1977. *The Child Savers: The Invention of Delinquency*. Chicago: University of Chicago.

Quinney, Richard. 1974. *Critique of Legal Order: Crime Control in Capitalist Society*. Boston: Little, Brown.

———. 1977. *Class, State and Crime*. New York: D. McKay.

Robinson, James, and Gerald Smith. 1971. "The Effectiveness of Correctional Programs." *Crime and Delinquency* 17:67–80.

Rothman, David J. 1971. *The Discovery of the Asylum*. Toronto: Little, Brown.

———. 1978. "The State as Parent: Social Policy in the Progressive Era." Pp. 67–98 in W. Gaylin, I. Glasser, S. Marcus, and D. Rothman (eds.), *Doing Good*. New York: Pantheon.

———. 1979. "The Progressive Legacy: Development of American Attitudes towards Juvenile Delinquency." In L.T. Empey (ed.), *Juvenile Justice: The Progressive Legacy*. Charlottesville: University of Virginia.

————. 1980. *Conscience and Convenience: The Asylum and Its Alternatives in Progressive America*. Boston: Little, Brown.

Scheff, Thomas. 1966. *Being Mentally Ill*. Chicago: Aldine.

Scull, Andrew T. 1977. *Decarceration: Community Based Treatment and the Deviant. A Radical Review*. Englewood Cliffs, NJ: Prentice Hall.

————. 1981. "Progressive Dreams, Progressive Nightmares: Social Control in 20th Century America." *Stanford Law Review* 33(3):1–16.

Sheldon, William H. 1949. *Varieties of Delinquent Youth: An Introduction to Constitutional Psychiatry*. New York: Harper & Row.

Staples, W.G. 1986. "Restitution as a Sanction in Juvenile Courts." *Crime and Delinquency* 2(2):177–185.

Sumner, Colin. *Reading Ideologies: An Investigation into the Marxist Theory of Ideology and Law*. London: Academic Press.

Tittle, Charles R. 1974. "Prisons and Rehabilitation: The Inevitability of Failure. *Social Problems* 21:385–394.

Visano, L. 1983. "Tramps, Tricks and Troubles: Street Transients and Their Controls." In T. Fleming and L. Visano (eds.), *Deviant Designations*. Toronto: Butterworths.

Von Hirsch, A. 1986. *Doing Justice: The Choice of Punishments*. New York: Hill and Wang.

Wolfgang, Marvin E. 1960. "Cesare Lombroso." In Hermann Mannheim (ed.), *Pioneers in Criminology*. Chicago: Quadrangle.

The Juvenile Delinquents Act, S.C. 1980, c.40.

The Young Offenders Act, S.C. 1980–81–82–83. C.110.

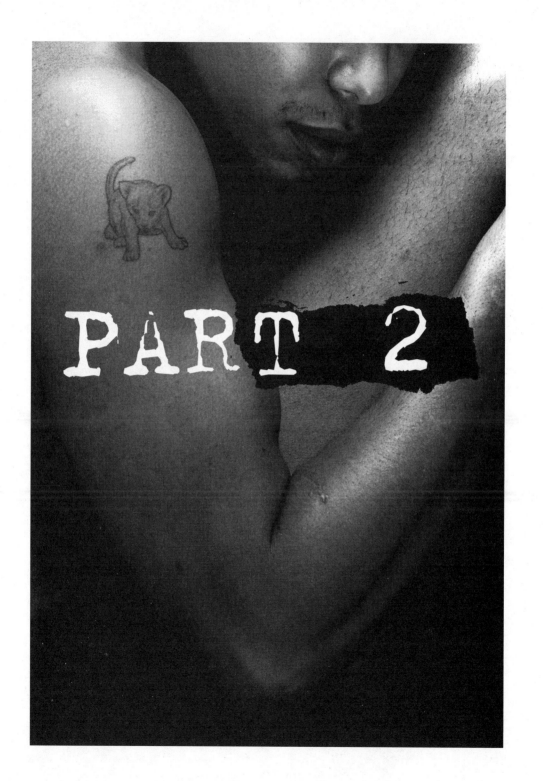

PART 2

Talking about Canadian Youth: Substantive Issues in Youth Crime and Deviance

The activities engaged in by Canada's young people are wide-ranging and diverse. The more socially acceptable forms of youthful behaviour (Girl and Boy Scouts, bowling, bingo, stamp collecting, etc.) generally escape the attention of sociologists and criminologists since they lean toward our society's view of conformity. In essence, society tends to believe that these activities represent what young people should be doing with their time. When publicized or witnessed, it is the deviant and criminal pursuits of young people that usually garner widespread attention. Media outlets of all types sensationalize them, politicians construct campaigns around them, members of society talk about them, the police complain about them, action groups protest because of them, and some Canadian social scientists attempt to understand them.

This section presents five specific studies of how and why some young Canadians commit deviant and criminal acts. While the entire range of such activities cannot possibly be covered here, I hope this section does highlight some critical examples of "bad" behaviour.

In Chapter 4, "Marking up the City," Teresa LaGrange looks at vandalism as a form of youthful expression. In Chapter 5, "Mean Streets and Hard Time," Dan Glenday presents a realistic portrait of youth unemployment in Canada and its relationship to crime.

Have you ever heard the term "maggot" used to describe a subcultural form of Canadian youth? Until I was enlightened by Rob Bowman, I certainly had not, and I thought I knew a lot about the leisure activities of Canadian youth. In Chapter 6, "Parliament/Funkadelic," Bowman describes and analyzes this subcultural form by focusing on its ultimate attraction: the funk music of George Clinton and Parliament/Funkadelic.

In Chapter 7, "In Cultural Limbo," R.S. Ratner examines the social problems encountered by native youths in British Columbia, and analyzes his very potent findings through the sociological lenses provided by the work of Jurgen Habermas.

Finally, in Chapter 8, "Bad Girls in Hard Times," Ann Duffy adopts a feminist perspective to address the rise of the female juvenile offender in Canada. Duffy rightly contends that traditional theories of criminology, being based upon male experiences and male-oriented research, are inadequate to explain women's involvement in criminal pursuits.

Marking Up the City:
The Problem of Urban Vandalism

Teresa C. LaGrange
University of Alberta

Last year an American teenager was convicted of vandalism in Singapore. His punishment? To be whipped six times on his bare buttocks with a cane. Human rights observers around the world protested the penalty, describing it as barbaric torture that would draw blood and leave permanent scars. In a *Newsweek* public opinion survey, however, 38 percent of those polled were in favour of the sentence; many wished it could be imported to North American cities (Elliott 1994:21).

In another case, a California newspaper was flooded with letters in response to a story about a boy who was killed during a vandalism escapade (Bortnick 1994:A1). "Reaction was swift and ... brutal," a shocked reporter wrote (Chavarria 1994:B1). One reader suggested that "D.O.A. ought to be spray-painted in huge, block, neon letters" on the body of the dead vandal. Another expressed the view that vandalism would be dramatically reduced if people were allowed to shoot vandals on sight.

As these incidents make apparent, many people are incensed by vandalism. Large segments of the public condone severe, even bloodthirsty, responses to what is a seemingly innocuous minor crime. We might well wonder why there is so much outrage about vandalism. This leads, in turn, to a number of questions: What exactly is vandalism? Who commits these acts? Most importantly, *why* do they do what they do? In this chapter, I will discuss these questions and several alternative answers. You might guess that the answers are self-evident, and in some respects they are. Most people agree on what is meant by vandalism, and almost everyone thinks that young people, especially teenagers, are the culprits. But the issue becomes more complex when efforts are made to move beyond the simple fact of youth. There is an enormous amount of literature about vandalism, and most researchers have tried to identify a particular *group* of teens: disadvantaged, socially deprived youths. Or alienated loners, seeking to leave some sort of mark in a sterile and uncaring world. Or highly aggressive, antisocial gang members who glory in destruction. Almost certainly of a visible minority.

Closely linked to each of these conceptions of "who" is a theoretical explanation of "why." Vandals as *individuals* are assumed to be different from their peers—lacking in self-control, having lower IQs, or suffering from emotional disorders. Or their *social circumstances* render them different. They may be of lower socioeconomic status, or come from broken homes. Possible *institutional* effects are sometimes identified, particularly the anonymity of modern social structures such as schools. Most laypeople subscribe to one of these views, often without giving the matter a great deal of thought. Yet as you read the material below, it may surprise you to learn that none of these explanations is adequate to explain vandalism. So many teens commit vandalism that, as one writer states, it seems to be "more or less normal behaviour" (Gladstone 1978:23). The reasons "why," then, may have little to do with the individual characteristics of offenders. In the last section of this discussion, we will return to that issue and look at some reasons why we should view vandalism as a consequence of the *routine social rhythms of the urban environment.*

✳ What Is Vandalism?

Almost everyone who studies vandalism offers his or her own definition, but all emphasize two elements. First, vandalism is wilful and deliberate rather than accidental. Second, it does not occur as a by-product of another crime; its apparent purpose is the mark or act itself. When a group of youths smash a pay phone to get the change out of the coin box, they've committed theft, not vandalism. When they smash the glass door and tear out the handset, *that* is vandalism (Geason and Wilson 1990; Jamieson 1987; Levy-Leboyer 1984).

We frequently read about vandalism in the papers, or hear reports on the evening news. A California newspaper article reported that "vandals have spray-painted a Highway 101 sign protected by razor wire for the fourth time this year." The writer described how the vandals must have clambered "monkeylike above traffic lanes and through reinforced razor wire barriers" in order to gain access to their overpass target (Green 1993). A news release from Florida related that four schoolchildren, all under 12 years old, broke into a local elementary school and did "about $100,000 in damage to classrooms and computer equipment" (Lindberg 1994). In Mississauga, Ontario, in a similar overnight incident, unknown vandals trashed classrooms, leaving an estimated $40,000 in damage in their wake (Ferenc 1993). Vandals in a rural area north of Edmonton, Alberta, stole a 35-ton crane and used it to damage a bridge pier, sparking a fire that caused $500,000 damage (*Edmonton Journal* 1994:A8).

These incidents are dramatic, so they make newsworthy stories. Their occurrence, and the news coverage given them, feeds the perception that urban vandalism is rampant, that it consists of horrendous sprees of destruction, and hence that vandals are wildly uncontrolled youths who must be stopped with drastic measures. But are these high-priced rampages typical of vandalism in Canadian cities? There is some evidence that they are not. In Edmonton, municipal departments spent $779,959.60 to repair damages from vandalism during 1990. More than half of this amount ($475,751.09) was spent by the transportation department on repairs to bus shelters, buses, and the transit system (City of Edmonton 1992). Yet these costs involved nearly 9,000 recorded incidents, at an average cost of less than $80 each. And these incidents were the *most serious ones*. Most vandalism occurs often enough, and is sufficiently minor, that no separate record is made each time it happens. Instead, it is simply cleaned up or repaired as part of general maintenance.

This type of destructive behaviour is not unique to modern times. Going back to the time of the Roman Empire, there have been incidents of purposeless destruction. When archaeologists unearthed the ruins of Pompeii, they found what looked suspiciously like graffiti on the crumbled stone walls (Roos 1992:73). In the last 50 years, however, many cities have experienced what has been described as an epidemic of this type of damage (Simpson and Hagan 1985). People write on walls and desks; carve their names on trees and benches in parks; mark up sidewalks and bus shelters; break windows in empty buildings and phone booths; and generally mark up, damage, or deface just about any available surface or structure, if given sufficient opportunity. In poorer urban areas, where repairs are not made quickly, the damage may accumulate so that entire areas appear to be endless tracts of vandalism.

Property owners in these areas are upset by damage to their own premises, and they worry that the value of their real estate is being lowered by vandalism in the surrounding neighbourhood. And since these poorer areas may also be racked by high street crime and other social problems, vandalism is viewed as a visible symptom of youth crime in general. A great deal of vandalism in an area sends a message, it is argued, that social control is weak or absent, that "no one is in control, and anything can happen" (Chalfant 1992:7). Add to these concerns the high costs of repairs for thousands of incidents of vandalism every year, as illustrated by the example of Edmonton, and it becomes apparent why the public is so irate about this behaviour. Their alarm is heightened by media articles like the ones referred to at the beginning of this discussion. The public is "fed up" with vandalism, and it is these factors which contribute to outraged demands for severe, sometimes vicious, action.

🐾 Who Commits These Acts?

Just as most people think they know what vandalism is, everyone has an idea of who the vandals are. We see on cable television young, minority gang members in shattered slums in American cities. These hardened, angry youths splash the surrounding neighbourhood with graffiti to proclaim their dominance over their territory. Or we watch rampages of destructive violence in the riots that periodically plague those same neighbourhoods. The typical vandal, we conclude, is probably a gang member, possibly a minority youth, most certainly an angry delinquent. But except for the fact that most vandals are young, this picture does not accurately reflect the typical vandal in the United States. Nor does it reflect the situation in Canada. While these angry youths do commit vandalism, they are not typical of most young people who do.

Far more typical is a young man I talked to a few years ago, who with his friends took a dog from outside his parents' apartment building (LaGrange 1989). The object of this kidnapping was not alive; it was an oversized mastiff carved of granite. One night, the youth was out late with his friends, one of whom had his father's van, and as a group they pried the dog loose and hauled it away. They "borrowed" it only long enough to embellish it with splotches of fluorescent spray-paint, and then returned it. The young man and his friends felt that what they had done was a harmless prank. They did not think that "borrowing" the granite dog was particularly serious. In fact, they thought it was highly amusing, and their efforts to return the dog surreptitiously were punctuated by a great deal of anticipatory hilarity, as they pictured the tenants' reactions to its changed appearance the following morning.

Unfortunately, their amusement was not shared by the building's manager. The police were called when the newly adorned mastiff was discovered the next morning. An elderly tenant on the ground floor, who had been awakened by the commotion caused by the boisterous teens in the middle of the night, had recognized her young neighbour when she peeked out her window. When she reported what she had seen, the youths were picked up by the police and taken down to the station. They were charged under the Canadian Criminal Code with "mischief," which refers to the wilful damage or destruction of property and is applied to the prosecution of vandalism.

None of these teens had a criminal record. They did not abuse drugs or alcohol, nor did they belong to a gang. Their ill-considered action was not so much "criminal" as it was foolhardy. Similarly, the teen in the case of the Singapore caning was, by all reports, an unremarkable young man, one who had been in a bit of trouble at school but who was not a habitual delinquent (Elliott 1994). The youth whose death sparked the California newspaper's landslide of angry letters was a 13-year-old boy who was described by his school principal as "a B-plus student who worked extra hard at school [and] enjoyed math" (Bortnick 1994:A10). That these rather ordinary youths are the most typical vandals is confirmed by self-report studies that ask large groups of young people, usually in schools, to report on their actions.

In one survey, conducted in Toronto-area schools a few years ago, 90 percent of elementary school students, and 88 percent of high school students, said that they had deliberately marked on, broken, or damaged something within the last year (Beaulieu 1982). The peak age for this type of behaviour was 14 to 16 years old. Students in this age range reported more than twice as many incidents as their younger and older peers—over 15 incidents each. Although these figures are somewhat higher than those reported by researchers in the United States and elsewhere, most studies consistently report that over 75 percent of their respondents admit to vandalism (Elliott et al. 1979; Erickson and Empey 1963; Gladstone 1978; Gold 1970; Short and Nye 1959). Most of the actions reported by these teens are minor, consisting of writing on walls, carving on benches, or breaking windows in an empty building. But the frequency with which vandalism is reported in these surveys underscores the fact that *vandals may be almost any young people, in some circumstances*.

Only a few of these youths are actually caught by the police and charged, as was the dog vandal and his friends. Vandalism does not take very much time, so unless someone such as an elderly neighbour sees them and recognizes them, there is little evidence for police to go on. And most vandalism is so minor that it is not reported; when it is reported, police usually do not bother to follow through on an investigation. For these reasons, official statistics on offenders may not be very reliable. Nevertheless, it is instructive to consider what sorts of persons are charged with vandalism, given the popular image of vandals as disadvantaged, minority teens.

In Canada, as well as in the United States, most vandals are males (90 percent); under 18 years old; and white (United States 1987; Silverman et al. 1991). It is widely thought that the criminal justice system is biased against minorities. Natives in Canada, and blacks in the United States, are greatly overrepresented in police statistics, in jails, and in prisons. Although this is for a variety of reasons, some writers have argued that neighbourhoods where minorities predominate are patrolled more extensively than white neighbourhoods.

In addition, suspects who belong to a visible minority are more likely to be charged than other persons (Chambliss and Nagasawa 1969; Hagan et al. 1978). If we assume that ethnic minorities are often consigned to poorer neighbourhoods, and that such neighbourhoods are overpoliced, and that vandalism is higher in such neighbourhoods, why are not arrested vandals white? It appears that our line of reasoning is incorrect—whatever our assumptions, *vandals may simply be ordinary young people.*

✸ Why Do They Do It?

As we stated before, the questions of "who" vandals are and "why" they do it are closely linked. When we view vandals as disadvantaged youths, we are implicitly attributing their actions to something about their circumstances. Similarly, if we assert that vandals act as they do because they wish to lash out against the institutional symbols of a society that has excluded them (Roos 1992), we are endorsing a statement about *who* those vandals are. What, then, are the implications of the findings reported above, which suggest that most teenagers may be vandals at one time or another? Or the assertion that most vandals are average young people? This question can be considered in terms of the theories most frequently used to explain vandalism.

Explanations most commonly used to explain why some people commit vandalism fall into three broad categories: (1) *individual traits* that characterize offenders; (2) *social factors* characteristic of the person's class or neighbourhood; and (3) *institutional factors*. You will recognize many of these explanations as having their roots in classical criminological theories about delinquency.

Individual Traits. According to this argument, certain youths are more likely to mark up or break things because of their personal deficiencies and weaknesses. They may have attention-deficit disorders, learning disabilities, low intelligence, or mental disorders. These traits are thought to contribute to the inclination to vandalism and other antisocial actions in two ways. First, these youths are assumed to be less successful in meeting the demands of modern life, especially in the critical arena of school. They may be inclined to skip school or drop out because of their problems; or if they stay in school they will spend less time studying. They will also be less able to form supportive personal relationships. Hence, it is thought that they will have more time and more inclination to hang around on the streets and get involved in such things as vandalism. Second, some researchers argue that youths with these traits are less able to weigh the pros and cons of certain behaviours, so they are more likely to act on immediate impulses. So, for example, when such a youth sees a window in a building and a rock nearby, he may immediately and unthinkingly pick up the rock and throw it, without really thinking the action through (Moser 1992; Van Vliet 1992).

Social Factors. A second type of explanation attributes vandalism to the social context of offenders. Some youths, it is argued, live in disadvantaged neighbourhoods or come from poorer families. Or they may have abusive, alcoholic, or neglectful parents. They may belong to an ethnic or racial minority, and have restricted access to the rewards and occupations of the more privileged. The commonplace stereotypes mentioned above, which portray vandals as angry rioters and youthful gangs, are based primarily on these social explanations (Challinger 1987; Christiansen 1983).

These perspectives, in turn, are most closely linked to more general theories of delinquency. The ways in which ethnicity, socioeconomic status, and family status contribute to vandalism thus depend on assumptions about the nature of crime in general. Some youths are thought to be unrestrained by *social control;* to experience *social strain;* or to hold *subcultural values* (Kornhauser 1978). Because of the impact of these social factors, such teens are assumed to be more inclined than most people to deface, damage, or destroy things. The minority gang member who splashes graffiti on a library wall does so because he is free of normal social restraints (social control theory); or because he is frustrated by his exclusion from normal avenues of achievement (social strain theory); or because of the value placed on such feats within his deviant social milieu (subcultural theory).

Institutional Factors. In contrast to the above explanations, which focus either on individuals or on their immediate social situation, some researchers suggest that vandalism occurs because of social and cultural factors embedded in modern society. School vandalism, in particular, is thought to occur in bigger schools, because the anonymity of large impersonal classes makes students feel anonymous. They therefore do not feel involved in the school, and are more likely to damage it or mark it up (Cohen 1973; Geason and Wilson 1990).

☀ Dispositional versus Opportunistic Factors

Each of the above explanations is primarily "dispositional." Some teens, because of their characteristics, are thought to be *predisposed* to commit vandalism. Because they are impulsive or aggressive; because they are frustrated and socially deprived; or because they feel socially adrift in an anonymous cultural context, they are assumed to be more likely to damage things than their less disposed peers (Clarke 1978). This viewpoint is consistent with most theories of delinquency, which try to understand what motivates some people to commit crimes. Theories of this nature seek to discover what distinguishes the delinquent from the nondelinquent. As explanations of vandalism, then, the orientation is toward discovering what distinguishes the youth who vandalizes from the youth who does not.

There is, without doubt, some validity in each of these explanations. Some youths who mark up or destroy bus shelters or phone booths are poor and are strongly motivated to lash out at a social system that excludes them. Similarly, youths who are not successful in school may feel rebellious vis-à-vis the educational system, and therefore feel little hesitation in breaking school windows or writing on classroom walls. Moreover, some vandalism is the work of gang members; and young people from dysfunctional families may express their turmoil in the destruction of property.

However, recall the evidence cited earlier—that as many as three-quarters of secondary school students report that they occasionally do these kinds of things. It does not seem reasonable to suppose that these sometime-vandals are all from dysfunctional families, or disadvantaged, or gang members, or fall into one of the other categories identified by these dispositional explanations. It is possible, of course, that some youths are motivated by one set of factors, and others by another, and so on. But it may also be that, as stated earlier, many of these youths are otherwise average, ordinary teens. Explanations for the "plague" of urban vandalism might have less to do with the motivation of individual offenders than with the nature of modern city life.

✳ Urban Social Rhythms

Some criminologists have suggested that crime trends in general are affected by a number of significant social changes that have occurred in the last few years (Felson and Cohen 1980). For one thing, there have been changes in the family: people have fewer children and there is more divorce. Also, more women now work outside the home. Moreover, the workforce has changed from a primarily agricultural one to one based on a wage economy and, as a result, people are working shorter hours and have more disposable income and more leisure time to spend with their friends. Because more people are moving from place to place, in search of work or career advancement, fewer people are well acquainted with their neighbours. This means they are less likely to intervene in their surroundings unless what they see directly affects them.

These factors have been identified as important elements in the occurrence of various types of crime. Two contemporary criminologists, Marcus Felson and Laurence Cohen (1980), argue that the place, time, and frequency of crime are directly linked to the *routine activities* that are characteristic of an area or neighbourhood. Each day, people follow specific schedules as they leave their homes to go to and from school, work, or leisure activities. These are, of course, individual schedules. However, since certain areas of a city are often inhabited by groups of people with similar social and demographic characteristics, these schedules often reflect on the daily routines of an entire neighbourhood.

Consider, for example, the different atmospheres and the different "routine activities" in Location A, an upper-middle-class commuter neighbourhood built a few years ago, and Location B, an older downtown business district with a number of bars, small businesses, and pawn shops. In A, most families have children. Daily activities revolve around the morning ritual of departure to work and school, and the afternoon return. People are in their homes most evenings, in order for everyone to have a regularly scheduled dinner and an early bedtime. There are few wild parties, and the parties that are held are unlikely to spill into the street. People tend to be acquainted with their neighbours, and strangers are carefully scrutinized. In such neighbourhoods, street crime is relatively rare. In contrast, in B, strangers are the norm. A variety of people gather on the streets at irregular hours of the day and night. There may be considerable activity and noise as patrons from the area's businesses come and go. In this type of neighbourhood, street crime is much more common.

These extremes exist in every city. In addition, even comparable types of neighbourhoods have different characteristics that reflect the lifestyles, ages, and social classes of their inhabitants. Some residential areas, occupied by families with young children, are relatively quiet, and a few people are at home around the clock. In other neighbourhoods, most of the residents are young adults, and homes are empty during the day as people work or attend school. Similarly, one downtown street may consist almost entirely of stores and businesses that are very busy during the day but relatively deserted during the evening. Others may contain businesses that cater to evening recreational and entertainment interests: video stores, theatres, restaurants, and bars.

According to Felson and Cohen, crimes occur when *potential offenders* come across a *suitable target* in circumstances of *reduced guardianship*. By "guardianship," they mean any person or object that prevents people from doing as they wish without getting caught. In residential areas where people are at home during the day, there is more likelihood that someone on the street will be observed. This increases guardianship, because a potential offender might be seen if he commits a crime. In an area where most people are gone during the day, and most homes are empty, criminals are less likely to be noticed. A business district that is teeming with customers during the day is unlikely to provide a suitable locale for crimes. But the same district might have few pedestrians at night. Research based on these assertions has found that personal crimes, such as robberies and assaults, are more frequent in areas where potential offenders and victims converge in circumstances of reduced guardianship: on dark empty streets, in parks, near bars or nightspots. Similarly, break-and-enters occur most often in areas where residents are out of their homes during the day (Bursik 1986; Engstad 1980; Felson and Cohen 1980; Harries 1993; Hartnagel and Lee 1990; Sampson and Groves 1989; Sherman et al. 1989).

What are the implications of all this for understanding vandalism? Consider again the case of the youth who, with his friends, took the stone dog from his parents' apartment building. In some respects this case illustrates how offenders, targets, and reduced guardianship converge to result in vandalism. These young men had the opportunity provided by a van, free time, lack of supervision, and the cover of darkness. In a number of other ways, however, this particular incident was atypical. It involved a specific target rather than one that was generally available; and it involved an investment in time and energy to nab the dog and later return it. Perhaps these factors contributed to the aspect of this incident that was *most* atypical: these youths got caught. Their perception of relative anonymity, which is implicit in the concept of guardianship, turned out to be false.

Most vandals, however, do not get caught—as few as 10 percent, by some estimates (Geason and Wilson 1990; van Vliet 1992). And very few are as purposeful as these young men. In the Toronto-area research cited earlier, most of the students who had vandalized something stated that they did not plan it in advance and had not chosen a specific target. They acted on impulse and wrote on or marked up whatever was handy (Beaulieu 1982). Vandalism seems to be a crime of opportunity. Although some vandals may be antisocial youths who deliberately seek ways to express themselves in costly rampages of destruction—as is believed by the public and portrayed by the media—many are ordinary youths who do their damage spontaneously and with little thought of its costs or consequences. Much of vandalism can be described as a "phenomenon of interaction" between young people and their immediate environment (Wise 1982).

In modern cities, young people have a great deal of freedom, and they spend much of their time away from home and their parents. Most teens attend school, and those who live in cities instead of rural communities often drive or take public transportation instead of riding school buses. Most young people still in school do not have time-consuming chores working in a family business or on a farm, and they often have difficulty finding part-time work. Generally, they can go where they choose, and they usually do so without adult supervision. Thus, they may have substantial amounts of free time to hang out with their friends.

In conjunction with the earlier assertion, that almost any teen may be a vandal in some circumstances, we might predict that vandalism is more likely when groups of young people are together in the absence of adult supervision. Support for this view comes from a number of different studies. One research project, conducted in Great Britain, examined the impact of child density on the level of vandalism in council housing estates in the London area. Council housing is the equivalent to North American low-income or public housing. In Canada, such housing is in extremely limited supply, and only a few of the poorest people qualify for it. There is a greater proportion of such housing in Great Britain; 30 percent of Britons live in public housing (Hough and Mayhew 1980). The estates vary in design and density, in how close they are to the city core, and in the social, economic, and racial composition of their residents. A study of over 50 of these estates revealed that in spite of all their other differences, the most significant factor in predicting the amount of vandalism was, simply, child density (Wilson 1978). The more children aged 6 to 16 years old that lived in an area, the more vandalism was recorded, above and beyond any differences that could be attributed to design or residential characteristics.

This research focused on residential vandalism, much of which might well have been the incidental product of normal play. A second indication of the opportunistic character of vandalism comes from an anti-graffiti campaign in Seattle, Washington (Bell, Bell, and Godefroy 1988). Local business people in that city started a volunteer effort to paint over graffiti in the downtown core each time it appeared. As the weeks went by, they found that certain areas required continual attention: around convenience stores frequented by teenagers, and along the bus routes that served the local schools. This suggested that vandalism occurred primarily in the course of routine daily activities.

Further support for the view that vandalism is opportunistic in nature comes from a much larger and more comprehensive study recently completed in Edmonton. This study mapped all of the vandalism inflicted in one year on transit shelters, parks, and public buildings throughout the entire municipal region (LaGrange 1994). As predicted by the view that vandalism reflects the routine activities of teens, significantly higher rates of vandalism were found around high schools, and to a lesser extent junior high schools. Also, the areas around malls were very highly vandalized. In Edmonton, as in many North American cities, teens congregate at shopping malls, and this also supports the argument that teen activities and vandalism are related (Engstad 1980; LaGrange 1994; Roncek and LoBosco 1983). Poorer neighbourhoods, where one might expect to find high crime according to the theories reviewed earlier, experienced more vandalism than more prosperous areas. But these factors were overshadowed by the presence of schools and malls, which draw masses of teens into the surrounding neighbourhoods on a daily basis.

These studies lend strong support to the conception of vandalism as primarily incidental to the activities of normal teens. The widespread public perception of vandals as out-of-control delinquents, who pose a threat to public safety as much as to public property, may be unfounded. In fact, such a perception may be largely a myth founded on media coverage of a few isolated incidents. Most vandalism can be seen as a product of the interaction between circumstances and opportunity, as ordinary young people go about their daily activities. That it seems to be "epidemic" in some cities or neighbourhoods may have more to do with the routines characteristic of those areas than it does with the criminality of certain groups of people. As groups of young people go to and from school, waiting in bus shelters or hanging around convenience stores, they may write on walls or carve their initials in a bench, but this is less because they are motivated to destruction than because the circumstances permit it.

This perspective has implications for the public attitudes noted at the beginning of this discussion. The idea that vandals would be deterred by extremely severe penalties seems unrealistic, given the frequency of the behaviour and the unlikelihood of getting caught. It may be more legitimate to address the fact that this is almost "normal" behaviour. Public education, both in schools and the media, may help to change attitudes. Recall that the youths who painted the stone dog viewed their actions as an amusing prank, one intended to shock their elders. They did not mean any permanent harm. After their arrest, they were forced to spend several hours each weekend doing community service under the direction of the very landlord whose dog they had decorated. Part of this work included the painstaking and labour-intensive work of removing all traces of fluorescent paint from every crevice of the stone dog's intricately carved surface. This type of consequence undoubtedly made a significant impression on these teens, one that will alter their future attitudes and behaviour. Far more so, it might be speculated, than permanent scars will alter the attitude of the American youth caned in Singapore.

References

Beaulieu, Lucien (chair). 1982. *Vandalism: Response and Responsibilities*. Report of the Task Force on Vandalism. Province of Ontario: Queen's Printer.

Bell, Maurice M., Merlyn M. Bell, and Kay Godefroy. 1988. "The impact of graffiti on neighbourhoods and one community's response." *International Symposium on Vandalism: Research, Prevention, and Social Policy*. Seattle, Washington.

Bortnick, Barry. 1994. "Adventure gone awry ends bright future." *Santa Barbara News-Press*. March 3:A1, A10.

Bursik, Robert J., Jr. 1986. "Delinquency rates as sources of ecological change." In *The Social Ecology of Crime*. James M. Byrne and Robert J. Sampson (eds.). New York: Springer-Verlag.

Chalfant, Harry. 1992. "No one is in control." In *Vandalism: Research, Prevention, and Social Policy*. Harriet H. Chistensen, Daryll R. Johnson, and Martha H. Brookes (eds.). Portland, OR: U.S. Department of Agriculture Forest Service.

Challinger, Dennis (ed.). 1987. *Preventing Property Crime: Proceedings of a Seminar*. Canberra: Australian Institute of Criminology.

Chavarria, Jesse. 1994. "Compassion necessary if we're to get along." *Santa Barbara News-Press*. March 12:B1.

Christiansen, Monty L. 1983. *Vandalism Control Management for Parks and Recreational Areas*. University Park, PA: Venture Publishing.

City of Edmonton Vandalism Prevention Committee. 1992. *Meeting Notes*. Edmonton: City of Edmonton Vandalism Prevention Committee.

Clarke, R.V.G. (ed.). 1978. *Tackling Vandalism*. Home Office Research Study No. 47. London: Her Majesty's Stationery.

Cohen, Stanley. 1973. "Property destruction: Motives and meanings." In *Vandalism*. Colin Ward (ed.). New York: Van Nostrand Reinhold.

Edmonton Journal. 1994. "Vandals cause $500,000 damage." February 15:A8.

Elliott, Delbert, Suzanne Ageton, and Rachelle Canter. 1979. "An integrated theoretical perspective on delinquent behavior." *Journal of Research on Crime and Delinquency* 16:3–27.

Elliott, Michael. 1994. "Crime and punishment." *Newsweek*. April 18:18–24.

Engstad, Peter A. 1980. "Environmental opportunities and the ecology of crime." In *Crime in Canadian Society*, 2nd ed. Robert A. Silverman and James J. Teevan, Jr. (eds.). Toronto: Butterworths.

Erickson, Maynard L., and Lamar T. Empey. 1963. "Court records, undetected delinquency and decision-making." *Journal of Criminal Law, Criminology and Police Science* 54:456–469.

Felson, Marcus, and Lawrence E. Cohen. 1980. "Human ecology and crime: A routine activity approach." *Human Ecology* 8:389–406.

Ferenc, Leslie. 1993. "Principal wages war on vandals." *Toronto Star.* June 17:A1.

Geason, Susan, and Paul R. Wilson. 1990. *Preventing Graffiti and Vandalism.* Canberra: Australian Institute of Criminology.

Gladstone, F.J. 1978. "Vandalism amongst adolescent schoolboys." In *Tackling Vandalism.* Home Office Research Study No. 47. R.V.G. Clarke (ed). London: Her Majesty's Stationery.

Gold, Martin. 1970. *Delinquent Behavior in an American City.* Belmont, CA: Brooks/Cole.

Green, Morgan. 1993. "Graffiti investigator may be signed on." *Santa Barbara News-Press.* October 10:B1.

Harries, Keith. 1993. "The ecology of homicide and assault: Baltimore City and County, 1989–1991." Paper presented at ASC Annual Meeting. Phoenix, Arizona (November 4).

Hartnagel, Timothy F., and G. Won Lee. 1990. "Urban crime in Canada." *Canadian Journal of Criminology.* October:591–606.

Hirschi, Travis. 1969. *Causes of Delinquency.* Berkeley, CA: University of California Press.

Hough, Mike, and Pat Mayhew (eds.). 1980. *Crime and Public Housing: Proceedings of a Workshop.* London: Home Office.

Jamieson, Bill. 1987. "Public telephone vandalism." In *Preventing Property Crime.* Dennis Challinger (ed.). Canberra, Australia: Proceedings of a Seminar (November 24–25), Australian Institute of Criminology.

Kornhauser, Ruth R. 1978. *Social Sources of Delinquency.* Chicago: University of Chicago Press.

LaGrange, Teresa C. 1994. *Routine Activities and Vandalism.* Unpublished MA thesis. Edmonton: University of Alberta.

———. 1989. Personal communication. Unpublished interview. Edmonton: University of Alberta.

Levy-Leboyer, Claude (ed.). 1984. *Vandalism: Behaviour and Motivations.* Amsterdam/New York/Oxford: North-Holland.

Lindberg, Anne. 1994. "Victims of vandalism." *St. Petersburg Times.* January 11:B1.

Moser, Gabriel. 1992. "What is vandalism? Towards a psycho-social definition and its implications." In *Vandalism: Research, Prevention, and Social Policy.* Harriet H. Chistensen, Daryll R. Johnson, and Martha H. Brookes (eds.). Portland, OR: U.S. Department of Agriculture Forest Service.

Roncek, Dennis, and Antoinette LoBosco. 1983. "The effect of high schools on crime in their neighborhoods." *Social Science Quarterly* 64:598–613.

Roos, Hans-Edvard. 1992. "Vandalism as a symbolic act in 'free–zones.'" In *Vandalism: Research, Prevention, and Social Policy.* Harriet H. Christensen,

Daryll R. Johnson, and Martha H. Brookes (eds.). Portland, OR: U.S. Department of Agriculture Forest Service.

Sampson, Robert J., and W. Byron Groves. 1989. "Community structure and crime: Testing social-disorganization theory." *American Journal of Sociology* 94(4):774–802.

Sherman, Lawrence W., Patrick R. Gartin, and Michael E. Buerger. 1989. "Hot spots of predatory crime: Routine activities and the criminology of place." *Criminology* 17(1):17–49.

Short, James F., Jr., and F. Ivan Nye. 1957. "Reported behavior as a criterion of deviant behavior." *Social Problems* 5:207–213.

Silverman, Robert A., James J. Teevan, Jr., and Vincent F. Sacco. 1991. *Crime in Canadian Society.* 4th ed. Toronto: Butterworths.

Simpson, John H., and John Hagan. 1985. *Evaluation of a Vandalism Prevention Project.* Ottawa: Ministry of the Solicitor General.

United States Federal Bureau of Investigation. 1987. *Uniform Crime Reports.* U.S. Department of Justice, Federal Bureau of Investigation: Washington, D.C.

Van Vliet, Willem. 1992. "The cherry question or the role of social science research in designing against vandalism." In *Vandalism: Research, Prevention, and Social Policy.* Harriet H. Chistensen, Daryll R. Johnson, and Martha H. Brookes (eds.). Portland, OR: U.S. Department of Agriculture Forest Service.

Wilson, Sheena. 1978. "Vandalism and 'defensible space' on London housing estates." In *Tackling Vandalism.* Home Office Research Study No. 47. R.V.G. Clarke (ed.). London: Her Majesty's Stationery.

Wise, James. 1982. "A gentle deterrent to vandalism." *Psychology Today.* September: 31–38.

CHAPTER 5

Mean Streets and Hard Time: Youth Unemployment and Crime in Canada*

Dan Glenday
Brock University

It's not madness, Ma'am, it's meat.
Oliver Twist

The April 2, 1993, edition of the *Calgary Herald* began its report on youth unemployment and crime in Great Britain with this headline: "Britain's 'Nasty' Youth Have Tough Time Ahead." The article quoted Home Secretary Kenneth Clarke as saying that Britain's young people are "suffering a loss of purpose and a loss of values." Kenneth Clarke was Great Britain's home secretary in 1849. *Plus ça change ...*

According to the article, unemployment for 16 to 25 year olds was running at 16 percent, while the figure for Great Britain as a whole was only 9 percent—almost twice the national average. Young people represented 31 percent of Great Britain's jobless. Income support for most 16 and 17 year olds had been abolished, and this worsened an already dismal picture; meanwhile, government promises to provide adequate funding for youth training for every teenager remained unfulfilled. The same article noted that in the previous ten years, the suicide rate among those under 25 had risen by 30 percent. Clearly, suicide is a tragic and unnecessary response to long-term unemployment, which was identified long ago as a solvable social problem. Another response the article alluded to was crime. Since the article appeared, little has changed. Is Great Britain the only country that acknowledges the relationship between unemployment and suicide and criminal activity among young people?

Recent newspaper headlines from western Canada have told us that "Tough Times Drive Kids Out of Class, into Crime" (*Winnipeg Free Press*, September 5, 1993). In the same paper: "Young Canadians have the highest unemployment rate, account for a large share of criminal activity and are especially vulnerable to economic downturns" (March 16, 1993:A3). The latter article went on to report that youths 12 to 17 accounted for 25 percent of people charged with criminal offences in 1992, up from 22 percent in 1987.

Also according to article, students who work more than 15 hours a week are more likely to drop out of school. It is widely recognized today that school dropouts do not develop good employment records. Even those who stay in school see grim prospects for good employment. Corey, a 15 year old, said that "there are more offers from gangs than offers of jobs." The article went on to say that "headlines heralding high unemployment and tough times sometimes lead kids to believe that crime and 'dirty money' offer the only future to be had these days."

Clearly, youth unemployment affects different young people differently; that being said, the relationship between youth unemployment and crime is real. But what types of crime are connected to prolonged periods of unemployment? Certainly, not all criminal offences. It is crimes against property that are most commonly related to unemployment. Prostitution is another course of action, especially for teenage women who have nothing to eat and nowhere to go. As will be described below, at both the societal and individual levels of analysis, persistent, high rates of unemployment for teenagers lead to increases in property crimes such as robbery, larceny, auto theft, and burglary. And poorly paid part-time and/or seasonal work leads many young adults to commit similar crimes.

Research into youth unemployment and crime has fallen into disrepute in North America. This is more true in Canada than in the United States, where pockets of sociological criminologists continue to advance research and policy alternatives. After reviewing the literature in North America, Great Britain, and Australia, I will present a portrait of youth unemployment and crime in Canada. I will follow this with a prognosis for made-in-Canada research and policy initiatives in this area of criminological sociology.

✱ Youth Unemployment and Crime: Theories, Evidence, and Remedies

This section includes a brief review of the North American sociological literature on adolescent and youth crime. This body of work crosses two time periods. The first stretches from the 1930s to the early 1960s, when unemployment was viewed as an important and unqualified factor in delinquency and youth crime. Methodologically speaking, researchers of that time were not afraid to "go to the streets" to investigate the social dimensions of youth crime and delinquency. Examples of research from this time period include Frederick Thrasher's *The Gang* (1927), William F. Whyte's *Street Corner Society* (1943), and James Short and Fred Strodtbeck's *Group Processes and Gang Delinquency* (1965). Ethnographic studies like these emphasized the harsh conditions facing street youth, especially young men. The lack of good jobs was a prominent theme in these studies, which offered rich textual detail about life on the streets, and moving accounts of despair and hope—the despondency spawned by the lack of legitimate opportunities and the lure of pocketfuls of money from crime. (See Ned Polsky's *Hustlers, Beats and Others*.) As important as this legacy is, the crux of this section will be devoted to the more recent statistically based studies that are critical of the research linking youth unemployment with crime.

Contemporary North American sociological criminology focuses on those background and developmental factors (e.g., single-parent families or lack of parental control) that are assumed to generate delinquent and criminal behaviour. Unemployment and poorly paid work seldom enter the picture as important independent causes of youth crime. It is more fashionable to dress up old theories in new clothes that feature "predispositions and propensities" in a person's or a group's culture as the causes of criminal behaviour—youth crime in particular—than it is to stress socioeconomic conditions such as dual labour markets, unemployment, and poverty. (A 1994 book by Herrenstein and Murray locates the decline of America in the prolific breeding habits of welfare recipients.) These academic novelties tend to resurrect dormant fears about dangerous teen gangs; meanwhile, comfortable conservatives and lazy liberals fall back on tired rhetoric that skirts economic conditions and instead proposes that when all else fails, you can always blame the poor! Lest we forget, the short time period when teen gangs in North American cities had the least impact on youth crime was *not* the 1920s, or the 1930s, or the 1940s, or even those "glorious" 1950s, but the latter half of the 1960s and early 1970s—a period of rapid employment growth, educational opportunities, and hope.

In the area of youth crime, the agendas and policy suggestions of most North American criminologists since the 1960s have been guided by what can be called "neostructural functionalism." This is a predominantly descriptive theoretical approach emphasizing "dysfunctional families" (usually defined as single-parent households) or the social antecedents of antisocial behaviour (one often used "example": the propensity for a parent's alcoholism to negatively affect the children's actions). At the level of individual behaviour, the strain theory of Richard A. Cloward and Lloyd E. Ohlin (1960) and the control theory of Travis Hirschi (1969) have dominated the general discourse. At the societal level, researchers have emphasized cultural factors or "milieu" effects in the generation of criminal activity among the young.

The first inclination of these modern sociological theories of crime is to emphasize individual backgrounds and developmental factors while disregarding situational circumstances such as unemployment rates. The focus is on the formative years of adolescence. Cloward and Ohlin (1960) propose that youths who cannot achieve material wealth by legitimate means turn to illegitimate (i.e., criminal) ones. Hirschi (1969) argues that delinquency occurs when a person's social bond to society becomes weakened or is lacking. Control theory focuses on the failure of the family and school to establish strong social bonds. Control theorists maintain that individuals who are excluded from society's mainstream remain free to offend (Box 1987). Recent commentators on youth crime stress *differential association theory* (i.e., a person's prior exposure to deviant beliefs), and *labelling theory* (i.e., a person's passage through successive stages of negative stigmatization). Simply stated, these arguments point out that keeping company with bad people can result in a person doing similar bad things.

At the societal level, consideration is directed not to what motivates individual criminal behaviour but to whether bad family or faulty community experiences have "milieu" effects that are associated with high crime rates (Logan and Messner 1987). In the 1950s, Robert K. Merton suggested that poor employment prospects could have a demoralizing impact on communities, with criminogenic consequences for those both inside and outside the labour market (Merton 1956). That is, poor labour market conditions, including high unemployment and insufficiently paid, part-time work, may generate indirect effects through the moderation of informal and formal community social controls. Unfortunately, the predominant view tends to emphasize "culture" (including single parents on welfare) while trivializing employment status and related immediate circumstances facing teenagers and young adults.

In more sophisticated studies, situational factors such as high unemployment and poorly paid work are acknowledged, but are assigned a secondary role in the causation of youth crime and delinquency. For example, Sutherland

and Cressy (1978) agree that "a person could define a situation in such a manner that criminal behaviour would be the inevitable result," but then immediately reverse field to conclude that "past experiences would, for the most part, determine the way in which he or she defined the situation" (1978:80).

As appealing as these neostructural functional theories may be, and as close to folk wisdom as they are, a number of researchers have felt obliged to scrutinize the empirical links between unemployment and criminal behaviour. A number of studies conducted in the United States during the 1980s, in an avowedly conservative political and economic climate, called into question the strength, significance, and direction of the unemployment/crime relationship (respectively, Orsagh and Witte 1981; Long and Witte 1981; and Cantor and Land 1985). Fox (1978) went so far as to question whether such a link even existed. What Theodore Chiricos (1987) called a "consensus of doubt" developed as a consequence of these analyses, which led most criminological sociologists to redirect their attention toward the disintegration of the "traditional" family and/or neighbourhood community, or toward "new" social psychological fads such as sociobiology.

Chiricos was an important dissenting voice in all this. He reviewed 63 studies that reported weak or vague statistical relationships between unemployment and crime (1987). Having looked twice at the data, he concluded that the evidence "*does favour* the existence of a positive, frequently significant Unemployment-Crime (U-C) relationship" (1987:203; author's emphasis). Currie (1985) observed:

> The grim prospects for decent work that afflict the marginal poor in America produce a potent breeding-ground for crime; ... as long as large numbers of people remain trapped in the dead-end of the shattered labour markets of the cities, we all have great difficulty in keeping them out of crime or at work" [1985:140]

The enduring relevance of the association between youth unemployment and certain types of crime will be explored in more depth later in this chapter.

In summary, research on youth crime has matured since the 1970s. Today it is commonplace for most sociological criminologists to discount the importance of economic factors in the theoretical, empirical, and public policy debates surrounding youth crime. *Nowhere is this more true than in Canada.* A few sociological criminologists in the United States are still convinced that unemployment and/or poorly paid work are independent situational factors in the generation of certain types of crime; Canadian researchers are virtually silent on the issue of youth unemployment and crime. I will explore some of the reasons for this silence later on. For the moment, I wish to say a few words about some of the more important methodological issues underlying North American research on youth crime.

A Methodological Note

The question of youth unemployment and crime is caught up in a larger ideological debate over the relevance of class analysis to questions of who commits what crimes and why. The primacy of class (i.e., employment status) has been criticized by structural functionalists, who contend that this emphasis trivializes the role of culture in social life. One of the drawbacks to stressing the independent role of rising unemployment in increasing criminal activity by teenagers and young adults is that some criminological sociologists perceive a productivist bias in this approach. That is, they tend to discount as axiomatic the notion that the central activity or expectation of the individual in our society is paid employment (see Glenday, in press, for an exposition of work as the determinant experience in sociology of work literature). These competing theoretical concerns have had an effect on methodological styles.

Methodologically, there are a number of research strategies and data sources to choose from, which fall into two broad categories: ethnographic or statistical. When sociological criminologists do macro-level research, they tend to rely on large data sets collected by government police agencies. However, crime statistics have been heavily criticized. The variability of criminal laws and therefore crimes over time and across jurisdictions, and inconsistencies in policing techniques and practices, are the more standard objections to these large data sets.

Exclusive reliance on school and home samples has diverted attention from less protected settings, like the street, that once formed an important focal point for delinquency research. (See, for example, Shaw and McKay 1942.) But the link between class and crime is only weakly (if at all) reflected in self-report analyses based on surveys of individual adolescents attending school, and this has led some to call for the complete abandonment of research to link class and crime.[1]

According to Hagan:

schools replaced the streets as sets for data collection; delinquency replaced crime as the behaviour to be explained; and parental-status origins replaced criminal actors' more immediate class conditions as presumed exogenous causes of delinquency. [1992:4]

One of the consequences of this move from direct participant observation on the streets to the self-report surveys carried out in schools is that status replaces class as the key theoretical concept. Used in this way, status explains the less serious criminal behaviours such as delinquency (which implicate school youths) rather than the more serious crimes reserved for street youths and young adults (Hagan 1992:5).

Not asking students whether they or their parents have experienced unemployment does not invalidate the claim that unemployment is a factor in criminal activity. Methodological ignorance is no excuse for poor practical or policy suggestions. To link delinquency and crime in self-report school samples, appropriate measurable concepts must be applied. Self-report surveys now measure youth employment status instead of or in addition to parental employment status. However, this is not enough, especially if students are dropping out of school *before* they are sampled. Any comprehensive research strategy must include a return to "the streets," with more sophisticated ethnographic studies across class communities and provincial boundaries. In addition, sociological criminologists should employ more frequently a "matched-pair" methodology. My own research in the sociology of work has benefited from this research strategy. John Hagan (1992) is among those Canadian criminological researchers who supports the use of this method.

At the level of individual behaviour, it is widely recognized that unemployment has a variety of negative effects on self-esteem, physical and mental health, and so on (Canadian Mental Health Association 1984). Paid employment is critical to people's self-definitions; unemployment is such a calamity that it can provoke criminal activity (e.g., street crimes, property offences) among teenagers and young adults.[2] More attempts to integrate the criminological with the social psychological (even psychiatric) data on unemployment might yield a more comprehensive theoretical model and better-targeted public policies.

At the societal level of analysis, more research is needed to map the link between unemployment and offending. Recent studies of the labour market that capture underemployment (Clogg 1979), and map out the dimensions of working-class stratification (Form 1985), show how some aspects of economic marginality may make illegitimate alternatives more attractive for young people. However, to my knowledge, none of these insights into the labour market has been exploited in analyses of youth crime.

✹ Employment Status, Age Cohort, and Crime

> When the long, dismal night came on, [Oliver] spread his little hands before his eyes to shut out the darkness and crouching in the corner tried to sleep ... and drawing himself closer and closer to the wall, as if to feel even its cold hard surface were a protection in the gloom and loneliness which surrounded him.
>
> *Oliver Twist*

When it comes to employment status, a number of simple theories have been expounded. The simplest idea is that unemployment causes financial hardship, which in turn causes crime designed to alleviate that hardship. This theory clearly predicts that unemployment is related to property crimes such as theft, burglary, robbery, fraud, and the fencing of stolen goods, rather than to violence or vandalism (see Orsagh and Witte 1981).

Another simple theory suggests that unemployed people have more spare time and hence more opportunity to offend. Marxists, for their part, depict crimes against property as an outcome of either absolute or relative deprivation. Theft is thought also to function as a form of social protest by the "have nots" against the more affluent members of society (Bohm 1983; Braithwaite 1979).

Strain and control theory in combination with employment status provide provocative proposals. One suggestion is that unemployed individuals may become frustrated or bored, and that frustration or boredom may be intervening variables that lead to crime. Specifically, poor labour market conditions (high unemployment or underemployment) may (a) render individuals susceptible to criminal behaviour for the purpose of overcoming economic hardship (see Brenner 1977) and/or (b) make illegitimate pursuits an attractive alternative to scarce or poorly paid work (see Block and Heineke 1975). Also, bored unemployed people may tend to spend their time in the company of other bored unemployed people—a grouping together that facilitates offending. Work tends to foster attachments to conventional social institutions; conversely, unemployment weakens people's bonds to society and leads to offending. (It should not be forgotten that certain types of employment may also provide opportunities for offending.)

Few contemporary researchers have heeded Radzinowicz's (1939) caution that the relationship between employment conditions and crime will probably differ across types of crime and social groups. For example, in Chiricos's (1987) review, the relative frequency of positive and significant findings is highest for property crimes (particularly burglary and larceny) and lowest for violent crimes.

As I see it, there are three dimensions to the relationship between labour markets and youth crime: employment status, age cohort, and gender. I begin with two age cohorts: juveniles 12 to 17 and young adults 18 to 24. According to Allan and Steffensmeier (1989), rates of both offending and unemployment are highest for juveniles and young adults. Their conclusion: "Full time employment is associated with low arrest rates, unemployment with high arrest rates" (1989:107).

At the same time, there is evidence that poorly paid employment may lead young adults to commit various property-related offences. Getting any job is not a sufficient deterrent. Sending those in their late teens and early twenties to do seasonal or part-time work could induce many to consider engaging in criminal activity as an "income supplement." A job with security and a future would discourage most from committing criminal offences. In other words, when talking about property-related crimes committed by young people, we must differentiate by age cohort. The younger the group, the more likely it is that any type of employment, including poorly paid and part-time work, will act as a deterrent to crime. However, similar employment opportunities for young adults may increase their likelihood of committing a crime to supplement their meagre incomes. Or, to paraphrase from Gary O'Bireck's (1993) ethnographic study of Toronto youth, "Why work at McDonald's when you can sell drugs or steal stereos?"

Juveniles are not subject to the same pressures as adults to succeed in the work world; however, they *are* subject to pressures to consume and to seek expression of their masculinity in the absence of adequate access to the labour market (Greenberg 1977). Work may be one outlet for these pressures, delinquency another. The types of delinquency engaged in by juveniles are typically exploratory, unlikely to provide more than pocket money—much like the minimum-wage service jobs available to teenagers. If suitable work is plentiful, some types of property crime may be unappealing as a source of spending money or consumer goods. At the level of the larger community, the greater the availability of work, the smaller the proportion of the juvenile population that will choose delinquent alternatives.

By comparison, poorly paid and part-time work may be insufficient to prevent young adults from committing certain property-related offences. For young adults, the choice of legitimate over illegitimate pursuits may be influenced more by the quality of employment than by mere availability. Low-wage and/or part-time work that is acceptable or even status-enhancing to juvenile first-job holders still living at home is seen as constraining and unsatisfactory to young adults seeking greater independence. Thus, the more an area is dominated by marginal employment, the greater the young adult population will be at risk. If the labour market is characterized by a supply of good jobs with adequate hours and pay, crime is less likely to attract young adults. Allen and Steffensmeier say as much when they point out:

> Dimensions of employment itself may encourage (or fail to inhibit) the growth of illegitimate alternatives. Where jobs are insecure, with low pay, few bene-fits, and minimal opportunities for advancement, work may provide few incentives for young people to form lasting commitments to conventional lifestyles, [so that] low quality of employment (inadequate pay and hours) is associated with high arrest rates for young adults. [1989:107, 109]

Few studies have attempted to follow individual young people over time to assess the impact of unemployment and/or underemployment on crime. Such studies as have been done provide intriguing evidence. West (1982) discovered that 43 percent of convicted youths aged 21 and 22 had been unemployed in the previous two years, compared to only 19 percent of unconvicted youths. In their longitudinal study of 411 London males, Farrington and colleagues (1986a) concluded:

> More crimes were committed by these youths during periods of unemployment than during periods of employment [and unemployment] was associated with a higher rate of committing crimes for material gain, but was not associated with a higher rate of committing other kinds of crime. [1986a:351]

Furthermore, an unstable job record at ages 18 and 19 predicted convic-tions at ages 21 to 24, independent of all other variables (Farrington:1986b). Finally, Bachman, O'Malley, and Johnston (1978) reported that unemployed youths at ages 22 and 23 had higher self-reported offending scores than employed youths. In a longitudinal survey of Montreal adolescents, Pronovost and LeBlanc (1980) found that dropping out of school, especially when it was followed by steady employment, led to a *decrease* in offending. Unemployment seems to be related to offending behaviour of individuals rather than to methodological problems such as measurement bias.

Lastly, in an important study of Toronto's homeless youth, John Hagan and Bill McCarthy (1992) offer a crucial analysis of the growing underbelly of youth unemployment and crime. They went "to the streets" and "to the schools" to assess the significance of "situational factors" such as prolonged unemployment on youth crime in Canada's largest metropolitan area. In their provocative study, they insist that homeless youths have fled from "one set of adverse situations (abuse in the home and conflict at school) only to find them-selves in another; that is, the difficult circumstances of life on the street"

(Hagan and McCarthy 1992:600). A growing number of homeless young men and women have been unable to find work in this city, and this has led many of them to commit specific criminal offences. Depending on the degree of hardship and gender of the offender, Hagan and McCarthy conclude that "hunger causes theft of food, problems of hunger and shelter lead to serious theft and problems of unemployment and shelter produce prostitution [for homeless women]" (Hagan and McCarthy 1992:597).

In summary, two problems of labour market marginality, namely, unemployment and part-time and poorly paid employment, carry different responses to property crime depending on the age cohort of the offenders. Juveniles are more likely to refrain from offending if sufficient part-time, seasonal employment exists that does not unduly interfere with studying. In contrast, young adults require higher-paying and more stable jobs with prospects for real advancement if they are to be kept from committing crimes against property.

✸ Employment Status, Gender, and Crime

The preceding review spoke about young males who commit property-based crimes. What about teenage girls and young women? Are their experiences with paid employment somehow different? Now that women have entered the labour force in such large numbers, are they increasingly involved in employment-related crimes such as embezzlement? Or do teenage girls and young women commit property-related crimes in periods of high unemployment, much like their male counterparts?

There has been scant research in this area of sociological criminology in Canada. On the other hand, in Great Britain and elsewhere in the developed world, the dramatic rise in female participation rates in the postwar labour market has led some analysts to hypothesize that women would account for an increasing share of white-collar crimes such as fraud and income tax evasion. Official British statistics indicate that the typical female crime is petty theft, not big-time embezzlement; also, typical offenders are poor, unskilled, undereducated, and unemployed (Chapman 1980). In her study of employment status, gender, and crime, Jane Chapman compared the female labour force participation rates from 1930 to 1970 with the arrest rates for the same period and found that the smallest increases in female arrests coincided with periods of sustained economic growth. This pattern suggests that the absence rather than the availability of employment stimulates female involvement in crime. In the United Kingdom, the longitudinal study of female crime from 1951 to

1980 by Steven Box and Chris Hale (1984) concluded that unemployment, rather than participation in the labour force, was positively correlated with female offending.[3] However, girls remain vastly more law-abiding than boys. In the case of females, while periods of unemployment appear to precipitate crime, there are clearly countervailing influences at work. According to Ngaire Naffine (1989), the low rates of female offending can be interpreted in terms of the schooling of females for a quiet, domestic life, the exclusion of females from male-dominated criminal subcultures, and the failure of society to teach girls the basic skills needed for crime. Thus, socialization rather than economic rationality has been adopted by some feminist scholars as the more important explanation for the significant differences between male and female criminal behaviour.

Referring once more to the important study of homeless Toronto youths conducted by Hagan and McCarthy (1992), the evidence points to gender-specific criminal activity. (See also Steffensmeier 1980.) While some teenage boys and young men worked as prostitutes, it was predominantly teenage girls and young women who earned money this way. Their conclusion:

> Situational concerns and difficulties are more likely to cause male involvement in theft and female participation in prostitution. That is, strains of the street are more likely to exert their effects along previously observed lines of gender specialization in crime. [Hagan and McCarthy 1992:605][4]

Clearly, males outnumber females in property-based offences and in the general prison population. While the research on employment status and gender is sorely missing on this side of the Atlantic, data from the United Kingdom (and on the homeless in Toronto) do show a relationship between unemployment and female participation in specific classes of crime, especially prostitution and larceny. While the numbers are not overwhelming, the evidence leaves few doubts.

✹ What Do We Know about Youth Unemployment in Canada?

For many young people, the transition from school to work means entering the labour market relatively unskilled and inexperienced, as well as weak in job search skills and unaware of what job opportunities are available. As a result, many will face unemployment. Their experience with unemployment will, however, vary by region, province, and city. Statistics Canada defines an unemployed person as someone who (a) during the week of the survey was unemployed and actively seeking work; (b) did not actively search for work but was on layoff for 26 weeks or less with the expectation of returning to work; or (c) was not actively searching for work but expected to start a new job in four weeks or less. As questionable as this definition is, we are, unfortunately, stuck with it. Based on this definition, the picture of youth unemployment in Canada is not encouraging. In 1992, for example, early school leavers accounted for about one-half of all unemployed young people. This group registered an unemployment rate of 24.5 percent, almost one-and-one-half times the annual average rate for all young people (Kerr 1993).

Between 1946 and 1965, the proportion of youths aged 15 to 25 participating in the labour force fell by almost 10 percent, from 57.3 to 48.1 percent. This downward trend was due not to recession but rather to state modernization that encouraged the continued education of teenagers (Glenday, Guindon, and Turowetz 1978). Education, especially higher education, was becoming possible for more and more young people regardless of class. It was also becoming a necessity in the employment market as Canada improved its position in the world economy (Glenday 1989).

Times have changed. The participation rates for teenagers and young adults increased substantially between the mid-1960s and the recession of the 1980s. As revealed in Table 5.1, the unemployment rate for both male and female teenagers and young adults has been increasing since 1970. The situation appears to be worse for those between 15 and 19 but is spread rather evenly between the sexes. It is alarming to note that between 1970 and 1993, the unemployment rate for those between 20 and 24 virtually doubled while the rate for teens increased by one-third. Competition for jobs by both males

Table 5.1

Unemployment Rates by Age and Sex, 1970–93

Age	1970	1973	1976	1979	1982	1985	1988	1991	1993
15–19	14.4%	12.2%	16.5%	15.4%	24.0%	18.1%	13.6%	17.2%	19.7%
20–24	8.0%	7.7%	11.3%	10.1%	19.1%	14.3%	10.4%	15.2%	15.7%
Gender									
Male 15–19	14.4%	12.5%	16.6%	15.3%	27.3%	20.4%	14.5%	19.4%	20.8%
Male 20–24	9.0%	7.9%	11.7%	11.0%	22.0%	15.9%	11.3%	18.3%	18.3%
Female 15–19	14.5%	11.9%	16.4%	15.5%	20.5%	15.7%	12.7%	14.9%	18.6%
Female 20–24	6.7%	7.4%	10.7%	9.1%	15.9%	12.7%	9.4%	11.7%	12.7%

Source: Statistics Canada, *Historical Labour Force Statistics*, 1993, pp. 258–385.

Table 5.2

Youth Unemployment by Province, Both Sexes, 1980–93[1]

Year	NF	PE	NS	NB	PQ	ON	MB	SK	AB	BC
1980	21.6%	17.1%	17.0%	18.3%	17.2%	12.4%	10.1%	8.5%	6.8%	11.8%
1982	28.5%	21.2%	23.0%	23.3%	23.2%	17.1%	14.0%	11.4%	12.6%	21.2%
1984	34.1%	20.5%	21.7%	23.9%	19.8%	14.9%	14.0%	15.0%	16.4%	22.6%
1986	31.1%	18.5%	21.4%	22.9%	16.9%	11.5%	12.3%	13.2%	15.2%	19.7%
1988	25.3%	18.5%	16.4%	19.2%	13.3%	8.25%	13.3%	13.4%	12.5%	15.5%
1990	25.0%	18.4%	15.9%	18.8%	15.0%	10.5%	12.5%	12.4%	10.9%	13.0%
1992	30.4%	20.6%	21.0%	20.6%	18.2%	18.2%	16.3%	15.2%	14.2%	16.5%
1993	37.7%	30.1%	24.9%	22.7%	22.8%	18.5%	15.1%	17.4%	16.7%	16.3%

[1]Estimates for P.E.I. are subject to a large sampling error. Consequently, the data for P.E.I. are not reliable and should be used with extreme caution.

Source: Kerr 1993:16.

and females in the 20–24 category is intense and will continue to be so for the foreseeable future.

Table 5.2 provides a breakdown of youth unemployment by province for both sexes. The one startling finding is the persistence of extemely high rates of unemployment for young people across the country. In any year, the Maritimes, but Newfoundland in particular, is the hardest hit region in Canada. The 1980s recession struck the eastern half of the country more severely than it did Ontario and the West. The 1990s recession, however, affected every province—none were spared. Moreover, according to Deborah Sunter (1994:35), the recent recession appears to have been:

harder on youths than the 1981–82 recession … where a stable number of close to 200,000 youths (72 per cent are women) who were neither in school nor in the labour force remain with low academic credentials [which means] they will face extremely limited [job] prospects.

These are the street kids of the near future. These are the young men and women with the fewest prospects for the future other than alcohol, drugs, and crime.[5] How many street kids are there in Canada? There are between 750,000 to 1,500,000 homeless youth in the United States (Shane 1989). Estimating from this, we can say that the numbers for Canada are somewhere in the neighbourhood of 75,000 to 150,000. Before the recent recession, estimates for Toronto alone ranged from 10,000 to 12,000 (Kelly 1989).

When social programs are slashed in the name of deficit reduction, or job training programs are either cut or are inadequate to meet the needs of employers, these young men and women are being primed for crime. More police and more prison cells is not the most appropriate response to this worsening situation for young Canadians.

✱ What Do We Know about Youth Crime in Canada?

Give him [Oliver] a little air! Nonsense, he don't deserve it.
   Oliver Twist

Canada's national statistical database on crime is housed in Ottawa. In 1986, the Canadian Centre for Justice Statistics began collecting data from most provinces and territories through its youth court survey (YCS). Today this material constitutes the primary database for youth crime statistics. In 1991 Ontario was included in the YCS. The following year, both British Columbia and Ontario were able to report between 95 and 100 percent of the caseloads in their jurisdictions.

The data derive from police reports of young persons between 12 and 18 charged with criminal activity. To complicate matters in the collection of information, Ontario and Quebec are the only two jurisdictions that have provincial police forces. The other eight provinces and the two territories rely on the RCMP. Even though there is cooperation between these police forces, each agency has its own approach to gathering data.

How do we define youth? This is not as simple a matter as it may first appear. For example, the Young Offenders Act (YOA) limits youth to individuals between 12 and 17 at the time of the offence. The police complain that they cannot charge individuals over 7 and under 12. The federal government maintains that the provinces have the power to treat these children under the child welfare laws. Therefore, data on youth crime derives from persons aged 12 to 17 appearing in youth court on federal statute offences such as drug offences, Criminal Code offences, and those found in the YOA.

What do we know about the types of crime engaged in by males and females in Canada in the two age groups reviewed above? Do property crimes predominate? What can be said about the relationship between unemployment, poorly paid work, and property crime? How do teenagers and young adults fit into the picture? Are patterns in Canada similar to or different from those in other countries such as the United States, Great Britain, and Australia? These are not easy questions and, unfortunately, we do not have the quality of data to answer them intelligently. However, the need to address these issues of work and crime has never been greater.

Table 5.3 provides evidence of the crime rates for violent crimes, property offences, and all other crimes (including drug offences and car thefts) committed by young people from 1986 to 1993. Clearly, the data confirm that violent crime is increasing. However, we must be careful when we interpret this data, since Ontario only began reporting to the Canadian Centre for Justice Statistics in 1991. The very large increase between 1990 and 1991 can be accounted for by Ontario being newly included. The category "other crimes" shows an increase until 1989, when the percentages begin to flatten out. Property crimes, by contrast, feature a marginal decline over the same period. However, property crimes account for a remarkable three of every five criminal convictions. I will say more about this trend later in this chapter.

I would like to say something now about violent crimes committed by young people. Contrary to popular belief, it is young people themselves who are most likely to be the victims of violent youth crime. Table 5.4 shows this: Canadian youths 12 to 17 are the largest group that are victims of minor assault, aggravated assault, and sexual assault. Are harsher penalties for young people the appropriate response to this tragedy?

The older the young offender, the more likely he or she is to be found in secure custody such as detention or prison. In 1992–93, over half of all cases (52 percent) with guilty findings involved youths aged 16 or 17. These same

Table 5.3

Crime Rate by Young People (12–17 years)[1]

Types of Offence	1986	1987	1988	1989	1990	1991	1992	1993
Violent crime	782 (9.0%)	826 (9.3%)	865 (9.7%)	908 (10.3%)	970 (10.3%)	1,056 (10.2%)	1,081 (10.8%)	1,079 (11.3%)
Property offences	5,528 (63.6%)	5,531 (62%)	5,419 (61%)	5,217 (59.2%)	5,593 (59.2%)	6,141 (59.6%)	5,890 (58.8%)	5,562 (58.5%)
Other crimes	2,382 (27.4%)	2,569 (28.7%)	2,603 (29.3%)	2,682 (30.5%)	2,891 (30.5%)	3,113 (30.2%)	3,044 (30.4%)	2.875 (30.2%)
All offences	8,692 (100%)	8,922 (100%)	8,887 (100%)	8,807 (100%)	9,454 (100%)	10,310 (100%)	10,016 (100%)	9,516 (100%)

[1] Rates are calculated based on 100,000 youths.

offenders were more likely to receive a term of secure custody than were youths under 16 years. One-sixth or 16 percent of these youths were sent to secure custody compared with 12 percent of youths aged 14 or 15 and 5 percent of 12 and 13 year olds (*Juristat* 1994:3).

✸ The Court System and the Young Offenders Act

Almost every developed country has its own equivalent of our YOA. Countries such as Canada, the United States, Great Britain, Sweden, France, and Germany all have YOAs. In 1984, the Young Offenders Act replaced the Juvenile Delinquents Act (JDA), which was first enacted in 1908. The latter treated young offenders not as criminals but as "misdirected [children] in need of aid, encouragement, help and assistance." The JDA could be invoked against any child over 7 and, depending on the province, under 16 or 18. The problems with the Juvenile Delinquents Act, as presented by advocates of change, included its arbitrariness and the fact that it denied young people basic elements of due process such as a clear right to counsel and definite as opposed to open-ended sentences. The resulting YOA is a considerably more detailed and explicit code governing criminal proceedings against young people.

The Young Offenders Act is federally enacted legislation but is administered through the provincial courts. Young offenders are tried in "youth courts," which are courts designated by the provincial government to deal with adolescents. As was the case with the JDA, criminal proceedings under

Table 5.4

Victims of Violent Youth Crime by Age, 1988–91

Age	Minor Assault	Aggravated Assault	Sexual Assault	Robbery
Under 12	12%	7%	60%	7%
12–17	50%	45%	35%	34%
18–25	15%	18%	3%	16%
26–36	10%	14%	2%	10%
37–45	9%	8%	0.5%	11%
46–64	4%	4%	0.4%	13%
65+	1%	1%	0.1%	8%

Source: Statistics Canada, Canadian Centre for Justice Statistics Incidence-Based Uniform Crime Reporting Survey, 1988–91.

Figure 5.1

A Chronology of Youth Crime Legislation in Canada

Year	Legislated Reports/Proposals/Enactments
1908	The Juvenile Delinquents Act adopted by federal Parliament.
February 1966	The minister of justice (P.E. Trudeau) tables the Report of the Department of Justice Committee on Juvenile Delinquency.
November 1970	A proposed Young Offenders Act (Bill C-192) was allowed to die after severe criticism in Parliament and across the nation.
October 1979	Legislative proposals to replace the Juvenile Delinquents Act are tabled in the House of Commons.
February 1981	A proposed Young Offenders Act (Bill C-61) is given first reading in the House of Commons.
July 1982	The Young Offenders Act receives Royal Assent.
April 1984	All of the Act except maximum age provisions is proclaimed in force.
April 1985	That all persons up to 18 are "young persons" is proclaimed in force.
September 1986	Substantial amendments are made to the YOA, including detention with adults until his/her first appearance in court, rules governing testimony, and so on.
May 1992	Bill C-12 amended several sections, including sentencing a youth for up to 5 years less a day for first- or second-degree murder and changing the Criminal Code of Canada to include life imprisonment for a person 18 years of age or under convicted of first- or second-degree murder.

the YOA do not require a preliminary hearing, nor is a jury trial a possible option. Parole is not available to young persons; however, the act ensures that all dispositions are periodically reviewed. On the whole, the YOA is a procedural statute; that is to say, it sets out the procedures (including rights and responsibilities) relating to young people that must be followed when an adolescent has been accused of a crime. The emphasis is clearly less on social intervention and more on the delineation of a young person's rights and obligations.

The YOA applies to all young people between 12 and 18. Like the JDA, it provides for the transfer of some serious cases to adult court. Tables 5.5 and 5.6 provide data on the age and sex of those found guilty in youth court. As expected, males outnumber females in every age category by as much as eight to one. Males 15 to 17 commit the most offences; females 15 years of age are the most likely to be found guilty of a criminal offence.[6]

Table 5.6 shows the number of guilty cases heard in youth court by gender from 1986 to 1993. Once again, remember that the large increase in the 1992–93 category is due to the inclusion of data from Ontario and the

Table 5.5

Youth Court Cases (Guilty) by Age and Sex, 1992–93

Age	12 years	13 years	14 years	15 years	16 years	17 years	Total
Male	1,754	4,455	8,822	13,039	16,956	18,114	63,642
	(2.7%)	(7%)	(13.9%)	(20%)	(26.6%)	(28.5%)	(98.7%)
Female	363	1,203	2,487	3,131	2,771	2,481	12,514
	(2.9%)	(9.6%)	(19.9%)	(25%)	(22.1%)	(19.8%)	(99.3%)
Total	2,117	5,658	11,309	16,170	19,727	20,595	76,156

Source: *Juristat* (March 1994):17.

Table 5.6

Guilty Youth Court Cases by Gender, 1986–93

Year	1986/87*	1987/88*	1988/89*	1989/90*	1992/93
Male	31,010	31,349	30,814	32,243	63,642
	(86.4%)	(86.2%)	(86%)	(86.1%)	(83.6%)
Female	4,862	5,013	5,015	5,187	12,514
	(13.6%)	(13.8%)	(14%)	(13.9%)	(16.4%)
Total	35,872	36,362	35,829	37,430	76,156
	(100%)	(100%)	(100%)	(100%)	(100%)

* Excludes Ontario and Northwest Territories.

Source: *Juristat* (November 1990/March 1994).

Northwest Territories. If these figures are discounted, the increase in numbers for both males and females over this time period disappears. Interestingly, they show a modest decline and certainly do not point to significant growth in youth crime in Canada.

What happens to children between 7 and 12 years of age? According to the federal government, provinces have the power to treat such children under child welfare (that is, family court). On the other hand, Ontario, for example, continues to prosecute young offenders between 16 and 18 years of age in provincial criminal courts.

In summary, older male teenagers commit the most crimes and are more likely to receive secure custody. While increases in violent crime have occurred, it is young people who are the overwhelming victims. Remarkably, about 60 percent of all youth crime in any given year relates to property offences.

✳ Youth Unemployment and Crime in Canada: A Profile?

Over the past three decades in Canada, youth unemployment and crime *have not* been carefully thought about either as a research agenda or as a public policy concern. For a number of reasons, criminologists in Canada have spent most of their energy on the politics of the Young Offenders Act or on specific issues related to youth crime such as alcoholism and drug abuse. Yet the evidence from the United States, Great Britain, and Australia all points to a link between youth unemployment and property crime. There is evidence that for juveniles, seasonal employment prospects that do not interfere with school can go far to meet the needs and consumer expectations of teenagers—needs and expectations that would otherwise be met through the committing of property-related offences. The same type of employment will not work for young adults, who require full-time work with reasonably good pay and fair chances for advancement. The experience of long-term unemployment encourages both groups to move into a life of crime.

Nowhere is this problem more pronounced than with our homeless youth. In their empirical study of Toronto's "street kids," Hagan and McCarthy (1992) note:

> Theft of food and serious theft increase with hunger; serious theft and prostitution increase with problems of shelter; and prostitution increases with unemployment. These effects are all significant and substantial and therefore increase our confidence that situational problems of *sustenance* and *security* cause street crime. [1992:623; author's emphasis]

Figure 5.2[6] combines the unemployment rates for males in the two age categories described above. In addition, the crime rates for property crime and violent offences committed by young Canadians 12 to 17 have been included. The trends shown offer little more than suggestions for future research. However, it is clear that while violent crimes continue to increase over the short time period selected, the rate of property infractions is more cyclical and appears to run in close tandem with the unemployment rates for both age groups. Certainly, there is a pressing need for more research to explore the links between crime and unemployment. Considering the large proportion of youth crime devoted to property-related offences, those who make public policy would be ill-advised to ignore the issue.

Figure 5.2
Youth Unemployment and Crime for Males, 1985–93

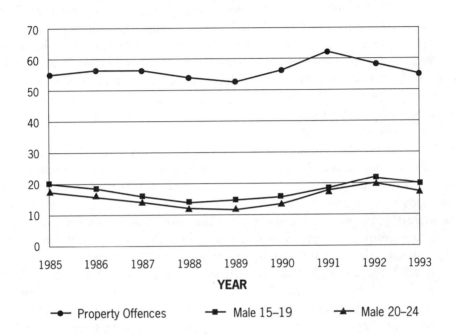

Why Not in Canada?

It is difficult to explain the lack of research by Canadian criminologists on youth unemployment and property crime. Nevertheless, it is important to try, because otherwise it will be difficult to persuade politicians, the public, and research-granting agencies to support more of it. I can postulate two sets of possible explanations—one environmental and the other discipline-based.

There are three major environmental factors—prosperity, a weak national social democratic party, and middle-class support for higher education as the most appropriate way to achieve social mobility. Unlike in many parts of Europe devastated by World War II, prosperity in North America during the late 1950s and 1960s meant low unemployment and clean streets. Linked to the prosperity of the 1960s was the rise of a youth-based "counterculture" that de-emphasized delinquency and crime by replacing it with "flower power," "soft drugs," "peace through music," and "the politics of the street." The spillover from these uniquely historical events may have "blinded" those of this generation, who have since become social scientists and policy makers, to the sociopsychological problems of teenage and youth unemployment and the "mean streets" of the 1980s and 1990s.

Great Britain and Australia have a strong social democratic tradition at the national level; Canada and the United States do not. The labour parties in both these countries have expressed concern over and are more sensitive to the links between youth unemployment and property crime. Indeed, Australia was founded on the backs of Great Britain's street criminals. Moreover, Great Britain has a literary tradition beginning with Charles Dickens's *Oliver Twist* that links youth unemployment and crime. Certainly, the Canadian literary tradition has been and still is very much attached to geography and identity.

In recent memory, middle-class support for higher education instead of training and job creation for these targeted populations has underpinned much of public policy dealing with youth crime, since unemployment is not as great a problem for middle-class kids as it is for the working class and poor in Canada. The larger political community tends to absolve itself from the responsibility of providing solutions to youth unemployment, and to concentrate on *individual* criminal activity (with its emphasis on police, rehabilitation, and experimental projects).

By discipline-based, I mean applied sociological research that relies on the dominance of structural functionalism. It is well understood that this theoretical paradigm carries with it a penchant for emphasizing the negative "cultural" characteristics of disadvantaged groups in society. Concentration on long-term cultural (especially family) factors reduces the situational or more contingent structural factors such as recent unemployment. Family factors accentuate lower-class and racial/ethnic factors (i.e., "dysfunctional families") and underpin the theoretical perspectives dominant in the sociological criminological literature. This argument implied that short-term unemployment for the young will disappear as a social problem once the economy rebounds from recessionary pressures. Therefore, there is no need to commit resources to overcome unemployment while dysfunctional families are with us. To date, structural unemployment factors lie outside North American sociological criminology. In addition, practitioners conversant with structural functionalism lean toward sophisticated statistical models while ignoring the experiences of the street. Close attention to individual attributes and family background underlines their collective approach to youth crime. Ironically, these individual criminal statistics quickly become stereotypes when criminal activity is combined with either ethnic background (the Mafia or Asian gangs) or both ethnic background and poverty (recent black immigrants and native people). This modus operandi supports conservative public policies that often "blame the poor" for their drinking, promiscuity, and drug addiction. Moreover, conservative social policies such as more police and more prison cells supplant "progressive" economic policies, such as job training and family allowances, which are aimed at tackling child poverty.

✸ Why We Need a Change in Priorities and Goals

McCarthy and Hagan (1992), as one example, have done a masterful and important job to move research into the study of what is referred to as "criminogenic circumstances," or situational factors. This can signal a significant shift in research and policy, because if many of the more serious problems of the street derive from

> the conditions of street life itself, including, for example, the problems of sustenance (hunger and food) and security (shelter) that street life produces ... [the] policy relevance [lies] in the fact that *street situations can be changed*. [1992:625; author's emphasis]

Canadian sociological criminologists should shift their focus and align their *research priorities* more closely with those of their progressive colleagues in the United States, the United Kingdom, and Australia. They can begin by, for example, requesting employment status of offenders from police; establishing longitudinal cohort studies of teenagers and the young; and initiating a number of "from the street" case studies.

Possible *policy options* to be publicly debated include these: the reinstituting family allowances and/or a guaranteed annual income; one year more of compulsory school attendance; regulating the amount of part-time employment reserved for high school students to work in establishments like fast food outlets. In terms of the latter, the overwhelming evidence shows that homework and juvenile crime are negatively correlated. In other words, students who spend more than ten hours a week at work spend less time on their homework. Once less time is spent on homework, the chances increase that individual young people will spend more time "working" the streets. R.H. Tawney (Szreter 1990) realized that compulsory school attendance was important in reducing the number of teenage males committing criminal offences. Considering the importance attached to education and job skills for the Information Age, another year of compulsory school attendance could be argued as fulfilling two significant public policy objectives: namely, decreasing youth crime and enhancing skills through public education and training. Finally, the reinstatement of family allowances and/or the creation of a guaranteed annual income are significant societal-level policy initiatives that must be publicly scrutinized and again widely debated. Together, these initiatives would signal a much-needed shift in research and public policy.

Notes

*I wish to acknowledge the assistance of Moira Russell and Gary O'Bireck.

1. In their survey of close to 2,000 seniors in three Canadian cities, Julian Tanner and Harvey Krahn (1991) conclude that teenagers with part-time jobs tend to report illegal activity such as alcohol consumption. However, they caution that some of this illegal activity such as alcohol use will become acceptable as soon as they reach the legal age. The more serious youth crimes "of the street" fall through their methodological cracks. If they are not at school, how can one know what these young people are doing? This is an endemic problem for those wedded to self-report survey research.

2. William Julius Wilson's (1987) study of the ghetto poor in the United States pinpoints the causes of crime and violence on the lack of good jobs. His study is made all the more important by his insistence that his argument is not confined to the black ghetto but to *any* group experiencing long periods of unemployment.

3. For conflicting results, see Naffine and Gale (1989) in their study of South Australian males and females. They conclude that "it is easier to make a case for

Year	1985	1986	1987	1988	1989	1990	1991	1992	1993
Property offences[1]	54.30	55.28	55.31	54.19	52.71	55.93	61.41	58.90	55.62
Violent crime[1]	7.31	7.82	8.26	8.65	9.08	9.7	10.56	10.81	10.79
Unemployment rate[2]									
Male 15–19	20.6	18.2	16.4	14.2	14.5	15.4	18.3	21.5	19.6
Male 20–24	17.0	15.5	13.9	12.1	11.0	13.0	19.2	19.3	15.6
Female 15–19	16.7	15.2	13.6	12.0	11.5	12.8	15.0	17.7	17.6
Female 20–24	13.4	12.9	11.8	10.4	9.1	10.5	12.3	13.6	12.9
15–19	18.8	16.8	15.1	13.2	13.1	14.2	16.7	19.7	18.7
20–24	15.3	14.3	12.9	11.2	10.1	11.8	15.9	16.6	14.3

[1] Rate per 1,000,000.

[2] Percentage.

Source: *Juristat* (August 1994); and Statistics Canada, *The Labour Force Survey*, 1986–93.

the theory that unemployment causes crime (that is, property crime) when analysis is based on male crime figures alone" (p. 154).

4. "According to these results, theft of food and serious theft increase with hunger; serious theft and prostitution increase with problems of shelter and prostitution increases with unemployment. These effects are all significant and substantial and therefore increase our confidence that situational problems of sustenance and security cause street crime" (Hagan and McCarthy 1992:623).

5. "Declining labour market opportunities for the less educated and participation in crime seem to reinforce each other for growing factions of less-educated young males" (Freeman 1991:18). The fact that similar research conclusions for Canada are unavailable, at present, does not invalidate the claim that Canada's increase in property crimes has similar roots.

6. The data for this figure are derived from the table on the previous page.

7. There is early American evidence from Schwartz and Skolnick (1964) that contact with the criminal justice system has especially negative effects for young working-class males. Therefore, when high dropout rates are combined with a shrinking labour market for uneducated youths, the likely result is a rise in income-supplementing crime.

References

Allan, Emilie, and Darrell Steffensmeier. 1989. "Youth, Underemployment, and Property Crime: Differential Effects of Job Availability and Job Quality on Juvenile and Young Adult Arrest Rates." *American Sociological Review* 54 (February): 107–123.

Bachman, J.G., P.M. O'Malley, and J. Johnston. 1978. *Youth in Transition* (Vol. 6). Ann Arbor: University of Michigan Institute for Social Research.

Baker, Geoff. 1993. "Streets Hold Thousands of Homeless Youth." *The Gazette*. April 15: A1.

Baron, James, and William Bielby. 1984. "The Organization of Work in a Segmented Economy." *American Sociological Review* 49:454–473.

Block, M.K, and J.M. Heineke. 1975. "A Labor Theoretic Analysis of Criminal Choice." *American Economic Review* (65)3:314–325.

Bohm, R.M. 1983. "Beyond Employment: Toward a Radical Solution to the Crime Problem." *Crime and Social Justice* (21):213.

Box, Steven. 1987. *Recession, Crime and Punishment*. London: Macmillan.

Box, Steven, and Chris Hale. 1983. "Liberation and Female Criminality in England and Wales." *British Journal of Criminology* (23).

Braithwaite, J. 1979. *Inequality, Crime and Public Policy*. London: Routledge and Kegan Paul.

Brenner, Harvey. 1977. "Does Unemployment Cause Crime?" *Criminal Justice Newsletter* (8)21:5.

Britt, Chester. 1994. "Crime and Unemployment Among Youths in the United States, 1958-1990." *American Journal of Economics and Sociology* (53)1:99–109.

Canadian Mental Health Association. 1984. *Work and Well Being: Perspectives on Mental Health and the Workplace*. Ottawa: Fort McMurray & Battlefords.

Cantor, David, and Kenneth Land. 1985. "Unemployment and Crime Rates in Post–World War II United States: A Theoretical and Empirical Analaysis." *American Sociological Review* (50):317–332.

Chapman, Jane. 1980. *Economic Realities and the Female Offender*. Lexington: D.C. Heath.

Chiricos, Theodore. 1987. "Rates of Crime and Unemployment: An Analysis of Aggregate Research Evidence." *Social Problems* 34:187–212.

Clogg, Clifford. 1979. *Measuring Unemployment: Demographic Indicators for the U.S.* New York: Academic Press.

Cloward, R.A., and L.E. Ohlin. 1960. *Delinquency and Opportunity*. New York: Free Press.

Cohen, A.K. 1955. *Delinquent Boys*, New York: Macmillan.

Currie, Elliot. 1985. *Confronting Crime: An American Challenge*. New York: Pantheon.

Farrington, David, et al. 1986a. "Unemployment, School Leaving and Crime." *British Journal of Criminology* 26(4):335–356.

———. 1986b. "Stepping Stones to Adult Criminal Careers." In D. Olweus, J. Block, and M. Yarrow (eds), *Development of Antisocial and Prosocial Behaviour*. New York: Academic Press.

Ferguson, Jonathan. 1994. "Young and Underemployed." *Toronto Star*. March 27: D1, D5.

Form, William. 1985. *Divided We Stand: Working Class Stratfication in America*. Urbana: University of Illinois Press.

Fox, James. 1978. *Forecasting Crime Data*. Lexington: Lexington Books.

Glaser, D., and K. Rice. 1959. "Crime, Age and Unemployment." *American Sociological Review* 24:679–686.

Glenday, Daniel. 1989. "Rich but Semiperipheral: Canada's Ambiguous Position in the World Economy." *Review: Fernand Braudel Centre*.

———. [in press]. "What Has Work Done to the Working Class? A Comparison of Workers and Production Technologies." *British Journal of Sociology*.

Glenday, Daniel, H. Guindon, and A. Turowetz. 1978. *Modernization and the Canadian State*. Toronto: Macmillan.

Greenberg, David. 1977. "Delinquency and the Age Structure of Society." *Contemporary Crises* 1:189–223.

Hagan, John. 1992. "The Poverty of a Classless Criminology—The American Society of Criminology 1991 Presidential Address." *Criminology* 30(1):1–19.

Hagan, John, and Bill McCarthy. 1992. "Mean Streets: The Theoretical Significance of Situational Delinquency among Homeless Youth." *American Journal of Sociology* 98(3):597–627.

Herrenstein, Richard, and Charles Murray. 1994. *The Bell Curve: Intelligence and Class Structure in American Life*. New York: Free Press.

Hirschi, T. 1969. *Causes of Delinquency*. Berkeley: University of California Press.

Howe, Wayne. 1988. "Education and Demographics: How Do They Affect Unemployment Rates?" *Monthly Labor Review* (January):3–9.

Kelly, F. 1989. "Drugs Darken Yonge St. Strip." *Toronto Star*. June 30.

Kerr, Kevin B. 1993. *Youth Unemployment in Canada*. Ottawa: Library of Parliament (Research Branch).

Kyvrikosaios, Deborah. 1993. "Plight of Vagrant Teens Called Crisis." *The Globe and Mail*. August 30.

Logan, John, and Steven Messner. 1987. "Racial Residential Segregation and Suburban Violent Crime." *Social Science Quarterly* (68):510–527.

Long, Sharon, and Ann Witte. 1981. "Current Economic Trends: Implications for Crime and Justice." Pp. 69–143 in *Crime and Criminal Justice in a Declining Economy*, Kevin Wright (ed.). Cambridge: Oelgeschlager, Gunn and Hain.

Merton, Robert K. 1956. *Social Theory and Social Structure*. New York: Free Press.

Naffine, Ngaire, and Fay Gale. 1989. "Testing the Nexus: Crime, Gender and Unemployment." *British Journal of Criminology* 29(2):144–156.

Nemeth, Mary. 1993. "Life on the Mean Streets." *Maclean's*. February 22:48–49.

O'Bireck, Gary M. 1993. "Richies and Reggies: The Family, the School, Peer Associations, Socio-Economic Status, and Adolescent Deviance Patterns: An Ethnographic Inquiry." Ph.D. dissertation, Department of Sociology, York University.

Orsagh, T., and A.D. Witte. 1981. "Economic Status and Crime: Implications for Offender Rehabilitation." *Journal of Criminal Law and Criminology* (72):1055–1071.

Pronovost, L., and M. LeBlanc. 1980. "Transition statuaire et delinquance." *Canadian Journal of Criminology* (22):288–297.

Radzinowicz, Leon. 1939. "The Influence of Economic Conditions on Crime." *Sociological Review* (33):1–26, 139–153.

Schwartz, Richard, and Jerome Skolnick. 1964. "Two Studies of Legal Stigma." In Howard Becker (ed.), *The Other Side: Perspectives on Deviance*. New York: Free Press.

Shane, Paul. 1989. "Changing Patterns among Homeless and Runaway Youth." *American Journal of Orthopsychiatry* 59(2):208–214.

Short, James, and Fred Strodtbeck. 1965. *Group Processes and Gang Delinquency.* Chicago: University of Chicago Press.

Sokol, Al. 1991. "Looking Street Kids in the Eye." *Toronto Star.* April 25:F1, F2.

Steffensmeier, Darrell. 1980. "Sex Differences in Patterns of Adult Crimes, 1965–77: A Review and Assessment." *Social Forces* (58):1080–1108.

Sunter, Deborah. 1994. "Youths—Waiting It Out." *Perspectives on Labour and Income* (Spring):31–36.

Sutherland, Edwin, and Donald Cressey. 1978. *Principles of Criminology* (10th Edition). Philadelphia: Lippincott.

Szreter, Richard. 1990. "A Note on R.H. Tawney's Early Interest in Juvenile Employment and Misemployment." *History of Education* (19)4:375–382.

Tanner, Julian, and Harvey Krahn. 1991. "Part-Time Work and Deviance Among High-School Seniors." *Canadian Journal of Sociology* (16)3:281–302.

Thrasher, Frederick. 1927. *The Gang.* Chicago: University of Chicago Press.

Visano, L. 1987. *This Idle Trade.* Concord: VitaSana.

West, D.J. 1982. *Delinquency: Its Roots, Careers and Prospects.* London: Heinemann.

Whyte, William F. 1943. *Street Corner Society.* Chicago: University of Chicago Press.

Wilson, William Julius. 1987. *The Truly Disadvantaged: The Inner City, the Underclass and Public Policy.* Chicago: University of Chicago Press.

CHAPTER 6

Parliament/Funkadelic: Entropy as a Deviant Creative Tool and Ideological Signifier

Rob Bowman

York University

Culture is generally defined as a way of life with a concomitant set of meanings and values. One of the functions of culture is to categorize the symbolic universe into publicly recognized patterns. As such, culture interprets or "mediates" experience. Deviant subcultural groups present an alternatively patterned symbolic universe. In doing so, they challenge the clarity of the symbolic universe as defined by the hegemonic culture. It follows then that the very concept of deviancy can be understood as the labelling by one group of another in a contest to determine whose definition of reality will be dominant. When "deviancy" is understood in this fashion, it becomes evident that deviance is defined differently from different vantage points: from a "deviant" subculture's point of view, it is the hegemonic culture that is actually deviant. What is really being contested from either vantage point is ultimately the site of power.

This is a battleground upon which many genres of popular music have waged war. Consumer capitalist culture axiomatically leads to stratification. Its very nature forces it to become disjunctive as, in our complex society, many different subcultures contest social and cultural space in a quest to legitimize their often conflicting behaviours, values, and lifestyles. Cultures in general, and subcultures very specifically, are attempts at solving the problem of carving out social space. By definition they are anything but neutral.

This chapter applies information theory to an analysis of the rhythm-and-blues group Parliament/Funkadelic and their "maggot" subculture. I attempt to link what the hegemonic society may see as entropic and deviant cultural behaviour to a deliberately constructed alternative ideology that functions in a positive context for those who define themselves as maggots.

Information theory as a discipline arose during World War II as an outgrowth of Allied attempts to unravel coded messages being transmitted by the Axis forces. In the ensuing half-century, various scholars have attempted to apply the basic tenets of information theory to a number of other disciplines, including historical musicology and sociology.

Canadian sociologist Orrin Klapp (1973) has borrowed a number of concepts from both information theory and biology and used them to construct models of social order that can be profitably applied to the study of popular music. Klapp contends that life is about winning and keeping order. To that end, every human action is oriented toward defeating entropy—in other words, to making order out of chaos. In this context, entropy is defined as the enemy.

The essential ordering process of life, according to Klapp's interpretation of information theory, is the encoding and decoding of information by the building of patterns. The mind naturally seeks pattern and, in doing so, creates probabilities based on both prior encoding and the stimuli of the moment. You are engaged in this process right now, as you read. These patterns are the means by which we make sense of the overwhelming number of stimuli that are present at every second of being. The ordering of the symbolic universe becomes an integral part of this patterning process.

The musical application of this concept is fairly obvious. Music is very patterned activity. We all process music constantly by subconsciously predicting harmonic, melodic, rhythmic, timbral, textural, linguistic, dynamic, and phrasing patterns, and so on. Our predictions are either met so that we feel a degree of satisfaction (or boredom); or they are thwarted, a small dose of entropy is administered, and we take pleasure in the stimuli of surprise. (If they are thwarted too often, the music will begin to appear as random.)

The notion of entropy as the enemy goes a long way toward explaining the dualism of good and evil (or hegemony and deviance) that so often permeates discourse about music. Most readers will have read accounts in which musical taste is explained in terms that approximate moral outrage (e.g., the Medieval labelling of the tritone as the "devil's interval," statements such as "so and so is ruining music," "rap is not music," "disco sucks," and so on). In cases such as these, moral approbation is expressed toward the deviant barbarian/sinner because his or her pattern violates one's own and thereby threatens entropy. Why else would a given set of social actors even care about what anyone else listens to?

There is one more aspect of information theory as extended into sociology that could be useful here. Living things signal to each other via communicated order through an environment that is full of irrelevant and unreadable information. Therefore, one of the central social problems of life consists of (a) finding one's own kind (those capable of relevant signals), (b) negotiating through these signals a readiness to act together in specifically ordered ways, and (c) developing enduring patterns of communication. This aspect of information theory can be directly applied to the formation and maintenance of musically based subcultures.

Sociological theory has long accepted that social identity is constructed via the social relations and meanings that surround social actors. Through primary socialization, these social relations and meanings are first inculcated in the social actor by the family. The social actor, in effect, inherits a meaning system whose ideology is embedded in the notion of "common sense." The mindset becomes, "This is the way the world is, it is patently obvious." This is the most insidious aspect of ideology. A given ideology's constructed, and therefore in a sense arbitrary, nature is not generally apparent to its adherents. In contrast, the subcultures that are tied to various types of popular music create, through the process of secondary socialization, an alternative *explicitly constructed* ideology that is often oppositional. This ideology, of course, becomes part and parcel of the essential subcultural gesture of difference.

If one puts Klapp's theories with regard to information theory together with those of the sociology of music at large, one can see the encoding and decoding process of patterning as a way of communicating meanings and values that effectively serve to create, articulate, and reinforce the ideology of a given subculture. Musical performances encode patterns that are decoded consciously and subconsciously by all involved in what Christopher Small (1988) has termed the "musicking" process whereby our ideal social relationships are modelled in the musical moment. With that in mind, it seems logical that if one can deduce the patterns of a given music and one dislikes it, it is because the patterns involved in that music model a different ideal society and concomitant ideal of social relationships than one is comfortable with. If one cannot deduce the patterns it is even worse—chaos (meaning entropy) is threatened. And, of course, if one can deduce the patterns and in doing so finds one's ideal relationships modelled in these patterns, a subculture is possible.

George Clinton and Parliament/Funkadelic actively embrace chaos/entropy for both creative and ideological reasons at a number of levels. The Funk Mob, as they are often referred to, was born in a barbershop in Plainfield, New Jersey, in the late 1950s. Originally a doo wop vocal group, the Parliaments recorded two singles for local independent New Jersey record labels in 1958 and 1959. In the 1960s the group's style changed with the times and the group recorded eight singles in Detroit for Golden World and Revilot that showed a substantial Temptations influence. In 1967, on Revilot, the group enjoyed a Top 5 r & b and Top 20 pop hit with "(I Wanna) Testify." Up to this point in their career, the Parliaments functioned as both a business and creative entity according to the then-current modes of mainstream r & b culture. Outside of the basic fact that to be black and working class meant that you were automatically outside the hegemonic culture, there was nothing particularly subcultural or deviant about the Parliaments' behaviour.

In 1968, in what turned out to be a decisive and successful attempt to circumvent the ensemble's contractual obligations with Revilot, Clinton decided that the group would cease functioning under the name the Parliaments. He proceeded to sign the group's backup musicians to Westbound Records under the name Funkadelic. The five vocalists who collectively were the Parliaments would "guest" on Funkadelic albums. A few years later, Clinton legally won back the right to the group's original name. Dropping the "s," he signed the vocalists, now known as Parliament, to first Invictus and then Casablanca. Funkadelic would "guest" on Parliament albums.

Necessity being the mother of invention, Clinton had stumbled into a situation where the same group of people recorded for two different labels under two different names simultaneously. At the height of the Funk Mob's popularity in the late 1970s, besides Parliament and Funkadelic, the same basic set of musicians recorded as Bootsy's Rubber Band, Fred Wesley and the Horny Horns, Parlet, and the Brides of Funkenstein. In addition, a number of members signed solo contracts with a variety of labels, recording still more product with the same basic set of musicians. What might be seen from the vantage point of the record industry as a deviant and entropic empire was born. Clinton had effectively turned the industry's version of slavery in the late twentieth century upside down and inside out.

In 1973, with an album by Funkadelic titled *Cosmic Slop*, George Clinton began to develop and articulate a funk cosmology that included such mythic characters as Dr. Funkenstein, Starchild, Mr. Wiggles, and Sir Nose D'Voidoffunk. On the 1976 Parliament album *Mothership Connection*, the WE-FUNK radio station was introduced along with the Lollipop Man aka the Long-Haired Sucker. Each new Parliament album contributed yet more characters as well as a series of events that pitted Dr. Funkenstein (Clinton himself) against Sir Nose D'Voidoffunk. Funkenstein hailed from outer space and represented the forces of funk, namely creativity, intelligence, and a healthy sense of uninhibited play, while Sir Nose represented the forces of boredom, blandness, and the hegemonic culture in general as seen from Clinton's vantage point. Various theories were advanced along the way. The Pinocchio Theory was simply that if you fake the funk your nose will grow (i.e., bullshit will always be manifest), while Funketelechy concerned the actualization of funk rather than its mere potential. By the *Trombipulation* album, released in 1980, Sir Nose had traced his ancestors (Cro-Nasal Sapiens) back to the pyramids and had begun to understand his own funky heritage. The potential for a grand metaphor where Dr. Funkenstein represents black culture and Sir Nose D'Voidoffunk represents white culture was not lost on many maggots.

To be a part of the maggot subculture, one had to become conversant with, and psychologically embrace, this cosmology. At the same time as this cosmology was being articulated on vinyl, the collective entity, variously known as a Parliafunkadelicment Thang, the P-Funk All-Stars, and the Funk Mob, began to stage elaborate two-and-a-half-hour hi-tech spectacles involving spaceships, pyramids, and the like that were metaphorically light years beyond anything previously experienced in the world of rhythm and blues.

Subcultural style is expressed in a number of ways that can be subsumed under three large categories: argot, demeanour, and image. Social actors select subcultural groups that provide attractive self-images. For would-be maggots, Parliament/Funkadelic presented radical alternatives to prevailing hegemonic ideas about image. The group's sartorial culture stood in sharp contrast to the r & b norm. Except for Sly and the Family Stone, which favoured hippie garb, r & b bands had traditionally dressed in matching uniforms that more often than not looked like dress suits. In marked contrast, the Funk Mob appeared onstage in fur, Cowboy and Indian gear, diapers, painted bed sheets, mop heads, Arab djellabas, Martian suits, and so on.

The P-Funk sign consisted of raised pointer and baby fingers. In the mainstream culture this gesture is commonly known as signifying "bullshit." Maggots embraced the gesture as conveying solidarity and, in so doing, turned the sign inside out on several levels: what was negative from the point of view of the hegemonic culture was celebrated by the maggots; and an attitude of recognition and cynicism was expressed toward the "bullshit" aspect of much of society.

Parliament/Funkadelic's demeanour was outside the norm in a variety of respects. The size of the ensemble on any given night would range from 13 to 17 musicians. Various members would trade off any number of instruments over the course of a performance,[1] and set lists were completely open and variable, being dictated by what was, in effect, the cosmic moment.[2]

By virtually any standards of arena rock and roll or rhythm and blues, this was anything but an ordered, predictable, smoothly running organization. On the contrary, it was chaos or entropy personified. One can easily advance the argument that such a presentation turns each night into an adventure of sorts for the musicians and consequently serves the needs of inspiration and creativity, counteracting the ennui of multiple nights on the road playing the same set in the same order with nary a hair out of place (which is the reality of artists as diverse as Pink Floyd, Ice Cube, and Metallica). All that is true, but even more importantly, the Parliament/Funkadelic mode of presentation also has ideological significance as a gesture of celebration. Parliament/Funkadelic's stage attitude, in both its visual and organizational modes, communicates at least four large-scale values: value is placed on the notion of a "rainbow nation" comprising a myriad number of personas; African-Americans are imaged as having the potential to be anything/anyone they want to be; differences are treated as things to be celebrated, not scorned; and craziness, play, and imagination are actively embraced as part of the celebration of life.

Not surprisingly, this creative and ideological use of entropy extends as well into the sonic and linguistic realms. Funkadelic's 1976 release "Let's Take It to the Stage" and Parliament's 1976 single "P-Funk (Wants to Get Funked Up)" provide a number of sample lyric lines that are worth singling out:

> Little Miss Muffet sat on a tuffet snorting some THC,
> Along came a spider, slid down beside her,
> Say what's in the bag, bitch?
> She said, "I'm laughin' at ya—Ha Ha!"
> ["Let's Take It to the Stage"]

If one uses information theory and interprets entropy as chaos resulting from the violation of pattern, that is exactly what has occurred here. Clinton regularly takes pop culture commonplaces of one or another mainstream and turns them on their head. Here he has redefined a hegemonic nursery rhyme within an oppositional frame of reference. Such a gesture is obviously deviant from the point of view of the hegemonic culture, but from the point of view of the maggot subculture, it is an empowering gesture and a patent example of appropriation reversal.

The same sort of process is occurring with phrases such as "Never fear McFunk is here" and "Say it loud—I'm funk and I'm proud." Both phrases are reflexive. The former contains references to the phrase "Never fear, McDuff is here" and to the McDonald's hamburger chain. The McDonald's reference connotes any number of attributes of and attitudes toward mass consumer culture, fast food, chains, and so on. "Say it loud—I'm funk and I'm proud" references James Brown's 1968 recording "Say It Loud—I'm Black and I'm Proud" and black militancy in general. Here, Clinton is valorizing Brown and positing P-Funk within the tradition that Brown epitomizes. If you do not know the original, you do not get the reference. Such linguistic gestures ultimately create difference and consequently distance between those who relate to the subversion or valorization of the pre-established code and those who do not.

To a similar end, P-Funk lyrics are rife with in-group jargon and inversions of "straight" logic. The following examples appear on either "Let's Take It to the Stage" or "P-Funk (Wants to Get Funked Up)": "New type thang," "post crazeo," "let's take it to the stage sucker," "Godfather, Godmother, Grandmother," "Snufus," "Slick and the Family Brick," "Fool and the Gang," "Earth, Hot Air and no Fire," "loose booty," "funk not only moves, it removes—dig?," "once upon a time called now," "I want the Bomb, I want the P-funk," "the desired effect is what you get when you improve your interplanetary funksmenship," and so on. All of these are reflexive within the world of rhythm and blues in general and the maggot subculture in particular and suggest both depth and tradition.

One of the finest examples of maggot logic can be found in the song "P-Funk (Wants to Get Funked Up)."

> Someone say is there funk after death?
> I say is 7-Up—Yeah!

Subversion is obviously occurring in examples such as these on the level of content, but it can also be argued that subversion or deviance is occurring on the level of logic. If one is equipped to understand these patterns, one can decode them on both content and logic levels and in so doing participate in the maggot subculture (even that term is an example of inverse meaning). Such constructions effectively shut out anyone who cannot decode the patterns. Such gestures are thus deliberately entropic/deviant for "outsiders."

Clinton also often articulated an explicit political agenda that would be labelled by some as deviant. An early Funkadelic album was titled *Free Your Mind and Your Ass Will Follow,* while the group's most successful chart single was 1978's "One Nation Under a Groove." Similarly, a popular P-Funk chant was "Think, it ain't illegal yet," and more recently Clinton has issued solo material that incriminates the CIA in drug dealing and suggests painting the White House black. Examples abound within the P-Funk canon. In the height of the disco boom Clinton dubbed the genre "the placebo syndrome"; "Cosmic Slop" approvingly portrayed a mother who turned to prostitution to feed her children. Deviant? Not to the maggots. Whether a subculture is ultimately viewed as positive or deviant is clearly simply a function of the given subculture's distance from the norms of the dominant culture.

The same sort of entropic logic (i.e., chaos resulting from *deviation* from understood and consequently expected norms) occurs on the sonic level. Just as the "Little Miss Muffet" nursery rhyme is appropriated, satirized, and inverted linguistically in "Let's Take It to the Stage," "Mary Had a Little Lamb" is inverted sonically on 1978's "Aqua Boogie." Further, Parliament will often play a three-strophe song and over time begin to play two or even all three strophes simultaneously. The following structure chart of the group's 1976 hit "Tear the Roof Off the Sucker (Give Up the Funk)" provides a number of examples of two sections being played singly and then later combined.

Section	I A C B A C B D A/C C C/D C C C/D C/D C C B A C
Bar length	8 8 8 8 8 8 8 4 8 8 8 8 4 8 8 8 4 8 8 4

Similarly, polytextuality is often employed, where two and occasionally three texts are sung simultaneously. As well, over the course of a performance keyboardist Bernie Worrell commonly plays lines that move further and further outside the song's rhythmic groove, textural norm, and tonal centre.

Ultimately, subcultures do the following: give ideology and form to "deviancy"; provide imagery that alters an individual's self-image; and create a community where individual social actors identify with immediate others and with distant, abstractly generalized others. The maggot subculture as created by P-Funk does all of this. In the case of Parliament/Funkadelic and their audience, solidarity is created through a number of homologies that embrace Clinton's overall concept/cosmology, performance practices, lyrics, and sonic gestures. The combined effect of all of this is to express an aesthetic of spontaneity, circularity, and constant multiple activities. For those mired in the hegemonic value system, this aesthetic adds up to chaos, entropy, or deviancy in its full glory. As such it creates a very real barrier or boundary between those who are "maggots," who are down with the funk, and those who just don't get it. The foregoing might go a long way toward explaining why between 1969 and 1981 Funkadelic could place 19 records on the r & b charts but only one on the pop Top 50; why between 1974 and 1980 Parliament could place a further 19 records on the r & b Top 20 but only two on the pop Top 50; and why between 1982 and 1986 the P-Funk All-Stars and George Clinton combined hit the r & b charts 13 times without ever reaching the pop Top 100. Entropy, as embraced by the Funk Mob, served as an ideological signifier of "deviancy" and deliberately left much of the pop culture audience in the dark. To be a maggot meant accepting and embracing funk as a cultural system that provided a coherent alternative set of values and way of life.

All of the above raises the much-debated issue as to whether a subculture "mediated" by the corporate and very hegemonic entertainment industry can be in any way oppositional. The argument has been advanced that such subcultural activity, by allowing small-scale expressions of rebellion, is actually serving as a safety value in the service of the hegemonic system.

I do not think the situation is that simple. The maggot subculture as created and fostered by Parliament/Funkadelic obviously did not create a large-scale revolution that fundamentally changed the society within which its adherents live. It did, though, have the potential on the individual, grass-roots level to provide an alternative/deviant perspective with regard to the symbolic universe. As such, it potentially provided the mental means for any number of social actors to make decisions that fundamentally affected the quality of their lives (quality here is used in a nonvalue-laden fashion). In this way, said social actors were, at least in a limited sense, freed from hegemonic ideology. That is oppositional and of great value. On perhaps a less permanent but certainly more massive level, the maggot subculture provided one avenue of coping with a hegemonically defined world that severely marginalized many young people. The importance of that function should not be underestimated.

Notes

1. In October 1989 I attended performances of the band in New York and Toronto held four days apart. Over the course of those four days three band members changed, a background vocalist in New York played bass in Toronto, the bass player played guitar, a rhythm guitar player took over lead chores, a saxophone player became a vocalist and MC, and so on. In both performances, various musicians played several different instruments at different points in the show.

2. I also saw the band in Cleveland in October 1989. As usual the set was different from any of the other shows I saw that year. What was particularly interesting about Cleveland was the way the show began. The group, as usual, was slow to take the stage. When it did finally appear, various members slowly made their way to the stage in no organized or predetermined manner, each picking up his or her instrument and beginning to play prior to the rest of the band appearing. That night a cadre of impatient fans began the chant from "Tear the Roof Off the Sucker (Give Up the Funk)." This song is normally reserved for a climactic part of the show. On this occasion the chant was taken up by most of the audience and maintained over about 15 minutes before the first member of the group ambled onto the stage. One by one, the members finally picked up their instruments, and

each began playing his or her parts of "Tear the Roof Off the Sucker." The effect was magical, bonding the band and maggot subculture in an intense fashion from the word go.

References

Klapp, Orrin. 1973. *Models of Social Order: An Introduction to Sociological Theory.* Toronto: National Press Books.

Small, Christopher. 1988. *Music of the Common Tongue.*

CHAPTER 7

In Cultural Limbo: Adolescent Aboriginals in the Urban Life-World

R.S. Ratner
University of British Columbia

As we approach the new millennium, we in Canada must take pride in the fact that the United Nations has designated us as the most liveable country in the world. Need we listen to the criticisms of those who would advise us, "Tell that to the Indians"? Yet it is one of the regrettable truths of this country's history that almost nowhere in Canada is it easy to live and die as an "Indian." Endless hearings, commissions, and reports crank up our collective guilt about the plight of native people in Canada; media accounts of child suicide, fetal alcohol syndrome, and native overrepresentation in penitentiaries threaten to awaken happily forgotten memories.

There are over a million Aboriginals in this country, and most of them are in bad shape. This is not to say that no Aboriginals are doing well; but whether on reserves or in cities, a shockingly high number are stupefied by drink, suffering or inflicting sexual abuse, selling themselves to obtain drugs, or lining up meekly to collect welfare checks instead of proclaiming their discontent. There are occasional outbursts, such as Oka, and political battles are being waged around native rights and land claims; even so, the number of Aboriginals sunk in a miasma of defeat and resignation is appalling considering the richness of this country and the paradoxically desperate condition of its first stewards.

Why does this dreadful situation exist in an age when awareness of wrongs can be easily publicized to induce contrition and compel redress? Perhaps we have inured ourselves to sorrow or have been immobilized by too much disturbing information. The problems may seem too massive to countenance, too severe to remedy. But if that is the case, *why* is it the case?

We need to step back from the countless reports and statistics. Enough data have already been collected, and we need have no quarrel with the pungency of existing accounts.[1] Instead, let us try to consider the problem through an analytic lens wide enough to reveal its enormity. I have in mind the theory of contemporary society developed by Jurgen Habermas in the second volume of *The Theory of Communicative Action* (1987). I will utilize this framework in relation to the experiences of urban Aboriginal youth, whose problems as an underclass are tragically easy to see.

✳ System and Life-World

One way of understanding the perilous conditions of Aboriginals in Canada, whether in cities or on reserves, is through Habermas's conceptualization of system processes and life-world. For Habermas, a second-generation Frankfurt School theorist, the legitimation problems of late capitalist societies were structural in nature and largely attributable to the absence of linkage between societal macro-institutions and the micro-interactional social order—that is, to the "uncoupling" of the life-world and system processes and the "colonization" of the former by the latter (Habermas 1987:Ch. 2).[2] In this formulation, life-world represents the everyday perspective of subjects and serves as the "context-forming background of processes of reaching understanding" through communicative action (1987:204). "System" refers to the functional interconnectedness of actions. It has its roots in the life-world, but develops its own structural characteristics sedimented in political and economic orders (state and economy). Ideally, the instrumental or formal rationality of the system processes complements the substantive or communicative rationality of the life-world, so that what people do and think in their everyday lives is congruent with system imperatives. Habermas argues, however, that as the impersonal steering mechanisms of money and power spread through the whole society, instrumental (means/ends) rationality comes to dominate all interactions, distorting and misrepresenting people's needs and normative expectations, thus "colonizing" the life-world. In Habermas's view, this outcome is fundamentally dissatisfying; however, resistance is not automatic, so it is the task of critical theory to document and expose how system processes have operated to colonize the life-world and thwart the potentially superior rationality inherent in the speech acts of communicative action. The solution, according to Habermas, lies in reconstructing the social order in less oppressive ways by stimulating "rational discourse" and thus rebalancing relations between life-world and system. This, in turn, calls for a revitalization of the "public sphere" through observance of an "ideal speech situation" in which actors possess all the relevant background knowledge and linguistic skills to communicate without distortion. Thus, through uncoerced dialogue, actors openly reconcile their differences and produce a more communicatively rationalized life-world that is able to amend system excesses.

Habermas's analysis of contemporary capitalist society invoked considerable interest and criticism. While much of his analysis identifies historical forces that undoubtedly hindered the expression of human freedom, there are questions about whether Habermas exaggerated the passivity of the public response to the media; there is also scepticism about whether all significant criticism has been suppressed in industrial societies, and doubt as to whether explicitly "rational" legitimations are necessary to sustain late capitalist society. Does the capitalist life-world truly fail to generate intersubjectivity in the context of system processes dominated by impersonal media of money and power? And do Habermas's expectations for the public sphere constitute a naive romanticism, given that his "ideal speech situation" is rarely attained in complex human affairs? Habermas defended his "project of modernity" as an unfinished task of the Enlightenment, containing unfulfilled emancipatory potential.

How do I contend that Habermas's analysis is relevant to the cultural impasse faced by Aboriginals in this country? Crudely, the Aboriginals' plight can be understood in terms of their chronic inability to access system processes and the impoverishment of their life-world. While degrees of malintegration exist for other ethnic and racial groups in Canada, and even for members of dominant groups to some extent, the "uncoupling" phenomenon is particularly acute for Aboriginals since ghettoization, either in cities or on reserves, isolates them from a supportive material base. Lacking institutional stability, Aboriginals also then experience a disintegration of life-world. The resulting motivational dilemmas are obvious. The question is whether they are without remedy, as many in this country seem to think. This predicament can be better understood by examining the daily experience of Aboriginal adolescents (primarily 12 to 18 years old) in the downtown core of Vancouver, British Columbia.

✸ The Vancouver Study

In 1989, I was commissioned by the United Native Nations, an Aboriginal urban advocacy group for nonstatus, off-reserve Native Indians and Métis, to report on the need for child welfare services in the Vancouver Aboriginal community.[3] The monograph that resulted was followed by research on the problem of native youth delinquency, an apparent extension of the lack of adequate and effective child welfare services for native children. The sequel study drew upon two main bodies of information: lengthy interviews with 80 professional and auxiliary staff working with various agencies servicing native youth in Vancouver,[4] and interviews with 50 native youths at five school or community centre sites who were known by their supervisors/teachers to have had some contact (or trouble) with the law.[5]

Interviews with agency staff revealed there were roughly 6,000 native youths living in Vancouver.[6] About half of this number were said to be "problematic," and at least 200 of them were regarded as "hard core" street kids "wandering somewhere" though officially living with relatives or in foster care. Many of the at-risk youths are reserve runaways, 12 years old and up, coming into the city from every reserve and band in western and northern Canada; often they are running from multiple abuses on the reserves and searching for cheap accommodation in the Downtown East Side area of the city, where substandard housing is concentrated and weakly regulated. Most of the reserve émigrés chose to flee the reserve and entertain dreamy expectations of the future—expectations that are quickly dashed, given that they lack work skills transferable to the urban area. Girls turn to prostitution and shoplifting; boys to car theft, stealing, and running drugs. Immersion in alcohol, sex, and drugs (often from the age of 12) ensures school failure, joblessness, and chronic welfare dependency. The predictable sequence for native youths caught in this spiral begins with entry into the child welfare system, advances to more serious delinquencies as the youths "rise" through the criminal justice system, and ends with a slow weaning off the latter, accompanied by burnout and apathy. Thus, the study of native youth delinquency epitomizes, with special poignancy, the obstacles to cultural regeneration faced by off-reserve Aboriginals. These adolescents languish in cultural hollows that reflect genocidal conditions that are continuous with the earlier assaults suffered by their parents and grandparents. They express their resignation in their specious embrace of "assimilation" as the logical alternative to native lifeways. Some of the youths we interviewed commented thusly on the relevance of native culture:

Lana (16): It's not really very interesting to me, even though I am a native. I'm not going to make use of it in my future.

Tanya (14): What the hell am I going to use my Indian background for? For nothing!

Joseph (16): I don't see how bein' native could help me out of trouble. Bein' native doesn't really help.

Mary (14): I don't go to powwows anymore 'cause they're boring and stupid.

Suzanne (13): The native language is mostly for the old people, and there aren't many old people left.

For those who come into the city from a reserve, lingering ambivalence induces some back-and-forth movement. Young teens often live with their mother in the city and with their grandparents on the reserve. The "big city lights" lure many, although the impetus to leave the reserves is usually cast in negative terms—the boredom of the reserve or the flight from sexual abuse.

Tanya (14): I want to get a good job ... and be rich ... and go shopping. The reserve is boring ... there's no shopping ... no nothing."

"Dominant culture" institutions—whether school or the courts—are perceived as authoritarian and alien, or regarded with brusque indifference:

Michelle (17): Things aren't that good at school. They kicked me out recently. I'm trying to get back in, but I think they don't want me there. I don't get along with the teachers. They're always telling me what to do.

As for the "fairness" of the court process which Michelle had recently undergone:

Well, I didn't think about it. I guess they were fair.

Charlie (15): The (non-native) students question anything you say about native cultures, native ways. We're nothing but "fuckin' chugs." They'll challenge anything you say about Indian culture.

On the ethnocentricity of white officialdom, Charlie added:

Politicians want to suppress the worth of the dignity of the pipe-carrier [Cree medicine man]. Then it will be suppressed in the people. They want you to learn *their* culture. This is the culture they've given us ... drugs and alcohol.

These responses, while not expressed by all the 50 youths whom we interviewed, evinced agreement that conventional institutions were irrelevant to processes of self-betterment. For many, the discovery of native identity was viewed as pivotal to personal change and development, although interesting differences marked their imaginings of this possibility. Some stressed, outright, the importance of acquiring native culture:

Mike (15): Yeah, it's important for the children. If they are to be the branches they have to know their roots. Before it's too late, before they go white ... like partying, drugs, boozing, wasting our lives. That's got nothin' to do with our background.

Benjamin (17): [Native culture and language] will help me learn about my family ... about before ... how it was a long time ago ... how they lived. You can't really learn it here in the city. I'm plannin' on movin' back [to the reserve] next year.

Others were less optimistic or deeply uncertain as to the value of learning about their native background. Many professed interest but were unable to define the purpose that such knowledge would serve:

Suzanne (13): I want to learn my language, but it's hard to do it being away from my grandparents. They speak the language all the time. It's just the old people that speak the language.

Dorothy (15): My grandpa talks to me. He tells me to be proud to be an Indian. He tells me, but I don't know this for sure ... he tells me that the Indians were the first ones in Canada ... but I don't know ... I just don't know.

Dennis (17): I wouldn't mind learning my own native tongue ... I guess. No, not really. Maybe, I don't know really. No, scratch that. I don't think it would actually help me.

A conspicuous strain of "High Plains" romanticism tinged the appeal of native culture for some of the youths in the sample:

Sonny (14): I'd like to be a drifter. Like, I'd like to drift into town ... like, give 'em wisdom ... drift out again.

A number of youths desired contact with elders on the reserve but were unable to say how this would help them. A few who skipped school to attend potlatches were unsure how their participation would benefit them personally.

Contrasting evaluations were made of the special native educational program offered at one of the high schools:

Christina (15): I feel like that's racism. They're always pushing the natives to one side at the schools ... putting all the natives in portables.

Roberta (14): I like the program here at Kumtuks. They help me solve my problems ... by talking to me ... by asking me what I want to do in my life.

Nearly all the youths who had participated in native enrichment programs felt comfortable in them and encouraged by them. The disturbing question, however, already occurring to students in these programs, was whether the knowledge they acquired would hamper or facilitate adjustment to the dominant system processes in which most of them would continue to function. Could they be more "Indian," yet legitimately garner the material rewards of the dominant culture?

The complexities of this cultural revitalization issue were a focus of the interviews with agency personnel. For Aboriginal youths and those trying to assist them, the world is full of complex riddles and painful choices.

✸ Bearable Options

Almost all of the 80 agency personnel interviewed in the Vancouver study cited "lack of identity" as central to the problems of Aboriginal youth. As one native educator and law student observed, "White kids think they're going from high school to college or into society. Indian kids think they're going to jail." Similarly, a native outreach worker noted: "The kids who are adopted out are afraid to identify with their native culture. They have no identity. They're not white—they're not Indian—they're nothing."

The school system has usually turned a bureaucratic blind eye to this identity gap, despite awareness that school activities seldom relate to anything that the native youth is doing at home.[7] Correctional "solutions" are equally shortsighted and fail to address the fundamental reality that socially based problems require *social* programs, not *control* programs.[8] But federal and provincial funding is almost never apportioned over the long term. As one correctional agency executive disclosed:

The provincial and federal governments sow disorganization or orchestrate chaos among the various Indian groups. If the [status and nonstatus] Indians could join forces, they would be extremely powerful. The governments know this, so they keep them apart, fighting over the dollar.

Even front-line social agencies contribute to the overall stagnation by turning into mere monitoring groups. As one frustrated street worker complained:

"We make the report, but is there anyone out there to do anything about it? You have to do something more than just identify the problem."

Many agency personnel now believe that the focus must turn to strengthening aboriginal heritage and identity in the urban setting, an approach that calls for new options aimed at the creation of a core native identity.[9] Such measures require the development of native role models and the inclusion of parents in programs with their children, since the identity problem of native youths is compounded by the fact that many nonstatus native parents are not eager for their children to be "native."[10] Moreover, for those youths raised off-reserve or in foster homes, the street life *is* their culture, so a native identity, though it be a gnawing void in their lives, is something they know little about except as a stigmatizing attribute. Also, native bands tend to take a sink-or-swim attitude toward youths who leave the reserves. Nonstatus Indians are written off by band leaders, and even off-reserve status Indians receive little help, since monies typically go to youths who stay on the reserve.

Within the social services, those assigned to managing the problems of Aboriginal youth arouse feelings of perpetual distrust. Most whites who work at the agencies (especially at the executive levels) reinforce the feeling among native clients that the systems are not user-friendly.[11] In this regard, simply increasing the number of trained professional and paraprofessional native personnel in the police, corrections, and social work agencies is a necessary first step in cultivating a native identity (notwithstanding the "Apple" label—red outside, white inside). Yet this alone cannot be enough, since the welfare and correctional systems are perceived by Aboriginals as extensions of white culture. More and more the idea is being advanced, even by waspish professionals, that natives must help natives and not expect whites to "fix" things.

But if native youths in the cities gravitate to dominant values, how can a native identity be fostered? The present tendency is for young people to live parasitically off the dominant culture, consuming its dubious benefits just as they had on the reserve. Still, the overwhelming majority of agency personnel insist that reconstructing native identity within the urban setting is the answer, and that this effort must begin quickly given the increased migration of native youth to the cities since the 1980s and the continuities developing between juvenile and adult patterns of native crime. Some native agency personnel stress the difficulty of revitalizing native cultural traditions in the city, and a few others maintain that "home is the reserve";[12] most, however, believe that "Indian-ness" may be the only route to self-esteem for urban native youth, and the only way to *prevent* "their feeling more comfortable as adults *in* jail than out." As one native respondent put it: "Without long-range visions, the kids can't see what their role would be as a young adult ... so they can't see how their delinquencies are incompatible with their future role as adults."And as one staff member of an urban native advocacy group truculently declared: "The sources of help need to be natives. The non-natives have had their chance. They blew it. We can do it on our own."

In sum, these agency workers visualize a whole panoply of social services that include "healing circles" and cultural, language, and skills development programs, but also instruction in the importance of observing dominant values when appropriate.[13] Romanticism is tempered by linking native cultural revival to adaptation in the urban milieu, by forcing recognition that some features of the native past cannot be carried into the present and, conversely, that some features of the dominant culture are also undeserving of support. Claims that native and white cultural values are incompatible are regarded by most agency personnel as premature or naive. Competitiveness, for example, is not seen as ruled out by the native stress on cooperation, since values of respect, courtesy, dependability, and honesty—esteemed in native cultures— ought not weaken the entrepreneurial spirit.[14] Indeed, Chief Len George of the Burrard Nation contends that the idea of the "hunt" can be reconceived as taking place in the city—organized around the motives of fending for self and family, followed by sharing with others, including the community in which the hunt occurs. As one native program developer put it:

> The assumption that the native Indian community is in conflict with the white materialistic community is dangerous. There are Indians who are entrepreneurs and individualistic, not just service providers. We shouldn't accept a stereotype that bunches us together in a particular way. We're all *individuals*, but we also have connections to our Indian roots.

Despite such affirmations, the question of whether native cultural enrichment would assist youths who remain in the city is not easily answered, though if adaptation depends upon the acquisition of a stable social identity, it is hard to imagine that it would not. In any such endeavour, the teaching of native cultural beliefs and language has a salient function. However, the possibility of establishing such programs is made less likely by the fact that the number of elders who can impart cultural knowledge is fast diminishing; moreover, such cultural teachers are often poorly paid. This is a reflection of the low regard many funding agencies have for their activities. As one elder observed:[15]

> There's a need for more funding. I've been teaching culture around here for years, and I don't really get paid by anybody ... but there's been a change in Vancouver since 1987. When I started a few years ago, there was nothing out there ... no cultural teachers, programs, and so on. Now they're cropping up all over the city. I'm still surviving on donations, but there's much less

opposition to what I'm doing, and a growing interest. It's heading in the right direction.

In sum, most of those whom we interviewed about the everyday experiences of native youth in the city argue that learning distinctively native values does not preclude adaptation to the urban milieu. On the contrary, native youths who acquire traditional values seem to gain self-esteem, improve their general sense of competency, adjust more effectively to the urban life-world, and enjoy a positive experience of their ancestral culture. Although the adjustment process is complex and involves a blending of values, it is believed that these cultural options can be meshed in a practical way.[16] Stubborn questions persist, however. In the next section of the chapter we return to Habermas's theoretical schema of system and life-world.

✳ Cultural Convergences

To recapitulate Habermas's thesis, reified social systems come to dominate the life-world, distorting communicative processes and vitiating the regenerative capacities of local communities. Ideally, system processes and life-world display *complementary* possibilities of rationalization, but in the actual history of capitalism, system forces overtake life-world, "pushing individuals to the fringes of completely reified systems" (Wellmer 1985:55). The counterbalancing effects of life-world traditions for preserving communicative rationality are gradually negated by systemic differentiation and the consequent decentring of world views (Giddens 1985:101). Thus, as Bohman (1989:391) notes:

> The imperatives of the increasingly independent systems begin to "colonize the lifeworld," taking over more and more of its integrative functions and producing "pathologies" (anomie, fragmentation of life, loss of meaning).

This disjuncture between system and life-world (or between material and symbolic reproduction) is extremely serious, given Habermas's insistence that systems must be anchored in the "institutional" base of the life-world. Not system, but life-world, therefore, is the more primary and encompassing order; but whether the failure to achieve balance between the two is attributable to system reification or to the passivity of life-world institutions, their differential force results in colonization of the life-world with deterioration of its inclusive "public spheres" and operative "validity claims." This is the fundamental problem underscored by critical theorists, and it is through reconstituting the life-world order that they believe a symbiotic relationship between system and life-world can be restored.

The crucial paradox in Habermas's analysis is that system differentiation yields *both* reification (which pathologizes communicative rationality) *and* societal evolution (which enables the further development of society and its institutional complex). Disruption of the life-world is regarded, therefore, as an unavoidable consequence of the emergence of modern society. While the pathological effects of "colonization" can lead to a complete detachment of system from life-world, rebalancing attempts are more likely so long as system processes generate the material foundation for institutional recomposition within the life-world. We may say that, up till now, and for most members of advanced capitalist society, system processes have managed to wrest legitimation from within its boundary domains. But the crises of "late capitalism" now present serious challenges to the manageability of system life-world relations, and, for some, the experience of deep disjuncture between system and life-world is familiar and ongoing. Returning to our empirical focus, the problems of urban Aboriginal youth demonstrate the potency of that rupture.

Many poignant accounts underline the fact that Aboriginal reserves, bereft of resources or the capital necessary to exploit resources, cannot sustain viable life-worlds; thus, the youths who flee to the city arrive with few cultural roots, low self-esteem, and considerable self-hate. Whether émigrés or city-born, they find themselves enmeshed in a system methodically geared to pulverize native identity, history, and culture. One might suppose that an institutional base in native traditions and values would provide a springboard from which native youth could acquire the cultural stability and personal resources to adjust to the urban setting. But the obstacles to such a reclamation of heritage are numerous: the "good riddance" attitude of bands conforming to the government-imposed status/nonstatus distinction; the "control" policies of the white justice sector, where, in the words of one native agency worker, "Kids just get hardened and come out [of jails and remand centres] intending to 'fuck society'"; the linguistic and cultural barriers between the different tribal groups in the city that prevent a shared native identification; the ready access to hard drugs in the downtown core;[17] the internalized prejudice of native youths against their own Indian identity; and, not least, the lack of coordination between federal, provincial, and municipal support agencies, which along with the predictable funding rivalries between local native organizations, ensures that the welfare of natives in the city never rises to the level where natives can fend for themselves.

In the midst of all this and more, can we even speculate as to what revitalization of what "public sphere" will restore native life-world? Will powwows, healing circles, potlatches, sweatlodges, and so on do the trick?

How can native youths in the city be encouraged to *seek out* traditional values? And *who* will transmit these values, given that most of the elders were of the residential school generation and had little chance to learn much of their own culture?[18]

Difficult as it is to identify starting points, some of the agency and support staff urge a rediscovery of the extended family—displaced as it is from the reserves—as one key area in which to commence the rebuilding of a public sphere. As one native youthworker put it:

> Today, it's no longer "bad" to be regarded as an Indian, but now we have to learn the ways ... get to know the "family tree," and maintain contact. The second generation of city natives is now trying to acquire the information they need to pass on to their children ... it's on the upswing.

The appeal of traditional and communitarian values, however, can ring hollow to native youth, given that these values are associated with the reserves, which boast little economic power. If commodity consumption is the aim, manipulating the urban system via Skid Row "vacations" (cheap accommodation and fast welfare checks) makes more sense to many native émigrés than storytelling and vision quests. The drift into an urban "underclass" and the subsequent crimes of misdirected vengeance may induce regrets, but even at this stage the reserve scenario cannot compete. Why gravitate to native values, which are likely only to interfere with the slim possibilities for success in the dominant "system" or to inhibit gratification in the transient pleasures of the urban life-world?[19] On this score, many of the native agency workers deny any necessary antagonism between native and white cultural values; they choose instead to highlight their convergent aspects. One native support worker argued that it was possible to "take the best of two worlds and live in the mainstream ... integration, not assimilation ... there's no need to go back to the reserves in order to be Indian." Others stressed that native values of sharing and strong extended family ties were worthy of incorporation in the dominant culture; that a collective rather than an individualistic competitive spirit could foster excellence and adaptability; that competition need not be stifled by spirituality; and that native values could help to slow down the maniacal push to achieve, *without* undermining productivity. All of these suggestions acknowledged the dominance of capitalist economic relations yet enjoined their amalgamation with native values. A native child-care worker expressed this viewpoint eloquently:

> I once heard an elder say, "There will never be the good old days, but the new ways can be good." We can't go back to hunting in the bushes, but you can

use the educational system as your hunting grounds. The food on your table is not what you killed in the bushes, but your bread and butter can be paid for by your accomplishment. It's important to let your conscience be your guide. Take the best from both worlds ... manipulate it in such a way that you're not hurting anybody ... that you're not being selfish ... that if you get something, you share it with your brothers and sisters. If it feels good, then that's what you need to do to succeed. You can be kind and gentle, but you can't be passive. You need to be assertive, but not aggressive. Treat people the way you want to be treated. Know both cultures and then combine them as you wish.

This theme of cultural convergence was a steady refrain in the thoughts of many of the native agency workers. Was it incredulously synthetic, pious, or hypocritical? Not, I believe, in their eyes. But relatively few of the native youths whom we interviewed were nearly so articulate or affirmative about linking native and white values as a means of living with hope and self-respect in the urban milieu. One wonders if it is simply a matter of *instilling* those values in order to impel an ideal adjustment, or whether the alleged predominance of system over life-world causes a debasement of communicative rationality that is impossible to forestall.

✳ Conclusions

What are the prospects, then, for creating a "public sphere" in which the problems underlying native youth delinquency in the city can be properly addressed? As implied throughout this paper, the priorities accorded to market and state suppress communicative rationality in the life-world experiences of these cultural vagabonds in their travels between city and reserve. Government ministries, battling over their budgetary allotments, engage in proprietary or "turf" wars in which, as one native agency worker put it, "The kids disappear between the cracks." Moreover, government economic priorities rule out the long-term planning that would be necessary for native cultural regeneration in the sprawling urban context. Consequently, native urban groups are left to compete over short-term funding and fail to develop the cooperative agenda that is vital to securing progressive change.[20] Band leaders, as noted earlier, are generally unwilling to cooperate with native urban groups, given their preoccupation with land claims and their conviction that economic independence is the only sure route to a restoration of native culture and pride. Opportunism, irony, and pathos do not deflect these leaders from their singular goal—more than 20 Indian groups in British Columbia plan to build or operate casinos as a lever to economic development.[21] Compunctions about profiteering and commercialism are balanced against the assumption that native revivalism (city or reserve) will not occur unless the reserves become bastions of economic power, even if this means replicating the morally dubious entrepreneurial initiatives of white society.

This drive for autonomy is spurred, too, by awareness of government efforts to blunt the momentum toward Aboriginal sovereignty, as exemplified by the recruitment of urban natives into the various state agencies—an ostensibly humane but latently "neocolonialist" tactic that further casts the identity and destiny of native Indians in the image of the dominant Euro-Canadian society.[22]

Against these contradictions, Aboriginal youths must consider whether to endure the degradation of living on in the city without creditable cultural roots (white or native); or to return to the reserves and experience the trauma of reverse cultural shock; or to make themselves available to the cultural bridging efforts slowly emerging in the native advocacy network. The latter option, should it continue to develop, would involve a long, trying process requiring exceptional individual tenacity and social supports—assets not now in abundance in the native urban milieu. Yet it may be preferable to the cultural limbo in which the great majority of urban native youths are now dangling. But to conceive of this third option is to take us back to the question of the alterability of system processes. Are the system mechanisms (visible in the ubiquitous media of money and power) unalterable and cut off from the agency of the life-world? Can the system be transformed by the growth of new self-reflective institutions in the life-world?[23] To argue that it cannot accepts, as Bohman (1989:399) observes, "an unwarranted totalizing view of systems and of their influence on the new possibilities for political life."

So the quandary of urban Aboriginal youth poses a much larger challenge than might have been originally supposed. It raises the question of whether we can devise more effective public spheres that will facilitate new courses of rationalization enabling a different relationship between system and life-world. Is there a dialogical "healing circle" that we can all enter in order to overcome the limits of our system-order so that native and "mainstream" values can enliven the same terrain? If we believe that systems cannot exist without actors who *will* them into being, then from the recesses of our life-worlds, we must answer in the affirmative and act accordingly.

Notes

1. For a particularly thorough and recent study comparing the Aboriginal inner-city experience in four Canadian metropolises, see La Prairie (1994). On the current situation in British Columbia, see also the backgrounder report issued by the Inter-Governmental Relations Division of the Office of the Premier, *Untangling the Social Safety Net for Aboriginal Peoples* (Mears 1994).

2. As well as Habermas's own discussion of system and life-world, I am relying on the summary accounts provided by Jonathan Turner, 1991, Ch. 3, pp. 254–281, and George Ritzer, 1992, Ch. 8, pp. 289–293, and Ch. 15, pp. 582–588. For a trenchant critique of Habermas's system and life-world concepts, see Bohman (1989).

3. See *Child Welfare Services for Urban Native Indians*, R.S. Ratner, December 1991 (Report commissioned by the United Native Nations).

4. This cross-sectional "snowball" sample includes social work and employment counsellors, correctional officers and administrators, lawyers, doctors, teachers, judges, community centre directors, city planners, nurses, psychologists, housing officials, native police liaison officers, Aboriginal chiefs of local reserves, native court worker counsellors, street workers, crisis intervention counsellors, ministry officials, band social workers, cultural revitalization teachers, and directors of various native-specific programs. Questions put to interviewees explored dimensions of the delinquency problem, including types and prevalence of native delinquencies, gang formation, continuities with child-welfare problems and with adult criminality, problems of discriminatory enforcement and culture conflict, impact of the Young Offenders Act, differential experience of status and nonstatus Indians, assessment of existing rehabilitative programs and outcomes, needed interventions, availability of funding and other resources, and native/white cultural convergence and dualisms. Obviously, it is possible to present only a selected portion of the research findings in this account.

5. The sample of 50 native youths included 29 males and 21 females; 24 were between the ages of 13 and 15, and 26 between the ages of 16 and 18. Interview sites were located at three community centres (18), an outreach alternative school (14), and a native education program located in portables of a secondary school (18). Interview questions focused on troubles with the law, difficulties in the transition from reserve to city life, problems with the police and courts, ambitions/aspirations/life plans, supports required to stay out of trouble with the law, problems of native identity and of augmenting knowledge of background/heritage, and the likelihood of committing adult criminal offences and going to jail. (I am grateful for the assistance of Keith Giauque, who conducted these interviews under my supervision.)

6. This brief description of the delinquent youth sample is paraphrased from my 1995 account.

7. Frank acknowledgment of this problem is reflected in the very recent proposal to establish a separate high school for native youth in Vancouver—an innovation likely to solve some problems and create others.

8. For example, the second level of deviantizing labels that comes with breaches of probation orders, a fairly predictable violation since many native youths are not raised to believe that punctuality has very great value.

9. At the same time, the expansion of a core identity must pay heed to the cultural differences between the 27 tribal groups in British Columbia, many of them represented in the downtown area.

10. It follows that many of the native youth also prefer not to be identified as Indian.

11. Indeed, many natives refuse to use the services provided for them.

12. Certainly, the settlement of land claims may eventually provide an alternative for urban Aboriginals since it would be impossible for them to return to strengthened reserves. For now, however, the housing shortage on reserves acts as a discouragement, even for those considering repatriation under Bill C-31.

13. In this regard, a native police liaison officer remarked that "there are some cultural differences that may be hard to change, especially the emphasis on time. In the old days, a powwow didn't start until the last person arrived ... some of those who got there earlier could be waiting for days. Lots of Indians today don't bother to wear watches. I know of several who have lost jobs because they couldn't get to work on time."

14. In an interesting aside, one community centre programmer commented that the "culture" of native youths who do drugs involves a sharing, generosity, and bartering that in perverted form revives some of the native cultural traditions and offers a deviant way of building a positive self-image when conventional employment opportunities are scarce or nonexistent.

15. This man, known as War Dance, was a venerated elder who stationed himself at the downtown Carnegie Community Centre. I bought him lunch and conducted the interview at a nearby Chinese restaurant. Before the proprietor would allow him to dine at his establishment, I had to pay for the meal in advance.

16. As one native court worker intoned, "From my own personal opinion, the culture conflict argument is bullshit. In a lot of cases, our native Indian laws are parallel to white laws. Some of the punishments meted out by native Indian tribunals would actually be more harsh. The kids *do* know that they're doing *wrong*. Crimes like auto theft and possession of stolen property are sociopathic behaviour ... period! Breaking and entering is not acceptable behaviour, whether you're in the village or the city. Children are taught the same fundamental rules on the reserves.

Soliciting by young girls is not acceptable in the Indian culture. Repeat offences are repeat offences."

17. Cocaine use in downtown Vancouver is estimated to have quadrupled over the past decade.

18. To this a native counsellor tersely replied, "If there's a will to learn, the knowledge can be found."

19. For comparisons of value differences between whites and natives, see Reed (1990:13) and Frideres (1988:269). A white Vancouver lawyer who represents native youths in court offers a rather categorical answer to this question: "The native Indian values won't add to their confusion. The adoption of white values has been a dismal catastrophe. Few native Indians have been assimilated and successful. It's been a complete failure to adapt to a white perspective. The native Indian values are coming in to fill a vacuum. Their own heritage would be a viable option. It would give them a sense of pride."

20. In 1989 an overview native organization—U.R.B.A.N. (Urban Representative Body of Aboriginal Nations Society)—encompassing over 50 native groups in the Greater Vancouver Area, was created in order to rationalize funding priorities and develop a common agenda. This coordinative body was beleaguered, however, by the chronic opportunism of its member-groups and by suspicions that it was affiliated more strongly with *one* of the charter members of U.R.B.A.N.

21. In British Columbia, 150 tribal or ban chiefs are furious about the provincial government's withdrawal from the negotiations on gaming policy on the reserves. The government argues that it will not accede to the licensing of major casinos ("Las Vegas-style") anywhere in the province (*Vancouver Sun*, May 13, 1994:B4).

22. In the past 20 years, a host of native paraprofessionals have sprung up: these include native foster parents, native police and prison liaisons, native court workers and counsellors, native outreach workers, and native cultural enrichment workers. These positions are usually short-term, poorly paid, and involve minimum training. They have not augmented the precious few native doctors, lawyers, and teachers. (On this point, see Frideres's discussion of "accommodation service organizations" (1985:276–280).

23. Wellmer writes: "It is precisely in this sense that Habermas reinterprets Marx's idea of an emancipated society: in an emancipated society the life-world would no longer be subjected to the imperatives of system maintenance; a rationalized life-world would rather subject the systemic mechanisms to the needs of the associated individuals. Only then, to put it in Marx's terms, would the dependence of the 'superstructure' on the 'base'—i.e., the dependence of the life-world on the system—come to an end" (1985:57).

References

Bohman, James. 1989. "'System' and 'Lifeworld': Habermas and the Problem of Holism." *Philosophy and Social Criticism* 15 (4):381–397.

Frideres, James S. 1988. "Native Urbanization." Pp. 257–280, in *Native Peoples in Canada*, Fourth Edition. Scarborough: Prentice Hall.

Giddens, Anthony. 1985. "Reason Without Revolution." Pp. 85–121 in *Habermas and Modernity*, Richard J. Bernstein (ed.). Cambridge, U.K.: Polity Press.

Habermas, Jurgen. 1987. *The Theory of Communicative Action*, Vol. 2. Boston: Beacon Press.

La Prairie, Carol. 1994. *Seen But Not Heard: Native People in the Inner City*, Reports #1–3, Aboriginal Justice Directorate. Ottawa: Department of Justice.

Ratner, R.S. 1991. *Child Welfare Services for Urban Native Indians*. Vancouver: United Native Nations.

———. 1995. "Drift, Delinquency, and Destiny." Pp. 332–340 in *Canadian Délinquency*, James H. Creechan and Robert A. Silverman (eds.). Scarborough: Prentice Hall.

Reed, Little Rock. 1990. "Rehabilitation: Contrasting Cultural Perspectives and the Imposition of Church and State." *Journal of Prisoners on Prisons* 2(2): 3–28.

Ritzer, George. 1992. *Sociological Theory*, Third Edition. New York: McGraw-Hill.

Turner, Jonathan. 1991. *The Structure of Sociological Theory*, Fifth Edition. Belmont, CA: Wadsworth Press.

Wellmer, Albrecht. 1985. "Reason, Utopia and the 'Dialectic of Enlightenment.'" Pp. 35–66 in *Habermas and Modernity*, Richard Bernstein (ed.). Cambridge, U.K.: Polity Press.

Bad Girls in Hard Times: Canadian Female Juvenile Offenders

Ann Duffy

Brock University

Can you imagine a world without men?
No crime and lots of happy fat women.
[Marion Smith, in Rimler 1993:109]

For many, female crime is a paradox. Women are socially idealized as passive, nonaggressive, and vulnerable—more likely to be victims than victimizers. Since men commit almost all crimes, female criminals are virtually forgotten. Within this societal framework, it is unthinkable that a young woman would intentionally kill her children, become a serial killer, or rob banks. The public furor that arises when such acts do take place reveals both the deeply felt social values that are being challenged and the enduring social commitment to a gendered reality.

Until very recently, this gendered perspective dominated traditional crimi-nology and blinkered criminologists. Women were essentially absent from research on crime and criminals. The few women who might warrant attention were dismissed as freaks and aberrations or as women led astray by their love for a bad man.

Since the 1960s, with the movement of increasing numbers of women scholars into the social sciences and with the massive social changes accompa-nying the contemporary women's liberation movement, this conception of women and crime has been steadily eroded. Indeed by the 1980s, there was a surprising about-face; some American analysts were calling attention to the "dramatic" increases in female arrests and speculating on whether women's liberation was triggering a "female crime wave" (Deming 1977). Today, researchers still complain about the lack of scholarly attention to female criminality, and most work still focuses on women as victims; however, there is now a growing body of research and an emergent feminist criminology (Smart 1976; Daly and Chesney-Lind 1991; Culliver 1993; Hatch and Faith 1989–90).

The new scholarship has not just brought women into its focus—it is examining how criminal behaviour reflects and reinforces the gendered nature of western societies. Deviance is rooted in societal conceptions of masculinity and femininity and in a patriarchal tradition. The kinds of crimes people commit, the weapons they use, and the reactions of the predominantly male police and judiciary are not gender neutral. For example, as Edwin Schur points out, our culture and its agencies have long been preoccupied with controlling female sexuality. While boys and men are assumed to "sow wild oats," women are expected to contain their sexuality within marriage and other long-term relationships. The criminalization of prostitution, abortion, and birth control, and the prosecution of prostitutes (but not their clients), are historical examples of this type of gender script (1984:220–221). These patriarchal traditions are seen today in society's continuing preoccupation with the sexual misbehaviours of female juvenile offenders.

These insights into the gendered nature of crime and deviance have combined with critical perspectives in criminology to shake the foundations of the discipline. Crime, policing, and the justice system are revealed not as neutral moral arbiters but as well-socialized reflections of the social power structure. Women's crime is socially constructed, rooted in women's social roles; influenced by the differences of class, race, age, (dis)ability, and sexual orientation; and embedded in women's relative powerlessness. Traditional theories of criminology, based upon male experience and male-oriented research, cannot adequately explain either women's involvement in crime (the generalizability problem) or their relative nonparticipation (the gender ratio problem) (Daly and Chesney-Lind 1991:412). In including women, we must find new ways of looking at the nature and origins of deviant behaviour. While the task of unravelling the role of gender and other differences of power is enormous, we will not understand crime and violence unless we make the effort (Messerschmidt 1993).

✳ The Female Juvenile Offender in Canada

The societal expectation that women will be virtuous and law-abiding also extends to children. Children, because of their physical limitations, are often assumed to be incapable of serious crime and more in need of protection than social control. Recent public outrage at the actions of young children who killed other children mirrors these deeply held beliefs. When the two social identities—gender and youth—are combined, it is not surprising that young women or girls are seen as unlikely candidates for criminal or deviant behaviour.

Young women, however, have long figured in the official reports of delinquency and crime. For example, in 1889 the mayor of Toronto reported that about 1,000 girls and boys were brought before the courts each year, and police figures during a ten-month period in 1890 reveal that 537 boys and 32 girls under 15 were brought before Toronto magistrates (Houston 1982:134). Clearly, boys were disproportionately represented and were the major concern of the police and social reformers of the time. However, even during the Victorian era, girls and young women were also engaged in behaviour defined as illegal.

In a period of pronounced social inequality and uncertain employment, childhood was a markedly class-defined event. Children of the well-to-do attended school and were protected from the adult world; working-class and poor children struggled for food and shelter. In order to survive in the absence of a social welfare net, poor families often were forced to abandon their children for periods of time at orphanages, or to engage their children in child labour so that they too could contribute to the family resources (Bradbury 1982; Copp 1974). Predictably, abandoned children, children whose parents were working or ill, and children who felt pressured to contribute to the family coffers might engage in behaviour officially defined as criminal.

In a time of tremendous social and economic upheaval, as immigrants flocked to Canada and industrial capitalism struggled to its feet, there was much concern about social unrest and social control. Well-to-do citizens looked to the police and the judiciary to protect the social status quo and to weed out threats to middle-class mores. These threats included "young ruffians" who engaged in petty theft, or who were transients and hung about in "gangs," getting into "mischief." Needless to say, police action was demanded for such direct threats to the Protestant ethic and property rights.

The crimes of women and girls were different. While they might steal and loiter, their more likely misbehaviours were against their sex. Typically, bad girls were girls caught rejecting traditional sexual mores by engaging in prostitution, by having illegitimate children, and by procuring or providing abortions.

Much of the social reform literature of the 1880s was devoted to warning young women of the perils of the white slave trade (prostitution). The first travellers' aid societies were established to protect young women, when away from home, from the designs of unscrupulous men. Similarly, young women were placed in reformatories and other institutions to ensure their chastity and purity until marriage (Schur 1984:222–223; Schissel 1993:11; Hatch and Faith 1989–90:443).

For a young woman from the working class, particularly if she was orphaned, or abandoned, or from a single-parent family, the constraints of Victorian femininity were often unrealistic. When she was fortunate enough to obtain employment, she often found that her low wages meant she must choose between hunger, homelessness, or part-time prostitution. Periods of unemployment left many young women with no alternative to the latter. Ironically, women with any aspirations for independence and success often discovered that the local madams were typically the only independently successful women around (Katz 1975).

It is perhaps surprising that so many of these early trends—the disproportionate male role in juvenile delinquency, the gendered nature of young women's crime, the socioeconomic roots of deviance, and the sexualization of female juvenile delinquency—remain with us today. Despite the women's liberation movement, the sexual revolution, and the massive movement of women into paid employment, the basic parameters of female crime remain remarkably fixed.

In recent years, women have constituted about one-fifth (18 percent) of all youths charged by police with Criminal Code and other federal statute offences in Canada (Conway 1992; Leonard 1993; Lesti 1994). Young women, today as in the past, are much less likely to be charged by police than their male counterparts.[1] Also, the specific nature of youth crime is heavily gendered. Predictably, almost half the police charges against female youths involved theft under $1,000 (overwhelmingly shoplifting). The next largest categories of offences were minor assault[2] (9 percent), break and enter (7 percent), and bail violations (5 percent). While theft under $1,000 is very popular among male juvenile offenders (constituting 27 percent of charges), males are charged with a variety of offences that are relatively unpopular with female offenders, such as break and enter (21 percent of male charges) and motor vehicle theft (7 percent of male charges) (Conway, 1992:4).

In particular, violent offences by juveniles are heavily gendered. Although they inspire extensive media coverage, "serious" violent offences—homicide, attempted murder, abduction, and so on—constitute an extremely small (0.1 percent) portion of all juvenile crime (p. 5). "Less serious" violent offences, notably sexual assault, are generally monopolized by male offenders. Of all violent incidents cleared by the police in 1989, 90 percent involved males. Seventy-nine percent of those charged with a violent offence were adult males and 10 percent were male youths. Adult females accounted for 9 percent of violent suspects, female youths for a mere 2 percent. In Canada in 1989, 458 men, 57 women, 43 male youths, and only 5 female youths were charged with homicide (Frank 1991:6,7). When young women are charged with violent crime, it is most frequently for minor assault (level 1), a crime defined by the relative absence of violence (Conway 1992:4). The world of violent crime appears to continue to be a distinctly male world (Hatch and Faith 1989–90).

✹ Trends in Female Youth Offenders: Toward More Crime and Violence?

Clearly, the popular notion that youth crime is a male domain is firmly based in social reality. Recent media reports of "girl gangs" and violent female juvenile offences[3] have led some to wonder whether this pattern is changing. In light of changes in the status of women in society, the movement of women into the paid labour force, the breakdown of the traditional family, and so on, it is widely speculated that girls are catching up with their male counterparts in the area of juvenile delinquency. It is precisely this line of thinking that has led some analysts to argue for a gender convergence theory. According to this perspective, social and historical changes in the status of women, the advent of the women's movement, and the increased participation of women in the public domain mean that differences in male and female criminality rates are gradually disappearing.

There is some evidence[4] of shifts in the official statistics. From 1986 to 1990, the number of female youths charged by police increased by 29 percent, against only 14 percent for male youths. During this period, with the general aging of the Canadian population, the number of female youths in the population actually *decreased* by 2 percent (Conway 1992:1). These figures suggest that there has been an increase in female youth criminality, or that police, for whatever reasons, are more likely than before to lay charges against female juveniles, or both.

The overall patterns of juvenile delinquency noted above lend some support to gender convergence theory; however, other research contradicts it. For example, homicide patterns indicate that young men are still more likely than young women to engage in lifestyles that increase their chances of violent victimization. The particularly violent arenas of organized crime and drug dealing are still overwhelmingly male domains. In fact, there is some indication that young women in Canada are "rejecting a lifestyle that would possibly increase their likelihood of death by homicide" (Maxim and Keane 1992:341–342).

If there is a trend toward increased criminal behaviour by young women and/or increased likelihood of charges against young women by police, it involves relatively minor offences.[5] In 1990 about half of the offences that involved young women involved theft under $1,000 (most of these were shoplifting charges). The next most common offence was minor assault (level 1).[6] This category accounted for about one-tenth of offences by young women (Conway 1992:4). Between 1986 and 1990 there was a dramatic increase (128 percent) in the number of minor assault charges against young women. However, during the same period there was also an increase, although not as extreme, in the minor assault charges against young men (78 percent). Whatever the gender changes in juvenile offences, they appear to be complicatedly interwoven with other factors.

The complexity of gender patterns is evident, for example, in provincial differences in charge rates. Women constitute about one-fifth of all youths charged in Canada. However, they are about one-tenth of all youths charged in Quebec and Prince Edward Island, and almost one-quarter of youths charged in the Yukon. Indeed, the charge rate (number of females charged per 1,000 female youth population) was three times the national average in the Yukon and more than twice the national average in the Northwest Territories. Clearly, various social factors, notably the proportion of native people in the population, directly affect patterns of charging female offenders and/or patterns of female offences (Conway 1992). Note also that native women, although only 2.5 percent of the Canadian female population, make up almost one-fifth (18.9 percent) of women in federal correctional institutions (Hatch and Faith 1989–90:449).

A variety of research confirms that minority racial status, poverty, inner-city residence, and residence on a rural reserve all increase the likelihood that a girl will face charges (Reitsma-Street 1991b:253). For example, social class appears to play a pivotal role in rates of incarceration. Elliott Leyton (1986) found that the overwhelming majority of juveniles confined to East Coast training schools were "poor kids"; indeed, most were from the "stagnant bottom" of society, and came from families that had long been locked into unemployment and welfare dependency. Clearly, gender identity intersects in a complex way with racial relations, attitudes toward social inequality, and patterns of social conflict.

Research based on self-reports of deviant behaviour reaffirms the inadequacy of present knowledge about rates of female youth offences. Not surprisingly, surveys that examine self-reports of criminal behaviour suggest that official crime statistics provide an extremely limited and class-biased representation of the "real" rates of illegal behaviour. Most girls in the general population engage in "at least one and usually more delinquencies" (Reitsma-Street 1991b:253; Tracy and Shelden 1992). Only a small minority of these instances ever enter the official record. Crime statistics seem to change more as a result of shifts in police attitudes, in the composition and size of police forces, and in the political climate as it affects police policies. It is by no means clear that statistical increases or decreases are helpful in pointing out trends in deviant behaviour in the general population.

☀ Explaining Female Youth Offenders

> The restricted powers of females in Western societies appear fundamental to understanding ... the epidemiology and etiology of female delinquency. [Reitsma-Street 1991b:269]

For decades, criminologists and social analysts have attempted to explain both the presence of female young offenders and how they differ from male offenders. Two fundamental questions are often asked: How do these young women differ from the majority (98 percent) of females who are (presumably) law-abiding? And how do these young women differ from offending males?

Needless to say, the literature on these issues has identified a wide variety of social, psychological, economic, familial, and peer-related factors. For example, Seydlitz argues from her research results that early adolescent female delinquency is more likely when girls "are expected to obey parents for whom they feel little affection" (1993:155). She argues that age, race, socioeconomic status, relationship to family, marital status, and history of abuse are key factors in determining whether offending behaviour will occur.

Theories that were popularized in explaining male delinquency have also been applied to females. Some analysts argue that patterns of differential association explain female delinquents; that is, these girls happen to become friends with deviants (girl gangs)[7] who both encourage them to engage in deviant behaviour and provide a group rationale for the offending acts. Others argue from a social control perspective that delinquent girls, because of the inadequacies of their family and community background, lack the social controls ("inner whips," etc.) that prevent delinquent behaviour in the law-abiding population.

Unfortunately, these various theoretical themes have not been very helpful in explaining female young offenders (Reitsma-Street 1991b:258). While they have identified important factors—poverty, domestic violence, poor friendships, and so on—they do not tell us why some girls from these backgrounds become delinquents while others do not, and why their patterns differ from those of their male counterparts. Certainly, much research reveals that female juvenile offenders are coming from childhoods that have been shattered by some combination of poverty, neglect, abandonment, and sexual and/or physical abuse. For example, studies of street prostitutes (male and female) show that the overwhelming majority are runaways. The families they have run away from typically are beset by problems such as "parental drinking, parental conflict, mental illness, spousal abuse and child physical or sexual abuse." A wide variety of research reports that female (and male) adolescent prostitutes are fleeing some form of childhood sexual abuse (Wolff and Geissel 1994:22; Webber 1991:98).

Repeatedly, case studies of female juvenile offenders reveal harrowing childhood experiences. An extreme but telling example is the life of Marlene Moore, the first woman in Canada to be declared a dangerous offender (Kershaw and Lasovich 1991). Moore was the tenth of thirteen children born to a poor rural-Ontario family. Neglected and impoverished, she grew up amid chaos and strife. Since she was a chronic bedwetter, her father routinely beat her. At one point he dangled her from a second-storey window and banged her against the house. Despite oppressive family conditions and her small size, Marlene was a fighter who came to the defence of her younger siblings and stood up for herself. Her aggressiveness may have helped her to survive in her family, where she was sexually abused for years by several older brothers; but it resulted in school authorities defining her as "belligerent," "wild," and "aggressive." Defined by her mother and school authorities as uncontrollable, at age 13 she was placed in secure custody at the infamous Grandview School for Girls.

Grandview was "an authoritarian prison for children" with "a distinct and persistent military ambience" (Kershaw and Lasovitch 1991:31) where uniformed girls were required to march from place to place and discipline was paramount. The locked doors, barbed-wire fences, and rigid routine made it clear to the inmates that this "school" was more a prison. Here Marlene learned to express her rage, despair, and loneliness by cutting, biting, and slashing her own body. More than 80 percent of Grandview girls were "carvers," and former inmates report that blood-splattered walls were commonplace.

Presumably, some of this widespread rage was a product of the sexual abuse the girls were subjected to at the "school." In the early 1990s, many ex-inmates charged school officials with sexual abuse and violation. Recently, for example, the school's former supervisor was arrested on six sex-related criminal charges involving former wards (*Toronto Star*, February 2, 1995:A8).[8] Whether or not Marlene was one of the victimized, the school did little to alleviate her misery. Predictably, the remainder of her life followed an unhappy pattern of victimization, aggression, and incarceration. She committed suicide at age 33 in the Kingston Prison for Women.

While Marlene Moore may seem like a worst-case example, Marlene Webber's interviews with 29 Canadian runaways reveal that horrific, multi-problem families and inadequate state responses are more the norm than the exception. As Webber comments, kids who run away and opt to live off the streets are typically the refuse of "destroyed and destroying families." Emotional, physical, and sexual abuse, parental drug abuse, and incessant parental conflict (wife abuse), along with unreasonable and rigid expectations, are common experiences. Ironically, child victims are often blamed for the abuse as "difficult," "bad girls," "stupid bitches," "ugly ducklings," and "sickly" (Webber 1991:61, 65). Schools and social and correctional services typically fail to ease their pain. Victims flee to the streets and learn, if they did not know already, that their survival probably depends upon victimizing others (1991:31). For girls, this means petty crime and, typically, street prostitution. Prostitution and drug use feed the female runaway's self-hate and set her up for further victimization and violence.

The pivotal role of "dysfunctional families" appears again and again in interviews and case studies. "Patsy" reports: "I was seven when the rapes started ... My parents were into alcohol and my brother was into incest." When her mother walked in on a rape, she let the brother finish and then hollered at Patsy, "'You slut ... Why are you doing this to your brother?'" (Webber 1991:80–81).

While family factors are clearly critical, their actual role in the epidemiology of juvenile delinquency is not clear. For example, some survivors of incest and abuse have not turned to criminal behaviour. Furthermore, oppressive families produce different patterns of offending behaviour in male and female offspring. Families themselves are simply intermediaries for the gendered realities of the larger social order. In short, family background is only one important piece of the puzzle.

In recent years, analysts have gone back to the original questions: Why do some girls and not others become offenders? And why do girls' patterns of crime differ from those of boys? It is possible that the questions themselves are misleading. First, it is not clear that many female juvenile offenders are so profoundly different from other girls who never face criminal charges. In a fascinating contribution to this line of research, Marge Reitsma-Street compared the experiences of 26 pairs of sisters: in each pair, one had been convicted in youth court of delinquent actions, and the other was free of convictions and had minimal social service contacts. Interestingly, she found that the "theme of commonality, rather than difference" emerged most clearly (Reitsma-Street 1991a:111; 1991b:264). Similarly, Marlene Webber's interviews with runaways led her to conclude that "street kids, on the whole, seem no sharper or duller than the general population" (1991:149).

Ironically, some of the differences that do emerge indicate that delinquent girls are sometimes more dynamic, innovative, and interesting than their nondelinquent sisters. The "good" sisters in Reitsma-Street's study were nice, quiet, and shy; the delinquent sisters "had guts" and were "boisterous," "exploring," "experimenting," and "rebelling against abuse and injustice" (1991a:115). These apparent differences between "bad" girls and "good" girls may need to be explored in terms of experiences inside the criminal justice system. Differences between the middle-class female juvenile offender whose shoplifting charge is stayed or dismissed and the poor female juvenile who ends up in a group home because she lacks a family who supports her may emanate as much from post-charge experiences as from any pre-existing patterns.

Second, analysts are questioning whether comparing female to male delinquents, and examining the differences between male and female delinquency patterns, is a useful line of inquiry. Why should male delinquents be considered the standard against which female juvenile offenders are measured? As pointed out in many contexts, women are not simply men who menstruate. Girls and women occupy a distinct social reality. In every major aspect of social existence, gender is a significant consideration. Whether reflected in differences in women's employment and wages or in the impossibility of male pregnancy, the lives of girls and boys and men and women are conditioned by significantly different factors.

In the area of juvenile delinquency, this gendered reality is apparent in the meanings and context of offences. A girl who shoplifts cosmetics so that she can live up to prevailing standards of female beauty ("fetishized female sexuality") cannot be understood as simply parallel to the boy who steals a car. While male and female juvenile prostitutes may both fear violence "on the job," female victimization is a dominant feature of the societal landscape. Thus, the typical male-dominated pattern of prostitution, where girls work for and are exploited by male pimps, is not usually found among male prostitutes, who generally work for themselves (Webber 1991:123). There are very different gender scripts at work here. Normal gender socialization has established the basis for these differences. When the prostitute looks to the pimp for affection and support and "thinks she is nothing without a man," she is honouring a well-established and "normal" gender prescription (p. 107).

From a wider vantage point, when a young woman resorts to street prostitution, this action must be located in the gendered context of patriarchal society. Low-income job ghettos for women, along with the commodification of female sexuality (from *Playboy* to MTV), mean that the "decision" to hook may be a "rational" response to an oppressive reality. "As for hooking, I can't afford to quit. With my education less than grade nine, what else can I do?" "How else can a girl like me [i.e., poor, black, ill educated] ever make any real money?" (in Webber 1991:87, 96). Sexually abused in the home, sexually assaulted on the streets, these youths may find it sensible to seek some crumbs in exchange for the prospect of ongoing victimization.

With these patterns in mind, analysts are arguing that female criminality must be "deconstructed" in terms of its meaning to actual lives of the women involved (Schur 1984). This means approaching female criminality in terms of the distinctiveness of the female experience and the realities of patriarchal social relations (Reistma-Street 1991b:272). Further, it implies that many of the traditional lines between victims and victimizers may be blurred. Research and analysis in this direction is still poorly developed.

☀ Responses of the Criminal Justice System

When a female juvenile offender comes into contact with the police and the judiciary, a wide variety of consequences are possible. These outcomes are highly gendered; that is, the dispositions of charges against females are different and are based on a societal conception of gender roles. Traditionally, police have been less likely to charge female offenders, but also more likely to charge female offenders with "status offences" (i.e., offences that relate to youthfulness rather than criminality).[9] Typically, half to three-quarters of girls who are caught by police are cautioned or referred to a community agency with no charges laid. Analysts have argued that there is in fact a chivalrous/paternalistic approach to female perpetrators. A police officer views the offender in terms of his [sic] own daughter, wife, or sister, and following traditional gender etiquette gives the girl or woman the benefit of leniency. However, if the girl is found to be acting in an unfeminine manner—"selling sex, behaving in a disorderly fashion"—she is more likely to face arrest than if she is simply caught stealing or robbing (Reitsma-Street 1991b:268).

The introduction of the Young Offenders Act (YOA) in 1984 appears to have resulted in some changes in this pattern. The new act sought to formally eliminate status offences such as waywardness and incorrigibility and to provide for a greater variety of possible dispositions, including absolute discharge, fines, compensation, restitution, community service, treatment, open custody (group home), and secure custody (Schissel 1993:129–130). Significantly, it made available to the courts a greater variety of noncustodial options. It is suggested that these "mild alternatives" have led police to be more willing to arrest young offenders, "especially nonserious female offenders" (Schissel 1993:25). Thus, legislative changes appear to have actually prompted increases in the reported rates of female juvenile delinquency.

While increasing the likelihood that female youths will be charged, the YOA does not appear to have eliminated police and judicial preoccupation with controlling the noncriminal behaviour of female (and male) juveniles. In practice, the act has not removed "status offences." Youths, particularly female youths, are still brought to court for noncriminal actions such as administrative offences (e.g., failing to appear), mischief, truancy, and breach of probation (Bell 1994:37–38).

Once youths are brought before the courts, gender patterns persist. Reviews of court decisions indicate that the courts are paternalistic and more inclined to "use the full weight of the law against males relative to females."[10] Consistent with patriarchal notions that men exercise power in society, male criminals are seen as a more powerful and serious danger to society; female offenders are treated with systematic indifference. Predictably, male juvenile offenders are much more likely to be held in custody; their female counterparts are more likely to receive probation, community service, absolute discharge, and the like (Schissel 1993:47, 52; Bell 1994:48; Hatch and Faith 1989–90:446, 449).

Within this pattern, the harshest sentences are "reserved for older males and younger females" (Schissel 1993:39). It appears that courts are most offended by young girls (15 years of age) who are "already" in trouble with the law and by older boys (17 years old) who are "still" in trouble (pp. 33–38). The gender assumption appears to be that by early adolescence young girls should be properly socialized and should have learned to control themselves. Boys will be boys, however, and only eventually are they expected to grow up and mend their ways.

The nature of the crime also impacts on court decisions.[11] For example, courts are inclined to treat male property and drug crimes as much more serious than female ones (p. 46). Conversely, sexual crimes (notably, sexual solicitation) are treated much more seriously when the offender is female (p. 46). Traditionally, female sexual deviance has always been seen as more socially threatening than male sexual deviance (excluding violence). Also consistent with traditional gender ideology, serious female violent offences (murder/manslaughter) result in higher rates of female than male incarceration. Serious female violence is in complete contradiction with prevailing gender scripts. For lesser violent offences (assault, etc.), the gender pattern is reversed (p. 47) and males are more severely punished.

Regardless of the severity of the offence and the criminal record of the offender, the gender appropriate or inappropriate behaviour of the female juvenile also appears to affect sentencing patterns. To the degree to which the female offender strays from a respectable and home-based existence (goes out with bad friends, does not live with parents, etc.), she is more likely to be treated harshly by police and judges (Reitsma-Street 1991b:268).

Finally, the actual interventions of courts into female offenders' lives tend to reflect traditional gender values. Group homes that emphasize improvements in personal appearance and sociability, counsellors who focus on sexual history, and educational programs that emphasize traditional female job ghettos all are rooted in the longstanding tradition of "policing girls to be good" (Reitsma-Street 1991b:168; Cain 1989). Ironically, being a good girl may translate into "going along with" the oppressive realities of patriachal social relations.

Similarly, the gender-appropriate make-up of the offender's family life may be taken into consideration in court dispositions. These gender factors are complex and intersect in a diverse manner with other elements, notably social class. Bell found that judges deal leniently with offenders who come from female-headed families if the offence is traditional and the family is economically disadvantaged—in other words, if the family fits the gendered stereotype of struggling single mom. Conversely, offenders from well-to-do families are dealt with harshly. Offenders who come from gender-inappropriate families— for example, those whose mothers are professionally employed—may incur greater ire from the judiciary (1994:53). Gender, social class, type of offence, and family structure all affect the reactions of the judicial system. Presumably, other dimensions of social power and powerlessness, notably race and sexual orientation, also impact on the gendered nature of court dispositions.

While researchers have clarified the social roots of court and police practices, we still know very little about the relative efficacy of these various dispositions or their differential impact on male and female juvenile offenders. We know that the system treats boys and girls differently, but we do not know whether or to what degree we are meeting the needs of either group (Reitsma-Street 1991b:269). Past history, such as the Grandview abuses, along with anecdotal evidence, suggests that the system has generally failed. Youth detention centres continue to be criticized for failing to meet the needs of young offenders, for helping them learn to "do crime better," and for providing an environment where self-esteem is based on being the "baddest of the bad." The persistent patterns of self-mutilation and suicide among incarcerated youths underscore the problems with the state's response of locking up young offenders (Webber 1991:194–196).

The appraisal from the street is devastating: "The kids make it on their own tenacity and survival instincts ... All the system ever does is judge them, deny them what it promises, set them up to fail, and reinforce failure when it happens" (in Webber 1991:100). Others complain of welfare assistance and court-mandated fines that necessarily lead juveniles to continue to sell themselves on the streets (Webber 1991:131–132).

✵ Toward the Future

> It's a free society, man. We're free to die down here and nobody give a shit. [in Webber 1991:248]

The criminal justice system is far from a dispassionate, gender-neutral arbiter of right and wrong. The police and courts have long been located in a patriarchal tradition. Repeatedly, research confirms that this tradition persists to the present day. The implications of these results are clear. The problem of female youth offenders is interlocked with the general problems of patriarchy and social inequality. Ultimate solutions, however seemingly unattainable, depend on dismantling the oppression and victimization that helps to create offenders. Within families, traditions of patriarchal privilege, including male violence and sexual abuse, must be eradicated. As Webber points out, "It is hard to imagine a serious street-kid problem would exist if male violence against women and children did not" (1991:248). Further, parental rights must be balanced by children's rights, and opportunities must be created for children to flee from violation and neglect into supportive, protective environments.

Such changes in the family would, in turn, require profound changes in the social order. Fundamental shifts in the economy are needed to counter current trends toward the feminization of poverty, and to enable mothers who flee abusive violence to support their families. Something better than McJobs must be created so that teens who flee abuse and exploitation can support themselves without falling into prostitution, or poverty, or coerced institutionalization. At the same time, support systems must be created to facilitate the transition from self-loathing to self-esteem.

Needless to say, the direct financial costs of even minor social program changes, such as increases in the minimum wage, prorated benefits to part-time workers, and neighbourhood "safe houses" for runaway teens (Webber 1991), would generate a howl of protest in a decade preoccupied with deficit reduction and political conservatism. The financial costs are dismissed as too onerous, and social commentators place the responsibility squarely on the shoulders of the offenders themselves. At the same time, the judicial system is being assailed for being too lenient, and the cry is for more and longer insti-tutionalizations.

Meanwhile, "hard times" translate into an increased chasm between the haves and have-nots; between the alluring consumer goods on display and the grim realities of many Canadians' lives (Ross, Shillington, and Lochhead 1994). Unemployment, poverty, inadequate housing, and family violence, along with increased social and racial tensions, colour the lives and deaths of more and more Canadian children. Poor children are more likely to drown, more likely to suffer from low birth weight, more likely to have a psychiatric disorder, more likely to perform poorly at school, and more likely to develop "a conduct disorder." Predictably, as teens these children are more likely to have an alcohol problem and to use drugs (1994:1–2). An unlucky few, like Marlene Moore, will run afoul of the law and have to pay the heavy social and personal penalties that come with being defined "bad girls."

Notes

1. There are also gender differences in the age distribution of juvenile cases. In general, the male caseload is older than the female. For males, the largest single age group is 17, while for females it is 16 years of age (Conway 1992:6).

2. Minor assault (level 1) refers to assaults that do not involve weapons or serious injury.

3. Much of this attention to violent female juveniles and girl gangs emanates from the United States (Harris 1994). However, even here, male violent juvenile offenders outnumber their female counterparts at least six to one (Tracy and Shelden 1992:33). Research suggests that high rates of violent crime in the United States, including relatively inflated patterns of female juvenile violence, are rooted in patterns of socioeconomic and racial inequality.

4. Evidence on changes in rates of female juvenile offences is difficult to obtain for a variety of reasons. First, in the early 1980s official Canadian statistics did not break down offences in terms of sex. Second, the official definition of juvenile offender changed with the introduction of the Young Offenders Act in 1984. As a

result, meaningful comparisons cannot be made between data obtained before and after this time.

5. Canadians often receive a distorted impression of crime, especially violent crime, from the American-dominated news media. In general, violent crime rates are notably higher in the United States. Further, American reports tend to restrict their category of "violent" crime to murder, forcible rape, robbery, and aggravated assault. The broader Canadian categorization (which includes minor assault) makes any comparions between Canadian and American youth crime statistics problematic (Frank 1992:6).

6. Similarly, in the United States research suggests that when female juvenile offenders are charged with a violent offence it typically (90 percent of charges) involves assault and battery. Most of these "assault and battery" charges were for "fighting" and the violence involved usually "no more than a bloody nose and a bruised ego" (Tracy and Shelden 1992:36). Predictably, given the nature of these "violent" offences, the majority were dismissed. However, any comparisons to the United States must be made cautiously, since that country is characterized by a rate of violent crime about five times greater than Canada's and since females constitute a slightly larger proportion of persons arrested (Hatch and Faith 1989–90:444).

7. Given the inadequacies of family life for many juvenile offenders, it is not surprising that they seek intimacy and social connection in other groupings.

8. Grandview does not appear to have been the exception. Similar charges have been laid regarding Saskatchewan's Bosco Children's Homes, St. Joseph's Training School in Alfred, Ontario, St. John's Home for Boys in Uxbridge, Ontario, and numerous residential schools for native children (Webber 1991:46).

9. Status offences are offences because of the age status of the offender. The offending behaviour—running away, incorrigibility, waywardness, curfew violation, sexual relations outside marriage, etc.—would not be considered a crime if engaged in by an adult (Bell 1994:57n).

10. Commentators complain that under the Young Offenders Act more youths (mostly male) are being placed in custody (including secure custody) for longer periods of time. Juvenile offenders served an average of 132 days in 1988 compared to 91.3 days before the introduction of the new act. Interestingly, adults that same year served on average only 74 days in custody. While violent youth offenders may be better off under the new legislation because of restrictions on maximum sentences (recently increased from three to five years), the overwhelming majority of non-violent offenders (who constitute 87 percent of all juvenile offenders) may not have benefited much if at all (Webber 1991:185–186).

11. As Bell (1994) points out, family characteristics also affect court decisions. Offenders from mother-headed families (particularly if the mother appears in court) receive more lenient sentences, while offenders from well-to-do families

(with parents who are professionals or managers) are dealt with more harshly. Similarly, offenders whose mothers have a record of conflict with the law receive harsher sentences.

References

Bell, Sandra J. 1994. "An Empirical Approach to Theoretical Perspectives on Sentencing in a Young Offender Court." *Canadian Review of Sociology and Anthropology* (February): 35–64.

Bradbury, Bettina. 1982. "The Fragmented Family: Family Strategies in the Face of Death, Illness, and Poverty, Montreal, 1860-1885." Pp. 109–128 in Joy Parr (ed.), *Childhood and Family in Canadian History*. Toronto: McClelland & Stewart.

Cain, Maureen (ed.). 1989. *Growing Up Good: Policing the Behaviour of Girls in Europe*. London: Sage.

Conway, Joan. 1992. "Female Youth Offenders, 1990–91." *Juristat* 12(1):1–14.

Copp, Terry. 1974. *The Anatomy of Poverty: The Condition of the Working Class in Montreal, 1897–1929*. Toronto: McClelland & Stewart.

Culliver, Concetta C. (ed.). 1993. *Female Criminality: The State of the Art*. New York: Garland.

Daly, Kathleen, and Meda Chesney-Lind. 1991. "Feminism and Criminology." Pp. 410–428 in Laura Kramer (ed.), *The Sociology of Gender*. New York: St. Martin's.

Deming, Richard. 1977. *Women: The New Criminals*. New York: Dell.

Frank, Jeffrey. 1992. "Violent Youth Crime." *Canadian Social Trends* (Autumn):2–9.

_____. 1991. "Violent Offence Cases Heard in Youth Courts, 1990–1991." *Juristat* 11(16):1–11.

Harris, Mary G. 1994. "Cholas, Mexican-American Girls, and Gangs." *Sex Roles* 30(3/4):289–301.

Hatch, Alison, and Karlene Faith. 1989–90. "The Female Offender in Canada: A Statistical Profile." *Canadian Journal of Women and the Law* 3(2):432–456.

Houston, Susan E. 1982. "The 'Waifs and Strays' of a Late Victorian City: Juvenile Delinquents in Toronto." Pp. 129–142 in Joy Parr (ed.), *Childhood and Family in Canadian History*. Toronto: McClelland & Stewart.

Katz, Michael. 1975. *The People of Hamilton, Canada West: Family and Class in a Mid-Nineteenth-Century City*. Cambridge, MA: Harvard University Press.

Kershaw, Anne, and Mary Lasovich. 1991. *Rock-a-Bye Baby: A Death Behind Bars*. Toronto: McClelland & Stewart.

Leonard, Tim. 1993. "Youth Court Statistics." *Juristat* 13(5):1–15.

Lesti, Tracey. 1994. "Youth Custody in Canada, 1992–93." *Juristat* 14(11):1–25.

Leyton, Elliott. 1986. *The Myth of Delinquency: An Anatomy of Juvenile Nihilism.* Toronto: McClelland & Stewart.

Maxim, Paul S., and Carl Keane. 1992. "Gender, Age and the Risk of Violent Death in Canada, 1950–1986." *Canadian Review of Sociology and Anthropology* (August 1992):329–345.

Messerschmidt, James W. 1993. *Masculinities and Crime: Critique and Reconceptualization of Theory.* Lanham, MD: University Press of America.

Ogrodnik, Lucie. 1994. "Canadian Crime Statistics, 1993." *Juristat* 14(14):22.

Reitsma-Street, Marge. 1991a. "Girls Learn to Care; Girls Policed to Care." Pp. 106–137 in Carol Baines, Patricia Evans, and Shila Neysmith (eds.), *Women's Caring: Feminist Perspectives on Social Welfare.* Toronto: McClelland & Stewart.

_____. 1991b. "A Review of Female Delinquency." Pp. 248–287 in Alan W. Leschied, Peter G. Jaffe, and Wayne Willis (eds.), *The Young Offenders Act: A Revolution in Canadian Juvenile Justice.* Toronto: University of Toronto Press.

Rimler, Marlene (compiler). 1993. *Women on Men.* Glendale Heights: Great Quotations.

Ross, David, E. Richard Shillington, and Clarence Lochhead. 1994. *The Canadian Fact Book on Poverty.* Ottawa: Canadian Council on Social Development.

Schissel, Bernard. 1993. *Social Dimensions of Canadian Youth Justice.* Toronto: Oxford University Press.

Schur, Edwin M. 1984. *Labelling Women Deviant: Gender, Stigma and Social Control.* New York: Random House.

Seydlitz, Ruth. 1993. "Compared to What? Delinquent Girls and the Similarity or Differences Issue." Pp. 133–169 in Concetta C. Culliver (ed.), *Female Criminality: The State of the Art.* New York: Garland.

Smart, Carol. 1976. *Women, Crime and Criminology: A Feminist Critique.* London: Routledge and Kegan Paul.

Tracy, Sharon, and Randall G. Shelden. 1992. "The Violent Female Juvenile Offender: An Ignored Minority Within the Juvenile Justice System." *Juvenile and Family Court Journal* 43(3):33–40.

Webber, Marlene. 1991. *Street Kids: The Tragedy of Canada's Runaways.* Toronto: University of Toronto Press.

Wolff, Lee, and Dorota Geissel. 1994. "Street Prostitution in Canada." *Canadian Social Trends* (Summer):18–22.

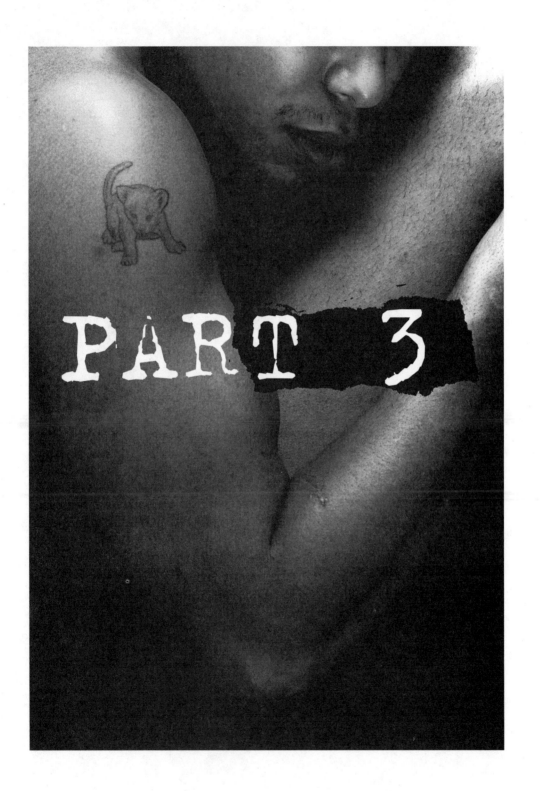

PART 3

Hearing the Voices of Canadian Youth: Empirical Studies of Crime, Deviance, and Subcultures

Constructing theories and forming contentions about young people from existing literature and from the empirical work of others is a perfectly acceptable method of "doing sociology." Conducting your own research requires a special set of talents. Not everyone is predisposed to imagining, creating, developing, and following through with the often trying demands of his or her own research. Acquiring the permissions, selecting the actors, developing a methodological strategy, and reviewing the literature can be time-consuming and frustrating. These things are usually done before data are collected in the field. Many social scientists, burdened with teaching commitments and committee responsibilities, simply don't have the time, however great their desire, to set up and carry out their own projects.

However, should time be allocated to the development of one's own research project (assuming, of course, that the desire is also present), and once the above-noted preliminary functions are completed, data collection, analysis, and writing can be a truly rewarding experience. Personally, my time spent in the field with Canadian musicians, rank-and-file police officers, a young offender convicted of a triple murder, detectives and informants, and (most notably) the many young people whom I studied for my dissertation has provided me with a wealth of current knowledge and valuable methodological experience, and with many fond memories as well. Some sociologists refer to this process as "applied research" and award it great value; others believe that other aspects of sociology are becoming more important.

It is my belief that conducting one's own research is the essence of "doing sociology." I always encourage students and colleagues to think creatively, to develop their own project ideas, to expand their horizons, to write up proposals, and to venture forth "into the trenches" and visit new social worlds by whatever methods they find most comfortable. Whether they employ qualitative, ethnographic, quantitative, survey research, or any combination of methodological strategies and theoretical perspectives is not of primary concern, as long as "the heart is in it and the body is able."

In this final section, six empirical studies are presented that explore, describe, and analyze different aspects of the Canadian youth experience. In Chapter 9, "If We're Not Gonna Kill 'Em," J. Michael Yates examines the Borstal concept as it has been applied to young male offenders in a youth correctional facility in British Columbia. Yates, who was a dorm supervisor at the facility about which he writes, provides both a historical account and recommendations for improving the state of corrections for Canadian youth. While this well-established writer and poet's scathing suggestions, wry humour, and candid approach may offend prison officials and politicians alike, Yates makes a multitude of valid points culled from his 12 years of experience as a guard in some of the toughest correctional facilities in Canada.

In Chapter 10, I present a comparative ethnographic study of the secondary school experiences of two groups of young people separated by geographic distance and socioeconomic status. "Preppies and Heavies in Bigtown" explores the attitudes and lived experiences of a group of working-class youth and compare them to a very different group of upper-middle-class actors. By spending approximately 15 months in the company of actors from both groups, I was allowed to peer into their social lives, observe their behaviour, and hear their voices in relation to their respective feelings about the function of secondary school.

In Chapter 11, "Kids, Cops, and Colour," Robynne Neugebauer-Visano examines the relationship between minority youth and the Toronto police. According to her findings, community policing is not accepted as a positive adjustment by most minority youth; rather, it is seen as simply another form of rhetoric. In this compelling qualitative inquiry, Neugebauer-Visano presents current Canadian data and analysis that clearly outline the lived experiences of a large group of minority youth.

In Chapter 12, "Youth Sports and Violence," W. Gordon West uses participant observation and interview research in a study of youth violence in sports (mainly hockey). West examines how physical force is tolerated and even encouraged in some aspects of sports, and how sports activities are constructed to embody various masculinities, how rules and regulations are learned regarding force and violence, and how these males progress through age-graded sport careers. Drawing on the interface of criminology and delinquency theory and research, gender studies, and sport sociology, West raises a number of questions that especially challenge our conceptualizations of sub-culture, masculinity, and violence.

Chapter 13 details the social world of and the deviant and criminal activities committed by cyberpunks as they relate to bulletin board systems found on the Internet. In the thought-provoking "Cyberskating: Computers, Crime, and Youth Culture," Kevin McCormick examines the swiftly changing nature of technology as it affects the leisure patterns of Canadian youth. Armed with both this new technology and the requisite knowledge, these young people routinely entertain themselves and, perhaps more importantly, commit a host of deviant and criminal acts that go largely undetected by agents of social control. By applying his vast knowledge of computer technology, McCormick contacted a wide variety of adolescent computer hackers by conducting research that took the form of "skating" around the Internet.

To complete both this section and this volume, Chapter 14 takes the reader into the subcultural world of three mutually exclusive youth gangs—Hommies, Housers, and Bangers—who all occupy a working-class neighbourhood of a large Canadian city. "'Ya Gotta Walk That Walk and Talk That Talk': Youth Subcultures and Gang Violence" details and compares their respective attitudes and lived experiences, but ventures further to suggest that the perception and self-perception of style is a major influence of subcultural formation and boundary maintenance. A historical retracing of the major influences of the youth of the 1950s is employed as a comparative approach to similar influences that impinge on the social lives of these young Canadian actors.

CHAPTER 9

If We're Not Gonna Kill 'Em

J. Michael Yates

If punishment makes not the will supple it hardens the offender.
John Locke

I became a prison guard because I make poetry, a practice widely known to pay less than crime—which is said not to pay at all. I had only to survive the shift at prison and the rest of the day was mine to write. Unlike university teaching, broadcasting, and various other jobs I have held to support the disease of fangling with words, corrections never required that I take work home: dissertations, theses, papers, and tests to grade; all-night scheming to pump the ratings of whatever radio or television outlet I was flacking, and so on. I worked at three prisons. Two of these were maximum security. The first was Oakalla, which was razed in 1991. It was held together by piss-yellow lead-based paint layered on for most of a century and by the experience of the line staff. The second—whose designers should have been razed before it was built—was Vancouver Pretrial Services Centre. Here the imagination and experience of staff were largely irrelevant. Physical structure and high-tech toys supplanted those things. Finally, I arrived at New Haven Correctional Centre, a 27-hectare open setting (no bars, no locks) that would draw on every molecule of experience I had as a teacher and a comedian, and from some resources I had no idea I possessed.

The Borstal philosophy is hardly a new concept. Named after the small town in England where the first Borstal Institution was established in 1908 (development began in 1895), the program grew out of a belief that it was in the best interests of the young adult offender that he be segregated from older, more sophisticated criminals. The Irish novelist and playwright Brendan Behan joined the outlawed Irish Republican Army at age 14 and wound up serving three years (1939–42) of Borstal time. He published a biography, *A Borstal*

Boy, in 1958. The film *The Loneliness of the Long Distance Runner,* with Tom Courtenay and Michael Redgrave, was released in 1962. Both of these offer some visceral sense of how the program worked in England.

The standard for Borstal classification in Canada is "first-time adult offender" between 18 and 23 years old. However, corrections in Canada is a numbers game. If the number of bodies incarcerated doesn't match the number of dollars allocated for corrections, then all standards are out the window.

In earlier times the fact of youth weighed lightly on the scales of justice. A hundred years ago in England, they could sentence a 15 year old to transportation (deportation to a penal colony) for life because he stole a pocket handkerchief. The disadvantages of prison were obvious: shortages of space and time made an all-round program of training impossible; there was much influence on young offenders by older ones; and the stigma of conviction was not easily erased. Probation was a real attempt to train the offender in free surroundings, but it was not always appropriate. Borstal tried to discover the possibilities of the offender and to develop them in as free a corporate life as the limits of an institution would allow.

A Borstal philosophy developed that involved education and training through constructive work, study, and sports participation; opportunities to develop self-responsibility; a promotional system leading to release on a "licence" (today's temporary absence permits); and aftercare programs in the community. The approach relies heavily on community participation and, in New Haven, on close inmate/guard interaction.

The pioneers of the Borstal system hoped that by stirring the qualities of the individual trainee (inmate) through leadership, educational, and vocational training, as well as the building of self-confidence and self-esteem, the trainee would have more success re-entering the community than if he had merely been moulded by a strict conformity to rules and set routines that often led to dependency on the "system" and negative peer group support.

The British Columbia Borstal Association of British Columbia was formed in 1948. These volunteers befriended trainees while they were at New Haven (a traditional "whist night" once a month, for example) and offered support if and when the trainees came to the Dick Bell-Irving Halfway House on parole.

Both in Britain and Canada, the Borstal program was predicated on the "definite indeterminate" sentence. The judge could specify a minimum sentence; the headmaster and staff of New Haven could then keep the offender until he had finished grade 12, learned a vocation, acquired sufficient life skills, and put together a solid "roots in the community" post-release plan. The time in the program could be extended to maximum of two years less a day. It was originally estimated that the average young adult offender needed nine months to complete the program. By the time I entered corrections (1981), the definite indeterminate sentence had been legislated away. New Haven attempted to pare the program down to an average of four months, but the crash approach was far less effective. The inmates who remained longest benefited most.

About this time, Borstal programs all over the world were disappearing. At present, New Haven's seems to be the last one on earth, and it is a mere shadow of the original paradigm. At New Haven, the Borstal program remains much the same as the one first established—*if you look for it*. Staff do not usually wear uniforms; they are assigned a "team" of young men with whom they form a close association. Guards are called dorm supervisors. It is impossible to teach a trade in the short time offenders are usually in New Haven, but they do become used to a full working day and grow handy with a variety of tools. Training attempts to stir the imagination, extend interests, and develop individuality.

In capsule, this is the Borstal drill:

- The inmate is classified to New Haven based on his rap sheet and age. Ideally, he is between 18 and 24 and a first-time adult offender.
- Locally (once he is classified to New Haven), his first-level status is that of junior or pre-junior depending on the nearness to Board Day (which is the day on which it is determined by administration, instructors, and line staff whether he will be promoted to the next level, retained at the present level, or demoted). An inmate earns 15 days of remission time for each 30 days served. Of these 15 days, the vocational instructors hold (i.e., grant or subtract) 6, the dorm supervisors 6, and the academic instructor 3.
- Above all (and this is the difference between Borstal and all other yahoo correctional models in the history of doing time), the program is *holistic*. The moment the new resident hits the campus, he is assigned to a team. The dormitory is divided into four teams of ten. Each has a team captain and an assistant captain, both of whom are at senior or senior/temporary absence level. The team captains report to the senior duty monitor, who reports to dorm supervisors. They approach staff only when their own chain of command fails to serve. The "new fish" is handed over to his team captain for orientation. His case manager interviews him (case managers have a low-ratio case load of 1:5) and assigns him to a work crew. He will report to his inmate crew foreman, then to the academic instructor.
- An appointment is made for him to punch in with the campus chaplain.
- An appointment is made for him to be interviewed by the campus psychologist.
- At the first doctor's parade, he is interviewed by the doctor and nurse. If he has skin problems or lousy teeth, or is overweight, or underweight, or has any other physical

problem that may affect his self-esteem, the problem is addressed as soon as possible.

- If he has substance problems, his case manager (guard/dorm supervisor) recommends—very strongly—that he attend one or more of the many 12-step programs.
- If he is to rise through the various levels from pre-junior to junior to intermediate to senior to, finally, senior/temporary absence—at which time he can have social passes, educational release (to trade school, vocational school, or university)—he must progress to dorm team captain and foreman of his work crew. Also, he must participate actively in sports. Any lagging behind and he will be penalized in promotion and/or remission time.
- His case manager assists in parole application. His plans (this means names, addresses, etc., of people contacted) must include where he will live, how he will pay for food and accommodation, educational plans, and so on. He doesn't require his case manager's permission to apply for parole after serving one-third of his sentence, but without a rave case manager's summary on his application, his chances of being granted parole are effectively nil.

The purpose of a Borstal Institution is to teach offenders to be self-contained individuals, to train them to be fit for freedom. It is impossible to train young men for freedom in a condition of captivity. There have been established, therefore, certain practices by which inmates are given greater freedom. There are no perimeter fences at New Haven. Trainees are given temporary absence passes after an appropriate length of time, which they may use for job searches, family visits, or some volunteer-led activity such as a hike, or just for walking through a local mall to "stay in touch" with the outside world. A few may fail, and every newspaper reader in the country will learn about the trouble that arises when offenders break away. The important fact is that the vast majority of trainees show that they can be trusted.

The recidivism rate out of New Haven during my time there was around 20 percent. Clearly, Borstal is the most effective method of dealing with young offenders that has been found to date. Of these successes, the world hears nothing. Most trainees pass into the merciful obscurity of the average honest citizen. The Borstal system should be judged by its silent successes rather than by its media-noisy failures.

✸ Mikey's Hoods in the Woods

In the good old days, they paid the staff at New Haven to take the trainees climbing and boating and on various other activities. By the time I arrived, money for such things was no longer available. There was a time when members of the Borstal Society, getting a bit long in the tooth now, would volunteer to take the kids here and there, but in my time the most active volunteer was Claude Gerriere. On his own time he organized such things as outings to hockey games for up-country kids who would likely never have another chance to see a pro hockey game. By and by it dawned on me, while talking to one of my shift partners who was a climber and who had been there for 20 years and remembered the good old days, that there had to be a way to get a hiking program together. But he wasn't about to do anything on his own time, not after having worked there during the better days of being paid to do it.

I worked up support among staff for the nifty new idea I had for a program. I bounced it off Claude Gerriere before taking a run at the director. I even went so far as to choose the first hike: Wedgemont, a local glacier north of Whistler Village near Mounts Wedge and Rethel. I collected a bunch of information and maps about the place. Then, materials in hand, I charged in to have a go at Angus Hawkins. It would mean taking only those who were senior/temporary absence, because I would have to be doing this on my own time, and they would have to be on leave—an important technicality. Otherwise I'd have to be paid, and there was no budget for such stuff. And it would have been overtime to boot.

"I like it," Hawkins said. "And I think Matthew Hopkins will like it. I'll take this material and present it to Matthew and see where we go from here."

Hopkins was our district director, and New Haven was the pride of his kingdom.

The hike I had selected was high—up to about 9,000 feet, to the very toe of the glacier—so we had to wait until the snow was off the trail. That meant late July or early August. It allowed plenty of lead time to put together equipment, select the trainees, and get everything approved.

It was the beginning of a wild odyssey of paperwork. Hopkins's first response was that the project was creative and we should start preparations while he chased clearance from Victoria. As soon as I mentioned it to the other staff—especially Gerriere, Peggy Bianco from the Borstal Society, and Norm Scott, who had recently transferred in from the Oakalla hospital—and to the trainees, there was all-around enthusiasm. The trainees began to calculate who was likely to graduate to senior/TA by the time of the hike, which was targeted for early August. We had a couple of months. When Stanley Juvastol, the PO who had been there for almost 30 years, heard of the hiking idea, he was sure that there were some old wooden-frame backpacks gathering dust somewhere on the campus. Eventually we found a pile of parts of packs high up on the third floor, in a room off the museum and personal-effects rooms. The trainees and I began to work on them, and we wound up with five complete packs.

We expected that the mandarins of corrections policy in Victoria would check their manuals of standards and operations and appropriate legislation and come back with a simple go or no. The idea had been pronounced "creative" by the district director. From a bureaucratic point of view, it was sound because it required no money to speak of. The kitchen would provide food, which it would have to do in any case. If we had one restaurant meal on the way back from the hike, it would be at the expense of the trainee participants, who would withdraw 10 or 15 bucks from their accounts as they would for any temporary absence. It was close enough—just above Whistler—that we could do the hike as a day hike. We would travel in an institution vehicle, thus covering everyone on government insurance. And since I would be doing it on my own time, it would not involve staff costs, nor would it set a dangerous budgetary precedent.

There were clear regulations for juvenile programs like Outward Bound, with guidelines for qualifications of staff, and so forth. Likewise for simple outings like bike rides through Stanley Park. But Victoria went nuts because what I proposed resembled an Outward Bound activity, and I didn't have formal certificates required for Outward Bound instruction.

Numerous questions came back through Hopkins and Hawkins. How many hours would be required? Did I have a certificate in survival first aid? It began to look as if it wasn't going to go. The probation officer, Jim Atkinson, was one of those people who is a wind sock; he guessed the direction of the power and jumped that way. And his attitude was rapidly changing from enthusiastic to "I don't think it will happen." He had mysteriously begun to hear the wrong kinds of noises and had started to pour cold water on the project. Hawkins said we should continue to plan until a final decision came in from Victoria.

Unfortunately, Hawkins was going to be away on holidays at the time of the hike. Then Hawkins was gone, the time was nearing, and there was still no decision—only more questions from Hopkins, who came in once a day to sign releases and do other paperwork of Hawkins's, and from Jim Atkinson, who had assumed the rest of Hawkins's duties.

Were there plans to climb in any areas where there was no clearly marked trail? No. This was a provincially designated and maintained trail that was well described and mapped and photographed, in documents that each of us would have. Did I have a topographical map? Yes. Compass? Yes. Altimeter? Yes. First-aid kit? Hawkins had gotten a fancy fanny-pack first-aid kit before he left.

Silence. Frowns from Atkinson. Finally, one day I came in on shift and Atkinson intoned, "Mr. Hopkins has some serious questions about your proposed hike."

"Where is he?"

"At the district office."

"You have the number?"

"You're going to call him at district office?"

"If you give me the number." I jumped on the phone and asked Hopkins how it looked.

"They haven't said a final yes."

"How would you call it?"

"Continue with your preparations. Just one last question: Have you hiked this trail yourself?"

"No, I specifically chose a trail I hadn't hiked so that my level of anticipation and adventure would be consonant with that of the trainees. I think this an important element. I have checked with the Federation of Mountain Clubs of B.C. to make sure that all bridges and parts of the trail are passable. No rock slides or washouts."

"Right, sounds good to me. I agree with your sense of spirit of the thing. I'll have something definite for you no later than tomorrow."

When I got down to the dorm, I found the five eligible trainees standing around the door looking down in the mouth. They said that Atkinson had told them the hike was pretty well off.

"I'll tell you when the hike is off. I've been fighting the paper war for all this time and I just spoke to District Director Hopkins, and he's in our corner. He said to continue preparing. Give me the checklist and a report on what things we still need." They brightened up, and I later ripped a strip off Atkinson and told him to keep his mouth shut. I was dealing with Hopkins directly.

One kid was just getting over mild pneumonia and had to be checked by the doc. Another was a physically lazy sort and I was surprised that he wanted to go along. Victoria had decided that one supervisor to five trainees was the maximum acceptable ratio, and we thought that was reasonable. I had tried to find another staff member who was free to go, but it wasn't to be. Those who would be willing to go had shifts the day of the hike. For later hikes I would find both staff and civilian volunteers.

The next day, Hopkins drove over personally to tell me it was a go—with a look in his eye that told me Victoria had been diffident and would be looking at the results of this hike very closely.

The sick kid wasn't allowed to go, and the lazy one bailed out. The three remaining had been pumping weights and running the track for a couple of months. I spent the next day with them going over the equipment. They had organized everything. Grady was foreman of the metal shop and had gone over the Suburban from bumper to bumper. Quinn had coordinated the food with the kitchen. And Dimitri had laid out all the equipment in the dispensary. We would be up at about 03:30 and leave the campus at around 05:00. That would put us at the trailhead easily by daylight.

There were a few final decisions about clothing and other incidentals. Dimitri and Quinn had been home and brought back their expensive cameras because I promised to bring a tripod and cable and give them some pointers. In a previous incarnation I had made a living as a photographer, and I was packing my two ancient Nikons.

They didn't have hiking boots, but they had agreed to wear two pairs of socks (the outside pair wool), as per good mountaineering protocol, and we were all going to wear moleskin patches on our feet's "hot spots." Mountaineers look to their feet above all.

Dimitri decided he would wear runners instead of boots. The four of us had a huddle about this. Said I: "Now, when we leave here tomorrow, aside from the joint vehicle and food, you guys are really on your own. You're on TA and I'm on a day off. Technically, we're just four guys going on a day's expedition. What you wear and what you do is up to you. We have no idea what we're going to encounter in the terrain. The work boots you guys decided to wear have shanks and steel toes. Probably better protection than my boots. If you were leading the rest of us on a pilot project that might have important implications for all outings to come, what would you advise the trainees?"

"Boots. I hate 'em, but I'll wear 'em," said Dimitri.

Thus we reasoned together about all details. They hit their beds early, fearing they might not be able to sleep for excitement, and I headed up the hill to my apartment, scarcely believing that the whole thing had finally come together. I spent the next several hours pacing up and down from bed to TV set worrying about what would go wrong, what we had forgotten.

The kitchen crew got up early and threw something together for breakfast for us. They had the packs loaded. We stowed them in the Suburban and hit the road.

I had brought along a portable tape recorder so that each of us could record his impressions on the trail and later write an article for the New Haven paper. I had also brought a handful of rock-and-roll tapes we could sing along with. They kept switching tapes and describing the view of the Squamish highway on tape. In Squamish we stopped for a quick fix of junk food; then we rolled on northward past Whistler Village (where we planned to have some hot food and check out the jet-set young ladies after we came off the mountain) and coaxed the old Suburban farther and farther up the logging road. The clearance of the vehicle was good, but it didn't have four-wheel drive, so we pulled off finally and donned packs and boots.

The dawn sky looked indecisive. It wasn't supposed to rain, but when you get above 5,000 feet, you enter white-out country. Cloud can drop on you in a matter of seconds, the fog so thick you can't see your feet.

The trail was steep and rough and surprisingly varied. I always hike with a ski pole and had brought one along for each of them. I thought it would be a war to get them to use them as walking sticks, but they tacitly agreed to humour me. I might just know something they didn't. After a couple of hours on the trail, it turned into root city. When you step on a wet root, your foot slides suddenly sideward, and it can be quite treacherous unless you have something to steady yourself. After about an hour over the roots, we hit an old rock slide. I slipped and banged my camera against a rock and jammed the lens cap. It wouldn't come off. Grady was the mechanic and Dimitri the electronics whiz. Between them, they finally unjammed it so that I could use the wide angle.

When we got to about 7,000 feet, we were walking through wisps of white-out and the sky was not visible. This gave me some pause, but we kept going because it didn't seriously affect our ability to see the trail.

On the lower parts of the trail, I had hit a pace and wouldn't budge from it. The kids whimpered and complained that it was much too slow. I had been hiking a good deal that summer and was in good shape. I tried to explain to them that all exercise is training-specific, and that while their running and weightlifting didn't hinder them, they still hadn't been walking trails. Quinn and Dimitri insisted on charging ahead. We agreed on a buddy system: you keep your partner on visual, and everyone had to stay within earshot. They flew ahead and then waited for Grady and me to catch up and razzed us. I insisted that they drink more water than they wanted and lectured them about water and hypothermia and heat prostration. By the time we were on the final approach to the lip of the lake and sight of the glacier, they were listening to every suggestion I made. And there was no more razzing. We were far above tree line, and the approach was a lichen-covered scree slope. Good place to rest and to have a drink and a bite to eat. Scree meant big steps up from boulder to boulder, and everything was wet from the fog condensation.

We had heard a Swiss couple coming up behind us comparing our Coast Mountains to the Alps and deciding that the Alps were much superior. We could hear their voices clear as a bell half a mile behind. The kids kept asking me what the Swiss were saying, and I had been translating. The kids were honked off at the foreigners, who didn't show proper respect for this grandeur. I told them to hang on and let them pass and just watch me. When the Swiss couple came by, they switched to English: "Hello. We're from Switzerland, visiting."

"*Ja, ich weiss. Schöne Landschaft, nicht?*" I replied.

They were visibly embarrassed. The kids loved it.

"What'd you say, Mr. Yates?"

"I said, 'Yes, I know. Nice landscape, eh?'"

"Right on. Do all the tourist assholes think that nobody in this country speaks anything but English?"

"Seemingly. Probably part of the Ugly American syndrome."

The redeeming aspect of the scree slope was the wildlife. When the first marmot whistled, Quinn thought one of us was a ventriloquist. I pointed out the varmint and it was telephoto time. Then I saw a rock rabbit, a pica. And then there were picas and marmots all over the place and we were all burning film like crazy. Dimitri decided he would make slow advance on a marmot. The whistling sound they make is what the village of Whistler is named after. Some of them are as big as badgers and wolverines. We stood quietly while Dimitri stalked one marmot with his Nikon. I couldn't believe how close he got. On two or three shots with a normal lens, he filled the frame. It took him half an hour to get that close. By then, it was final-ascent time. Quinn and Dimitri scrambled for the top almost in a dead heat, but Dimitri was more nimble and vanished over the top first. Quinn popped over a couple of minutes later.

Grady was glad enough to hang back and proceed at my pace. He was the skinniest of the bunch and also the heaviest smoker. Good kid. He was in jail as a victim of his own metabolism. The doctor had given him some medication, and he had had no way of knowing it wouldn't mix with the beers given him by his fiancée's father. Before he came down, he had stolen a police car and there had been a high-speed chase with bullets flying all over hell. He was lucky to be alive. Grady had no prior record of any kind, unlike Quinn, who had once broken into the home of a famous Canadian movie star for booze and found all sorts of amazing and unexpected items, and Dimitri, who had a long juvie record. I'll always remember Grady saying to me with a big grin as we started up the last 100 yards of near-vertical scree, "Guess we've pretty well got her beat now, eh, Mr. Yates?"

"Roughly 25 percent," I said, traversing my way up.

"I mean we're almost there."

"Yup." I stopped and looked at him puffing up behind me with a disbelieving look on his face. Then I looked up at the hovering white-out and hoped we'd get a good look at the glacier before we were socked in.

We were now exposed to the wind that was whipping around the col. When we were perhaps halfway I heard a noise and looked up. There was Quinn's upper body and head looking over the edge. He was shouting something, but I couldn't make out a goddamn word. Then he was beckoning us up furiously. What raced through my head as we sped recklessly up was every possible disaster. I thought perhaps I had misread the topo map. The ground was supposed to flatten out at lake level on top. In my mind's eye, I saw Dimitri hit the top and instantly drop off a cliff ... and Quinn had stopped just short.... The closer we got to Quinn, the harder the wind blew in our ears. Then we fired over the top. And there was the turquoise lake from which flowed the stream we had been following all day. And the refuge hut, and even an outhouse. And in the distance, the Swiss couple heading back toward us. I was standing beside Quinn, who was pointing at the lake and glacier: "Ah, fuck, Mr. Yates, isn't that the best, the most beautiful fucking glacier in the whole fucking world ..." He was jumping up and down and slapping his thigh, sweat rolling down his forehead from his hairline and into his eyes.

"Do you mean to tell me that you almost gave Grady and me heart attacks just to get us up here, where we were coming anyway, to see your glacier?"

"Well, isn't it the most beautiful glacier?"

"You said you've seen a glacier before."

"Pictures."

"Yeah, a great looking piece of ice." We started toward it. Dimitri was booting toward a trail along the left side of the lake toward the toe. I cupped my hands and whistled as hard as I could. He turned around. "Stay away from that trail to the ice. Wait for us." He stopped near the hut and waited. The Swiss nodded as they beetled back toward the ridge. When we caught up, I unslung my pack and reminded them, "What did we tell Hopkins about the flight plan? We said no technical climb. Glacier climbing requires crampons, different boots, ice-axes, and jumars. We eyeball the glacier. We don't step foot on it."

"Aw ... just at the edge?"

"Nope, I did that once on Helm, but at least I had an ice axe. It was foolhardy. I slipped once, but I arrested with the axe. I was lucky to get off with my old ass still alive. We just shoot pictures this time. If this hike goes well, maybe we can get a guide to rope us up and take us across a glacier on some later trip."

They all dumped their packs. And we began to dig into the huge lunches that Moe Waddington, the kitchen program instructor, had prepared for us: sandwiches, all kinds of fruit, even macaroni salad in plastic containers held together with strong rubber bands. We had been packing a hell of a lot of weight. Moe must have given us ten pounds of food each.

We ate and relaxed and rested and shot pictures. But before we could finish lunch, the white-out dropped on us.

"What now, Mr. Yates?"

"Let's go have a look at the cabin." It was a tin chalet. Rugged as hell. Enough floor space for 10 or 12 people to sleep on the combined footage of the loft and main floor. We could get through the night here if the white-out didn't lift. But when we looked out the door, it was already lifting, and we heard voices in the distance. A couple of very athletic and very gay hikers were headed toward us. These kids were not very enthusiastic about homo folks. They were already looking at one another.

The two were very pleasant, but much preoccupied with each other and with getting their gear inside in the loft. They were definitely staying for the night.

We went back outside and continued with lunch. The white-out returned and was fogging up my glasses. I could just imagine a night in the refuge cabin with the cons and the couple. I could hear Quinn saying to Grady, "I didn't know gearboxes climbed mountains." I could see the headline: "Old Poet-Guard Dies Refereeing Fight Between Convicts and Gays at 9,000 Feet." They were all about the same age, early twenties.

The next ball of fire in the sky was the arrival of a couple of Alberta cowboy caricatures who had climbed in full Stampede gear, except they wore hiking boots. They bade us "howdy" and took their gear into the hut. Now the nightmare was in Technicolor. My B.C. cons—like me—were trying to imagine the nightlong hurricane of drunken cowboys and athletic gays sorting out space and views of the universe as we know it. And the four of us were seeing ourselves huddled in the eye of the storm. It was clear that the cons considered the cowboys much goofier than the gays.

The white-out got thicker, and the kids had that "What now?" look. I had told them that white-outs can last a few minutes or keep you on a mountain for a couple of days. I sure as hell hadn't highlighted the possibility of a white-out when putting together the proposal for Victoria. We would be fine for the night in any case.

Then the white-out blew off as quickly as it had dropped. It still hovered overhead. I cleaned my glasses and suggested we all fill our water bottles in the lake. Because of the fog, we couldn't see the very tops of the spectacular spires of volcanic rock around the lake, nor could we see the very top of the glacier, but we still got some superb photographs.

The gays had vanished into the refuge cabin and were arranging the loft to their liking. In it was a logbook for visitors. We had all entered our names and the date. Dimitri had stayed in for several minutes. We got on his case about what he was doing.

"Writing a note to my girlfriend telling her how I really feel."

"Is she going to helicopter in to check it out?" Quinn asked, and we needled him to hurry up. The white-out was looking nasty again. I was making odds on whether we could make it the couple of hundred yards to the ridge before it dropped.

Mercifully, the white-out lifted and we could see the rim. I suggested we grab our packs and go for the gusto. We hit the trail just as the cowboys were gathering up their gear to go in the cabin. We hot-footed it to the rim and started down the steep scree. Skeins of white-out were hanging here and there. By the time we got by the big rock slide, I figured we were in the clear.

Back down on the protected trail, it was windless.

Our conversation rocketed from one topic to another. Dimitri had the idea that he could take a nine-volt battery and get massive voltage from it and then return the voltage to the battery, which would recharge it. It would be a limit-less source of energy.

"Dimitri, do you know what you'd have if you made it work?"

"A perpetual motion machine," Quinn jumped in.

"Right. And if you perfect the perpetual motion machine you'll be staring at the nose of Looie Freeman" (the name of God for agnostics in custody—another of my inventions for purposes of conversation with case managers).

We were back down on the rooty part of the trail. I was just ahead of Quinn, who was bringing up the rear. I stepped on a root and invented several new balletic routines before landing squarely on the expensive fanny-pack first-aid kit. Instantly the kids were warning me to watch it. "You got us in here; now you have to get us out." We had already made a plan that if some-thing happened to me, one would stay with me and the other two would take the keys and go for help.

The condensation from the white-out was falling in huge drops from the boughs of the trees. Grady went down, then went down again while getting up. Dimitri was in the lead; he went for a skate and then fell.

Never have I lectured on as many subjects as I did that day. Quinn had a million questions about photochemistry and journalism. Grady wanted to know why if he stopped smoking he would have better wind. Dimitri's mind was always whirling. He was writing a novel longer than *War and Peace* that we were serializing in the newspaper. They wanted to know about the lichens hanging from the trees, and that led to my childhood and the Spanish moss hanging from the cypress trees in the swamps in South Carolina, and that led to Tony Joe White, which led to a general discussion of music ranging from

Metallica to Bach. I had to keep sending down the bucket into the well of memory to remember the name of every alpine flower we encountered: Indian Paintbrush, Foxglove, Cow Parsley, Pearly Everlasting. It was endless and exhilarating and the talk helped because Grady and the others were beginning to see what I meant about climbing up being only 25 percent of the hike. They were leaning on their ski poles heavily and trying to lower themselves down step by step without bending an ankle. Then they began to complain out loud and asked why I wasn't complaining.

"I'm tired and sore too, but I do this all the time. Quinn, what happens every time you bump up another ten pounds on the bench press and try to break through a plateau?"

"I'm a little sore the next day."

"But not sore enough to make you give up pumping iron?"

"Naw."

"Remember that tomorrow."

The last couple of miles on the trail were hilarious. It was getting pretty dark. The three of them would beetle ahead of me and out of sight. I'd come down the trail and they'd be lying on their backs, resting on their packs. I'd walk past them and they would jump up, charge on ahead, and then lie down again.

It was a short drive from the trailhead to Whistler, no more than five miles. Dimitri and Grady were dead asleep when we arrived for the hot meal.

We had been 14 hours on the mountain. I called the joint to let afternoon shift know we were O.K. and headed home. Grady and Dimitri couldn't get out to eat. Quinn and I found a pizza place and got a big one and some pop. They were bagged.

When we got back to New Haven, everyone there was asleep. We had been a total of 22 hours away from the campus. The others dragged their asses to their bunks in the dorm and slept with their clothes on, leaving me to unload the gear and stow it back in the dispensary. Then I drove up the hill to bed myself.

Dimitri stayed in bed for a day and a half. Grady booked off work for half a day. Quinn went to work, but when I came down in the afternoon he hobbled over to me.

"Damn, Mr. Yates, aren't you sore?"

"Yes, but not as sore as you are. You did things with your muscles and ligaments yesterday that you don't customarily do. You just have to get some blood to the places you exercised. Go to the main building and go up the stairs two at a time and come down the stairs two at a time. Do that 20 or 30 times and tell me how you feel."

This was a revelation. He felt a lot better after he'd tried the stairs, and trotted off to persuade Grady and Dimitri they should do the same.

When all the film was developed, we had a magnificent album for New Haven, which Hawkins sprung for, as well as duplicate prints. There were many other hikes with plenty of adventures and silliness and great memories, but none was as memorable as the day Uncle Mikey's Hoods in the Woods was born. I still write to two of the three kids who were with me that day, and see them from time to time when they come to Squamish to challenge me at table tennis.

✳ 1995

The outlook for the Borstal program in Canada is dim to piss-poor. For reasons which go something like this:

- So long as corrections remains vulnerable to changing political winds, no program can be stable. The cost to the taxpayer of the New Haven program is hugely reduced because the trainees plant and harvest their own produce and raise and slaughter livestock. With the creation of "greenbelts" in B.C., it was fondly thought that the location at New Haven was safe. However, in the past ten years, property prices in South Burnaby have skyrocketed. The New Haven location has become a wet dream for speculators and developers.
- Since the founding of the British Columbia Borstal Association in 1948, the volunteer program has gone steadily downhill. The success of the program depends on constant replenishment of the volunteer base from community groups, businesses, and so on. Instead, the administration of the BCBA has been plagued by overpaid opportunists who pander to a network of contractors ("consultants").
- The Borstal program at New Haven has been savaged by the placing of other "programs" on the campus. There is what is imaginatively called "the Parallel Program." These are older inmates who can be either federal (two years or more) or provincial (two years less a day, "deuce-less"). Aside from the fact that they eat in the main dining room and are housed differently, there is nothing parallel about this program. They work on the various crews (thus defeating the premise that younger offenders should not be in contact with older ones). They are not required to participate in the strictest elements of Borstal structure, and this is deeply resented by the Borstal trainees.
- As if this weren't enough, temporary housing has recently been set up for intermittent inmates ("weekend warriors"). These are largely drunks, lightweight druggies, and fathers who fail to pay child support. They come in on weekends because they

have jobs (the vaunted "roots in the community" premise is sometimes vastly over-valued). It is useless to attempt to get them to work. They come into contact with trainees and with the parallel inmates and make deals to bring in booze and drugs. It makes for a nightmare. These elements contribute to the further maceration of the Borstal philosophy.

- The most critical job in corrections is that of classification officer. At the provincial level, remand classification officers may classify as many as 16 inmates a day to sentenced units. The federal system sends federally sentenced inmates to Matsqui, where they are observed for several months before being classified to a destination institution. The most egregious example of bad classification to New Haven was the Danny Perrault case. As a juvenile, Perrault had literally stomped an old man to death. Because of a complicated political situation (a warden running for federal office), two wardens arranged to have the alerts removed from his electronic file; they then pressured classification to send him to New Haven, from which he promptly walked away to commit sexual assault and various other crimes. This led to the Prowse inquiry of 1994, which resulted in a good deal of musical bureaucrat, though no one was fired.

- A great day in a warehouse unit is one in which, simply, the lid has been kept on. A great day at New Haven (when the program is functional) is one in which a case manager shows signs of progress. As I write this, I am in close touch with friends who are still at New Haven. They tell me that a new director has been brought in with a mandate to fill the 68 hectares with bodies. The physical plant (as I have recently seen) is a filthy shambles. When grounds and physical plant go to hell in a correctional centre, the morale of inmates and staff follows it down.

- There should be a maximum of 40 trainees—teams of ten—at New Haven. On weekends, with the intermittent inmates, there are as many as 100. Older, "parallel" inmates have been moved into the dormitory with trainees. At present, it is difficult to find much evidence of the original Borstal paradigm. In other words, New Haven is becoming an open-setting warehouse.

- More and more, to paraphrase George Carlin, corrections suffers from NIMBY (Not In My Back Yard). Since 1937, few institutions have enjoyed the community support that New Haven has. However, in recent years, crap-shoot classification has resulted in many maximum inmates arriving at New Haven only to walk away and commit more crimes. As a result, confidence in the New Haven program is waning in the surrounding community.

☀ The Yates Plan

- Never in Western history have prisons been so full. This has produced an atmosphere that is a mix of nihilism and bafflement. Falling in step with the United States, we have begun double-bunking in maximum institutions, despite ugly experience with this in the 1960s and 1970s. We have imported the practice of the Electronic Monitoring Program (a computerized anklet that responds to a central computer on modem; this form of house arrest is a lot like being sent to your favourite room as punishment), but without establishing any real criteria to decide who should be under house arrest and who should be sentenced to intermittent time. We are building more and more prisons, some in urban areas (such as Vancouver Pretrial Services Centre), others in the boondocks (such as Fraser), away from services, and a few (such as Surrey Pretrial Services Centre) in suburban areas, where all the residents are up in arms over the proximity of the institution. There is no pattern, no overall plan anywhere in Canada that I can discover.

- Criminologists are proving to be useless. They lapse into publish-or-perish delirium, never getting any closer to crime and punishment than the newspapers. The media rarely consult them about anything. Dense as the media can be, they intuit that the inductive mess at hand cannot be changed by deductive ninnies.

- Until recently in the history of civilization, we have killed criminals. (In Maoist China, the drug problem was solved by lining up all known dealers and all those alleged to have used drugs and shooting them.) We have not detained them and made them a burden on the citizenry after their conviction. If the state does not kill lawbreakers, then rehabilitation must be pursued, scientifically and imaginatively. There are many new directions being tried in this field. Most have had to do with warehousing people in different ways. They have had very little to do with offering skills that might lead to options other than crime. Programs such as the Borstal program at New Haven, in Burnaby, British Columbia, indicate the better road, albeit there will always be a few cons who are not amenable to any type of rehabilitation.

- Given the low recidivism rates of yore and the high rates of today, the Borstal program must be retooled along the lines of original intention and success. In the early days of Borstal (from 1908 through the 1970s), inmates 15 to 21 were trained with success. Since repeal of the definite-indeterminate sentence, the age has been extended to 24 in Canada. In the age brackets indicated, we know that Borstal *works*. We know that what we are doing in juvenile and maximum institutions *does not work*—we are merely subtracting people from society. We warehouse them until parole or mandatory supervision. Then we must deal with them again—and with their replenished arsenals of antisocial attitudes and experiences.

- To my knowledge, no *holistic* (in the spirit of early Borstal) program has ever been attempted at the juvenile or maximum levels. Most juvie programs point to their high school classes and their gymnasiums and claim that what they are doing is holistic. That is bullshit.
- I would first fix up the Borstal model at New Haven and encourage Borstal-model institutions elsewhere in British Columbia and across Canada.
- Since I am more comfortable with young adult and adult corrections, I would begin at this level. Into a maximum-security institution I would take a team of experienced corrections personnel, with a minimum of ten years' correctional experience and two years of postsecondary experience. During the time that we had degree programs in federal corrections, the practice of bringing in M.A.s and Ph.D.s with no corrections experience has been less than felicitous. One of the primary objectives of team members would be to help teachers adjust to the maximum-security environment. I would also expect them to help inmates make postsecondary decisions and to provide "disincentives" for inmates to con teachers into divisiveness with security staff. This team would ensure as seamless an environment as possible between program and security people. The same issues of self-esteem, vocation, academic education, and physical education would apply at the maximum level as at Borstal.
- Then would come the critical processes of internal classification. Those inmates who considered themselves institutionalized and had no desire to participate in any rehabilitative avenue would not remain to pollute program units. They would be segregated in units where they could smoke, play cards, and vegetate as per hard-time tradition. With this proviso: a hard-case who changed his mind and wanted to have a shot at the program would get that shot.
- I would repeal the Young Offenders Act and re-enact the Juvenile Delinquents Act (and this I would do today, were it in my power) as an interim statute until something intelligent could be created and legislated. I would then go through the juvenile system with a vengeance, reforming and reconstructing almost everything. Time and effort spent at this end will eventually pay off at the other. It is about time that someone did something with the goddamn long run in mind. Politicians do not think beyond the ends of their present terms.

In travelling across the country doing the publicity idiocies for *Linescrew,* I was often asked what changes I favoured for corrections. Again and again I said I would like to see the Borstal model applied to both juvenile and maximum-security adult institutions, very much as I have outlined it above. Invariably this dialogue ensued:

"But won't this cost a lot of money?"

"Do you believe that the States will ever pay off more than three trillion dollars of national debt?" I ask.

"No."

"Then talk money to me."

Gravid pause.

Then I inquire: "How about life then? Can you put a dollar value on life?"

"No."

"Well, so far we have ignored Tom Malthus from 1798 to 1995. How much do you think your life is worth if we continue spewing ex-cons out the other end of the system in numbers which increase exponentially? Ex-cons with ever newer and better ways to commit crimes of person and property. Maybe some things are beyond money. Maybe some things are simply and self-evidently matters of life and death. Your life, incidentally, and your death."

CHAPTER 10

Preppies and Heavies in Bigtown: Secondary School Experiences

Gary M. O'Bireck
Lakehead University

Findings from a 15-month qualitative study of two groups of youth in a Canadian metropolis reveal striking differences in the perceived value of the secondary school experience. In an exclusive section on the west side of "Bigtown," one group is referred to as the "Preppies" since its members are the offspring of upper-middle-class and upper-class families. Approximately 40 kilometres to the east is the second group, referred to as the "Heavies" since its members are the offspring of middle- and lower-class families who reside in a working-class neighbourhood. Both groups comprise male and female actors between the ages of 13 and 18 years who currently attend public secondary schools in their respective areas.

Between February 1992 and April 1993 I observed individual and collective behaviours at two youth hangouts in each setting. The methodological concept of triangulation (Denzin 1978)—that is, incorporating a variety of different methods and viewpoints when perusing a single empirical situation—was considered to be the best method applicable in these particular settings. A total of 52 adolescents (26 in each group) were observed in their natural settings, informally interviewed, and involved in many group discussions.

Throughout data collection, a selection of general themes continuously emerged from the raw database. As these themes began to repeat themselves, cross-references were established on an ongoing basis with two informants in each setting and a small selection of adolescents from other geographical areas within Bigtown. In addition, I frequently consulted the proprietors of each observational setting (a pizza palace, a convenience store, a souvlaki restaurant, and a submarine-sandwich shop) for descriptions of valuable social events that I may have missed.

All actors were guaranteed strict anonymity from the outset. During interviews and group discussions, no last names were ever mentioned, and most actors referred to themselves by nicknames. To further protect the identity of these actors, I adopted the sociological practice of substituting pseudonyms for actual first names (Sutherland 1961:111; Heyl 1979:37). Further, I assigned to actors in both groups the first names of stars from the television soap operas *The Young and the Restless*, *The Bold and the Beautiful*, and *Knots Landing*. All identifiable locations have been assigned pseudonyms.

✳ Theoretical Considerations

The link between school failure and an adolescent's propensity to deviant activity is a central feature of a variety of theoretical perspectives. Strain theory posits that the environment of the school frustrates the goals and aspirations of adolescents, which results in adolescents turning to deviance to relieve this frustration (Cloward and Ohlin 1960; Cohen 1955; Merton 1938). Social control theory suggests that an adolescent's lack of commitment to parents and teachers and a weak commitment to goals within the spheres of education and occupation result first in school failure and eventually in delinquency (Empey 1982; Hirschi 1969). Conflict theory contends that an educational system that provides an inferior education to poor and minority adolescents breeds deviance among these groups. Societal reaction theory suggests that the negative labelling of school failures and troublemakers increases the likelihood that these youths become delinquent (Gove 1980). With this variety of theoretical perspectives in mind, my aim in this article is to explore this link between school failure and deviance as it applies to descriptive comparisons of the two groups of youth studied in this inquiry.

From a Durkheimian perspective, Hargreaves (1979) concludes that the "hidden curriculum" of schooling rests in this institution's ability to provide—in addition to basic knowledge, discipline, ethics, etc.—further socialization of students to meet social expectations. For both Durkheim and Hargreaves, the school represents the vital preparatory link between the general insulation provided by the family and the potential social coldness often found within the wider community. Within the group setting of the school, each adolescent is afforded the main socialization required for a complete moral adult life.

The main function of this hidden curriculum is to grant each adolescent the clearest possible concept of the groups to which he/she belongs during these school years and to which he/she will belong in the future. In this excerpt,

Hargreaves explains his conceptualization of Durkheim's words in relation to the actual function of the school:

> Perhaps the most significant part to be played by the school in moral education concerns the attachment to social groups. The school is the bridge between the family and the wider community; in its own group life can rest the main preparation for adult life. School, suggests Durkheim, must above all give the pupil the clearest possible idea of the groups to which he belongs and will belong ... The key function of the school is "to breathe life into the spirit of association." [1979:28]

In the absence of this spirit of association, deviance and criminality develop from the unchecked or uncompensated individualism that characterizes modern social life (Hargreaves 1979:26–29).

If the hidden curriculum of adolescent schooling lies in socialization preparations for later life, then the clearly visible function must reside in adolescents acquiring measured amounts of specific information, learning specific academic skills, and having these accrued abilities tested by conventionally sanctioned academic professionals. Other clearly visible functions of the school are succinctly summarized by Finn et al. in their recent study of 104 juvenile offenders:

> It is well understood that schools establish a set of performance expectations, accompanied by formal and informal reward structures, that result in some students being characterized as successful and others as less successful, even to the point of "failure." [1988:150]

The common yardstick in quantitative research for measuring the degree of adolescent success or failure with regard to the overt functions of the school is the student's grade point average (GPA). In a general sense, the experience of mandatory school attendance (until age 16) is translated into numbers or letters that reflect each student's level of success or failure.

This standardized practice has been considered and employed as a rather potent indicator of an adolescent's propensity toward or away from deviant involvements. Generally, it is posited from a social control perspective that higher levels of academic performance lead to a higher stake in conformity. This in turn tends to predict lower levels of deviance and criminality. Conversely, lower degrees of academic performance tend to contribute to a lower stake in conformity. As a result, deviant and criminal behaviour becomes highly predictable (Hirschi 1969). To buttress this social control perspective, Braithwaite (1981) discussed a variety of causal factors believed to contribute to adolescent deviance and criminality. He concluded that "the weight of empirical evidence that school failure is a strong correlate of delinquency is beyond question" (1981:50).

These contentions in the literature should not be assumed to be universal. In the event of more sophisticated varieties of deviance and criminal activity (e.g., computer theft, creating false identification, cyberpunking, etc.), high levels of academic achievement may greatly facilitate success in these areas. High levels of academic achievement may in fact be required in order to attain any level of operational success while simultaneously avoiding failure, discovery, and/or arrest.

With this in mind, Agnew (1990) included academic achievement as a component of adolescent resources. Research findings reveal that high levels of adolescent resources are strongly linked to delinquency involvement. These resources include amounts of spending money, cars, stereos, tapes, compact discs, and clothing; but in order to attain these resources (sometimes legally, but often not) the majority of adolescents in his sample were most often required to possess above-average intelligence. This level of intelligence is often reflected in high academic achievement. These findings appear to directly contradict past conclusions that predict a tendency to conformity for adolescents who do well academically.

From a symbolic interactionist perspective, Chambliss's (1973) two-year longitudinal study of upper-middle-class and lower-class males reveals contradictory findings in relation to the school–deviance linkage. Chambliss observed that the upper-middle-class actors (the Saints) tended to earn relatively high GPAs (B to A averages) and the lower-class actors (the Roughnecks) tended to earn relatively low to average GPAs (C averages). However, through observation and interviews, Chambliss concluded that

> the Roughnecks were constantly in trouble with the police and community even though their rate of delinquency was about equal with that of the Saints. [1973:24]

This finding suggests that academic achievement is less of a determining factor in relation to adolescent deviance and criminality than previously believed. It also strongly suggests a class-based difference in the societal perception of both groups.

While Chambliss notes that the rate of delinquency remained approximately equal for both groups throughout the two years he observed them, the societal perception of the groups and their deviant acts was very different. The upper-middle-class group's members were most often considered in reality to be "good boys who just went in for an occasional prank" and boys "out sowing wild oats" (1973:24–26), while the lower-middle-class group's members were often considered to be "tough young criminals headed for trouble" (1973:27). This class-based societal perception had legal ramifications as well. While no arrests were recorded for the Saints, the Roughnecks were constantly in trouble with the police.

In the same spirit, Crespo's (1974) Canadian inquiry into the nature of school truancy identified academic performance as a contributing factor in deviance and criminality. Data were collected during an eight-month period of participant observation and interviews with 45 truants in a low-income area of east-end Montreal. Crespo concluded that the link between academic performance and deviance is greatly mediated by the process of adolescent labelling that accompanied the tracking system present in most Canadian secondary schools at that time. Students streamed into lower tracks by author-ities were therefore systematically labelled by the administration, teachers, other students, and themselves. As a result, lower-tracked students were routinely considered to be less intelligent than higher-tracked students, were expected to acquire low GPAs, were generally believed to possess low levels of self-esteem, and were perceived to be more prone to skip classes. Crespo's find-ings revealed that, while most students attempt to resist this labelling process, students successfully labelled in this way eventually acquire

> a view of self as unfit for school. At this point, systematic skipping becomes a matter of identification rather than commitment, as students become more and more identified with a version of themselves as marginal to school life. When the skipper finally views himself as the school views him, he drops out. [1974:145]

Crespo concluded that, while a construction of deviance is developed within the context of the school through skipping, and as many as 82 percent of these students eventually drop out, other deviance patterns are usually maintained or experience a mild increase after the dropping out.

Similarly, Gaines (1991) studied the subcultural environments of "jocks" and "burnouts" in Bergenfield, New Jersey, and her analysis reveals few criti-cal differences in this area. Gaines describes jocks as being generally sports-oriented, clean-cut, and appearing to conform to norms established by our wider society. Burnouts, on the other hand, are described as being alternatively attired, music-oriented, and appearing to deviate from accepted societal norms. For these two social subgroups, "subcultural affiliations are expressed through clothing and music, coded in signs" (1991:92).

Using participant observation and interviews, Gaines found that the levels of both academic achievement and deviance and criminality remain fairly equal between these two largely disparate and highly stereotyped social groups. A major cause of most acts of deviance for burnouts is adult (especially teachers) labelling and societal reactions to previously affixed labels, rather than low levels of academic achievement. Gaines found that for one of her "burnout" actors, the labelling process was a powerful stigmatizing force:

> Like her friends, Jeanne hates school. "They judge you by the way you look. Forget it. If you smoke a cigarette then you're considered a burnout. And then the teachers treat you like you're stupid ... And your friends, well, they're losers, truants, druggies, dropouts." But she knows she's not. Because she dresses unconventionally, she understands that it means she will systematically get less. [1991:112]

For Chambliss's "Roughnecks," Crespo's "skippers," and Gaines's "burnouts," the overall effect of these negative labels appears to foster a sense of powerlessness in adolescents who are systematically and negatively designated. Matza's (1964) concept of "drift" captures this sense by arguing that it contributes to the further development of adolescent deviance patterns:

> Being pushed around puts the delinquent in the mood of fatalism. He experiences himself as effect. In that condition he is rendered irresponsible. [1964:89]

Academic achievement as a variable on its own does not appear to provide a strong prediction of adolescent deviance and criminality. There seems to be more to it. Perhaps greater consideration should be awarded to a mixture of what Hargreaves referred to as the school's hidden curriculum of socialization and adolescent academic achievement. The research of Hargreaves clearly indicates that both aspects of the school experience are inextricably bound together.

Findings from this present inquiry clearly lend support to this contention and reveal that, for the most part, the school serves as a both an institution for learning academic skills and a site for developing social skills. Status points are accrued for proficiency in both areas. However, while academic performance is evaluated formally by school officials in terms of grade point averages, the development of social skills is evaluated informally by other students in terms of popularity, clothing styles, choice of music, types of hair fashion, material possessions, etc., which lead to peer acceptance and the availability of opportunities for social interaction. Because school brings many like-aged adolescents together for long periods of time, it does not seem unreasonable to believe that both types of learning are essential for the complete socialization of adolescents. However, other theoretical perspectives (e.g., strain, social control, conflict) seem to indicate that the bulk of emphasis should be placed on the side concerned with academic learning.

☀ The Heavies in School

Overall, the social aspects of school tend to outweigh the pursuit of academic excellence for the Heavies. In contrast, Preppies tend to employ alternative sites for social purposes and attempt to concentrate more energy on academic pursuits. Academically, the Heavies report a GPA at slightly below C, while the Preppies possess an average GPA of slightly above B. Approximately one full letter grade separates these two adolescent social groups academically.

Other factors may help account for this disparity. For instance, findings reveal that Heavies generally appear to sustain more punishment for longer periods of time for institutional infractions. Detentions, enforced visits to the principal's office, suspensions, and expulsions appear to be charged more frequently to them throughout their school experience. Preppies, on the other hand, tend to suspend their misdeeds at roughly the grade 11 level. Other comparisons may also be drawn. What follows is a comparison of the opinions of these actors that reflects the perceived value, functions, and explanations of their personal secondary school experiences.

I was first concerned with asking Heavies about their overall impressions or opinions of their school experiences. From many personal observations, it appeared that most Heavies considered the classroom to be less important than socializing in a variety of recreational pursuits while at school. Interview data revealed that the majority of Heavies are not able to fully grasp (or refuse to accept and believe in) the advertised function of their school experience. In this excerpt, Jack's feelings are representative of the majority of views portrayed by these actors:

> They call it high school, but it really makes you feel low. Teachers treat you like shit ... and they teach you shit you're never gonna need in life. Look at my dad! He's doin' all right and he never needed his schooling! He told me that one day. All the stuff he learned in school went right out the window when he got his first job ... right out the fuckin' window ... told me he never had to use it again and he makes good money! So I can't see this thing about school bein' so fuckin' valuable.

This view is corroborated by the words, feelings, and opinions of Rex and Ashley, who maintain a friendship even though they attend different schools. Both actors were approached immediately after leaving their respective schools for the day. In this excerpt, Rex wonders whether his schooling will help him deal with survival as an adult. Ashley, though she is rather quiet by nature, clearly agrees with Rex:

G.O.: How was school today?

Rex: The same as always. [looks at Ashley and laughs] Boring, boring, boring! I wonder why I go!

Ashley: Yeah, me too.

G.O.: All the time?

Rex: Yeah ... some days are better than others, but usually it's the shits. Same at [Ashley's school], Ash?

Ashley: Yeah ... it's bullshit.

Rex: I'm old enough to quit and so is Ash, but we keep on going. I guess I'm going 'cause I hope it'll get better ... you know, the teachers will get better or they'll teach better stuff. I don't really know ... like do I really need it? Is this shit s'posed to be preparing me for life in the real world [mockingly]? Life's gotta be better than this. I just keep going like it's a bad habit, or something! [laughs]

Ashley: Yeah ... me too.

Similarly, Neil and Olivia seriously question the potential worth of concentrating their best efforts in the direction of academic pursuits when current economic conditions may inhibit them from attaining suitable (and legal) employment after graduation. This attitude took me somewhat by surprise, so I asked about the perceived sense of risk involved in approaching adult life without the benefit of (at least) high school matriculation. The majority of Heavies insist that greater value is currently awarded to the possession of a strong working knowledge and performance in the area of street norms. Armed with this informal knowledge, most Heavies believe that they can better survive as adults. Neil and Olivia summarize this approach to preparing for their future existences as adults:

G.O.: What do you mean, school's not important?

Neil: I know school is supposed to be your ticket to greatness, but I don't know ... fuck, there's no jobs out there anyway, so how's school gonna help you get a job? I think it's more government hype ... they can't give you a job so they tell you to stay in school so you can get a job later on, I don't know ... mostly I think school is boring. Our teachers are really boring ... they're fuckin' tweaked, man ... it's the same shit year after year and for what? To go on unemployment? Or welfare? Our guidance teacher's always talkin' about these great careers in fashion design or computer marketing, but I don't see myself anywhere near that shit. Maybe a welder or an ironworker, but even that's stupid to consider because we're in a fuckin' recession! Nobody's building anything anymore, so why should I get trained to be a carpenter or something? I think it's stupid really.

G.O.: So why do you go?

Neil: I go [to school] to hang out mostly ... my marks are shit 'cause I don't really listen to the teachers that much ... only when I have to. There's better things to think about so that's what I do. I don't give a fuck about school because I know I'll make out anyway ... I always get by one way or another 'cause I know what's happening on the street ... that's where it all happens, dude.

G.O.: Do you feel the same way, Olivia?

Olivia: Yeah ... you know that's right! Neil's ... [says to Neil] I guess that's why everybody likes you, man ... you right on! I mean, lemme ask you ... what am I gonna do after high school? Work at McDonald's? Not me. You ain't gonna see me there ... no way ... so I gots to prepare myself. I'm all right, because I know what to do out here [points to the pavement], ... I got respect out here, so I'll do all right ... I'll survive and it won't be because o' school! I don't need school that bad.

Considering these attitudes, it was not surprising to discover that for some Heavies a pointed display of apathy marked their demeanour when they expressed opinions of their school experience. In some cases, the topic of school was too bothersome and somewhat annoying to discuss during valuable recreational time. For these Heavies, school was regarded as a function that had to be performed in order to placate parents or guardians, authorities, teachers, etc., and to ward off potential trouble for not attending. Thus, any mention of school was met with a groan or, at best, a brief comment. However, more persistent probes were often reluctantly or flippantly responded to in a fashion represented by Deanna's inconclusive comments:

Deanna: I'm not sure what to say! School is school! What'cha wanna talk about this shit for anyway? It's something you just gots to do. I don't really like it that much, but then again I don't hate it. You know what I'm sayin'? It's some place you have to go to every day ... sometimes it's good ... sometimes it's real boring. But, like I got lots of friends there so we usually have a good time. That's more important for me.

G.O.: What's more important to you?

Deanna: Hangin' out with my friends.

G.O.: Why's that?

Deanna: I don't know ... it just is! [pause] But like ... I don't do homework ... I never do it. But I never get in trouble for it because I don't give anybody a hard time. I don't say too much at school. It doesn't take a rocket scientist to figure out gettin' mouthy's not worth it. Lots of my friends cause shit at school and pay for it! So, like, then the teachers go out of their way to make their lives a living hell! That's not my idea of a good time, so mostly I keep my mouth shut. I just smile and don't say nothin'. Most of my teachers think I'm O.K., I guess ... or maybe they just don't notice me ... I don't know ... and I don't care really. School is just school ... know what I'm sayin'?

Although Deanna readily admits that school offers little stimulation and consequently warrants even less dedication, she clearly states that greater value is attained through the social aspects easily generated within the context of her school peer group.

Similarly, I was curious about the majority of Heavies who rained praise on the social benefits offered by time spent at or around the school, while simultaneously denigrating academic responsibilities. Most of their criticisms were levelled at course content and the perceived inability of teachers to explain and contextualize material in ways that could be easily and quickly understood. Students who fail in curriculum learning appear to quickly replace academic endeavour with effort directed at social success. Academic learning and adherence to formal institutional norms seem to be swiftly supplanted by concentrated efforts directed at social learning and the consistent adherence to informal street norms. In the following excerpt, Nat expressed an attitude that was frequently stated by many Heavies. He clearly differentiates between the societally sanctioned value of formal academic learning and the socially modified necessities provided by informal skills that Heavies are often forced to employ outside of school:

Nat: School's a great place to be ... like even though I don't get great marks, I still like it. I just don't work at it, I guess. But I'm not too worried about it, the marks part of it I mean ... I like the social aspect better. Like I'm on the student council ... hangin' out, bein' around people ... shit like that. That's more important to me as far as I'm concerned because it makes you a whole person. Like you get some of the [people] at our school ... they really freak me out because all they do is study, study, study ... fuckin' dweebs! And sure they rack up A's and A+'s, but they're lost once they hit the real world. That's not what I think education should be about.

G.O.: Really? What do you think it should be about?

Nat: Education should be about helping boys become men and girls become women ... I mean getting everyone ready for the real world out there [points to the street]. Because, like once you get out of school you have to go out and do something useful and you can't do anything if you can't communicate with other people an' shit. Get what I mean?

G.O.: Yeah, communication is a big part of it, I guess, but how do you mean?

Nat: [Some of the dedicated students] never learn how to deal with anyone who's not like them ... but they get A's so that makes them smart? Bullshit ... it's not fair ... it's fuckin' bullshit. I think my C's are more valuable to some employer than [those] A+'s any day, 'cause I know about the world ... I know what time it is ... [gets excited] I know what's goin' on out there, man! They don't. [pause] I know how to communicate. I'm a people person.

Growing out of the concentration on the social aspects of school is the tendency for the majority of Heavies to become unclear on the subject of higher education after graduation. The highly ordered, generally accepted, and socially sanctioned concept of academic excellence in high school, followed by acceptance at university or college, followed by university graduation, followed by increased occupational opportunities, does not appear to be a widely accepted program of activities for these actors.

Findings reveal that most Heavies have difficulty comprehending or believing that there is validity in this ordered sequence of events. In short, they substitute instant gratification for deferred gratification. My observation of this substitution resulted in a series of probes, and I discovered that many Heavies interpret the perceived inadequacies of high school learning as a template for all upper-echelon academic pursuits:

Steve: I don't like school. I think it's fuckin' useless 'cause it doesn't give you anything. At least at a job, even a shitty job, you get something out of it ... like your pay. But at school there's nothin' good about it except the girls. It's a good place to see lotsa babes, but most of them are either dweebs or bettys [skaters' girlfriends]. Some of them are hot though ... at least at my school.

G.O.: Well, that's a good point, isn't it?

Steve: [pause] Yeah, but the teachers are cracked at my school. They teach such boring shit ... but I don't care, I just use the place to operate ... make plans ... do shit. I do some good business outa that place! Seriously, dude ... I don't see any use in it ... like learning shit you're never gonna use on the street ... that's bogus. But I still go ... it keeps my Mom happy, I guess. She wants me to go to college, you know, like keep on learning! I don't know. Don't think I could handle it 'cause it's probably worse than high school! If it wasn't for the babes at my school, I'd quit. Like everyone says you need school to get a good job an' all that shit, but I don't get it ...

As evidenced by Steve's comments, advanced learning at the college or university level is generally evaluated in the same light as the academic dimension of their high school experience. This would indicate that learning academic skills for any reason and at any level is of secondary importance to developing strong social skills within the collective school experience. Findings reveal that for some Heavies, these prominent social considerations soon become transformed into and entangled with displays of deviance and criminality in the form of recreational drug and alcohol use, truancy, vandalism, shoplifting, assault, extortion and car theft. Some Heavies become entrepreneurial and predatory and begin to conduct forms of "business" within the formal structure of the school. In this exchange, Michael describes a typical chain of events:

G.O.: Michael, you really hate school so much?

Michael: But yeah, man ... there's been a lot of heat [police] up there [at school] lately. So I been stressed out ... so like I don't give a fuck about anything, really ... just care about my business ... why should I give a fuck about school? I don't give a fuck about school. It's a fuckin' waste o' time ... the classes, an' shit ... like, I don't talk to my teachers when they talk to me. I don't even look at them. I just sit there an' look at the floor. I got in so much shit for givin' it to them an' talkin' back ... so now I don't say shit ... fuck them ... someone else can answer their fuckin' questions. I don't give a shit. They say I gots to be there, but I don't have to talk ... they call it participate ... nobody says I have to participate [gets aggravated] ... So what?

G.O.: Chill, man! Michael, it's O.K., I'm not from the school board ... so, if it upsets you so much, why even go? It doesn't make a whole lotta sense to me ...

Michael: I got to! [pause] Yeah ... like I was sayin' about participation [laughs] ... I participate in my ways ... like hangin' is participatin' as far as I'm concerned! [laughs louder]. But it never used to be like that. I used to do O.K. in school when I was younger ... like, I never really loved it, but I could put up with it better. Now it's a real pain in the ass, the school part. [gets quiet] But now I got my business there ... you don't gotta know what it is, sucka ... maybe I deal [drugs] a little ... maybe I don't. Who cares? That's my business ... an' it gets me by. But it can be a dangerous place if you're not careful! [laughs] But my business is there so I gotta go, 'cause school's where the money is! [laughs]

A multitude of group observations tend to add credence to this notion of adolescent "business" affairs. While most critical activity appears to be conducted in a highly covert manner within a collection of privileged "insiders," some street transactions were visible. Those witnessed by this researcher involved the sale of marijuana and hashish and stolen compact discs. Other drugs (cocaine, heroin, LSD) and larger items (car stereos, VCRs, leather clothes) were discussed and overheard by this researcher but not witnessed. Field notes revealed the following:

I wonder how these kids can afford to dress like this! Scott just walked in with a new leather jacket with a Chicago Bulls crest embroidered on the back. It even looks valuable! He's telling his friends he got it at ____ for $380. Scott is not the type of guy to exaggerate, as far as I can see, so it probably cost at least that much. It baffles me how he can afford to lay out that kind of money ... he's only 16 years old and he doesn't have a part-time job. Last week he told me his father just got laid off [he's in construction], so it looks like something strange is going on here. [Later] I see Scott hand another actor a small plastic bag and get some paper money in exchange. He stuffs it into his jeans in a very nonchalant manner. Scott comes over to my area and sits at a table close to me, reaches over and slaps my hand in a friendly greeting and we start a conversation:

Scott: What's happenin', dude?

G.O.: Zip, just hangin'. What's up with you? Nice jacket!

Scott: Thanks, dude ... jus' got it.

G.O.: Looks great on you ... looks like it costs a lot ... did you win the lottery?

Scott: Nah ... jus' payin' attention to business, that's all ... nothin' serious. You gots to look good to be successful [laughs].

G.O.: Yeah, I guess so! But how can you afford it?

Scott: Like I told you, I look after my business an' it looks after me. Got that?

A very small contingent of Heavies reported that they had been able to secure student welfare assistance. This enables these actors to leave the family home and take up residence in a government-subsidized housing unit and to receive approximately $600 per month in welfare benefits. A critical condition to this arrangement is mandatory secondary school attendance.

To most Heavies, these living arrangements are considered high status, as they relieve them of parental influences and restrictions. In essence, the government awards these arrangements to adolescents who have complained of physical and sexual abuse, malnutrition, neglect, and generally unsafe living conditions. However, those Heavies who are adept at tricking government officials into believing they are truly abused or neglected in order to receive "a seriously rad party place" and a monthly stipend of "free government money" are awarded high peer status. The perceived downside to this trickery is mandatory school attendance, but group observations reveal that these adolescents often deal with this situation in this manner:

I noticed Brandon saunter into Convenience Store B in a very good mood. He joined his friends at the video games and they started laughing and hand slapping. I heard Danny ask Brandon how he "pulled it off." I thought they were talking about a theft so I moved closer. Victor saw me out of the corner of his eye.

Victor: Can you believe it, man? Brandon just got his new place ... it's just up the street ... and it's all his ... right, Brandon?

Brandon: [proudly] Yeah ... got it today ... I can move in tomorrow!

Danny: Fuckin' eh! Party down, dudes!

G.O.: What do you mean, got your own place? You rented an apartment around here?

Brandon: Well, I didn't get it myself ... student welfare. They got it for me.

G.O.: Really? How does that work?

Victor and Brandon together: Ah, you just tell 'em your Mom doesn't feed you 'cause she spends all her money on crack or somethin' like that, or your Dad kicks the shit outa you. Then you go home and cause a lot of shit so when welfare calls, if they do, then whoever answers the phone says you're sleepin' in the garage or somethin' like that. It's real loose, an' you get an emergency cheque ... then a place. It's real easy, but it takes time to get it all together. But you gotta go to school ... that's part of it.

G.O.: So what's wrong with that?

Brandon: Nothin', except school's bullshit. I fuckin' hate it. But I'll go to keep this deal goin' [laughs]. I don't have to learn, but I can hang with my friends, make plans, do a little business. That's the good part of school.

In one instance, student welfare was employed to facilitate the opportunity for educational advancement for Eve, an adolescent single mother. She was forced to leave secondary school in her second year to give birth, but she returned the following year to continue her education. This opportunity would have been denied her had it not been for government assistance. Regardless of this societally perceived "saving grace," Eve's opinion of the value and functions of secondary school does not appear to have been altered by her absence to any large degree:

G.O.: Eve, now that you've had your baby and you're back in school, does goin' to school mean more to you now? Do you like it better? Do you think it's worth more?

Eve: I never liked school before, and to tell you the truth I don't really like it now! It's so fuckin' boring! And, like it doesn't make sense because like most of the shit they teach you in school you can't do nothin' with! Like, today we were talking about this Bosnia shit. Well, sure I feel sorry for those people, but really ... is that shit gonna help me feed my baby? So what if I know about Bosnia—is that gonna get me a great job? I don't fuckin' think so! But they make you learn shit like that all the time ... call me an idiot, but I can't figure out what that's got to do with my life. But I don't say shit about stuff like that anymore. I just keep my mouth shut and do what they tell me, but I don't have to like it! And I don't like it, but if I wanna keep my student welfare thing goin' I have to go to school, so what am I gonna do ... know wa I'm sayin'? I just gotta keep goin' and keep my mouth shut. I never used to be so quiet! [laughs] I used to tell everyone to go fuck themselves. All this school shit was boring. [raises her voice] Yeah, I used to let everyone know what I was thinkin' an' it got me into lots of trouble at school. But that didn't bother me ...

G.O.: Gettin' heat at school didn't bother you? Why?

Eve: 'Cause my friends thought I was cool so that's all I cared about. That's the most important thing in life. Friends. Way more important than doin' good in school. If you have 'em you're O.K., but if you don't you're fucked.

It seems fairly clear that, for this group of Heavies, the general concept of academic learning has been supplanted by a variety of social aspects within their collective school experience. They appear to prefer the instant gratification gained from "hangin' with friends" and participating in a variety of deviant activities to striving for academic excellence in the hope of gaining acceptance at university or college and making career plans. This inquiry reveals that Heavies often seriously questioned this widely advertised, generally accepted, and socially sanctioned concept of deferred gratification, and generally rejected and socially modified it also. These youth gain status through adherence to subterranean value systems congruent with their subcultural affiliations. In essence, adolescent street norms tend to prevail over the structured academic norms within their collective high school experience.

✹ The Preppies in School

Through interviews and observations, I found that Preppies tend to approach their experience at school in a slightly different manner. While strong similarities can be drawn between the school-related deviance patterns of young Heavies and Preppies (up to the approximate level of grade 11), more mature Preppies have begun to embrace the tenets of and beliefs in academic excellence. In a comparative sense, findings reveal that, in the early stages of high school, both groups display approximately equal levels of desire for immediate gratification in terms of recreation, enjoyment, and popularity. The words of 18-year-old Brooke contain personal behavioural descriptions that indicate this similarity:

Brooke: When I was younger I was a really bad student. I couldn't pass a test if my life depended on it! I wasn't at school very much and the days I went I was usually high. We'd usually smoke a few joints before class and fuck around with the teachers. It was fun but not very productive, to say the least. I got sent to the office more times than I can remember for being "insolent"! I didn't know what that meant, but I figured out real quick it wasn't good! So after a while I stopped going and went to Robbie's apartment every day to get high.

When my mother found out she was really pissed and grounded me. She even drove me to school every day even though we only live three blocks from school. But I figured a way out of that!

G.O.: How'd you get around that?

Brooke: I went to my first class and then skipped out after it ... like, for the rest of the day. She was really pissed when she found that out, but I didn't care as long as I didn't have to go.

Both groups also display a high level of risk-taking behaviour in early adolescence and appear to be very willing to sacrifice career goals in order to attain these instant pleasures. While the Heavies appear to retain, develop, and nurture this attitude into a highly meaningful subcultural concept as they advance through high school, these findings indicate that Preppies do not. Instead, these Preppies appear to jettison this approach to social living midway through their high school experience and turn toward parent-induced and socially accepted behaviour. An excerpt from an interview with Sonny, whose former subcultural affiliation was with the skinhead movement, clearly demonstrates this trend by contrasting his own descriptions of past and present social life:

Sonny: But that's nothing, nothing compared to what I used to be like. We used to skip all the time! And get drunk in school or get really high and laugh at the teachers when they're tryin' to teach a class [laughs]. That was really funny 'cause it got everyone laughing in the whole class! But we'd have to pay for it ...

G.O.: How d'ya mean?

Sonny: Ah, the usual. We got the detentions an' shit, an' like my buddy got suspended a few times. I was lucky 'cause I never got suspended, but I came close. [pause] But I'm not like that anymore ... and I don't hang out with those dudes anymore either ... but like the skinhead thing is dead anyway, as far as I'm concerned, so it doesn't matter really.

G.O.: Do you miss it ... those good old days?

Sonny: Nah. Even if it was happening now, I wouldn't be a skin ... or even a skater ... most of those guys got into skateboarding, but I didn't. I didn't like the whole idea of it so I never got into it ... but ... yeah ... school. Yeah, about school. It's a necessary thing. All of my friends realize it's just something you gotta do. You gotta have it or else you just go nowhere. Your life just goes nowhere without an education. There's nothin' you can do about it! It's just that simple. Like smoking causes cancer? A good education can get you a good job.

G.O.: It's that simple?

Sonny: Yeah ... it's as easy as that! You can't fight the system 'cause that's the way it's set up. So you might as well go along with it and get a free education ... so that's why I kinda changed my attitude a bit ... you know, like about school an' that. I don't think it's too smart to be a fuckin' clown anymore 'cause you miss too much school ... then it's too hard to catch up ...

In characteristic Preppie fashion, Claudia describes her early adolescence as adventurous, turbulent, and ultimately unsatisfying as a result of negative labelling from two major areas prominent in her life. In the first instance, her continued association with known deviants resulted in negative group labelling from school officials. This often resulted in unwanted attention and negative sanctions from teachers. Secondly, the wider adolescent society affixed a decidedly unflattering label to her based on what they perceived to be inappropriate behaviour, namely her sexual promiscuity (real or imagined). In this interview excerpt, Claudia reveals how this combination of very potent negative labels contributed to a marked change in her personal actions in, and her attitude toward, the remaining years of her school experience:

Claudia: That was a bad time for me all around. I was hanging out with some really strange people and, like, you kinda always do what they do, I guess. They were always in trouble at school so I guess I kinda did the same things or at least tried to do some of the same things. That's what we were, I guess ... you know, kinda like shit disturbers. But some of it was real because the teachers treated us like shit and gave us a hard time even if we didn't do anything. But I guess I wised up ... 'cause when I started grade 11 the word was out on me ...

G.O.: What do you mean? Who put the word out on you?

Claudia: Everyone! Like, everyone was talkin' about me and callin' me a real slut, you know, like a "ho." So I had to make a real hard decision. I couldn't deal with these school problems on top of people calling me slut and spreading bad things about me. So I just kinda woke up, I guess.

G.O.: Sounds like lotsa pressure! How did you handle it?

Claudia: I started hanging around with different people. I got real quiet at school and the teachers stopped bothering me. That was a relief! And that's the way it is now. I don't say much in school so I never have any problems anymore. And I guess that's what makes it more fun. I think about better stuff now ... like my future.

In direct opposition to the general attitude displayed by the majority of Heavies, the value and functions of school appear to be fairly clear to this group of Preppies. Specific subjects or teachers may remain unclear to them for various lengths of time, but these findings reveal that the overall function of high school is generally perceived as preparatory for advanced education at the college or university level.

This attitude may be supported by additional findings that reveal that most actors claimed generally to enjoy their personal school experiences or at least find them relatively tolerable. Very few Preppies reported that they "hated" school. In fact, most Preppies believe that academic success can easily be translated into future career success by applying to and being accepted into university or college. For most actors past grade 10 or 11, it appears that this highly ordered, widely advertised, and socially sanctioned sequence of events is considered valid and highly valued as a way to structure life processes. For these Preppies, then, gaining acceptance to the university of their choice appears to be highly valued, seriously considered, and the next logical step after high school.

In the following group discussion, Thorn, Robbie, and Tommy express views representative of the majority of Preppies queried about the validity of this linkage. Most truly believe in the progressive pattern of striving for academic excellence in high school, of university attendance and graduation, and of future job success:

Thorn: That's one thing my dad drilled into my head and I'm thankful for it. The only way to the top is with an education. He says you can't do it any other way and I believe him. I remember [pause] I heard him tell that to my older sisters when they were growing up ... over and over ... like when they were going on dates too much and flunking courses and shit ... then he started in on me and I guess it worked 'cause I really believe him.

G.O.: I can see that! But is this the only way to the top? Don't you think there are other ways to go places?

Tommy: No fuckin' way! You ain't goin' nowhere without good marks. If you think you are, you're cracked.

Thorn: Nope! It's impossible to go anywhere without a good education ... and ya gotta get good marks 'cause you won't get into university with shitty marks ... everybody knows that! I don't fuck around. School means a lot to me.

G.O.: Seems to be fairly obvious! [we both laugh] Why is that? What's the big deal about doin' so good in school?

Robbie: Well, who wants to be a fuck-up? Do you wanna be some fuckin' no-brainer for the rest of your life? I don't, no way! If I do good in school maybe I'll have a chance to do something good, like live a good life like my dad. If I don't I'll end up bein' a fuck-up. I don't want that—

Thorn: [cuts in] I don't want a shitty job ... like I don't want to work for some asshole and have him tell me what to do all the time. I want to be the guy doin' the telling!

Tommy: Yeah, me too. Workin' for someone else is the shits ... I did it last summer—

Thorn: [cuts in] And that's easy to do ... just get a good education ... you know, like good marks and stuff.

Research findings reveal that, for the majority of Preppies, the primary motivation behind concerted efforts at academic excellence in high school stem from parent-induced and adolescent evaluations of potential occupations. This indicates that not all occupations are viewed in the same light and awarded similar credentials. Those occupations that have offered stability, a level of security, and eventual financial freedom in the past (e.g., lawyer, doctor, accountant, etc.) seem to be popular choices for these adolescents. It does not seem sufficient to attend school aimlessly or even to work casually toward a general career area. Rather, status is gained by having firm career goals in place by late high school. Ridge, a grade 12 student, demonstrates his dedication to an integrated program of achievement that has already been put in place and acted upon:

Ridge: That's my real love ... computers ... but not just playing games and stuff, but getting into the guts of them and modifying their function capabilities. Designing software is my dream and I've already started a little. I designed a package that my dad uses at his architectural firm.

G.O.: Sounds impressive! What do you do with it—or should I say, what does it do?

Ridge: It records and processes small orders upon receipt. I'm now going to expand it to include a list of features my dad wants. He says it really helps his business ... he told me his friend in San Francisco is using it for his plumbing business and it's working out very well. That makes me real excited because there's a lot of money in software and I'm sure there will be for a long time. But I need my education first and that's about where I'm at right now. That's the only thing holding me back right now, but that's O.K. ... I'll get there.

Similarly, Alexandria has organized her school curriculum so that it leads to a formatted set of career goals complete with justifications for many of her future career decisions. In one of our informal discussions, she informed me that her adult career would probably be devoted to an area of social work:

Alexandria: There are tons of problems in this world, like people problems, and I really think I can help out somewhere. I like school. In fact, I really like it because it stimulates me.

G.O.: In which way? [we both laugh]

Alexandria: It really makes me think. Like, it makes me think about the future, like, not just my own future but the future of the world. Most people don't really care what happens in the world except to themselves ... like their own little world, and I don't think that's very good. Education should be designed to help change that whole way of thinking. I want to be a social worker of some kind ... and in order to get that high up I'm going to need an education and good marks. I pay attention to that because it's what my future depends on.

Field notes recorded during observation sessions add support to this Preppie notion of appreciating the inherent value of school as it relates to future life goals. A typical lunch-time session in Souvlaki Joint A reveals that, by and large, a strong social attitude exists among these youth that is based on doing well in school. In short, conforming to school norms and attempting to excel is the "cool" or "rad" activity, while avoiding school for alternative activity is perceived by these adolescents as "bogus," "cracked," or "tweaked" (deviant).

This is wild! These kids talk about school a lot! Well, I guess it is their domain for six hours a day, five days a week, and this is a school day ... but it seems to take up a lot of their conversation. Some of them can be real "keeners." I know that, but here comes Robbie and Valene and they look like they had a real party type of weekend. At first they don't say too much to each other. There seems to be anger in the air. This is rare because these two are usually good friends ... maybe there's a problem. [five minutes later] They are joined by Willie, Nick, and Seanna, and their discussion begins. From what I can see and overhear, Robbie and Nick are considering cutting class this afternoon to see if they can get into the sports arena to see the professional team practise.

Valene reminds them that an important test (or series of tests, I'm not sure) is coming up and the teacher is giving a one-time review of the course material that afternoon in class. Up until Willie, Nick, and Seanna arrived at their table, she didn't say much, but now that they are present she starts berating Robbie and Nick (especially Robbie, who I think she cares more for) about being very irresponsible. She mentions that they can always watch "that stupid team" on television and that her father owns season tickets. Seanna and Willie agree with Valene, so she gets more vocal. She mentions more than once that neither of them can afford to fail this test. (How does she know their grades? I never discussed my grades with anyone, but they seem to know each other's as a matter of habit!) These five actors actually spend their entire lunch period arguing about Robbie and Nick cutting class to watch a team practise! As they leave Souvlaki Joint A to return to school, the issue appears to be settled based on their happier collective dispositions. Valene, Seanna, and Willie have convinced Robbie to abandon the idea. I see these four get into Valene's car and drive off toward their school while Nick stands in the parking lot looking like he is trying to decide what to do. After about five minutes, he gets into his car and appears to head towards his school. Whether he went back to school or to the arena, I don't know.

As this group observation session indicates, these strong subcultural norms exist, in part, because they are considered by these youth to contribute to future life goals. In addition, these norms are considered to be an element of what they feel is a reliable formula for success and because they appear to emulate the words and actions of these actors' parents.

It appears that the wide variety of social aspects found within the school experience of the Heavies is conspicuously absent from that of the majority of Preppies. While socializing at and during school is still considered a large part of their school experience, these Preppies overwhelmingly report that the most critical social activities occur away from the setting of the school. Social activities often move into group congregations in family households, neighbourhood "youth hangouts," area movie theatres, Souvlaki Joint A, and Sub Place B. In this interview segment Taylor, Tammy, and Jayne provide a representative series of reasons for this socialization movement away from the school:

Taylor: Mostly school is all right, but I spend my time thinking about other things …. makin' plans for after school, stuff like that, goin' places, doin' things, meetin' my friends. The other kids all want to hang out with us 'cause they hear about our social life through the grapevine. I guess they all want to know where we go and what we do, but we never let on about our secrets.

G.O.: Secrets? Why the cloak-and-dagger thing?

Tammy: 'Cause we don't want coolies hangin' with us! We don't need the aggravation. [laughs]

Taylor: That would wreck it for us, so we don't say nothin'. Everybody thinks they're special, I guess, but, yeah, we don't hang out at school. No way ... never! Nobody hangs out at school. Only dweebs do that! [laughs] And low-class scum. They hang around after school an' get high, whatever ... do the gang-banger thing [laughs]. But not us.

G.O.: Really? Why is that? What's the rush?

Jayne: There's nothing interesting to do. Only dull people hang at school when they don't have to ... there's a big world out there—or haven't you noticed? [they all laugh]

Taylor: It's not a cool thing to do. When school's over we're outa there and into something better. Even at lunch we get outa there ... like, you just go to school for the marks ... for the diploma, know what I mean? You hang with your friends in better places than school ... like [Burger Joint A] ... that's a quality place. I see you there all the time!

In contrast to the Heavies, whose school experience is characterized by a highly charged and extremely active social atmosphere, the Preppies define the school as a setting in which academic goals are set out, strived for, and, they hope, accomplished. While within the confines of the school, Preppies seem to enjoy acting socially, but they do not rely on the school to serve social functions. Instead, Preppies appear to set themselves apart from other youth by seeking out and establishing alternative sites for concentrated social interaction. During an informal discussion, Stephanie underscores this major difference by her clear demarcation between, and preference for, the social and academic functions of her school experience:

Stephanie: Like, the social part of school is what I don't like, but most of my classes are interesting and the teachers are really good.

G.O.: So the school part of school is O.K., but the social part stinks, right?

Stephanie: Right.

G.O.: Why is that?

Stephanie: 'Cause the cliques are really bogus there, because they prejudge people all the time. You don't have to do anything to get them to pick on you. I don't prejudge anybody, but they have a major laugh doing it. We don't have much in common. They're real sick fucks up there, so me an' my friends don't hang out at school at all.

G.O.: Where do you go to have fun? What do you do?

Stephanie: We go out! Like ... shopping, partyin', whatever. I'm only there for the education part of school ... 'cause that's all that matters anyway. The rest of it's all bullshit.

✳ Discussion

Some major differences between the Heavies and the Preppies surfaced in relation to school experiences and collective social lives. For the most part, school functions for the Heavies more as a site for social activities (some deviant, others not) than for acquiring academic skills. In contrast, Preppies tend to view the school almost exclusively as a site for acquiring and testing academic skills; they spend most of their leisure time away from the school setting.

Second, Heavies tend to consider the social aspects of schooling to be of greater value in acquiring familiarity with informal street norms as opposed to striving for (or even attempting to fit in with) the formal and established institutional norms of the school. On many occasions, Heavies were heard to comment that, in their view, the only way they could make some form of personal impression on the wider society was by way of the informal street route. Based on my frequent interactions with them, I tend to believe that many Heavies intrinsically believe that they are systematically denied performance opportunities very early on in their educational development.

This opinion is based on recollections provided by some actors who state emphatically that, throughout their early years of schooling, adult power figures (teachers, school officials, parental figures, baby-sitters, etc.) often treated them in ways that evoked expectations of their eventual failure. As a result, these actors were frequently singled out for public criticism and monitored closely in school. Other students undoubtably witnessed this frequent castigation by adult authority figures and themselves created situations marked by mocking, barbed remarks, a perception of secondary status, and lower popularity rankings with peers. In response to these predominantly negative reactions, the Heavies developed a negative impression of the school system, repeatedly reinforced over time. As a result, they gradually opted for the ways of the street in order to attempt to gain some level of status, personal pride, and inner satisfaction that they believed they were earlier denied. The gradual shift from attempting to adapt to the norms of the school to embracing the street as their primary frame of reference began in the early years of their secondary school experience and continued increasing throughout high school.

With Preppies, conversely, some social needs are met during time spent at school, but their primary concern is on working within the established, parent-approved norms of the school in pursuit of good grades and overall academic advancement. In short, while Heavies appear to be more concerned with "makin' it in the street" (instant gratification) and using this informal knowledge as a basis for their future, Preppies tend to be more concerned with "makin' it in the world" (deferred gratification) by attempting to earn conventional or socially acceptable credentials.

Although these findings reveal that the average grade point averages for these two groups differed by over one full letter grade (Preppies higher than Heavies), young Preppies and young Heavies appear to display very similar patterns of deviance and criminality. This finding appears to strongly contradict previous theoretical assumptions (mentioned earlier) that link failure in school to an adolescent's propensity to deviate. Other factors (possibly social, familial, economic, peer-oriented) must therefore contribute to adolescent deviance patterns in addition to academic considerations alone.

Findings clearly indicate that it is not until approximately the late grade 10 or early grade 11 level that Preppies tend to turn away from deviance and begin to embrace the wider society's view of conformist behaviour. Up until that time, however, many Preppies report attitudes toward, and much of the same participation in, deviance and criminality that are similar to those reported by young Heavies. In short, the process of reform that affects the majority of young Preppies part way through secondary school appears to affect few Heavies in quite the same fashion. While both groups certainly mature over time, Heavies tend to maintain or increase their deviant pursuits while Preppies demonstrate marked decreases in their individual and collective involvements.

Observations, group discussions, and extensive interviews over time with both groups lead me to believe that one of the major reasons for this disparity is that maturational reform is class-based. Most of the Heavies come from lower-middle and working-class families. These family units report their total annual family income as ranging from $25,000 to $45,000. The majority of Heavie parents, step-parents, and guardians work at unskilled, blue-collar, or semiskilled occupations. No professional occupations were reported by these actors for this group. Actors often informed me that their parents were working overtime (or holding two jobs) to "pay the rent," working part-time instead of full-time, suspended by the union, temporarily laid off, unemployed for long periods of time, or collecting social assistance. A few actors reported that parents had had long-term jobs terminated or phased out due to computerization or other forms of automation. These unsettling occupational circumstances are essentially conditions of working-class survival. They are bound to affect these parents' offspring in a variety of ways, either directly or indirectly.

Despite these unsettling economic conditions, many Heavies still seem intent on emulating the lived experiences of their parents. They accomplish this by consciously (and, I suppose, subconsciously) adopting and then projecting many of their parents' attitudes toward our larger societal institutions. For example, Jack's view is clearly representative of this trend and the prevailing Heavie attitude toward secondary school. Based on his father's informing him that nothing the father learned in school was ever applicable to his occupational setting, Jack, in the above excerpt, seriously questions the value of an education. In effect, Jack accepts his father's view ahead of the societal view of the value of formal education.

Similarly, Olivia and Neil are concerned only with societal survival and recreation. Both sets of their parents (and step-parents) work at unskilled jobs and generally live week to week. Therefore, any image that these adolescents may have held of growing and thriving within conformist career goals has been replaced by an attitude geared toward mere survival. Both believe they have a better chance of surviving in this world by gaining respect on the street.

Nat feels much the same way as most Heavies. He questions the value of a formal education based on his belief that his skills as a communicator or "people person" will guide him through his adult life. His father is a frequently unemployed sales representative and his stepmother has been sporadically employed in the hospitality industry for much of her life. In the same spirit, Eve openly questions the relevance of class discussions on "that Bosnia shit" to feeding her newborn baby. In a generational sense, one may wonder what example Eve will set for her offspring to emulate should they complain about the validity of their secondary school education.

In direct contrast, the majority of Preppies come from upper-middle-class and upper-class families. Actors from these families report annual incomes ranging from $85,000 to $150,000. In some cases, actors reported amounts higher than this average, but, admittedly, these were considered to be estimates. The majority of Preppie parents or step-parents have worked for long periods of time at professional occupations, own their own businesses, have taken early retirement, or occupy white-collar jobs. After leaving behind their brief forays into displays of deviance during early adolescence, most of these Preppies seem proud of their parents' accomplishments and speak openly about them. In this setting and at this time, there is a pronounced feeling among these youth that mere survival as an adult is insufficient to attain any measure of social status. To be considered successful, one must thrive.

However, during early youth Preppies tend to be very aware of their superior class status. Actors reported that in grades 9 and 10 in a public secondary school setting, their parents' affluence made them feel very conspicuous. Most Preppies report that very early into grade 9 they were labelled "rich pricks," "candy asses," or "rich cunts" by other envious students. Some reported that they believe teachers treated them differently from less fortunate students. These negative assessments were usually based on last names and addresses, clothing styles and quality, choice of music, available visible resources, and their initial choice of peers. Findings indicate that these perceived prejudices usually weighed very heavily on the consciences of individual Preppies.

In order to counteract the social pressure of being routinely singled out and negatively labelled, many Preppies report that in a show of defiance they gradually rejected their parents' ideals, became rebellious, altered their appearance and peer associations, adopted different forms of deviant activity as a pastime, and began to emulate patterns of behaviour more characteristic of classes lower than theirs. In essence, they looked away from the norms and values of their family unit and examined those of the overall youth culture in an effort to increase overall acceptance. While it was reported that, by and large, overall peer acceptance did increase for these Preppies during the examination of these new norms, so too did their participation in deviance and criminality. The majority of Preppies freely admit to engaging in a wide range of group-oriented deviance and criminality during this period.

But why do these Preppies routinely report that they "came back" from this life of temporary deviance—a life initiated by clashes within the school and controlled by peer norms—to their present existence, an existence characterized by conformity to parental and societal norms? All actors who experienced this normative shift report that, while in this rebellious stage, they never once considered embracing their parents' norms again. Although they continued to live under the family roof, most disliked their parents and publicly referred to them as "rich snobs" or "capitalist pigs." In effect, they blamed their parents for their social hardships and transferred their negative labels onto the shoulders of their parents. But why did they not remain this way? What caused them to change again?

Findings reveal that over time (approximately 1.5–2.5 years) the majority of Preppies began to feel guilty about their deviant behaviour. Most began to seriously question the validity of their actions and began to feel badly about themselves for causing embarrassment to their parents. Some realized how fortunate (economically and parentally) they were in comparison to peers in other classes. In response to this self-questioning and self-reflection, most report they soon realized that all the privileges of their class position were directly attributable to their parents.

In response to these realizations, Preppies report that they gradually gained renewed respect for their parents, their achievements and accomplishments. Over time, it became clear to them that they themselves were the fortunate ones because their lives were currently much easier than others' and could remain that way in the future. As well, many realized they possessed the opportunity to develop some form of power in the future if they desired. In effect, Preppies began to truly believe that they could really "be somebody" if they began to heed their parents, reaccept their parents' norms and values, and adapt them to their personal modes of behaviour. Without this parental influence, guidance, and support, Preppies realized that their own row would be much harder to hoe.

These contentions are clearly supported by the database on Preppie actors. But within the specific school setting, interview segments and group discussions involving Brooke, Sonny, and Claudia detail the shift from early attitudes and acts of deviance to later (and present) situations of parent- and peer-induced conformity. In a similar fashion, Thorn, Robbie, and Tommy freely admit to having these concepts of conformity "drilled into their heads" by their fathers and finally accepting them. As well, these actors are in agreement when they present evidence representative of parental respect and emulation by clearly distinguishing between "being a no-brainer fuck-up" and "living the good life, like my dad."

Ridge and Alexandria clearly internalized their class position and began making it work for them. In effect, they narrowed their interest in a field of possible future occupations, chose an area to cultivate, and directed their efforts toward future life goals. Both believe that education is the key to their success. Ridge attributes his promising computer software career to a high level of parental influence, guidance, support, and involvement.

To set themselves apart from the majority of less fortunate students, these Preppies routinely and consciously socialize away from the school setting. Why? Observations and group discussions suggest that these Preppies socialize in this way because of their resources. Parental financial support—in the form of weekly allowances, cars, credit card accessibility, etc.—allows these Preppies to behave with a strong sense of exclusivity: to have lunch in restaurants instead of school cafeterias, to travel to malls to shop, and to go to movie theatres, video stores, trendy bars, dance clubs, and sporting events. Because these avenues are accessible to them, they take advantage of them and incorporate them into their daily routines.

I also got the strong sense that these actors did not want to have their newly reaccepted norms and values contaminated, criticized, or made fun of by those not privy to their views of the keys to success. It must be remembered that most of these Preppies in their early adolescence experienced life as a rebellious deviant. Most report that they "came back" and no longer wish to exist in opposition to family and social class norms. Continuing past associations is generally considered to be counterproductive, since those associations contain the potential to "reinfect" their newly cleansed lives.

With this concept in mind, Preppie actors Taylor, Tammy, and Jayne describe their social lives as "active" and their social settings as "secret, quality places." They take great pains to remove themselves from school property after classes to avoid the "aggravation" of "coolies, dweebs, low-class scum, and gangbangers." In approximately the same spirit, Stephanie is adamant about having a separate set of friends away from her school because she considers the "cliques" to be very distracting. She considers the function of her school experience as strictly academic and considers social relations within her school to be "bullshit." In essence, these findings provide reasons why the school does not function as a social setting for these Preppies. For them, the school is instead employed mostly as a means to achieve future life goals by attaining academic credentials.

My analysis of the prevailing atmosphere within both groups, Heavies and Preppies, as it relates to their separate views of the school can be closely aligned to societal reaction theory. Initially conceived by Tannenbaum (1938), societal reaction theory takes into consideration the power possessed by one's audience (in this case, the teachers, school officials, parental figures, and classmates of Heavies and Preppies) in defining and redefining one's social existence. To be more specific, Tannenbaum states,

> The process of making the criminal is a process of tagging, defining, identifying, segregating, describing, emphasizing, making conscious and self-conscious; it becomes a way of stimulating, suggesting, emphasizing, and evoking the very traits that are complained of. The person becomes the thing he is described as being.... The persistent suggestion, with whatever good intentions, works mischief, because it leads to bringing out the bad behaviour that it would suppress. The way out is through a refusal to dramatize the evil. The less said about it, the better. [1938:19–20]

Of fundamental concern to societal reaction theorists is the distinction between primary and secondary deviance. According to Lemert (1967), primary deviance refers to initial acts of deviance that may or may not lead to one being labelled as deviant. Based on the societal reactions to these initial acts of primary deviance, secondary deviance is constituted when acts of primary deviance produce patterns of behaviour that place the offender in a societally defined deviant role. To be more specific, Lemert states,

> Primary deviation is assumed to arise in a wide variety of social, cultural, and psychological contexts, and at best has only marginal implication for the psychic structure of the individual; it does not lead to symbolic reorganization at the level of self-regarding attitudes and social roles. Secondary deviation is deviant behaviour or social roles based upon it, which becomes a means of defense, attack or adaptation to the overt and covert problems created by the societal reaction to primary deviation. [1967:17]

Providing explanations for the variety of reasons people commit acts of primary deviance is not generally the concern of societal reaction theorists. However, the commission of acts of primary deviance is often attributed to incompatibilities within a particular social structure, the quest for hedonistic social states, or to plain ignorance of the widely agreed-upon social rules. Acts of primary deviance do award one's audience with the opportunity to judge the particular behaviour and then the power to assign it a deviant or nondeviant label. The power awarded to the social audience is succinctly outlined in this passage from Erikson:

> Deviance is not a property inherent in certain forms of behaviour; it is a property conferred upon these forms by the audiences which directly or indirectly witness them. The critical variable in the study of deviance, then, is the social audience rather than the individual actor, since it is the audience which eventually determines whether or not any episode of behaviour or any class of episodes is labelled deviant. [1962:11]

Similarly, the contentions of Becker (1963) add support to the claims made by many Heavies when reflecting on the reasons for their negative impressions of the academic aspect of the school. They routinely blame their gradual marginalization on labelling power awarded to adult power figures and classmates during their earlier school experiences. Becker, in the explanation for deviance that follows, would seem to agree:

> Social groups create deviance by making rules whose infractions constitute deviance, and by applying those rules to particular people and labelling them as outsiders. From this point of view, deviance is not a quality of the act a person commits, but rather a consequence of the application by others of rules

and sanctions to an "offender." The deviant is one to whom the label has successfully been applied; deviant behaviour is behaviour that people so label. [1963:9]

While these contentions may help explain why the majority of Heavies attained deviant status initially, it does not explain why they tend to remain in opposition to official school norms. Nor does it cast light on why most Heavies eventually shift their focus away from academic pursuits at school and toward deviant activities on the street. According to Becker and Erikson, following the process of stigmatization that results from being successfully labelled deviant, a self-fulfilling process is inevitably initiated. As a result, other students, teachers, school officials, parental figures, etc., would regard these Heavies as deviant and respond to them in this fashion (Becker 1963:34; Erikson 1962:311). According to Becker, this occurs because the deviant status conferred on most Heavies becomes a master status. This master status tends to override all other social perceptions in relation to how other audiences react to these Heavies (Becker 1963:33). In short, the majority of Heavies were treated as "bad apples" before they gained a chance to demonstrate whether they were actually good or bad.

Based on the recollections of Heavies concerning their early school experiences, it is my opinion that many were labelled deviant after suffering degradation at the hands of adult power figures at school. In essence, these Heavies experienced a "profound and frequently irreversible socialization process" (Gove 1980:13) throughout their early adolescence. As a result, they acquired an inferior status in terms of their wider society and developed a predominantly deviant view of the world. In turn, and by virtue of their present adherence to informal street norms instead of school-related norms, they possess and are continually developing the knowledge and skills to accompany their deviant world view.

This contention is supported in a general sense by the empirical research of Chambliss (1973), Crespo (1974), and Gaines (1991), mentioned above. In a specific sense, an important conclusion appears in the findings of Chambliss (1973):

The community responded to the Roughnecks as boys in trouble, and the boys agreed with that perception. Their pattern of deviancy was reinforced, and breaking away from it became increasingly unlikely. Once the boys acquired an image of themselves as deviants, they selected new friends who affirmed that self-image. As that self-conception became more firmly entrenched, they also became willing to try more extreme deviances. With their growing alienation came freer expression of disrespect and hostility for representatives of the legitimate society. This disrespect increased the community's negativism, perpetuating the entire process of commitment to deviance. [1973:31]

In addition to the differences already described, another major difference stands out between these two groups of youth. It appears to be predominantly class-based, although I believe that additional factors contribute as well. This major difference, simply stated, is that during early adolescence, both the Heavies and Preppies admit to experimenting in similar forms of deviant behaviour and sharing relatively negative impressions of the value of school. However, at approximately the midpoint of their high school experience, the Preppies turned away from their deviant designations and returned to relative conventionality. The Heavies, by contrast, seemed to continue acting out in a deviant (and often criminal) manner through to the end of grade 13—that is, if they did not drop out before they reached graduation.

Why the majority of Heavies and not Preppies are ultimately and increasingly subject to predominantly negative evaluations based on societal reactions to primary acts of deviance is a question of considerable concern. In the opinion of the vast majority of societal reaction theorists, even if the Heavies were so inclined, the majority of them are simply unable to relinquish their deviant designations. According to Gove, this inability to effect positive change may be determined by the fact that

> those on the margin of society, particularly those who have little power and few resources, are those who are least able to resist a deviant label and are therefore most likely to be channelled into a deviant role. [1980:11]

In much the same spirit, the empirical research conducted by Chambliss (1973) is closely aligned to this theoretical approach. The results of this inquiry allow Chambliss the opportunity to offer a general conclusion and the ability to speculate about what may happen to his groups in the future. In the closing passage of the article, Chambliss states:

> Selective perception and labelling—finding, processing and punishing some kinds of criminality and not others—means that visible, poor, nonmobile, outspoken, undiplomatic, "tough" kids will be noticed, whether their actions are seriously delinquent or not. Other kids, who have established a reputation for being bright (even though underachieving), disciplined and involved in respectable activities, who are mobile and monied, will be invisible when they deviate from sanctioned activities.... It is more likely that their [Roughnecks'] noticeable deviance will have been so reinforced by police and community that

their lives will be effectively channelled into careers consistent with their adolescent background. [1973:31]

❋ Conclusion

This examination of the secondary school experiences of these actors provides a brief and general explanation of the major differences between the Preppies and Heavies in Bigtown. The exploration, description, and analysis of these experiences may or may not be applicable to other adolescent social settings in Canada. It was never the intent of this inquiry to provide such applicability but, instead, to exist as

> a relatively modest project whose humility is not quite recognized by the proponents of other schools. It does not seek to capture the essence or spirit of society; it does not claim to master the basic logic of social life; it does not pretend to address issues of majesty. It merely tries to cast some light on those tracts of sociation which might yield tenable knowledge. [Rock 1979:231]

Contrary to the popular adult phrase "kids are kids," knowledge gained from this inquiry indicates that these "kids are not just kids." Instead, adolescent social life in these two settings is fraught with intrinsic differences firmly rooted in other social institutions such as socioeconomic status, the family, peer associations, etc. It appears quite safe to speculate that reverberations from other social institutions, in turn, help to shape the sense of self, the social existences, and the secondary school experiences of both Preppies and Heavies in Bigtown.

References

Agnew, R. 1990. "Adolescent Resources and Delinquency." *Criminology* 28 (4):535–564.

Becker, H.S. 1970. *Sociological Work: Method and Substance*. Chicago: Aldine.

Becker, H.S. 1963. *Outsiders: Studies in the Sociology of Deviance*. New York: Free Press.

Becker, H.S., and B. Geer. 1970a. "Participant Observation and Interviewing: A Comparison." In *Qualitative Methodology*, W. Filstead (ed.). Chicago: Rand McNally.

Becker, H.S., and B. Geer. 1970b. "Participant Observation and Interviewing: A Rejoinder." In *Qualitative Methodology*, W. Filstead (ed.). Chicago: Rand McNally.

Blumer, H. 1970. "What Is Wrong With Social Theory?" In W. Filstead (ed.), *Qualitative Methodology*. Chicago: Rand McNally.

Blumer, H. 1969. *Symbolic Interactionism*. Englewood Cliffs, NJ: Prentice-Hall.

Braithwaite, J. 1981. "The Myth of Social Class and Criminality Reconsidered." *American Sociological Review* 46:36–57.

Chambliss, W. 1973. "The Saints and the Roughnecks." *Society* 11:22–31.

Cloward, R.A., and L.E. Ohlin. 1960. *Delinquency and Opportunity: A Theory of Delinquent Gangs*. New York: Free Press.

Cohen, A. 1955. *Delinquent Boys*. New York: Free Press.

Crespo, M. 1974. "Career of the School Skipper." Pp. 129–145 in *Decency and Deviance: Studies in Deviant Behaviour*, J. Haas and B. Shaffer (eds.). Toronto: McClelland and Stewart.

Denzin, N. 1978. "Sociological Methods: Critical Reflections." In *Sociological Methods: A Sourcebook*, N. Denzin (ed.). New York: McGraw-Hill.

Denzin, N. 1970. "Rules of Conduct and the Study of Deviant Behaviour: Some Notes on the Social Relationships." In *Deviance and Respectability*, J. Douglas (ed.). New York: Basic.

Empey, L.T. 1982. *American Delinquency: Its Meaning and Construction*. Homewood, IL: Dorsey.

Erikson, K.T. 1967. "A Comment on Disguised Observation in Sociology." *Social Problems* 12:366–373.

Erikson, K.T. 1962. "Notes on the Sociology of Deviance." *Social Problems* 9:307–314.

Finn, J.D., M.W.R. Stott, and K.T. Zarichny. 1988. "School Performance of Adolescents in Juvenile Court." *Urban Education* 23(2):150–161.

Gaines, D. 1991. *Teenage Wasteland: Suburbia's Dead End Kids*. New York: Pantheon.

Gove, W. 1980. *The Labelling of Deviance: Evaluating a Perspective*. Beverly Hills, CA: Sage.

Hargreaves, D.H. 1979. "Durkheim, Deviance and Education." In *Schools, Pupils and Deviance*, David Hargreaves (ed.). London: Kegan Paul.

Heyl, B. 1979. *The Madam as Entrepreneur*. New Brunswick, NJ: Transaction.

Hirschi, T. 1969. *Causes of Delinquency*. Berkeley, CA: University of California Press.

Lemert, E. 1967. *Human Deviance, Social Problems, and Control*. Englewood Cliffs, NJ: Prentice-Hall.

Lemert, E. 1952. *Social Pathology*. New York: McGraw-Hill.

Matza, D. 1969. *Becoming Deviant*. Englewood Cliffs, NJ: Prentice-Hall.

Matza, D. 1964. *Delinquency and Drift*. New York: J. Wiley.

Mead, G.H. 1934. *Mind, Self and Society*. Chicago: University of Chicago Press.

Merton, R.K. 1938. "Social Structure and Anomie." *American Sociological Review* 3:672–382.

Rock, P. 1979. *The Making of Symbolic Interactionism*. London: Macmillan.

Sutherland, E.H. 1961. *White Collar*. New York: Holt, Rinehart and Winston.

Tannenbaum, F. 1938. *Crime and the Community*. Boston: Ginn.

Kids, Cops, and Colour: The Social Organization of Police–Minority Youth Relations

Robynne Neugebauer-Visano

☀ From Community Policing to Policing Youths

The relationship between the community and policing is a major focus of sociological inquiry. Clearly, an examination of the community is basic to an understanding of policing. This chapter examines the policing of youth and the role of race in police–community encounters.

The study of policing enjoys a rich intellectual history. Traditional perspectives on policing have delineated various vantage points—various conceptual lenses through which we learn to appreciate the phenomenon of social control. Early criminological approaches highlighted the relationship between the police and the community. A review of several key themes indicates that the nature of policing shapes and is shaped by the nature of the wider community. Classical theorists such as Emile Durkheim stated that the community provides a pervasive belief system that preserves social harmony. Within the community, social ties are integrating "forces" that constrain criminal propensities ([1897] 1951). Policing in primitive and undifferentiated societies involved the moral and social integration (which suggests that policing is influenced by the quality and quantity of intimate affiliations). In such groups, all individuals were firmly anchored in extensive close-knit networks that served to maintain a shared "communal" order—the "community." This moral integration, especially the sharing of beliefs, values, and rituals, reinforced and promoted common conceptions. This social solidarity was the basis of a community that kept social order intact.

In more contemporary and complex societies there is a weakening of the collective moral conscience and a general decline in social integration. Within these major societal transformations, the collective conscience of traditional societies has gradually been replaced by the division of labour and the assigning of highly specialized roles to ensure harmony. Social differentiation promoted solidarity (Durkheim 1933:395–406) by creating an entire system of binding obligations replete with duties. Urbanization, accompanied by capitalist practices, ushered in a new social order. Dislocation, contradictions, and alienation contributed to "criminogenic" conditions (Gordon 1973:163) that required police intervention.

For Max Weber, the dissolution of the feudal order by rational and bureaucratic forces had produced a retrograde urban environment that obeyed its own laws. Weber's concerns with the negative effects of bureaucratization were also articulated as expressions of alienation (1958:55; Giddens 1973:43). In analyzing the development of legal authority, Weber noted that domination becomes impersonal and legalistic so that the institutional character of authority has largely, if not wholly, displaced the personal one. In analyzing the qualitative experiences of new urban populations, the early writers were fundamentally attentive to the distinctions between traditional (rural) and modern (urban) communities. Pivotal to Weber's (1946) discussion of this impersonal order is the coercive character of organizations whose primary task is norm enforcement. The police as a bureaucratic, legal, formal, and rational institution began to assume different functions as a result of both industrialization and urbanization.

The first modern police force, the London Metropolitan Police, was established in 1829 in Great Britain. The philosophy and practices of this "new model" were adopted in Canada and the United States. In the interests of social control, according to one of the early architects of modern policing, Sir Robert Peel, "the police are the public and the public are the police."

Throughout this century, efforts have been made to make police forces more accountable to the communities they "serve and protect." The concept of community policing emerged in this context. Good community relations enhance the intelligence-gathering process. It follows that police functions—law enforcement, peace keeping, order maintenance, and social services—are performed better, the more communities participate in the process. In the last few decades there has been a growing realization that policing is a shared responsibility.

Transformations of society (Park 1952; Park and Burgess 1925), notably the rapid rise of cities and immigration, have altered the bases of social order in the community. Rapid migration, anonymity, and stimulus overload have produced alienation and anomie, and other symptoms of social disorganization. Community policing initiatives are carefully constructed responses to increased public cynicism. Within the last few decades police forces have been actively promoting a "community-saved" argument (Wellman 1979:1205). That is, the community has emerged as a set of common ties or modes of relationships, and a prevailing normative value system promotes a sense of belonging, cooperation, and distinctiveness.

Community policing and police–community relations have become interchangeable. The former term has always occupied a central role in police work. Genuine expressions of community policing characterized the premodern forms of policing; the authority of policing was actually located in the community. Contemporary control strategies are in actual fact designed to police the community; to this end, they euphemistically allude to the rhetoric of the community. "Police–community relations" refers to levels of relative understanding and respective accommodations on the part of both the community and the police. In a society where individuals, institutions, and structures are linked through many ties, it is grossly misleading to discuss the community as spatially confined. Social order is far too frequently decontextualized and extricated from the larger processes of urbanization and industrialization, from the attendant divisions of labour (Wellman and Leighton 1978:3), and from changing property relations which loom large in structures of social relations (Kahne and Schwartz 1978:474). Likewise, analyses of policing and crime must not be limited to the efficacy of foot patrol officers and neighbourhood-based stations; also considered must be the wider community, historical trends, and social structures such as political economy, culture, and law. Nonetheless, much attention has been directed to the promises, prospects, and paradoxes of community policing.

The motto "to serve and protect" can now be seen as confusing. How is a community served and protected simultaneously? To serve is to defer and attend to the wishes of the other. Implicitly, service to the other denotes subject–authority relationships. Officers in Canada would easily argue that they do not serve the individual members of the community. Rather, the police serve the law and the Crown (the sovereignty of the people). They enjoy an independence of office that is not readily surrendered to any community. This independence ensures a sense of freedom from political interference. The act of protecting—that is, providing protective services to all in the community—is also a convenient slogan. This activity requires the development of dependency relations. The police will protect when called on only according to their own frame of reference. The police serve and protect those elements in the community which have demonstrated an investment in the existing order. Other constituencies in the community are perceived as troublesome. Irrespective of

285

these challenges, much has been written about the efficacy of community policing. For the past few decades, politicians and police administrators in Canada and the United States have generally supported community policing. According to their logic, one can prevent crime by encouraging the beat cop to work with residents and merchants in the neighbourhood. All over North America, there has been much talk about putting more police on the streets. Ideally, community policing will provide better service to the community as a result of personal contact, commitment, and continuity. As part of community policing, officers are assigned to specific areas of the community on a long-term basis to develop relationships with the various groups residing in and working in those areas. Healthy police–community relations are a product of social processes whereby actors learn values and skills; they learn to identify their own activities as different and to appreciate the integrity of others.

However, the community concept tends to gloss over the heterogeneity of community members, stratification, and differential rates of participation. In other words, from large-scale collectivities in the urban setting to neighbourhood street corners, the single chorus of the police is often met with a multiplicity of voices and strikingly different experiences. In this regard, youths generally represent a challenge to policing. And youths defined as trouble present a set of difficulties to the authority of the police.

Juvenile laws were historically designed to redirect youths in trouble within a "child-saving" protectionism. The Young Offenders Act in practice has always been a punitive measure, contradicting the principles of "doing good." Juvenile laws have long had difficulty balancing "doing justice" with "doing good," getting serious with getting tough.

In addition to the biases inherent in regulating youths, racism has become increasingly implicated in police–minority youth relations. As in many other contexts of Canadian society, race appears to be a liability in the business of control. The interests of both the police and the community are such that the phenomenon of "policing youths" *should* consist of professional, fleeting, emotionally detached, and legalistic exchanges; in practice, these encounters are disturbingly coercive, and replete with bias, threats, and power imbalances. The social construction of race influences the following: original decisions (discretion); selection of options (penalties); performances (demeanour and deference); levels of exchanges (negotiations, trust); and outcomes (formal and informal processing). In Canada no comprehensive attention has been paid to how race affects police–juvenile encounters. However, there is empirical evidence that minorities are disproportionately represented in all aspects of the juvenile justice system, from suspicious stops to secure detention facilities (Crichlow and Visano 1994; Jennings 1993; Lewis 1992; Ontario Ministry of the Attorney General 1987; Solomos 1988; Visano 1995).

Interestingly, although minority communities routinely rely on the police, the police tend to be unresponsive to their needs. In North America, blacks are far more likely than whites to be violent crime victims. To reduce disproportionate confinement of minorities, the community has been encouraged to work together—to address the causes by enhancing prevention and diversion programs and expanding alternatives to secure detention and corrections, particularly in minority neighbourhoods. Local initiatives involving families, neighbourhoods, and community-based agencies serving minority youths have been developed and implemented in urban centres throughout North America. But these policies, laws, and practices need to be reviewed—and, as necessary, corrected—to ensure that race, ethnicity, and gender do not "make" decisions to punish. Strategies to reduce the disproportionate confinement of minority juveniles have included the use of risk-and-need assessment instruments, cultural competency training for law enforcement officers (and other juvenile justice professionals), and individualized home-based care. Other strategies include mentorship, therapeutic foster care, community-based family-oriented services, reintegration services for juveniles placed outside the home, and job training.

In examining the extent to which race plays a significant role in the control of young offenders, a number of questions are asked. How does the dominant order script police–minority youth relations? To what degree do police perceive colour as an incongruity in their moral assessments? To what extent are the police defined as an "occupying army"? (On this subject, see Di Manno, 1994, on Metro Toronto Police Commissioner Arnold Minors.) To police, does colour signal trouble? Our data indicate that all youths in our sample, black and white, believe that the police "exploit" colour as a "resource." That is, police officers generalize situations in terms of fixed racist stereotypes located in both the occupational and the popular culture. Specifically, black youths note that police see their power as partly based on white supremacy. How do black and white youths vary in their perceptions of the police? To what extent has youth become a commodity and colour a liability in the "market" of police exchanges? In general, youths feel that they must accommodate the arbitrariness of police authority. How different are these views from those of the wider community?

✳ Methods: From Naturalistic Inquiries to Action-Based Research

The material in this chapter is part of a larger, ongoing five-year longitudinal project designed to track developing relations between police and various ethno-racial communities. In the course of relating to the police, communities adopt a wide variety of strategies, from easy accommodation to direct confrontation. These qualitative and quantitative contacts vary according to each group's *vertical* (power; prestige; privilege) and *horizontal* (institutional completeness; historical investment; cultural proximity to the "dominant" Anglophone and Francophone heritage; linguistic, racial, and ethnic differences) location within the Canadian mosaic.

This specific study of police–minority youth relations incorporates a multi-method design, with the following elements: informal interviews with youths conducted between May 1994 and February 1995 in Metropolitan Toronto and York Region; observations at community centres; street-corner transactions; and structured diaries. We adopted a flexible "theoretical sampling" scheme (Glaser and Strauss 1967) that was well suited and convenient. This sample was collected primarily by "snowball" techniques, which generated leads to well-informed contacts. Researchers also made independent introductions by going directly to the natural settings (various community centres and community-based organizations). For comparative purposes, systematic observations and interviews in mainstream and ethno-cultural settings were conducted.

The sample consisted of 63 youths, 37 of whom identified themselves as black and 26 as white. Forty-two of the participants were boys between 15 and 18; 21 were girls from 16 to 19. The white cohort (26) identified themselves as follows: ten Anglophones; three Francophones; six Italian descent (three foreign-born); two Portuguese descent; two Greek descent; and three Jewish descent. The black group comprised 24 Canadian-born (parents from Jamaica); five Canadian-born (Trinidad); six Canadian-born (Guyana); and two youths born in Somalia.

There were few age-specific distinctions for the two groups. Whatever the validity of claims about police harassment, what youths say, imagine, or believe regarding the police is very integral to the way youths and police relate to each other. Validity was enhanced by sharing data with the participants in an effort to capture more accurately "their" diverse perceptions. At different sites, cross-comparisons and interviews were conducted with key informants. Thus, services providers, teachers, community activists, police officers, politicians, religious leaders, social workers, and lawyers ensured reliability of the data. Ethnographic tools facilitated a close cultural description of the social organization of police–minority youth interactions.

☀ Policing the Encounter: Criminalizing Colour

The policing of youths, as a social process, exists in interactions that reflect both unique and generic features. The situational characteristics of encounters shape their definitions and outcomes. These characteristics include demographic, organizational, and situational factors. For example, the following factors are relevant: the deference and demeanour of the actors; age; colour, class, ethnicity; appearance; number of youths; gender; number of police officers; and age and years of service on the police force. Also significant in this regard are style of patrol (legalistic or peace keeping); experience in dealing with youths; characteristics of the situation; nature of the suspicious circumstance; presence of bystanders; location; time of day; whether the event is repeat or first-time; and organizational pressures. As a result of repeated interactions, both officers and youths learn from their more seasoned colleagues how to "take the edge"—that is, how to maximize gain with a minimum of effort in negotiating the encounter (Visano 1990). Exchanges are contextually determined.

For youths, there is a youth-oriented street culture that is reinforced by the media-driven popular culture. In the study, 90 percent of youths indicated that their definitions of the police were similar to and supported by their friends. For the police, the occupational culture with its attendant roles and rules affects definitions of situations. Yet the influence of this culture has been overlooked in studies of youth–police exchanges.

In addition to stopping and searching individuals, the police seek to "contain" or control certain communities through surveillance and intelligence gathering. A policing strategy that regards blacks as intrinsically criminal and potentially threatening to law and order paves the way for even greater police overreaction (Institute of Race Relations 1987:12). The police culture, with all its myths, provides a general frame of reference that is used to justify street stops. This framework is a source of direction with prescribed expectations that guide police–youth relations. Moreover, the subterranean values of the police culture act as a defence mechanism that protects the police from the negative attitudes of outsiders toward them. The stopping of a black motorist or pedestrian, often on a flimsy pretext, is one of the most frequent stop-and-search situations. Police stereotypes assume that blacks cannot own cars or must be up to "no good" when driving in white areas (ibid). Once stopped, these "suspects" are questioned in a rude, hostile, and provocative manner. Frequent stop-and-searches create considerable anger and frustration. This frustration is interpreted by the police as a sign of guilt. Equally significant is that black suspects are automatically checked out on the police computer (ibid 13). These random stops tend to initiate lengthy confrontations. Arbitrary arrests characterize many of these encounters. Blacks are seldom told why they are stopped or searched. When they resist these arbitrary arrests, they are subjected to unfair interferences, including charges of assaulting a police officer. Violence or excessive police force, therefore, is presented as an inevitable aspect of arrest (ibid).

As 18-year-old Joe commented:

> I came from Jamaica, that's cool. There the cops are tough. They pick on the poor. People know that. The government and cops are corrupt. But here in Canada it's different; Canada is a free society. I don't expect to be roughed up simply because I'm black.

Ultimately, the victims are blamed. Colour becomes "commodified." The police interpret colour as an expression of a troublesome social identity. According to the youths, colour for the police signifies class and imputes a debased or "spoiled" status. Black youths see the police as shallow. Police reportedly draw conclusions on the basis of clothing, accent, and appearance. Moreover, they often "assign" personalities to "superficial appearances." As Sylvester, a 17-year-old black from the inner city, recalled:

> Just 'cause we look tough don't mean shit. But you see the police use that to say we're dissing [disrespecting] them. Even if we are, that's no crime. So we wear clothes in a different way. What does that mean? We deserve to be harassed for that? They don't think that just maybe we don't like their stupid uniform.

Stewart, a 15-year-old white from the suburbs, elaborated:

> Cops are on my case a lot. At night when I'm hanging out, just swinging, a dick will come up and ask why I wear my handkerchief. What gang I belong to. They say I'm in their "face." Sure, hassle the shit out of me when I'm doing something. But not for nothing. They're a bunch of lazy fat asses who think they're big. We don't got the attitude, *they* got it.

In many ways, appearances "manufacture" trouble. Once the encounter is initiated (and especially if the police initiate it), youths feel compelled to cooperate with a hostile party. According to black youths, whenever they communicate with the police they are treated with contempt. Even in casual banter, youths sensed the distrust and discomfort created by the climate of suspicion that police bring to encounters. The gestures, tone of voice, and overall demeanour of the officer indicate trouble. Black youths commented that the police go "out of their way" to be rude. Signs of impending trouble are immediate and noticeable in all police encounters. Youths are constantly on guard and required to learn quickly how to respond to police.

Josephine, an 18-year-old black woman from a more privileged background, stated:

> The cops like to see us squirm. We hate it. But we are forced to accept their reasons for stopping and searching us. White kids walk away after their nasty dealings. For them it's bad but they get up and dust themselves off. It just reminds them of who they really are in the eyes of the police—white trash. For us, it's not just making a mistake. We can't just get up and walk away. For black kids the hurt is a big deal. It's a reminder of who we aren't. It really hurts when you have to agree with what the officer says. If you don't, they'll get even. Plant some dope, maybe. Call me a dumb-assed whore. It isn't worth it. It really hurts. It really makes me mad.

Interestingly, youths who described themselves as victims of violence generally refused to register a complaint against the police. This was for many legitimate reasons, including fear of reprisals, insensitivity of the criminal justice system, and inadequate or limited options. Though well-established police-complaint procedures are at hand, all youths perceive themselves as disenfranchised. Clearly, they lack the requisite intellectual and political modes of resistance as well as the resources to proclaim an effective counterhegemony. Youths have learned to be accommodating while fully realizing their opposition to definitions police impose.

White youths tend to "play it safe" and derive some pleasure from practicing the traditional "ceremonies" of deference to the "office," which are without a real purpose or goal. Unlike their male counterparts, white girls tend to "play the game," "go along" or "do the time." White males talk of the boredom of the police hassle. After repeated encounters, they become inattentive and accept this routine as a growing pain. Jeff, a 19-year-old white, added:

> What's the beef? It's a price we all gotta pay. Don't kid yourself; it happens when you're older too. They act like hotshots. Expect us to give them infor-

mation. Run when they come. It's a hassle. They're like cowboys or sheriffs, running us out of town. With blacks, they chase them too but only after shooting them first.

White youths—especially the young women—express doubts regarding levels of police violence in this study. Their black counterparts articulate a more profound degree of psychological cleverness. This cynicism is a survival skill and is used to outsmart abusive authority figures.

Police–youth encounters are full of images, props, and special language. During the investigation of a suspicious youth, the police officer expects the suspect to take the back seat of the cruiser. This means that encounters are no longer visible to the general public and therefore are beyond external interference. The cruiser is part of a tightly articulated system of control. The locked back door, the cage, the police radio, the visible presence of the revolver (and in some instances the rifle mounted on the dash), note-taking behaviour, and the computer-check ritual constitute a coherent set of symbols that display a monopoly over physical force. In this context, processes of negotiation and mediation are more circumscribed. Exchanges outside the cruiser are less coercive, less predictable, and more productive. Skilled police investigators tend to rely less on coercion (the physical features of control) and more on consent.

Once encounters move away from the more public street-corner locations into more private settings, their content changes. In private settings the police are better able to establish immediate control over youths. The police maintain a position of power by resorting to exaggerated displays of legal power and physical prowess. Armed with legal expertise, they take charge by imposing their preferences and by directing the rhythm of the exchange. This control minimizes the danger of being exploited by youths who refuse to cooperate and threaten to use violence. Also, control serves to reduce any ambiguity about the roles established by the police. The police rely on persuasion in addition to direct commands. Initially, they routinely manipulate these youths and gently prod them into submission. By flattering the youths regarding their knowledge about drugs or weapons, these officers hope to be rewarded. Younger black and white boys will concoct ingenious hard-luck stories to elicit favourable responses from the police. Seventy percent of the youths (boys and girls) admit that they fabricated information about themselves to encourage a more lenient police response. In turn, older youths talked about "how they stayed out of trouble." Younger youths failed to realize that the police are not reluctant to use force if encounters become problematic. The low visibility of these encounters enables the police to use threats of physical violence. Although all youths perceive a willingness on the part of the police to use force, only 10 percent of them said that physical force was applied to secure compliance. As Foucault (1977, 1980) argues, a "confessional" examination is more effective than physical punishment in achieving power and discipline. Once the police strip youths of their anonymity, they are able to ensure a greater degree of compliance. The police establish dependency relations wherein the youth feels obligated to provide some information. The police use the leverage of law to manipulate relations. The language of law mystifies youths. Foreign legalese and even police occupational argot compel youths to seek clarification from these officers. As the police respond, they impose their own definitions of trouble. Mark, 16 years old, recalled:

> Just before the cop told me anything, he put me in the back of the cruiser. Who knows. I'm not going to fuss. It seemed that it was the law. Later I found out that's harassment.

Parenthetically, policing is information gathering. Thus, strategies are necessarily invoked to stimulate the flow of information from youths about serious offences; this is different from hassling youths during "fishing or hunting" expeditions. More experienced officers, especially in the homicide and hold-up units treat suspects as good sources of information. Uniformed and patrol officers have yet to establish lines of communication that develop community contacts.

In brief, the following substantive issues were confirmed: all youths reported varying degrees of police harassment; and all youths were suspicious of police. White and black youths agree that the level of police abuse (physical and verbal) corresponds to the ordering shown in Table 11.1.

All youths believed that the category "black male alone" suffers the greatest degree of police harassment. Anecdotal evidence from white and black youths suggests that colour figures prominently in police–youth encounters. So does gender; and so does gender *layered with colour*. Fourteen out of the 37 black youths noted that the police subscribe to both racist and sexist stereotypes. The police are more inclined to stop and search a male black youth with a female white youth than two female black youths or two female white youths. Fifty-two mentioned that the police behave in this problematic manner in order to demonstrate their disapproval of any mixing. As Damian, a 17-year-old black, succinctly observed:

> The cops cannot stand to see a black kid with a white girl. It's not that they're jealous, they just don't like it 'cause they think like the white supposed to be superior or something. It scares the shit out of them. They have to wake up—that it isn't their fucking business.

Table 11.1

Focus of Police Harassment: Perceptions of Youths

Category	Percentage of Respondents
Black male alone	100
Black males together	100
Black and white males together	100
Black males and white females	90
White males together	80
Black and white females	70
Black females together	70
White males and white females	50
Black female alone	50
White female alone	50
(N=63)	

Michele, a 19-year-old white, concurred:

I've gone out with black guys all my life. So what? But you can see that when you get pulled over, the cops keep staring. I get the feeling that they think I'm a prostitute. They stare and give my date a rough time.

White youths reported occasional stops; black youths (both motorists or pedestrians) indicated that they are routinely stopped and questioned by the police. The police tend to be more hostile in dealing with motorists than with pedestrians. Black and white youths agree that the more serious charges are reserved for black youths. Georgette, a white 18 year old, said:

It's like this. They hassle anybody who is young and looks out of place. With me they'll talk about me being on a joy ride thing. But with blacks they call it car theft. No big deal. What sounds worse in court? Joy ride is having fun. But stealing cars is breaking the law.

The provincial Highway Traffic Act and municipal by-laws, and other legislation, provide the police with the legal authority to initiate an investigation. Drivers are under more legal obligations than pedestrians. Pursuant to the Highway Traffic Act, every driver is required to carry his or her driver's licence while driving and to produce it, together with proof of insurance, when requested by a police officer. For example, the police have the right to stop a motorist for the purpose of determining intoxication, or in the lawful execution of duties, or to demand a breath sample. If there has been no accident and you are stopped by the police, you need not give any statement to the police but you are required to produce your driver's licence and proof of insurance and to blow into a breathalyzer (McDonald 1984:18). Often, youths complained about being pulled over for reasons not related to their driving. As Georgette, an 18-year-old experienced driver, summarized:

> They ask where we've been, where we're going, what we've been up to, and lots more. Cops are stupid. They ask if we got drugs. Sure, I'm going to say for sure. Give me a break. No really, they stop me and my friends all the time. They make up some phony reason. They talk. They're checking it out. That's cool. But if we're clean, get away and leave us alone. Go have your doughnuts and free coffee. I don't care.

In contrast, there is much more friendly discussion and good-humoured teasing with the foot patrols. In our focused group discussions, it was pointed out that these officers satisfy more than legalistic requirements: they are also a form of public relations. These officers are expected to maintain a degree of cordiality, civility, and community interest, at least in the public eye. Officers in cruisers do not appear to be as concerned with projecting a "public relations" image to youths that satisfies organizational propaganda. Community policing assumes a different meaning for officers in cruisers than for officers on the beat. White youths discussed their difficulties with the police in terms of exploitation. They feel exploited at first: they are expected to respect the authority of the officer. However, once the youths show a willingness to cooperate, the officers assume a different stance. Although they never compromise their authority, they are willing to negotiate with individuals they define as cooperative. White youths noted that the police treat them as if they were corrigible. These youths indicated that they were more able to manipulate the police once the officers adjusted their definition of the situation. Amanda, a 17-year-old black, elucidated:

> White kids are lucky. They can always pretend to be afraid of the police. Cops believe them. Cops see some bonds with them. All the white kid has to do is fake it. They can play better. My brothers and sisters can't play along. They don't know how. They're too hurt. Too suspicious of the cop. African Canadians are never trusted any time. Even when they're innocent they're guilty. They are made to feel guilty. I'm not saying that white kids love the police or the cops like all white kids. All I'm saying is that black kids have a hell of a time connecting with the cop. It's deep. Really deep. Cops don't get it.

Police–minority youth relations exist within wider social contexts. Policing is one of many institutions that attempt to subordinate the self-esteem of black youths. Within the circular logic of a racist hegemony perpetrated from academic institutions to the popular culture, black youths are reminded that they do not belong because they are different, and that they are different because they do not belong. As 16-year-old Maurice suggested: "Because I'm black means I'm like too different. Not just different but too different, like dangerous." Black students feel like strangers in their own land. They don't feel connected, nor are they made to feel connected. These youths experience little confidence and credibility in their dealings with the police.

The Canadian criminal justice system reflects structures of dominance. History teaches these youths that they are not as attractive, intelligent, or capable as whites. Their painful search for individual worth in Canadian society is thereby frustrated. Black youths indicated that because they are socially pressured to perceive themselves as poor, ill informed, and more delinquent than whites, they sense a "cultural distance" in their encounters with police. Incidents like the following inform the opinions of many youths. On November 14, 1991, in Montreal, police officer André Sevigny slammed a 14-year-old black teenager against a window and held a revolver to the boy's throat. In October 1994, in response to this brutality, a tribunal of the Quebec Police Ethics Commission merely handed down a guilty verdict with a seven-day suspension without pay (*Toronto Star*, October 18, 1994:A12). This penalty does not convey a message of condemnation. All minority youths in this study have experienced inappropriate treatment by the police. Policing black youths meshes well with the policing of the poor and unemployed. This means that black adolescents grow up under a system of police surveillance. In other words, as Brake (1985:142) identified, "the ongoing problem of policing the blacks has become, for all practical purposes, synonymous with the wider problem of policing the crisis." Since arrest statistics are high in minority neighbourhoods, crime becomes a justification for racist attitudes (ibid 128). Throughout Canada, the United States, and the United Kingdom, black youths are typically depicted as fragmented, dysfunctional, or delinquent by most police officers.

In the Greater Toronto Area, police officers attribute many problems to Jamaicans. In 1994, in Toronto, two events occurred that enabled them to make this connection. The first was the Just Desserts killing. Vivi Leimonis was shot to death in that downtown café during a robbery. Oneil Grant was charged with manslaughter. Grant, a Jamaican immigrant, had been ordered deported in 1992 after being convicted several times for assault and for drug offences, but a member of the Immigration and Refugee Board had granted him a "second chance" (*Toronto Star*, June 17, 1994:A19). Also in 1994, Constable Todd Baylis was killed with a stolen handgun while on community patrol. Clinton Junior Gayle was charged in this death. Gayle, a 25-year-old Jamaican, had been ordered deported in 1991 after being convicted on nine charges. He was also convicted on five more charges after the deportation order was issued; most of the charges were drug-related. Through bureaucratic error, he was never deported. Note that these two men came to Canada as children—Grant at the age of 12 and Gayle at age 9. They were *not* recent immigrants. The stereotype continues to flourish that Jamaicans are dangerous, and this quickly spills over into misperceptions that all blacks are potential criminals.

This normative frame of reference informs police assessments and ultimately affects modes of interaction. The problem for black youths occurs well before the encounter. Many police officers inaccurately equate colour with crime. As evidence of their beliefs, they often cite (refutable) crime statistics from the Jane–Finch area of Toronto. As a result, they have a poor appreciation of African-Canadian culture. This poor understanding includes the assumption that there is one homogeneous black family type and one homogeneous black community.

✵ Individual Rights, Institutionalized Responses, and Community Rage

Whenever youths feel less attached to and involved with institutions of authority like the police, they are more likely to be less committed to them and less likely to trust them. Moreover, aside from occasional public gestures of accommodation such as sporting events, youths are generally not encouraged to participate meaningfully with the police. Interestingly, throughout elementary school, children look forward to the visits of friendly police officers who come and talk about safety concerns (Block Parents, traffic safety). Yet during the teenage years a growing cynicism about the police develops. This is partly a result of personal experience. However, the youths in our study also cited the following examples of police failing "to take their views seriously": the case of teenager Marlon Neal, who was shot for failing to stop at a police radar stop; the police presence in secondary schools in Metropolitan Toronto as a result of the perception that school violence is increasing; and the failure of the police to accept the legitimacy of community initiatives such as the Guardian Angels.

Notwithstanding this mutual distrust, statistics reveal that black male teenagers (that is, boys and young men from 12 to 19) are more likely to be violent crime *victims* than any other group. Their average annual rate is 113 victimizations per 1,000, or almost one in nine. For white male teenagers the rate is 90 per 1,000, or about one in eleven (Visano 1995).

The type of community in which a youth lives also affects his or her likelihood of becoming involved in hostile police encounters. Youths living in better neighbourhoods do not have high rates of police encounters. Economically disadvantaged areas tend to be flooded with social workers, private security measures, and police officers.

According to Giddens (1992), modernity produces "risk cultures," "differential access to empowerment," "exclusion," and "marginalization." Accordingly, relationships in these contexts are called upon to provide "inoculations" and to act as "protective cocoons" for community members (1991:3–4). For both the police and youths, community and peer cultures act like "protective cocoons" and "inoculations" that screen out potential trouble and also provide a framework for interpretation. These cultures also produce marginalization and enhance their own differences. In addition, for youth—especially for black youth—peer cultures provide important protection against powerlessness and exclusion. A priori conditioning incites intolerance. Police–youth exchanges are represented as a "risk." The common-sense knowledge and beliefs about policing are problematized. Additionally, policing is perceived as an intrusion into the lives of others. Both youths and police provide staged performances, differentially manipulated by wider narratives of trouble that demand intolerance, closure, containment, and coercion. Moreover, the nature of police authority is a barrier to effective communication precisely *because of* its absolutist, dysfunctional, bureaucratic, paramilitaristic, and corporate interpretive frameworks.

Police exchanges are ideologically constituted in the interests of the state. Law serves and protects this privilege. Accordingly, youths are denied meaningful participation. Youths are criminalized commodities, by-products of a system that seeks to recruit only informants. Minority youths are further oppressed by the imputation that they are dangerous and therefore worthy of discipline. For the police, however, these impaired relations are related to faulty family, school, peer, or work socialization. In this regard, four of the ten officers interviewed noted that society is pathogenic by nature. As Michel Foucault (1977:175) reminded us, this pathological orientation serves to inspire a whole mythology for the police that in turn justifies exaggerated crime panics. For the police, society is unruly, predatory, and unprincipled. Crime, manifested in social disorganization, is sometimes perceived as a product of decaying transitional neighbourhoods plagued by "alien" cultures and diffuse cultural standards. Natalie, a community organizer, aptly maintained:

Youths see themselves as scapegoats. They are impotent while the police are incompetent. It's understandable. The police have been around as a very conservative institution while kids always test and challenge authorities. The police have difficulties in dealing with challenges to their authority. They are not professionals if they allow themselves to be annoyed by a belligerent kid. They are no better. In my business I see the police looking for trouble. They want trouble. Some [police] are real bullies.

The police find it difficult to regulate encounters with citizens without some threats of sanctions. Should persuasion prove to be ineffective, they resort to threats to restore order in the interaction. Verbal intimidation is the most common tactic used by the police to control youths defined as resisting of authority. Such intimidation is designed to embarrass and to create fear. Police officers expect youths to debase themselves by assuming a degree of blame. By feeling ashamed, they contribute to their own pacification.

Police–minority youth exchanges are inherently unequal. The failure of youths to cooperate with the police is related to the wider societal practices of discrimination based on age, gender, and race. These exclusionary forms relate to issues of access to social and political structures. For youths, the following features of the police and the law are systemic barriers: the cultural distance of police officers; the complexity and bureaucratic nature of the legal system; variations among youths in knowledge and understanding of their rights, resources, benefits, and entitlements; and the bewildering multiplicity of human rights organizations and agencies, with their complex and confusing eligibility rules regarding complaints against the police. Youths also believe that the legal system perpetuates these tensions by sustaining repression and punishing resistance.

The consistent denial of fundamental rights contributes to a lingering rage that partly explains why riots occur. Black youths noted repeatedly that the seductive police campaigns concerning community consultation, partnership building, ongoing dialogue, innovation, accessibility, accountability, and cross-cultural training have become empty slogans of legitimation. As 17-year-old Jerome added:

Put that shit about community policing on the billboards. Make the whites think they're doing something. Make the new chief think that he's really down there working with the people. What shit! Tell the chief and his men that we know that he can't be that stupid to think that we're buying that shit. Maybe he thinks that! Most whites think that—come down, shoot the shit, and that's cool. All of a sudden we're going to forget police brutality ... oppression. Talk about getting us out of this misery, not this shit about community. We're poor. Talk about that, not community policing crap.

Likewise, 16-year-old Manley added:

What kind of dumb fucks do they think we are. Piss on us and then expect us to respect that shit. Times are changing. I think that is what the cops want. They want us to declare war. They want me to be mouthy. They want something on me. Why give them an excuse to fuck you. Just be cool. Take the heat.

Poverty creates a despair that, if unchecked, challenges the conventional order. Discrimination in the criminal justice system only serves to exacerbate the disadvantages that minority youths already suffer. The overrepresentation of black youths in the criminal justice system is the result of racial and economic inequality and a deteriorating economic situation (Philips and Votey 1987; Adler, Meuller, and Laufer 1991:47). Criminalization is directly linked to the production of race relations. For the criminal justice system, colour signifies danger:

The low power and more disadvantaged position of blacks make some of their criminal actions more likely to be seen as rebellious attacks on an alien order by disgruntled outsiders. Blacks are also regarded as having deviant characters even before any criminal involvement, and their higher official rate of offending confirms their deviant character. White crimes are likely to be viewed as temporary deviations from character. [Kempf 1986:43].

Marginalized communities are stressed communities. As the youths in this study argued, rage is a logical response to stress. Riots are situationally defined coping mechanisms for dealing with structured physical and psychological abuses. When confronted with a set of circumstances supported by clear evidence of systemic oppression, various coping strategies are adopted. Within a functionalist framework, the forces of repression, rage, and riots encourage an appraisal of available managing styles. This frustration/aggression model locates the problem in the abilities, aggression, and failed expectations of affected individuals and groups. Although this situation precipitates urban rioting, more structural elements warrant analysis.

A focus on the "ideology of hopelessness" (Massey and Denton 1993:5) must implicate the economic, political, and social structures that perpetuate all forms of inequality, including racism. The push/pull factors contributing to exclusion, alienation, and disengagement involve employment prospects, education, and recreation, to name only a few. Youths have at length commented on the hopelessness of their encounters with the police. Racism is the root of all riots, which are expressions of collective political protest. Typically, the state attempts to distract communities with the empty promises of pluralism/multiculturalism and equality. Even if disadvantaged communities were to submit grievances, why should they trust the white power structure, given the lessons of history and current exclusionary legal practices? Drug abuse has always provided a good excuse for state intervention. Crime control has become grounded in this overstated fear of youths. Moreover, policing youths has been transformed into an instrument of oppression. Anger, frustration, and resentment characterize youth–police exchanges.

Stigmatization or the collective designation of discredit has extensive consequences for any individual's self-concept. A label, once affixed by powerful interests not only shapes identity but remains so firmly attached that it becomes difficult to remove. Specifically, labels generate new definitions of "self" for the particular person, his or her reference group, and the larger societal audiences. Furthermore, when these individuals fail to shed the designation, they often "personalize" or internalize their labels by organizing their lifestyles around the assumptions associated with the labels. A "master status" emerges that overshadows all other aspects of identity.

Conscientization, as a form of resistance, is long overdue as a means to minimize the exploitation of stereotypes that has long been found in police–youth encounters. This conscientization is reflected in the lyrics of Public Enemy's (1990) "Fight the Power," which confront the realities of daily life for many youths, whether in south-central Los Angeles or on the reserves of Canada:

> To revolutionize make a change nothin's strange

• • •

> Power to the people no delay
> To make everybody see
> In order to fight the powers that be
> Fight the Power.

Likewise, Ice-T (1991) advised:

But you don't understand,
You're still a slave to the Man,
Prepare for revolution ...

Throughout the 1960s and 1970s, animosity toward police was a condition necessary for transforming one's identity. Policing is still perceived as oppressive in the 1990s. Social change has been extremely slow—and in some instances reversed—largely because of a white police agenda. The prospects of "solving" racism are not good as long as corporate economic power can simply move from blatant forms of containment to piecemeal, shallow strategies of accommodation—a form of liberal inferiorization.

Recently, the Toronto police have come under considerable media and public scrutiny as a result of the comments by one police commissioner, Arnold Minors. Minors, the only black member of a seven-person board, indicated that white officers fear blacks. He is reported to have told the *Bermuda Times* that "black people [in Toronto] have been shot and killed per capita disproportionate to any other community" (*Toronto Star*, September 4, 1993:A4). Minors, a consultant in race relations who teaches antiracism courses for the Attorney General, also commented on the lack of cooperation police received from witnesses to a shooting of three men at an after-hours club frequented mainly by blacks. In reference to these concerns, he said:

> There is a long, long, thousand-year history of people not speaking to occupying armies ... but I do know that when police officers talk about "These people won't speak to us," it is precisely the same thing that occupying armies talk about: "These people won't speak to us." [*Toronto Star*, October 20, 1994:6]

Minors was simply illustrating the "perspective that some people might have" (ibid). According to Lennox Farrell, a well-respected community activist and a former candidate for mayor of North York, the idea that the police are an occupying army is a "widely held perspective" among blacks who have experienced the racism of the criminal justice system. Spokesperson Akua Benjamin, representing a coalition of African-Canadian groups, added: "We strongly condemn the recent vitriolic attacks by the media and the unfair actions of some government officials toward Mr. Minors" (ibid, October 26, 1994:6). In response to the police slogan "to serve and protect," the feeling among blacks is that the motto of some police officers may as well be "to harass and oppress (Head 1976:1–7). In reference to these claims, the following findings emerged: black youths perceive the police to be an occupying army; black and white youths perceive the police to be hostile; black and white youths accept too readily that they are unfamiliar with available legal remedies and complaint services; black youths highlight cultural factors in explanations of why they are reluctant to cooperate with police; and only four youths had anything positive to say about the police. Specifically, youths identified a number of obstacles to improving youth–police relations, including a lack of information, communication problems, and inaccessible services.

In North America, policing in black communities is qualitatively different from policing in other communities, especially since formal social control is a reflection of historical and colonial attitudes toward blacks. Police forces rely on stereotypic classifications and mental images that corroborate their negative beliefs. These views reflect wider sociocultural conditioning, institutionally sanctioned police practices, and informal, occupationally derived subcultural attitudes.

The process of moral integration, especially the sharing of beliefs, values, and rituals, reinforces conformity and promotes common conceptions regarding appropriate behaviour. Thus, a collective dominant conscience based on similar social circumstances, feelings, and interests directs individuals to internalize these collective sentiments. In general, police officers share a perception that blacks are lazy, drug addicted, incompetent, and untrustworthy. This set of values is closely linked to identification with the police subculture. In the field, police officers are expected to surrender to the subculture's expressions of social values. The police assume that everyone is tied to "the" same conventional order—an encompassing common stability. Yet some corporate image experts say racial harmony is a marketing fad—and only firms such as Benetton are expected to remain committed to it after other social issues come into vogue.

✸ Remedies: Orwell's *1984* versus Huxley's *Brave New World*

Community policing cannot be appreciated without a fundamental concern for knowledge, especially in the grounding of interbureaucratic perspectives. The apprehension and articulation of knowledge as truth governs relations and subsequently accounts for control. The police task, therefore, requires a scrutiny of what knowledge is needed by the corporation. Integral to community policing is the assignment of public safety officers to specific areas of the community on a long-term basis to develop relationships with the various groups living and working those areas. These officers work together with community members to define and solve problems and to develop proactive strategies to reduce crime. Officers also implement special programs to address specific needs of the community. Community-based programs like Block Parents encourage parental participation in making neighbourhoods safe for their children; Neighbourhood Watch is another voluntary program. Consistent with and inseparable from social services, team policing is designed to improve intelligence. Thus, with increased budgetary cutbacks and dwindling resources, the police are required to rely more heavily on the community in an effort to improve public safety.

Studying the conditions of successful police–youth relations requires the development of a framework for identifying contexts and processes—influences on the decision-making options of all parties. It would be fruitful and challenging to build on this research and develop an inventory of factors that could be analyzed in an effort to close the gap. Police–community relations is a dramatic example of the production of items for display and the display of these images for mass consumption. This research demonstrated that the disguising of police as authoritative knowledge brokers serves to create and maintain the collective conscience of a community—a concentrated normative moral consensus. As Habermas (1974) indicated, the meanings and symbols of the dominant ideology prevent critical thinking by penetrating social processes, language, and individual consciousness. Ideology transforms the self into a subject—individuals adopt versions of the truth for themselves. But, as a sophisticated means of control, the dominant ideology succeeds in creating processes of self-subordination. The actor represses, deprives, and denies self-autonomy by projecting a deindividualized conception of self. This advances the vulnerability of the individual.

Where do we then go from here? The following is a partial list of remedies, short- as well as long-term. It is incumbent upon all segments of society to understand the significance of cultural factors, to confront insidious forms of white supremacy in all institutions, and to become conscious of the impact of institutionalized racism, sexism, and age discrimination. Furthermore, we must challenge white power and privileges in their relationships with all minorities and strive toward coalition building between oppressed groups. In other words, we must connect all forms of oppression in order to provide a more powerful unified movement toward full equality for all oppressed groups. Lastly, we should move toward connecting the social institutions of the state—especially immigration, education, housing, health care, welfare, and the law and order apparatus—to better serve the needs of oppressed groups.

This research corroborates the findings of James (1990:4) that white and black youths do not receive the same treatment. Racism within the juvenile justice system functions to foster solidarity and collective conformity and to justify further exclusionary exercises. The prevailing ideologies, perceptions, and values within facilities incorporate strategies of survival within and assimilation to alien cultures. Youths are compelled to abandon distinctive ethnocultural traits in favour of widely held dominant values. It is an ideology not simply of differences (physical and cultural) but of superiority that denies the meaningful participation of black youth.

This study confirms Bolaria and Li's (1988:212) findings that black youths feel categorized as a problem group by the police, who are more likely to question or arrest them; that the police use excessive physical violence in their dealings with black suspects; and that the police perpetrate popular rumours about the involvements of youth.

Nonblack ethnocultural groups expect the state to protect fundamental rights. Systemic discrimination refers to inequalities deeply rooted in the operation of society. As a built-in feature of all institutions, systemic racism reinforces racist attitudes and behaviour; in this way it excludes people of colour from significant participation in these institutions. In juvenile justice there is a streaming of youths defined as a problem. Punitive options are ineffective. Youths are discouraged from participating in the legal system. Equally superficial is the hiring and promotion of more blacks. Tina, a 17 year old, added:

> We ain't going to help 'cause they're not black but now they're blue. Really it's like the cop cars in Metro. Check the colours out—blue on white. No black colours here. Pushing for blacks alone won't change the rules.

Police reform is long overdue. Better training of police, as well as the recruitment and promotion of nonwhites, cannot on its own eliminate institutional racism, the roots of which are embedded in the culture and in the socioeconomic conditions that require change. Youths must recognize the limits or weaknesses of existing police initiatives. It would be fruitful for them to move toward a model of both community and self-development. By becoming well tutored in the law and advocacy, coalition building, and professional affiliations, youth can convey a vision. Andrea, a 19 year old, summarized:

> I don't have much to feel proud about. Tell me what there is? Nothing seems to change. Look at the States. That's our future. We really can't expect anything different. Look at our history and then tell me to feel good about the cops. Cops haven't changed. We're still treated differently. Go to court and just watch who is there. Find your solutions not here in the black community

but in the white place. We can't do it. It's a white problem. Look at yourselves first. Ask yourself if the white man really wants to change.

On the basis of the empirical findings in this exploratory study, and in the interests of critical pedagogy, the following questions are asked as a means to stimulate further criminological dialogue and research.

- To what extent is the discussion of community policing a distraction? Highlight how an analysis of police roles is central to a more comprehensive appreciation of the structures and processes of racism.
- To what extent are the police accountable to the rule of law?
- How is the police occupational culture an accommodation to both the norms of the organization and wider hegemonic imperatives?
- How is the policing of youth a function of the needs and demands of the wider political economy?
- Assess the concept of "community policing" in terms of prevailing crime control ideologies, effectiveness, and the "blurring and reshaping of institutional boundaries."
- Racism has become a pervasive feature of modern policing. Discuss the significance of racism for social control. Address the difficult relationship between the institution of policing and property.
- How is policing a process of intelligence gathering?

References

Adler, F., G. Mueller, and W. Laufer. 1991. *Criminology*. New York: McGraw-Hill.

Bolaria, Singh, and Peter Li. 1988. *Racial Oppression in Canada*. Toronto: Garamond.

Brake, M. 1985. *Comparative Youth Culture*. New York: Routledge and Kegan Paul.

Crichlow, W., and L. Visano. 1994. "A Liberal Text of Equality and Subtexts of Oppression." Unpublished paper. OISE and York University.

Di Manno, R. 1994. "Minors' defenders adopt the tactics they condemn." *Toronto Star*. (October 26):6.

Durkheim, E. [1893], 1933. *Division of Labor in Society*. New York: Free Press; 1964 edition with Free Press (NY).

Durkheim, E. [1897], 1951. *Suicide*. Translated by G. Simpson. New York: Free Press.

Fagan, J., E. Slaughter, and E. Harstone. 1987. "Blind Justice? The Impact of Race on the Juvenile Justice Process." *Crime and Delinquency Journal* 33.

Foucault, M. 1977. *Discipline and Power*. New York: Pantheon.

Foucault, M. 1980. *Power and Knowledge: Selected Interviews and Other Writings 1972–1977*. Edited by C. Gordon. New York: Vintage.

Giddens, A. 1973. *The Class Structure of Advanced Societies*. New York: Harper and Row.

Giddens, A. 1991. *Modernity and Self-Identity*. Stanford: Stanford University Press.

Glaser, B., and A. Strauss. 1967. *The Discovery of Grounded Theory*. Chicago: Aldine.

Gordon, D. 1973. "Capitalism, Class and Crime in America." *Crime and Delinquency* (April) 2:163–186.

Habermas, J. 1974. *Theory and Practice*. London: Heinemann Educational Books.

Head, W. 1976. "Perceptions of Police Attitudes and Practices toward Blacks and Other Visible Minorities in Metro Toronto." In *Law Enforcement and Race Relations*. Social Planning Council.

Institute of Race Relations. 1987. *Policing against Black People*. London: Institute of Race Relations.

James, C. 1990. *Making It: Black Youth, Racism, and Career Aspirations in a Big City*. Oakville, ON: Mosaic.

Jennings, K. 1993. "Black Youth in Police Crosshairs." *Covert Action* 45 (Summer):50.

Kahne, M., and C. Schwartz. 1978. "Negotiating Trouble: The Social Construction and Management of Trouble in a College Psychiatric Context." *Social Problems* 25 (June):5.

Kempf, K., et al. 1986. "Older and More Recent Evidence on Racial Discrimination in Sentencing." *Journal of Qualitative Criminology* 2 (1):29–47.

Lewis, Stephen. 1992 (June). *Report on Race Relations in Ontario*. Toronto: Queen's Park.

McDonald, M. 1984. *Know Your New Rights*. Toronto: Fenn.

Massey, D.S., and N.A. Denton. 1993. *American Apartheid: Segregation and the Making of the Underclass*. Cambridge: Harvard University Press.

Neugebauer, R. 1992. "Misogyny, Law and the Police: Policing Violence against Women." In K. McCormick and L. Visano (eds.), *Understanding Policing*. Toronto: Canadian Scholars' Press.

Ontario Ministry of the Attorney General. 1987. *Task Force on the Law Concerning Trespass to Publicly Used Property as It Affects Youth and Minorities*. Raj Anand (Chair). Toronto: Ontario Ministry of the Attorney General.

Park, R., and E. Burgess (eds.). 1925. *The City*. Chicago: University of Chicago Press.

Park, R. (ed.). 1952. *Human Communities*. New York: Free Press.

Philips, L., and H. Votey. 1987. "Rational Choice Models of Crimes by Youth." *The Review of Black Political Economy* 16 (1–2):129–187.

Solomos, J. 1988. *Black Youth, Racism and the State—The Politics of Ideology and Polity*. Cambridge: Cambridge University Press.

Taylor, I. 1981. "Crime Waves in Post-War Britain." *Contemporary Crises* 5 (1):43–62.

Visano, L.A. 1990. "Crime as a Negotiable Commodity." *Journal of Human Justice* 2(Autumn)1:105–116.

Visano, L. 1995. *Beyond the Text*. Toronto: Harcourt Brace & Company.

Weber, M. 1946. "Class, Status and Party." In H. Gerth and C.W. Mills (eds.), *From Max Weber: Essays in Sociology*. New York: Oxford Press.

Weber, M. 1958. *The City*. Translated and edited by D. Martindale and G. Neuwirth. New York: Free Press.

Wellman, B. 1979. "The Community Question: The Intimate Network of East Yorkers." *American Journal of Sociology* 84(5):1201–1231.

Wellman, B., and B. Leighton. 1978. "Networks, Neighbourhoods and Communities." *Research Paper #97 Centre for Urban and Community Studies*. University of Toronto.

Youth Sports and Violence: A Masculine Subculture?

W. Gordon West

Rittenhouse Foundation (for Transformative Social Justice)

Consider the mounting evidence that organized sports and the sports mentality—from little kids' leagues to college teams to TV spectacle—have become a major cultural pollutant. Everyone has noticed, and commented on, the disturbing overlap of sports and military lingo ... Why do we condone our spouses' or children's massive TV indoctrination into glorified aggression and greed? ... "If you can't beat 'em in the alley, you can't beat 'em on the ice," said Conn Smythe. For those of us who do not believe in beating anyone, the question must be: how can we delegitimize this North American ceremony of blood and conquest? ... Now and then, when you observe youngsters amusing themselves without an audience or a prize, you can see the real spirit of sports: the fun, the exhilaration, the joy and self-forgetfulness of a physical challenge freely undertaken.

[Michelle Landsberg, "Team Sports Merely Glorify Violence, Greed," *The Toronto Star*, February 2, 1991]

Late in the 3rd [period], [Stan] got bodychecked cleanly, [after he] had been "swearing" about "getting that guy." After the body check, he [illegally] high sticked [the other player] in the neck under the face mask. The other kid fell down, but the referee reprimanded the other kid, not Stan! When Stan returned to the bench, I told him "Look, you got a dirty check, but you can't hit the other kid back, or you'll get a penalty."

[Field observation, February 1992]

✻ Introduction

Recently, many issues regarding males and violence have been raised in the political context of male violence toward females and increasing male youth violence (but see West 1993, 1995, forthcoming, for critical discussions). The Landsberg quote expresses a common opinion; the field note would seem to provide an example of such senseless violence. Sports have been particularly identified as enhancing "the worst" of patriarchy: elitism, competitiveness, sexism—and violence (Gruneau and Whitson 1993). Whatever our personal interest in sport activities or our moral stance toward them, since so many males do play sports and are so enthralled by them we need to investigate how various males experience sports, and we need to understand their bodily engagement in them, if we are to change social (including gender) relations in positive directions (Lenskyj 1986; Hall 1987).

Although violent behaviour by males has become a topic of considerable theoretical and practical interest, and although organized recreation has not infrequently been accused of encouraging such violence, little empirical research has been done regarding how males learn such activities and understand their physically aggressive aspects. What we do know from criminological research linking males and violence demands that we clarify both our concepts and our political projects. Why are some males more violent than most females (and most males)? How do they become so? We still understand very little empirically about the lived relationship between masculinity and violent behaviour.

In this chapter, I report on participant observation and interview research conducted over three years, focusing on males involved in baseball, shinny, "ultimate" (frisby football), scouting, and especially hockey. Ages of subjects ranged from 7 to 50, with the focus on preadolescents and adolescents. Subjects were members of five teams, one scouting group, and three informal pickup shinny sites. Some girls and women were also observed and will be used in comparisons.

The major sociological approach to understanding (especially youthful) male violence has been subcultural theory. This paper will examine the extent to which traditional sociological subcultural theories of male violence are adequate. I will argue that they need to be dramatically revised by interactionist and gender-sensitive conceptualizations to account adequately for the data on males, sports, and violence. Drawing on criminology and delinquency theory and research, and on gender studies and sport sociology, I will raise a number of theoretical questions, especially regarding our conceptualizations of subculture, masculinity, and violence.

🕸 Theoretical Perspectives on Male Violence and Adolescent Sport Subcultures

Criminological Data, Biology, and Psychology

> violence: 1. the quality of being violent; 6. the unlawful exercise of physical force.

> force: 1. power, exerted strength or impetus; intense effort; 2. coercion or compulsion especially with the use or threat of violence ... [*Concise Oxford Dictionary for the Nineties*. 1990. Oxford: Clarendon.]

Various strands of literature do present material indicating that, indeed, *some* males are more violent and aggressive than *most* females and *most* males. The sources—criminology, police statistics, historical war data, women's sources (rape crisis centres, halfway houses for battered women and children, etc.), media analyses, social psychological development studies, and teacher accounts—all concur that males perpetrate violence more than females (see West 1984). Criminologically, the great majority of violent criminal offenders are male (for instance, some 90 percent of those who commit homicide). It is hard to deny that something about "male-ness" makes it more likely that males will commit violent acts. But how and why?

Sociobiological explanations must be noted, especially given their current popularity (e.g., see *Time* 1992; *Newsweek* 1992; Givens 1992; Steinhetz 1992; Kline 1985). There are some biologically identifiable differences in levels of testosterone and a few other hormones associated with aggression; even so, it is clear that such differences are few compared with similarities between males and females. Whereas the findings are statistically "significant" beyond expected levels of random probability, the statistical "associations" are very weak: any causal claims are weak (the explanation of variance is minimal) and of almost no use in prediction. Furthermore, the few biological differences found (e.g., in testosterone levels) can be influenced by social activity: more exercise increases testosterone levels, leaving the causal ordering quite unclear! While biological explanations of disproportionate male violence may explain some differences (Treadwell 1987) and cannot be ignored, the few male–female biological differences are socially channelled and directed, so in this paper I focus on social learning experiences.

In addition, the discourse surrounding male–female differences has been overly informed by and invested in psychological research that ignores the social and historical organization and practice of gender relations (Thornton

1992). Adherence to lists of masculine and feminine role traits, for instance, does not explain how and where such sex-differentiated traits arise, or how particular individuals adopt them. Women are not concerned only about those few males who are psychotic; rather, they point out how "normal" male violence is. Although we will incorporate social psychological aspects of learning into our analyses, we need to go beyond psychological theories.

Within the criminological statistics, there are major "interaction effects" (West 1995, forthcoming.) For instance, methodologically sophisticated self-report studies have found that working- and lower-class young people, both male *and* female, are more likely to commit street violence than middle-class young people (Byles 1969). Even the crude criminological statistics do not baldly support notions that "violence" is something that males do to females.

Rather, violent behaviour tends to be an intragroup rather than an inter-group phenomenon. While males perpetrate most individual violent street crimes (murder, assault, rape, arson, robbery), and while some of the most violent acts are suffered by females, the victims of violence in general are significantly more likely to be males, not females. Males are three to four times more likely than females to be assaulted, and three times more likely to be murdered (Miles 1991:8). The group most likely to be severely censured for criminal actions is young, ethnic- and racial-minority males: some 25 percent of American black men aged 20 to 29 are in jail, on probation, or on parole. But this demographic group is also the most likely to be victimized by violence (Lerman 1978).

But—within all these caveats—how, or under what circumstances, do (some) males commit violent acts? Within the small literature that does empirically document lived males' experiences, little has been done to integrate theoretical perspectives (from criminology, feminism, and sport sociology) and empirical data showing how males learn "masculine" behaviour, such as violent behaviour.

Adolescent Subculture Theory: Sports or Violence

The classic sociological formulation for conceptualizing group adolescent deviant behaviour has been subcultural theory (Dorn and South 1983). Early sociologists (Thrasher 1927; Rogers 1945) gave considerable attention to the delinquent gang as the social organization most involved in crime and in carrying a subculture accepting violence. In part this attention was due to police concerns about errant street-corner youth: such groups *have* carried out serious delinquencies; in part, these groups piqued the curiosity of middle-class sociologists who were fascinated with describing what the mysterious and threatening working class was up to; in part, however, it was also because such groups were clearly social (as opposed to psychological) causes of delinquency. Walter Miller (1958) continued this theme when he argued that working-class young people were attracted to gangs as alternatives to their inadequate (fatherless) families, and that such gang members carried on the particular value system of their lower-class parents, which was oriented around such focal concerns as toughness, fatalism, having smarts, generating excitement, and so on. Violent behaviour was seen as validated within a lower-class subculture.

Cohen (1955) synthesized differential association and anomie/strain theories into a subcultural theory to explain the higher rates of official delinquency among young urban males of the working class. He argued that working-class youths are disadvantaged by their home preparation for competition in school. Consequently, they are more likely to fail and to suffer a resulting loss of self-esteem and status. Boys, especially, feel this lack of self-esteem and status, since they are socialized to be particularly achievement-oriented. When a number of young people experience these problems and interact regularly, they are able collectively to work out a common solution to their common problem. Since the middle-class school and its teachers have rejected them, these youths are likely reciprocally to reject their teachers and the values for which they stand. Teachers embody such middle-class values as hard work, effort being required for rewards, respect for property, deferred gratification, and so forth. In rejecting their rejectors and their values, failing working-class youths undergo a psychological reaction formation and adopt the contrary values: hedonism, nonutilitarianism, negativism, and so on. They then act out such values, in particular engaging in acts of delinquency that appear meaningless and senseless to adults (such as vandalism, senseless violence, substance abuse); their focus is on defying adult middle-class authority.

This theory was elaborated by Cloward and Ohlin (1960), who argued that one needed to examine not only the absence of legitimate means or opportunities, but also the absence of *illegitimate* means. For working-class youths who were not prepared well enough to succeed at middle-class schools, but who lived in relatively stable, older, integrated ethnic neighbourhoods, organized crime offered a relatively stable alternative route to economic viability. Without such illegal opportunities, they argued, young people had to devise their own status system, and it is this which led to violent gang behaviour. Finally, those who lacked the physical prowess and fighting skills necessary for participating in such a conflict subculture might turn to "retreatist" activities such as substance abuse or sexual deviance.

In recent decades, these theories have been subject to much criticism (see West 1983, 1984). Although some early research found adolescent gangs that fit Cloward and Ohlin's types (Spergel 1966), most researchers have concluded that real-life gangs tend to be much more loosely organized (Yablonsky 1959) and much less differentiated. Short and Strodtbeck (1965) had difficulty locating any purely criminal or retreatist gangs in Chicago. Even most delinquent youths spend relatively little of their time participating in gang activities. Self-report research on delinquent behaviour has shown that it is much more frequent than the official statistics indicate, and much more spread throughout the social-class structure (Vaz 1965; Morton, West, and Gomme 1984).

Even more serious criticisms have been levelled. Kitsuse and Dietrick (1959) pointed out that the subcultural theories are really concerned about explaining the origins of deviant subcultures, and hence are untestable since origins by definition are lost in history. Nonetheless, these theories can be used to explain recruitment to and maintenance of such subcultural forms through the motivation of new recruits. The data on sports participation across age groups presented here provides some needed insights on this issue of recruitment by observing both pre-adolescent and adolescent subjects. Sykes and Matza (1957, 1959) offer more devastating criticisms, pointing out that it is very difficult to describe the boundaries of subcultures or the interaction boundaries of group members who hold subcultural values. Holding subcultural values does not predict behaviour very accurately, given the weight of situational factors on behaviour; the view that values straightforwardly determine action is overly deterministic. In particular, Sykes and Matza argue that the so-called delinquent values outlined by Miller and Cohen are not unconnected with mainstream social values; rather, they are "subterranean" values within mainstream culture. Sport and leisure recreation activities exemplify such values. What is key is to explain how *particular* values are invoked as justifications for *particular* situated actions. They list a series of "techniques of rationalization" that could be invoked to excuse particular delinquent behaviours: denial of responsibility, denial of injury, denial of the victim, condemnation of the condemners, appeal to higher loyalties, and so on.

The involvement of working-class young people in delinquent gangs has been an ongoing interest of sociologists of deviance; middle-class youths involved in peer group activities and adolescent subcultures have been more actively researched by sociologists of education. Early work by Hollingshead (1945) and others revealed the heavy impact that family social class and gender have on teenagers' relationships with schools and with leisure activities. The recognition that middle-class teens were heavily involved in delinquency (Vaz 1965; Byles 1969) coincided with more extensive research as fears about an independent, anti-adult adolescent society became more widespread. Coleman (1961) deplored the subordination of academic pursuits to sport activities (for boys) and to social activities (for girls). Somewhat confusingly, those who had been "good kids" in the delinquency studies became "bad kids" in adolescent subculture research! But it is just such "normal" male violence that feminists have raised concerns about.

Elkin and Westley's (1955) study of Montreal teens provided an early challenge to these notions, pointing out that most adolescents are more conventional and adult-oriented than suggested by "youth culture" theory. Young people seem to share many of the leisure values of adults (Matza and Sykes 1964), although their active participation in such "adult only" activities as drinking and sex have made many adults quite uncomfortable. And those who are heavily involved in such activities do tend to be more likely to commit other delinquencies (Hirschi 1969:168–169, 193.) Since adolescents as a group tend to have much leisure time, their orientation to subterranean leisure values is quite understandable. But the depictions of adolescent subcultures as distinctly different from adult ones would seem to describe the belief systems of only a small minority of youths (West 1983, 1984).

More crucially, there is almost no research on how adolescent subcultures and socialization are linked to pre-adolescents' experiences. While some excellent discussions of children's and young people's participation in sport are available (e.g., Gruneau and Whitson 1993, Chapters 6 and 8 especially), there is a dearth of grounded empirical data. In part, this is because there is barely any sociological research on pre-adolescents. Similarly, there is little research on the topic of how 6 to 12 year olds learn about gender, even though this is considered a key time for basic skills development in a number of theories of human development (see Erikson, Piaget, etc.). Furthermore, this age group "spontaneously" participates in sport and recreation groups that are assumed by our society to be "naturally" sex segregated, and that presumably are the sites where "boys learn to be boys." Yet very few studies in the sociology of sport and recreation have focused on pre-adolescent males (see Hall et al. 1991 for a review) and their transition to adolescent sports activities. Understanding this younger age group is crucial to the study of sport violence among adolescent males, as almost all adolescents active in the sports studied first began participating as pre-teens.

Within the sociology of sport, there has been some recent interest in violence in discussions of sport as a socializing agency (Smith 1983). Gruneau and Whitson (1993:177) give short shrift to the popular NHL argument that hockey's body contact arouses tempers that inevitably explode in fighting beyond the rules. They opt instead for a "violence begets violence" perspective:

Aggressive behaviours are viewed as products of environments that arouse aggressive sentiments, provide role models of aggressive behaviour, and place people in situations where aggression visibly "works" and is rewarded, and that sanction and even applaud aggressive behaviour.

But they then assume that mass-media professional hockey represents all hockey, and provide very little empirical data on the sport at younger age levels. They recognize that most boys leave competitive organized hockey during adolescence—very often citing its increasing emphasis on physicality in the older age levels. But they fail to consider seriously the implication: does that mean most males are rejecting such a hegemonic masculinity? The data demand that we ask, given their argument that the displays of strength and toughness in the sport reinforce one traditional notion of hegemonic masculinity. This research will try to ground such speculative theorizing.

Gender Issues

Few studies of adolescent culture problematize violence as masculine, nor do they conceptualize it in gender-sensitive terms (Dorn and South 1983, 1988). While feminist theory has greatly enhanced our understanding of females (e.g., Barrett 1980; Smith 1987, 1988; O'Brien 1981), only recently has attention been devoted to the study of *males'* active participation in constructing gender inequality, or to the social construction, constitution, and regulation of masculinity (see Connell 1987). Sex is not gender; as a social construction, hegemonic heterosexual "masculinity" is an ideological construct (Frank 1991); it is also an institutionally idealized and assumed reference point that is actually realized by few if any living males. Real males use their bodies in active processes of social construction of their own persons, selectively referencing various aspects of masculinity (Connell 1987:83; Connell 1992; Varpolitai 1986).

While there is much "grand theorizing" about *the* male condition and *the* masculine in the burgeoning literature on masculinity and men's studies (Kaufman 1987; Blye 1990; Keen 1991; Clatterbaugh 1990, Chapter 4 *Wild Men*), there is still little empirical research on the variety of lived experiences and understandings of males about their being male, about how they are constructed (and construct themselves) as masculine. Much of the existing research and writing on masculinities is deeply flawed by this conception that there is a unitary, noncontradictory masculinity and femininity (Thornton 1992). In this area there is a great need for detailed ethnographic research.

Conceptualizing these male experiences as "socialization" into "masculine roles" is not very useful (following Connell 1987); sex and gender are differently organized and defined across situations—even within the same institutions and activities, and for the same persons under different circumstances (Thorne 1986). Listing a set of supposedly "essential" masculine characteristics and then checking off their absence or presence is not particularly descriptive or useful, as it fails to explain the historical origins or the particular actor's use of the gender role characteristic of interest. Instead, we need to examine the situations in which such ideological constructions are invoked by particular actors in their social interaction (see Short and Strodtbeck 1965 regarding the situational invocation of gang fighting). And just as class is a concept assuming relationships (see Thompson 1963), this invocation of gender needs to be understood as basically dialectical: "masculinity" is invoked in opposition to "femininity," "heterosexual masculinity" is invoked in opposition to "homosexual masculinity," and so on.

In studying how sex is transformed into gender, I want to raise and suggest provocative questions about any easy assumptions of mind/body splits. I wish to emphasize how these male bodies are learning (as "intellectually" as their minds) what it means to be and act as masculine: their bodies are as intelligently embodying masculinity as their minds are imagining it. This of course raises very central questions about learning, socialization, education, and social change. I am suggesting that "embodying" is as crucial as "knowing" in the construction and maintenance of gender (see Foucault 1977, 1979).

Something very complicated seems to be taking place here whereby boys learn to understand bodily knowledge—and more specifically force and violence, which is profoundly gendered. Haug (1992) argues that moralities have at least two genders. We suggest this is crucial in understanding differences in male versus female understandings and experiences of pain and violence, which is a politically central yet theoretically unexplored topic (but see Dryden 1983; Hall et al. 1991; Messner 1992).

I have chosen these various pieces of ethnographic data to illustrate how (especially younger) males learn about their bodies, force, and violence in multiple ways in sports. I am not arguing that playing sport is only about claiming and being claimed by "masculine" power and violence. To make such essentialist claims is to condemn us to accepting that there are no possibilities for changing sports into nonviolent relationships. Even more problematic epistemologically, it suggests that we researchers can "know" prior to and outside of the lived and experienced activities of people. It also denies the validity of "embodied" knowledge present in sports, and falsely privileges "mental" knowledge.

Sport as a socially realized practice of men and boys represents a series of contradictions. For instance, sports encourage safe play, and danger. While claiming to inculcate values of "good citizenship," "morality," "character development," and so on, other issues of health, injury, and violence are embedded in its day-to-day practices. There have been very few ethnographic studies of males' experiences of their bodies as forceful in the context of sports—in aggression, violence, and pain, but also in joy, exhilaration, communal caring, and the like (but see Pronger 1991; Messner 1992; Fine 1987).

✸ Research Methods

I am an adult "straight" male, age 49, maritally separated with an 18-year-old daughter into travel and world development, a 12-year-old son into baseball and hockey, an 11-year-old stepson avidly involved in hockey, a 16-year-old stepson much more into girls and computers than sports (although basketball is some distraction), and an 18-year-old stepdaughter near Olympic standard in swimming and the toughest blueliner on her high school hockey team. I have also been a past Cub and Scout and an avid baseball and hockey fan and coach (and occasional aging player). I have had head stitches from being bottled, lost two teeth to hockey pucks and two to soccer heads, and suffered a chronic knee cartilage injury and broken an ankle in football. Otherwise, my health is good(!?)

I am not a stranger to aspects of violence and injury from sport, or to the gender and political implications; hence, I have a certain "personal under-standing" of it. I still actively participate in shinny hockey. I am politically committed to transforming gender relationships: I believe that understanding males' experiences of bodies, sport, and violence can contribute to this. I have explicitly stated my own sports experiences to alert readers; on the other hand, I definitely believe that understanding masculinities cannot be based simply on anybody's personal biography, including my own. More extensive and repre-sentative research is demanded, even if the exploratory nature of the topic demands intensive ethnographic research.

Over the past three-and-a-half years of standard participant observation and informal interviews, the immediate subjects of this research have been some seventy-five 7 to 16 year olds involved in five organized hockey teams; some fifteen 8 to 9 year olds on an organized baseball team; some dozen 8 to 11 year olds in Wolf Cubs; and their coaches and leaders (numbering about ten.) There have been a couple of girls on the hockey teams and some dozen girls scattered over the six teams in the baseball league, although none on the specific team observed. Perhaps 5 percent of the shinny players have been girls. Some 75 games, 15 practices, and 10 pack meetings have been observed, as well as preparatory and "clean-up" activities. The fact that I have participating offspring and have served as a coach has granted me further access as well to young people's peer group activities outside the formal ones (after-school play, occasional sleepovers, weekend and summer cottage visits, and so on).

The shinny hockey subjects number perhaps a hundred, at three sites, although most observations focused on some three dozen regulars aged 10 to 30 years old. About 10 percent were female.

The hundred adult "ultimate" players tended to be upper-middle-class university students, with some young employed professionals. About 80 percent were males. Some two dozen games were actively participated in, another three observed. Additional intensive retrospective interviews were conducted with some dozen adult men; league documents, forms, newsletters, and manuals were also consulted.

Most of the subjects have middle- to upper-middle-class family backgrounds; the vast majority are white (there a few Chinese, East Indians, and blacks). One hockey team is mainly Jewish, religiously and culturally. The leagues officially forbid sexual discrimination; the hockey leagues have explicitly outlawed bodychecking for pre-teens, enforcing it with penalties. Of course, bodychecking is illegal in shinny. We cite this sampling to openly admit that it is not "random": we are using instead a variety of intensive participant-observation ethnographic collections and analyses of data. One must be careful not to generalize from these studies; on the other hand, the teams, pack, and participants seem quite typical on all other dimensions except those noted. This can be seen as a kind of theoretical sampling procedure.

I have avoided studying "professional" athletes. I have also avoided addressing the dominant mass-media presentations of sport violence and of elite/professional athletes, whose relationship with sport is quite different from that of the general population who actually play sports (see Gruneau and Whitson 1993, who argue that the professional presentation hegemonically dominates all who play).

We are also highly sensitive to the problems of analyzing "discourse" and assuming it represents self-evident ethnographic reports (see Foucault 1981). Film and video material has been collected on the hockey, shinny, ultimate, and baseball activities. "Masculinity" has not simply emerged from the research as the central organizing feature or "product" of these youths' participation in sports. The material could equally well have been organized in quite different ways: for instance, according to perceptions by adults, parents, coaches, league officials, and young people. Also, the "usual" sociological categories of race, sex/gender, and class could have been used more centrally.

I have, if anything, emphasized *age* as a relatively underutilized category with significant social import. By intentionally spreading my theoretical sampling across age ranges, I was able to observe and retrospectively interview informants concerning questions of recruitment into and retirement from various sport activities and their subcultures. Very few other studies in the sociology of sport and recreation have examined data on the violent sports activities of pre-adolescent males and their relation to those of adolescents; in the same way, few have included males from across the age span (see Hall et al. 1991 for a review). When we study only adults—as in almost all the literature on gender—we are ignoring more than half of the relevant population on a world scale. This makes it harder for us to understand how First World males construct themselves biographically.

✸ Some Ethnographic Data, Some Suggestive Analyses, and Many Questions

While this research is ongoing, some initial findings, with illustrative field notes, are presented below. I have organized the material into a dozen main findings, grouped into four major issues: the adult context of youth sports and culture; the embodiment of force in sports; participants' exuberance and control of violence; and masculine sport subcultural socialization regarding violence. While this grouping is not at all arbitrary, neither can I claim that it simply "objectively" reports on the social realities of these boys' sport experiences. Obviously, these are working hypotheses that invite comment and need further research, modification, and corroboration.

The Adult Organized Context of Sports

Although children's play activities have always been allowed some independence by adults, one of the central reasons for organizing sports for young people has been the concern of some (mostly middle-class) adults that (some, often working-class) youths were not being properly socialized in their play. The British elite "public" schools' use of sport to "capture" their charges' interest and exuberance was carried into not only the state schools provided to control the middle and lower classes, but also into social reform efforts (in the

YMCA, Boy Scouts, settlement house work, etc.; see Musgrove 1965). This adult concern and control continues.

Sports Are Sponsored by the Wider Adult Community

Almost all competitive sports are sponsored by the most "legitimate" organizations. Governments and leading corporations, both national and local, use our love of sports and desire for health to win our loyalty through displaying their support for helping youths become healthy, civic, and trouble-free. Uniforms, prizes, and the like are usually donated by local businesses. (One hockey team sponsored by a neighbourhood delicatessen awarded a salami each week for the best player of the game: "The best gets the wurst!")

Parental support is strongly encouraged; in fact, it is essential:

> A number of parents were here this game: more than most: James', Allan's (also a coach), Terry's, John's (who helped in the practice), Barry's mom dropped him off (he's the only other kid with 2 home telephone numbers, indicating separated parents), Sam's (coach), Ken's grandparents, Rob (coach), Kevin's (coach.) [Se14/91]

On the face of it, then, it is to be expected that sport activities would reproduce or support basic community and parental values. In an age-graded society (see Berkeley, Gaffield, and West 1977; Cierri, Gonzales, and West 1988), this is not a novel finding, but in a society that systematically ignores and denies the domination of adults over children in both obvious and subtle ways, it needs to be reasserted.

Parents, Officials, and Coaches Try to Control Boys' Sport Experiences

If parents do not like the activities promoted through recreation for their sons, they withdraw support and their youngsters:

> M: [M. has an older son, 13 or 14, totally uninterested in hockey.] I took Ron out of Cubs because it was so wild and lacking discipline. [De13/91]

Most parents want sport and recreational activities to promote their children's health without causing injury or harm. Most coaches do concentrate initially on "health": how to fall down, how to curl up on a bodycheck, how to roll over and get back up on skates, how not to hit the boards, how not to get your wind knocked out, how to protect your knees, and so on. Boy Scouts and Cubs have always had a similar emphasis. Admittedly, this reflects a concern with legal suits, but it also reflects a genuine adult concern with young people's well-being:

> The dressing room as usual is so chaotic, and crucial: the timing for ice time is exact, the required equipment precise (no elbow guard, no play!) (yet with some idiosyncratic adjustments: e.g., taping shin guards or socks; lacing adjustments, etc.). But basically, all this plastic and webbing has to be strapped onto these little bodies in some 20–30 minutes, so it feels comfortable and ordinary, yet of course it's mass produced and they outgrow it, etc. And the key equipment items: skates and sticks, and puck, can be deadly weapons! [Oc01/90]

Discipline is required, in the sense of rationally controlling passion:

> WGW: [over to Tom] Listen, what did the convenor tell you last week about body checking?
>
> T: Well, not to, but I didn't.
>
> WGW: Listen, go for the puck, try and score, but remember you can't hit anybody, and you have to be in control of yourself out there.
>
> T: Okay, but I didn't. [De15/91]

"Discipline" (in a more social sense) remains an ongoing issue, in part because of the danger of physical injury:

> In this, Shawn hit Jack near the eye, resulting in a few tears, which Balloo cleared up; Jim and Jack got into a rambunctious chair pushing scene, kicking them over, etc: nothing really done re damage, but Bill tried to cool it out by gathering chairs up, asking Jim not to; grabbing him a couple of times: he basically ignored the request, jerked his arm away when Bill grabbed him (with a "take your hands off me" look): he is a handful of exploding challenging, disobedient energy: cute when you're not in charge. [Oc21/91]

Publicly at least, parents expressed concern about conflicts between young people. Certainly, none publicly endorsed violence.

At the curriculum night, the issue of kids having disputes was raised by Sharon, Dan's mom; Will chimed in, supporting her suggestion that "We as parents would like to know about such events when they are major, or kids are having trouble with each other." [Oc16/91]

But this is not a simplistic transmission of a monolithic, unified "value system." There are sharply competing definitions between various adults concerning the appropriate limits of injury, force, and violence:

Well, this game, the other team really was physically strong, some dirty body-checking; the kids complained about this, and also about how loud the other coach was, whom I tried to cool out, standing some 3 feet from him. [Oc/90]

The significance of illegal force is a frequently debated topic in activities that privilege force.

WGW: I talked to the referees about calling penalties. He said, "Oh, just the last 2 minutes to go, so we didn't."

ADT: I talked to the other coach. He said, "Oh, I didn't see anything on purpose."

WGW: He hasn't played hockey!

ADT: He had a tan! [Meaning he had just been to Florida!]

WGW: Well ya, but on the other hand, ritual [balancing of penalties] might be important in the construction of social order.

ADT: I just don't like ritual.

WGW: That is not the question: we're not talking about what you or I like, but about how sometimes dirty hockey works. [Ja/92]

Such disagreements among adults extend beyond the sports arena:

Ken [to dentist]: this is also a hassle: Ken's regular dentist never played sports and is quite down on Ken playing, so he is absolutely freaked about this chipped tooth; the specialist (some $60 later) played hockey and is missing a couple of front teeth like me, and we see absolutely eye to eye: nobody wants to lose a tooth, but let's not quit living to make sure we don't! [My24/91]

Whatever their disagreements about the legal and moral classification of particular activities, however, both adults and young people agree that physical contact sports inherently "suspend" conduct rules prohibiting the exercise of bodily force under certain conditions.

Adults' Concern with Moral Socialization Genders Embodied Force

A third aspect of these boys' activities that is essential to understand is the pervasive and profound gendering of embodied force through sport. Sport activities have traditionally been organized along sex/gender lines, partly because of traditional notions of propriety regarding sex differences. Separate dressing rooms acknowledge the social concern with sexual differences. The integration of girls into traditionally all-male hockey and baseball change rooms for pre-adolescents curtails nakedness, but it does not stop the youths from noticing the different construction of genital protectors. "Innocent" equipment failures can become morally charged:

> Sean somehow also lost the plastic cup of his jock strap on the ice: how symbolic! The ref picked it up, a few other kids laughed: not really in any mean way, but just sympathizing with his embarrassment. Back on the bench, fellow coach Martin and I asked him to check himself as to the cup's absence: he shyly agreed. So I was left to untie his pants, and told him to fumble around as to where the cloth container was.

> [This was difficult:] Hockey pants ride high, well above the waist; then there are unusual things like sock garters and the straps to the socks; then they all wear their own individual things: some in their underwear, some not, some in their pants, some in long underwear, some not, etc. But legally in the league he can't play without it, and morally, it's actually the piece of equipment which in many ways parents are most concerned about! (Something like "My kid can lose an arm, but I don't want to lose my possibility of grandchildren!") I ask him to take off his gloves.

> WGW: Make sure the cup is fitting securely. You don't want to get hurt there, it would really hurt.

> He fumbles around, and presumably gets his equipment organized, smiled and thanked me. He goes out and the game continues. [Oc/91]

Boys do essentially have some different bodily parts that are particularly sensitive in some sports. By adolescence, separate dressing rooms are used wherever possible.

Even though the leagues have adopted policies of no discrimination on the basis of sex, and uniforms and equipment disguise the sex of players, sex remains a notable feature: an excellent play by a girl is likely to be acknowledged with more surprise; girls are not expected to perform as well, or as physically. Contrarily, a boy who does not perform aggressively is still more likely to be reprimanded. And the continuing numerical predominance of boys in sport activities reflects the continuing higher value of sports for boys. The guys are "handsome, heroic" warriors," and the girls "cute, gorgeous," and so on in the spectators' minds.

> Ruth just went wild [with admiration in spite of the fact that] her favourite team lost: we had to go down and check them out, each one, how sweaty, how smiling, how well built, etc. This was a sexual ritual, crudely put. [Mr21/93]

Sport prowess, then, continues to be taken up in the social construction of gender.

These sport activities are one forum for an increasing concern for young people's behaviour in public. These boys are moving out of spending most of their time with their families, have usually gone to day cares, all go to school, and are being introduced to "community organizations" by their parents. But there is also a "new mixture" that combines family intimacy (in the locker room or tent) with public display (on the ice or the baseball diamond or parade route).

There is a lot of body work and learning about sexuality. In the social construction of gender, the sports arena is utilized not only in establishing masculine-feminine contrasts, but also in delineating "normal/heterosexual" and "homosexual" stereotypes. In part, this results from issues raised by the frequent physical contact and bumping, especially in situations of intimacy.

> There was a lot of body contact among the kids: a lot of rough and tumble, firing the puck, chasing each other, bumping, bouncing, punching, and passing gas ... [Oc14/90]

Among pre-adolescents, the tackles and rules are so inchoate that after-whistle wrestling, fumbling, and hugging is frequent, with jokes, cries of 'let up" and "don't tickle me," and so on. At the same time, there are rules of intimacy, such as "Tickling is okay, but no kissing!" It has to be "rough" and "without commitment." But it leads and educates "toward" not only football and hockey (with the contact seen as violent), but also toward adolescent love and intimacy, whether heterosexual or homosexual.

In sum, the initial involvement of these young males in sport was controlled by important and powerful adults. The basic structures of these youths' relationships to sport are not contracultural. As these young people pass into adolescence, there is some relaxation of adult control, and some assertion of independence, but it remains tightly controlled by adults even then:

> My friend and work-colleague was in emotional disarray on Monday morning: her 16-year-old son, Jack, who stars on his hockey team, has been suspended for a week for "unsportsmanlike conduct": he apparently insulted the referee after a penalty call by riding his stick around the rink in an obscenely suggestive fashion. [De15/92]

Sports Involve Bodies and Physical Force

Embodied Force

Most sports involve the forceful movement of physical bodies in space: baseballs are hit, pucks shot, discs propelled, beanbags tossed. The "basic skills" of any sport involve proficiency in exercising physical force upon an object.

> They can all now hit [the baseball], and all can direct the hit, even if they signal it outrageously in terms of foot placement and looking. Still, they've learned it. [Se14/91]

Sportspersons' bodies are drilled to exercise such physical force in the most efficient and effortless ways possible: get up and move your arms and legs in places; exercise muscle movements; exert; and so on. What clearly is prized and learned in these activities is how to perform definite physical skills (skating, shooting, puck carrying, scoring; throwing and catching a ball, hitting, running, sliding; similar "wide game" skills at Cubs, but also "curriculum" skills such as woodcraft, leadership, and "general development").

Different sports emphasize different particular skills. Although some sports (such as tennis) do not involve direct competition for physical space, most popular sports do (e.g., hockey, football, basketball, baseball). Getting one's body to a particular spot before one's opponent can is crucial.

326

Mick: When the puck is in our end, I want to see one defenceman in front of the net, and one going after the puck or puck carrier in the corner. The winger on that side is on the boards at the hash marks, looking for the pass; the centre is covering or helping out, and the other winger covering the slot. When we got the puck in their end, we want to put it in front of their net and shoot. The first guy in goes for the puck. Where does the second guy go?

Kid: The front of the net.

Mick: Right. And where does the third guy go?

Kid: Deep slot, in case the second guy misses or we get a rebound. [De15/91]

Even when games are "under control," and the kids are playing well, in tough defensive-style games the kids are learning as early as age 6 or 7 to hurl their bodies into the fray to save the team:

He dove into the boards once in our end, and got his stick in his gut and lost his wind, cried with pain, but got up and chased the play which he has helped to set up. He rushed to cut them off coming out of their end, and smashed into the boards again; he positioned himself just right, the puck came, and then he lost his balance on shooting, never got the shot off, and fell down (so embarrassing!) He got another chance to fire from inside their blueline, and lost his balance again, and fell. Don (another coach) looked at me appreciatively down the bench as we both sighed. [No24/90]

Team sports complicate this by demanding the coordination of such bodies. One of the central tasks of coaching or managing is to arrange your players' bodies into positions so that your team's force (physical strength and skills) is exerted against the opponent's weaknesses. This maximizes your advantage within the rules of the game.

We as coaches have also learned how to put them into batting orders: a lead off grounder [grounded baseball] aimed to 3rd [base] (from which the throw to first is very long for this age group), perhaps a middle hitter, then a clean-up person; and repeating this over through the line-up. We missed out on doing this the second and third last games, and failed to get runs because our line-ups had too many grounders leading to second base force-outs. [Se14/91]

The kids are clearly exhausted—just two forward lines, anchored in the [strongest players as] centres, John and Ian, and the others digging like crazy; [by necessity,] Bill was rearranging the defence shift after shift—but they were just eating it up and rising to the occasion—the buzzer—and we've done it 5–1. Second place! They came off as soon as they could; they were exhausted! [No24/90]

Interestingly, in many sports, a kind of bodily knowledge is developed before the understanding can be verbalized: players "know" how to perform without being able to articulate that knowledge.

> Kevin: [The coaches] told us when it was offside. They did their hardest to cheer for us. They told us what position. They showed us what we did wrong. That is all I can think of.
>
> WGW: What does "offside" mean?
>
> K: When people are at one side and one other person is on the other. Of the rink. [No04/90]

While this boy knew how to abide by the offside rule, his verbal description would provide totally inadequate guidance for performance. That some such embodied knowledge precedes "verbal" conceptualization indicates a preliterate aspect of sports and suggests that mere "attitude" changes or a resocializing of cognitive values would be inadequate to change males' understanding of force.

The Preparation, Care, and Maintenance of Bodily Force

These bodily forces are nurtured and maintained, especially by parents. It takes much family organization to feed players, do the bathroom stuff, clothe them, and get them looking presentable at the ball park or arena. Athletes must be well rested and healthy to perform well.

> Matt was equally good: he constantly chased the puck, I had no sense of his on-ice play slowed by his flu, even though he was incredibly subdued on the bench, Harriet checked his forehead once, and gave him a cough drop; his mother came along after a few minutes to check. [De07/92]

The sports equipment attempts to protect the players' bodies, and the kids test each other out in the dressing room, swinging sticks and practising shots at the goalie, ritually "slashing" (hitting) his pads with their sticks to "build up his courage." (They do this on the ice too, just before the first whistle, or after a goal.)

Ted into physicality, Trevor whacking Bob's pads: I think the uniform/body thing is really interesting in that dressing allows them to become "supermen." [Mr14/92]

The uniforms and equipment accentuate their sense of invulnerability. Even though bodychecking was outlawed in the hockey leagues studied for youths under 13, and the rule was strictly enforced, the physicality of the activities inevitably led to bruises. Younger kids constantly bump around in all sports activities. They clearly love the "impenetrable" armour of their hockey equipment, playing out fantasy roles, hitting and tapping each other with sticks, and so on and realizing it doesn't usually hurt!

Furthermore, while the best sports equipment and armour does not entirely eliminate pain, it does foster an "other-worldliness." The kids clearly recognized this at the end of each game:

Sometimes the physicality of the game is overwhelming, dazing, and other-worldly: they quite obviously can't "see straight" (even rushing the wrong end, shooting the wrong way, etc.).

These kids today were taking hits: even with all the equipment, etc., some of them were seeing stars: they got up dazed, skated the wrong way, etc. This is with all the equipment, which they use to think of themselves as supermen, beyond pain, yet in games they like this bodily experience—*pain*! As in every time Stan or Lewis or Harriet goes out to play: they may well win, but they also know already that tonight, it will be liniment time. It hurts. [Mr28/91]

Every parent senses this physical aspect of the threat to his or her own child's precious—and much cared for—body:

Parent: God, much as I love the game, my heart was in my throat, tossing my little kid out on the ice to face all that rubber and steel blades, praying he'd somehow remember all he's learned in our fun time practices, and would get a bit of luck and be okay. [De01/90]

Gender Differences Accentuate Embodied Force

Boys are biologically different from girls. Sports accentuate these differences and we socially accentuate them even more. This should not be such a big surprise, but it is worth repeating:

The "big hitters" are also usually the biggest [kids]: basically the kids standing up in the team photo; they can run faster too, have a bigger reach for catching, etc. There are some exceptions: little Harold is good catching and throwing; the big kids seem to miss as many sure grounders as the little guys; Kent and Sam are such highly wired sparkplugs their enthusiasm rubs off. [Se14/91]

One might note how the team uniforms obliterate persons to some extent, at least in terms of their off-ice characteristics.

When "little" [i.e., one year younger and physically smaller] Peter initially [in uniform] saw Ken crying, he was surprised, but saw him as equal; when they had stripped down, he "reconstituted" him as an older boy, and did not know how to intimately support this older [bigger] boy in his obvious pain. [No24/90]

One might begin to investigate how such situations begin to restrict males' being able to express emotion and support and intimacy. Contrarily, these young males *are* expressing emotion very openly, have just thrown their bodies literally into the fray to "save the team," have hugged each other, and are "breaking down" crying, as well as cheering each other. Simplistic analysis through preset categories is simply inadequate.

The Sport Participants' Experiences

Exercising Embodied Force Is Experienced as Having Fun

In all of these activities, the youths are revelling in learning how to move their bodies. Cubs learn to run, jump, climb ropes, scramble through bushes, swim, canoe, and so on. Baseball players learn how to hit home runs, throw, and catch. Hockey players learn how to rush, push, bull on through, and score.

A lazy morning, Ken typed a few stories and played with his Leggo; then off to his ball game, where he played well (4 hits, including a double; 2 runs, one on a really brightly played tag-up on a pop fly, then sprinted home from second; three or four good catches and a couple of good throws ... he has improved so much over the year), but they lost 36–33. [Se14/91]

Players actively seek to maximize their enjoyment of the activities:

He did complain of a pulled muscle and didn't go out in field for 2 innings; I sensed he was faking, but then only after did it strike me that he was bitchy for not playing catcher! Nonetheless, he had a good time as close in rover [an extra position in T-ball] backing up second and made two excellent outs. [Jn14/91]

Although sport is "rule-bound" in many ways, it also allows for spontaneous pleasure and fun. And there is such fun in less rule-organized activities, too:

The cubs ran around playing their spontaneous rule-less "rugger" among the circle of chairs ... A lot of physical contact here, and some sense of rules: i.e., not to get tackled before throwing or handing off [the ball] to anyone. But a lot of play wrestling after the tackle: and nobody got hurt [or has been hurt in the three months: literally if adults did this for 15 minutes, somebody would get really bruised: the cubs already have learned how to fall, how to concede you are caught, how to apologize and help the opponent up, how to tickle and joke while playing the game, as well as the more obvious things of running, dodging, passing, catching, etc. This is quite literally the play wrestling stuff which kids this age love (and John forbids at home despite Ken's and Andrew's attempts). [De19/91]

This stuff is very concretely an exercise of physical contact, force, and bodily intimacy. It's the kind of experience upon which more formal "sports" like football and hockey build. What they are clearly learning here is how to be physically aggressive and assertive, yet without hurting each other, without breaking "the rules" even when the rules are not explicit—when they make them up as they go and can renegotiate them. Behind the more superficial rules (when to throw, who has possession of the ball, etc.) lie deeper rules of fair play and having fun.

But such "roughhousing" tends to be seen differently by men and women:

Bill: [joking] Candy, isn't this like Brownies.

C: Are you kidding? We never did any of this sort of stuff.

B: Well, at least Ken has learned the rules (as he passed off on being tackled).

C: Ugh! [with concern]

B: It's okay, that's his best buddy Don pulling him up. (Don was literally giving him a hand up as in pro football or rugger.) [De19/91]

This gender difference often continues into adulthood:

Louise was surprised ... asking why Bill [as an adult] likes shinny [with all its physical injuries]: he replied: "It's interesting, unpredictable, exciting, uses skill, endurance and intellect, and fun, and a laugh with friends." [Fe/93]

Balancing Exuberant Force and Pain

While a seemingly intrinsic part of the pleasure of sport consists of the exuberant exercise of force, uncontrolled force can easily result in injury and pain. Often this results simply from accidents, without intentional acts of violation.

... A great rush by Harriet, and a goal mouth charge, and a goal mouth scramble with a near goal, they shot out and got a near breakaway; I can't remember who cut them off but we did. After the whistle, I noticed one of our guys being dug out of their net by the ref, their goalie being concerned, and Matt comes skating/limping back. As he approaches the bench, we all became concerned, and I realized [through the wire on his helmet] he is crying. The ref says he hit the post on his neck, turns him over to the other coach and me at the fence gate. Matt's father appears behind the glass, immediately here and concerned. Martin the coach then comes down the bench, and Mick the other coach.

I ask how he is, "What happened?"

M: I hit my neck on the post ... I just want to sit for a minute: it's just a bruise.

Father: Okay, see how he is in a few minutes.

WGW: Okay ... That was a great rush, you were really terrific. [I was self-consciously trying to cajole him into continuing here, I realized then and now.]

Matt: [sob sob] Okay, yeah. [No30/91]

Thousands of boys, girls, men, and women participate daily in sports of one kind or another without serious injury or pain, or violence. They learn how to minimize such pain and injury by taking precautions, learning how to fall, wearing the correct protective equipment, and so on.

They got an early goal on a scramble ...

Ken still out of shape, and not into the routine of play, but working his butt off (he collapsed coming off near the end; and then the next shift lay on the bench he was so winded).

That got us fired up. The kids dug and dug; the defences pinched; they got a breakaway or two. On one Jerry cut the guy off and wouldn't let him cut to the net, ended up hitting himself into the boards, and Don (bless his soul) went running out to make sure it was okay. (It was appropriate for a coach to do— but I know he also did it because Jerry is like a son to Don). Then okay: cheers, Jerry is okay. [Oc/90]

The injury can also be social, especially given the public nature of sport. Embarrassment and shame are not far from defeat, incompetence, or weakness in competitive sports:

The other kids were also learning a lot through all of this: they had also been caught up in the play; they were silently concerned when Matt came off crying. There was absolutely *no* putting him down for this: they all "felt" for him in empathy and were concerned. ... they looked quietly down the bench; the kids near him "emoted" concern with looks, a touch or two, a little tap on his pads with their sticks, and "Are you okay?" [No30/91]

Besides the learning of physical control of embodied force, competitive sport requires the development of a set of mental attitudes in a social context. This is a learning of subcultural understandings:

He went out on his next shift, some two minutes later: skated more gingerly, not his usual rambunctiousness. Came back to the bench half hurting, half smiling.

WGW: How'd it go? You looked pretty good, made a great pass down the boards there. How are you feeling?

M: Okay. Thanks. I'll be all right [with a kind of grudging half-falling, half-conscious tapping me with his stick]. [No30/91]

One learns how to incorporate being hurt within the continuation of the activity. One learns how to play with pain and injury:

AT: You said something about hurting yourself before ... Have you ever hurt yourself playing hockey?

HA: Well, I do, but I try to get up. I don't really like to ... stop the play.

AT: So you never cut yourself or sprained an ankle?

HA: Well, I sprained an ankle a couple of times in hockey, but I managed to get up. And uh, once in squirt [level] ... Once I got nailed, a skate hit where there is no padding. And um, I almost went up and got up, went to the bench. (ADT: Uh-hum.) I don't really like stopping the play. [Oc29/92]

Learning to Control Violence

One main way of controlling possible injury and pain is to outlaw dangerous actions through rules. In organized hockey, for instance, bodychecking is outlawed for preteens.

AT: What do you think of the rule that says "no checking"?

AH: No checking? ... Since I'm small, I guess that's a good rule, but just this summer I learned to bodycheck. I don't know ... [Oc29/92]

In sport, winning has a high value, and there is a constant pressure and temptation to "bend" or even break rules—including rules that don't pertain to violence—in order to win:

We got up late, did pancakes, then I took Alex and Ken for baseball, and a movie, then took Ken shopping while Jack dealt with Ian: Ken and Alex were incredibly competitive: changing rules, invoking new rules, playing off against each other using (abusing) their different ages and skills, different baseballs even, arguing about whether this was a practice or a real game, etc. Alex was a real jerk in using his intelligence with words to compensate for his lack of physical skills to dominate Ken, and Ken felt really badly over this. [Jl13/91]

This is often interwoven with adult interests and investments in winning:

We lost also from some "technicalities": two of our last at bat runs were disallowed for the kids not tagging up: technically correct, but really pushing the rules by the other coaches; we had one tie at first called out; then one of theirs

334

similar to ours called safe; also a questionable out at second on a force. Their coaches were really aggressive towards the umps (who are 11- to 14-year-old kids). Their coaches had called earlier in the year for kids not to play if they were not wearing hats; 3 of their kids didn't have hats today. [Se30/91]

In learning "legitimate" physical assertion of force, players are also developing very explicit notions of illegitimate force, which in part consists of learning to manipulate the rules, exploiting their ambiguities so as to break them without getting caught:

It raises a big philosophical question: are the kids playing to have fun, or just to win? Obviously they like to win, but the opposing coaches (in our collective opinion) really took the competitiveness too far. We persisted in rotating players and respecting the umps' calls; they didn't. [Se14/91]

This continues into adult participation, where it can become a playful game within the game:

And we did have a fun game: about a dozen guys, from 16 to 47, most in 20s, and good humour to the point where we could "cheat" or "shove" as a joke, and admit defeat or being outmanoeuvred, deked, etc. [Fe/93]

But the exertion of illegitimate force can easily be expanded to include more violent actions:

AT: Some of the other kids said they had a lot of fun playing hockey. Do you have fun or do you find that it's fun without the teams?

HA: Well ... I sort of except this game I got checked ... I got, ummm ... David nailed me. And then I got tripped again and it took me a hard time to get up and one more time, ummm ... Oh, the time I was on a breakaway I was tripped from behind, then I went feet first into the boards. I [got] killed! Took a long time for me to get up ... [Oc29/92]

They sort of knew they'd blown it/or we (coaches included) had "blown the victory": but they also knew—somehow viscerally knew—that they had really worked: they were really tired, they'd tied a hard fought game with a team using dirty tactics of bodychecking; we were missing our star skater and scorer. [Fe/91]

The increasing use of interpersonal force in older age groups is one of the primary reasons why many youths drop out of competitive sports when they reach their teens. (Other significant reasons: they realize they will never be Wayne Gretzky; increasing pressures from school; and the availability of other leisure pursuits, especially those involving girls.) The violence inherent in many sports actually repels most male teenagers—quite the opposite from what classical subcultural theories would lead you to expect.

AT: So what sort of future do you see in hockey?

HA: Well, I see a lot of injuries in both sports [hockey and baseball]. [Oc29/92]

Sport Subcultures, Violence, and Legitimacy Across Ages

Sport "Subcultures"

In a number of ways, these boys' leisure activities are staged, preset, and organized by adults, not infrequently along race, class, and religious lines (see Fine 1987). One hockey team, for instance, in a Jewish neighbourhood, was regarded as just one more avenue for developing well-rounded youths; as such, it competed with music classes, dancing, lessons, and so on. On another team it was assumed that hockey would be the youths' primary commitment.

GW: How is [the other league] different?

Max: Maybe more positional, serious. [De13/91]

The arena in this neighbourhood was more of a community centre; it was physically integrated into a town centre, being located beside the library, the high school, and the local town council. Few parents had played hockey actively themselves; most of them gathered at the arena in the heated cafeteria to gossip and informally discuss business; they paid relatively little attention to the game itself. In any case, the seats were poorly designed, draughty, and poorly located. In contrast, another arena had excellent seating, and walls resplendent with banners, team trophies, and autographed pictures of professionals who had visited. This arena drew players and parents from across the metropolitan area, and the talk (among parents who "knew" the game) was much more centred on the sport itself.

Different sports emphasize different ideologies: "community baseball" versus "real hockey" versus "friendly shinny" or "the spirit of the game" (in Ultimate). And individual leagues and coaches give these aspects different styles and interpretations:

> The new [baseball] coach reminds me much more of Ron: straight, honest, and into the game rather than winning. Much improved compared with the old team: he taught the kids throwing skills, some signals, and base-running, then batting during a rain break. The whole attitude is so much better. [My25/91]

From the young people's collective experience, friendships develop and, from these, an ongoing peer social structure:

> The kids have become friends with each other through the whole thing: they were having fun and hanging loose and cheering each other on, and teasing each other, etc. Kevin also got a big up by finding Grant's lost glove in the washroom. [Se14/91]

Coaches, parents, peers, girlfriends, and so on clearly play a key role in all of this. Many critiques of "patriarchy" have tended to see "it" as some sort of "objective power/gender structure out there." Yet these boys can participate in sports and Wolf Cubs only because their parents—mothers as well as fathers—actively support them in sport competition.

In most of the sports studied, almost all participants started playing as young children before or during elementary school—that is, as pre-teens. They learned skills and formal rules, and attitudes toward the game and toward the exercise of physical force (both legitimate and illegitimate or violent), *before* becoming adolescents. These knowledges were then carried over and "applied" to whatever particular circumstances they encountered as adolescents.

While almost no ultimate players had participated in the sport as pre-adolescents, almost all had learned the key elements of the game at that age: how to throw a disk, and the basics of positional team play (such as found in basketball or touch football). While ultimate prides itself on being nonviolent, it is fundamentally an exercise in competitive, team-coordinated bodily force. Upon analysis, the same issues of the use of illegitimate force seem to apply (see Thornton 1993 for more detailed analyses).

People do not simply "abandon" these sport subcultural understandings as they become adult. For most, sports become subordinated to other concerns (school, interpersonal relations, jobs) and occupy both less time and less mental "space" in their lives. Even so, they usually continue to participate in sports (perhaps at a "reduced level," such as by playing shinny instead of hockey), and they remain appreciative fans. The subcultural understanding initially acquired in childhood, perhaps developed in adolescence, thus continues into adulthood.

The subcultures connected with the sport activities studied are thus much more integrated with school, family, and community than was implied in the classical theories. They are also much less cohesive and clearly defined, and vary greatly in their value orientations across the range of sports. Rather than assuming an essentialist set of core sports values, we must document empirically which participants' understandings come into play in differing circumstances to permit enough understanding for the continuation of the collective activity.

Learning the Rules Implies Learning How to Break Them Violently

The type of violence described in the opening field note is endemic to playing hockey (and sports in general). Learning about health and injury, rules and legitimacy, also means learning how to use these to one's social advantage:

> Another shift: Stan clearly dominating. He also did a couple of slashing stick checks: he was also dominating the play so much that they would be going for him.

> Stan: I'm tired. I don't think I'll get many goals this game. They're hitting me a lot. A lot of elbows and stuff. [Fe/92]

When players are very unequal, or when games are very lopsided and hence already decided, rule-breaking (including violence) becomes more likely. It also becomes more likely in extramural games, where opposing players do not know each other well. It also becomes more likely in high-stakes games, which tend to occur toward the end of the season, especially in playoffs.

Rule-breaking also increases when it is culturally sanctioned through the buildup of collective talk, especially when the referees are seen as not fairly and equitably enforcing the rules:

> The talk on the bench in the third period was about dirty plays and cheating and getting hooked, slashed, bodychecked, etc., and how they are "playing dirty" on us, and the ref isn't calling anything.

WGW: I saw at least 6 or 8 bodychecks [which are illegal at this level]: with the hit kid falling, and about 3 to 6 hooks, about 6 slashes, about 6 trips, finally Stan losing the puck the second time in 15 seconds. [Fe/92]

Intermediary steps at retaliation are often used. Besides using minor retaliatory assaults, players will often dramatize their victimization to draw the referees' attention:

ADT: He fell.

WGW: He took a dive!

ADT: Yeah, virtually throwing up his hands. That's what he was doing. We weren't doing anything effective.

WGW: I was beginning to yell at the referees, about calling penalties; I was maybe too restrained, not wanting to cause a scene with the 14-year-old referees. [Fe/92]

When individual and authoritative appeals to the referees have failed, and minor retaliation hasn't worked, and the dramatic portrayal of oneself as victimized is to no avail, more serious violence may occur:

Late in the 3rd [period], [Stan] got bodychecked clearly, [after he] had been "swearing" about "getting that guy." After the bodycheck, he [illegally] high-sticked [the other player] in the neck under the face mask. The other kid fell down, but the referee reprimanded the other kid, not Stan! When Stan returned to the bench, I told him, "Look, you got a dirty check, but you can't hit the other kid back, or you'll get a penalty." [Fe/92]

I have purposely repeated the opening quotation to show that what appeared in isolation to be a senseless act of violence can better be understood as a carefully modulated response socially constructed over a period of time in reaction to others' social behaviour:

By this time, our kids were so angry at losing 9–1, and the referee not calling penalties, that they basically had decided to take the game into their own hands. I was afraid there would be a real fight.

ADT: I didn't feel that way, Orest and Jim were even-tempered.

WGW: By the third period, I was trying to just cool them out. I was saying, "Look it's only an exhibition, who cares, don't get hurt, don't hurt anybody else." I was going beyond that, because they were actively talking on the bench about "going out to *get* that guy!"

ADT: It was 6– or 7–1.

WGW: I mean that it was building up to a fight. Simply put. I was praying for the clock to run out first.

ADT: Not necessarily a fight?

WGW: No, a fight! They were just hot to trot.

ADT: Do you mean a fight? Two people bopping each other, taking gloves off?

WGW: Yes—Stan and David especially were talking about "get that guy!"

I don't know whether this team of pre-adolescents actually would have known "how to fight" on the ice, but Stan had probably watched enough hockey to have a pretty good idea: when he highsticked the other kid, he knew just how to do it to avoid the protective face mask.

Yet the activities are not simply competitive, or hostile, or aggressive, or nasty. There is also a lot of physical touching in a friendly, comradely manner: patting each other, giving "high fives" after a goal or run, hugging the goalie or each other on winning (or losing, for that matter). At least as much as learning how to use violence in certain circumstances, these youths are learning how not to hurt each other, how to control their exertion of physical force and channel it into legitimate expressions—of assertion, but also of affection.

Body Chemistry and 'Team Chemistry'

Common understandings of "how the game is played" allow for the teamwork that is key in most sports. In pickup shinny, for instance, even when almost no players have met before, good players have a background mental map of "how the game is to be played": experienced players, without even looking, "know" not only where teammates but also opponents are "supposed to be" when certain events happen (for example, in a breakout, a pinch along the boards, or a give-and-go pass). In the same way, good shortstops and second basemen know their reciprocally supporting roles for turning double plays. Every sport has its standard plays, which are often listed in skill-building books. But for these standard plays there are also standard counterplays; thus, in high-skill-level games, success is achieved by "raising the play a notch" and varying these standard plays to exploit particular players' exceptional abilities to the full (e.g., by utilizing speedy skaters in breakout passes in hockey). The quick responses required in the heat of the play, however, demand that such skills be highly "embodied," "reflexive," or "automatic." This is why plays can be executed successfully only if practised extensively.

Such social learning about bodily force cannot be divorced from "mental" attitudes and "team chemistry." "Team chemistry" refers to relatively intangible ways in which team members interact; it depends on seemingly effortless, common subcultural understandings of the technical aspects of the sport, combined with individual biographies and team history in a reciprocal play-back of social coordination:

Mick the coach: The flu has been sweeping around, and we know Harriet and Manny won't make it.

At 5 minutes to go or so [before game time], in came Jack and Alan. Mick did a chalk talk, as I drew the rink outline on the board, and I thought he did a really clear and inspiring kind of talk.

Mick: Listen: we're short of players today, but that means you'll each get lots of ice time. Okay?

Kids: Hey, okay! [They tap each other on the pads, and take a few swipes at Bob, our goalie, with their sticks: outside of a hockey dressing room, this would hurt, be legal assault, and cause injury.]

I'm not quite sure exactly how, but I felt a kind of "Okay guys, this is it, dig down deep, do our best, carry the flag, etc." A kind of surge: sort of "we have to carry on through and have fun," and a sense of peaking just at the right time of the season and before the game. Maybe because we did the talk at 5 minutes to [game time], and closed the door [which prevented interruptions]. We trooped out a couple of minutes early, and they were *up*. A sort of deep breathing, jostling each other, and concentration. I could just feel it as they waited, so anxious to get on the ice, a kind of tension and energy building. To top it off, at this moment, Orest arrived, all dressed but skates and helmet. He put on his skates at the corner of the stands.

I had to keep Ken and Orest back from the gate: they were just champing at the bit to get out there: they came wanting to play! The other team came out: they were just kind of wandering around in contrast to our guys: they mingled, and a few friends/acquaintances talked, but I didn't feel that same sense of energy. I somehow *knew* right then and there that barring misfortune, we were gonna—as they say—"whip their butts"! It raises an epistemological question here: how did I "know" that? [De15/91]

Since gaining first advantage is often crucial, dressing room preparation is key:

There really is a "zen" about this: the hype and adrenalin in going to the toilet and getting dressed; then the relaxing, deep breath of cool instructions; quiet talk (it could be a prayer), a sort of togetherness, and meditation, letting the adrenalin build up. Then the ritual of order: things are together, and the walk out on stage/ice/diamond. Then how much they rely on routine on the bench to keep going: the coaches run the lines, they have to play it out there, but with some absolute confidence upon the coaches. [Ja24/91]

The privacy and ritual of the dressing room are crucial aspects of this development of team spirit and collective understanding and appreciation. This "jelling as a team" is crucial to success in competitive sports. These common understandings and team chemistry provide interpretations for painful events, injuries, and violence:

The major deke beat the goalie [and scored], point taken, but the interesting thing is that the kid who scored that goal crashed into the boards, but nonetheless popped right up! [In an elation which overcame his pain.] [Oct01/92]

Interpreting personally painful events as collectively joyous, as in this instance, is one example of what is variously called "team spirit," or "giving it all for the team." There are many more dramatic examples of such collective reinterpretations of pain incurred through the exercise of bodily force. Not only goalies are lauded for blocking pucks; blueliners are also taught to drop in front of shots; alternatively, forwards are intentionally put into the line of fire to "screen" goalies by distracting them; similarly, linemen in football and "grinders" in hockey "take out" opponents to allow scorers through.

The exercise of physical force, then, becomes fully integrated into the collective understanding of how the game should be played. Furthermore, "gentlemen" players congratulate their opponents on their play, however forceful it was, when they are beaten by them. The exercise of physical force thus becomes fully legitimated.

✱ Some Conclusions (and More Questions)

[Stan, one of our star players, went down after an illegal bodycheck, and lay on the ice without getting up.]

WGW: "Taking a dive": this is interesting epistemologically: I "knew" he was "taking a dive."

ADT: I didn't see it.

WGW: I saw him go down after he lost the puck, and he fell "harmlessly": the only possible hurt/injury would be a twist.

ADT: I thought it was Matt?

WGW: No, I anticipated Stan was building up for this.

[Epistemologically how did I know? From the bench talk, his body movements, his frustration, and playing hockey myself.]

WGW: The other kids also "knew" he was "faking" ... Or was he? They gathered round in some concern, but a survey would have given 50-50 response. When I lifted his head, he winked at me and smiled! The little devil! He got up, took a couple of strides, then realized he should "limp"! He indicated to me that I should hold his arm on the way back to the bench, check out his knee, etc. He could walk in 15 seconds, took the next shift, no problems.

In the ongoing debate concerning masculinity, sports, and violence, I wish to raise a number of questions about the considerable slippage of meaning over terms that require some conceptual clarification and precision in use. "Violence" has always been defined as the *illegitimate* use of force: it is not simply the use of force.

Neither is "violence" an objective description of behaviour; rather, it is a social action with meaning only within a social relationship between knowledgeable actors. Groupings of such understandings among distinguishable actors constitute a (sub)culture. These understandings are reciprocally meaningful among participants, both teammates and opponents.

Sports players experience a common problem of regulating the use of force so that it provides for accomplishment in the particular sport activity, with pain and injury limited by regulations socially developed and meaningfully understood in active processes of collective understanding. The sport subcultures studied do not sanctify violence, but rather the exercise of force collectively understood as legitimate under specified conditions. The research evidence here shows how such organized activities teach these boys how to consciously use the physical force of their bodies while avoiding pain and injury, and how *not* to use illegitimate force or violence so that others suffer pain or injury. Most do not usually use force illegitimately, nor do they require coercive responses.

Sports involve mastering a kind of embodied knowledge that relies less on language than many other human activities. Some key elements of knowledge in any given sport tend to elude all but active participants. Understanding embodied knowledge is essential to understanding how boys learn differentially about their bodies, force, and violence, in part through sport.

There are some very complex relationships between families, schools, and other leisure activities of these young people and what happens during their organized leisure in sports and scouting. This chapter described how these formulations are used by actors to constitute themselves as male persons. By encouraging and even requiring physical coercion or force by players, sports do teach participants how to use their bodies forcefully. One might speculate that males who develop some facility in using their bodies forcefully in sport might be more likely to carry this facility over to nonsports activities, but such a hypothesis is beyond the scope of this paper.

The boys and men studied, however, do not seem to be anomic "failures" looking for another arena in which to build their self-esteem, as suggested by some theories of subcultures. Most are middle class and do reasonably well in school; their sport activities are integrated with other legitimate leisure pursuits. Nor do sports constitute a subculture unique to adolescents. The people studied began to learn about sports and the surrounding values as pre-adolescents and will carry this learning through into their adult lives. The critiques of classic subculture theories by Sykes and Matza, and by Elkin and Westley, seem corroborated by this research.

Gender relations are at least as complicated as the class ones that are so focal in classic anomie-type theories of subculture. Any simplistic conceptualization of "patriarchy" as a male-perpetrated system of domination based on force must be corrected by recognizing that males are not only inordinately the perpetrators of violence and bodily injury, but also inordinately the victims (see West 1993a, 1993b). We need to be suspicious immediately of facile and simplistic explanations (such as claims that males are inherently more violent, or that sport makes them violent). "Patriarchy" is not just being "imposed": these activities are actively sought out by these young people, who find them enjoyable. Fundamentally, if the activity were not personally attractive, the young person would not continue to volunteer for it.

Playing sports is one of many options available to boys and girls. Historically and culturally, achievement in sport has been more encouraged for males than females. Adults do "engender" sport activities, and contextualize these with concerns about "moralities." Since sport does privilege larger and more muscular bodies, males are more likely biologically to be more successful; that being said, there is an enormous range of overlap. Some aspects of competitive team sport, such as increasing use of force in body contact sports among older age groups, discourage most males past early adolescence from continuing to pursue them competitively. (They nonetheless continue to enjoy less competitive sports into and throughout adulthood.)

Much more empirical research must be done regarding exactly how young males learn about force and violence in such activities as sports. The point would be to learn how they use their bodies, handle pain and frustration, obey authority, understand rules and regulations, and so on. Detailed ethnographic work would seem to be the appropriate research method.

This research has been supported in part by the Social Science and Humanities Research Council of Canada, the Ontario Institute for Studies in Education, the Centre of Criminology at the University of Toronto, and the Education Centre of Bath Institution, Correctional Services Canada. Particular thanks is due to Andrew Thornton, especially for help with the ideas in the section on gender theories, and for collaboration on much of the data collection. Thanks also to Elizabeth, Matthew, Martin, and Rosemary Flanagan, Till M'Geachie Capell and Deidre Cruickshank, Tony and Arleen Schenke, Michael Bach, James and Isaac Fowlie, Aaron Rousseau, Kyle and Carey West, Greg Barnett, Chris Purdue, Eldon Bennett, Brent Rutherford, Blair Harley, Fiona, Brian, and Michael Hart, and Mary Morton regarding gender relations, health, and sport. And special thanks to the boys, girls, men, women, parents, coaches, and leaders in the various organizations who shared with us some of their lives. Of course, none of them can be held in any way responsible for the above analyses.

References

Askew, S., and C. Ross. 1988. *Boys Don't Cry: Boys and Sexism in Education*. Milton Keynes, U.K.: Open University.

Berkeley, M., C. Gaffield, and W.G. West (eds.). 1977. *Children's Rights: Legal and Educational Issues*. Toronto: OISE.

Cierri, M., L.E. Gonzales, and W.G. West (eds.). 1988. *Modernizacion: Un Desafio Para La Educacion*. Santiago, Chile: CIDE/PIIE/UNESCO-OREALC.

Clatterbaugh, K. 1990. *Contemporary Perspectives on Masculinity: Men, Women and Politics in Modern Society*. Boulder, CO: Westview.

Cloward, R.A., and L.E. Ohlin. 1960. *Delinquency and Opportunity*. New York: Free Press.

Cohen, A.K. 1955. *Delinquent Boys*. New York: Free Press.

Cohen, A.K., and J.F. Short, Jr. 1971. "Crime and Juvenile Delinquency." In R.K. Merton and R. Nisbet (eds.), *Contemporary Social Problems*. 3rd Edition. New York: Harcourt Brace Jovanovich.

Cressey, D.R. 1971. "Delinquent and Criminal Structures." In R.K. Merton and R. Nisbet (eds.), *Contemporary Social Problems*. New York: Harcourt Brace Jovanovich.

Connell, R.W. 1983. *Which Way Is Up?* Sydney: Allen and Unwin. (Esp. Chapter 2, "Men's Bodies.")

————. 1987. *Gender and Power: Society, the Person, and Sexual Politics*. Oxford: Polity Press.

————. 1990. "An Iron Man: The Body and Some Contradictions of Hegemonic Masculinity." In M. Messner and D. Sabo (eds.), *Critical Perspectives on Sport, Men, and the Gender Order*. Champaign, IL: Human Kinetics.

Corrigan, P.R.D. 1988. "The Making of the Boy: Meditations on What Grammar School Did With, To, and For My Body." *Journal of Education* 170(3).

Dryden, K. 1983. *The Game*. London: Sports Pages/Simon and Schuster.

Elias, N., and E. Dunning. 1986. *Quest for Excitement: Sport and Leisure in the Civilizing Process*. Oxford: Blackwell.

Fine, G.A. 1987. *With the Boys: Little League Baseball and Preadolescent Culture*. Chicago: University of Chicago Press.

Foucault, M. 1977. *Discipline and Punish*. New York: Vintage.

————. 1981. *The History of Sexuality*. Vol 1. New York: Vintage.

Grant, James P. 1991. *The State of the World's Children*. New York: UNESCO/Oxford.

Hall, A., T. Slack, G. Smith, and D. Whitson. 1991. *Sport in Canadian Society*. Toronto: McClelland & Stewart.

Keen, S. 1991. *Fire in the Belly: On Being a Man*. New York: Bantam. (Esp. Chapter 15, "Travel Tips.")

Kidd, B. 1987. "Sports and Masculinity." In M. Kaufman (ed.), *Beyond Patriarchy: Essays by Men on Pleasure, Power, and Change*. Toronto: Oxford.

Kimball, A. 1991. "A Time for Men to Pull Together." *UTNE Reader* 45 (May/June).

Kitsuse, J.I., and D.C. Dietrick. 1959. "Delinquent Boys: A Critique." Pp. 213–215 in *American Sociological Review* 24 (April).

Kotz, L. 1992. "The Body You Want." *Artforum* (November).

Lenskyj, H. 1986. *Out of Bounds: Women, Sport and Sexuality*. Toronto: Women's Press.

Messner, M. 1992. *Power at Play*.

Miedzian, M. 1991. *Boys Will Be Boys: Breaking the Link between Masculinity and Violence*. New York: Doubleday.

Miles, M. 1991. *The Rites of Man: Love, Sex and Death in the Making of the Male*. London: Grafton.

Miller, Walter B. 1958. "Lower Class Culture as a Generating Milieu of Gang Delinquency." *Journal of Social Issues* 14(3):5–19.

Pronger, B. 1990. *The Arena of Masculinity: Sport, Homosexuality, and the Meaning of Sex*. Toronto: Summerhill/New York: St. Martin's Press.

Psych, C. 1992. "The American Man at Age Ten." *Esquire* (December):115–130.

Reasons, C., et al. 1981. *Assault on the Worker*. Toronto: Butterworths.

Short, J.F., and F.L. Strodtbeck. 1965. *Group Process and Gang Delinquency*. Chicago: University of Chicago.

Sykes, G., and D. Matza. 1957. "Techniques of Neutralization: A Theory of Delinquency." *American Sociological Review* 22(December).

———. 1959. "Techniques of Neutralization: A Theory of Delinquency." *American Sociological Review* 24(2):208–215.

Thorne, B. 1986. "Girls and Boys Together ... But Mostly Apart: Gender Arrangements in Elementary Schools." In W.W. Hartup and Z. Rubin (eds.), *Relationships and Development*. New Jersey: Lawrence Erlbaum Associates.

Thornton, A.D. 1991. *The Accomplishment of Masculinity: Men and Sports*. Unpub. MA thesis. Toronto: OISE/University of Toronto.

———. 1992. "Masculinity as Ideological Practice: How to Not Talk about Men." Unpub ms., course 1917. Toronto: OISE.

———. 1993. "Going Ho! Pedagogies of, to, and for the Body." Unpub. ms. Toronto: OISE.

———. 1993 (March). "Rethinking the Links: Sports, Schools, and 'Violence.'" In W.G. West (ed.), "Violence in the Schools: Schooling in Violence." Special issue of *Orbit*. Toronto: OISE.

————. 1993. "The Accomplishment of Masculinities: Men and Sports." In T. Haddad and L. Lam (eds.), *Men and Masculinities: A Critical Anthology*. Toronto: Canadian Scholars' Press.

Thrasher, G.M. 1927. *The Gang*. Chicago: University of Chicago Press.

Treadwell, P. 1987. "Biologic Influences on Masculinity." In H. Brod (ed.), *The Making of Masculinities: The New Men's Studies*. London: Allen and Unwin.

Varpolotai, A. 1986. *Sport, Gender and the Hidden Curriculum in Leisure: A Case Study of Adolescent Girls*. Unpub. Ph.D. thesis. Toronto: OISE/University of Toronto.

Vaz, E.W. 1965. "Middle-Class Adolescents: Self-Reported Delinquency and Youth Culture Activities." *Canadian Review of Sociology and Anthropology* 2 (February):52–70.

West, W.G. 1979. "Adolescent Autonomy, Education and Pupil Deviance." Pp. 151–172 in L. Barton and R. Meighan (eds.), *Schools, Pupils and Deviance*. Driffield, U.K.: Nafferton.

————. 1984. *Young Offenders and the State: A Canadian Perspective on Delinquency*. Toronto: Butterworths.

————. 1993a (March). "Social Problem or 'Moral Panic'? A Critical Perspective." In W.G. West (ed.), "Violence in the Schools: Schooling in Violence." Special issue of *Orbit*. Toronto: OISE.

————. 1993b. "Boys, Recreation, and Violence: The Informal Education of Some Young Canadian Males." Pp. 277–310 in T. Haddad (ed.), *Men and Masculinities: A Critical Anthology*. Toronto: Canadian Scholars' Press.

————. 1995. "Youth and Violence: The Recurrent Construction of Canadian Moral Panic." In T. O'Reilly-Fleming (ed.), *Post-Critical Criminology* (forthcoming).

Yablonsky, L. 1959. "The Delinquent Gang as a Near-Group." *Social Problems* 7(Fall):108–170.

CHAPTER 13

Cyberskating: Computers, Crime, and Youth Culture

Kevin McCormick

York University

Cyberspace: A new universe, a parallel universe created and sustained by the world's computers and communication lines. A world in which the global traffic of knowledge, secrets, measurements, indicators, entertainments and alter-human agency takes on form: sights, sounds, presences never seen on the earth blossoming in a vast electronic night.

Michael Benedikt, 1993

For today's young people, the Information Highway has had a dramatic effect on the communication process. Youth culture has become electrified. Countless "cyberskaters" are spending hours each day on their home and school computers linked with a myriad of information systems. The electrified culture has given these technology literate youths the means to transcend physical and social boundaries. Interestingly, the Information Highway has also enabled some youths to expand their deviant and sometimes criminal activities.

Computer break-ins by teenagers of military databases and of files of international banks are now widely recognized as a new form of youth resistance. Thousands of young people now regularly try to break into information databases. This "hacking" (Makus 1990; Forester and Morrison 1990) is seen by many young computer users as a rite of passage, as part of the process of becoming accepted by the "cyberskating" community. Often, young people must prove themselves to a "virtual community" (Halal 1992) by committing criminal acts such as information theft, software theft, and virus "assault."

The ever-changing world of electronic communications has swallowed not only individuals but entire subcultures. In this chapter I will demonstrate that computers are more than a mere convenience: they have profoundly changed how young people interact with one another. Because of computers, many teens are socially (and criminally) more powerful than they could possibly have been a generation ago. Specifically, the computer has opened up far more sites and targets to young offenders.

To show how youth crime has become electrified, I will take the reader into the "virtual communities" in which deviant youths interact. Specifically, I will utilize the Information Highway as both a site of investigation and an instrument for interviewing members of the subculture. First, I will examine computer bulletin boards as sites for social and criminal activities. Then I will look at hacking, software pirating, and the dealing of illegal goods and services—all three activities take place on these systems. I hope to demonstrate that as technology has changed, so has youth culture—and so has youth deviance.

✹ Computer Bulletin Boards: Electronic Presentations of Self

In the past decade, researchers have noted the impact of the home computer on communication (Heise 1981; Postman 1992; Meyrowitz 1985). Many young people have noticed that electronic bulletin boards are conducive to legal and illegal activities. As the number of people owning computers increases, the number of these boards will grow exponentially.

In the 1980s, research on bulletin boards focused mainly on their potential as message exchange systems (Myers 1987; Greenstein 1987). There was little examination of the effects this new medium would have on the culture into which it was being introduced. The studies that were written amounted to users' manuals. However, researchers soon began to examine the interactive (i.e., "social") abilities of computers and their effects on various subcultures, including youth. For example, Gaines and Shaw (1984) studied the "dynamic" relationship users have with electronic media. However, this perspective focused on individual–computer relationship; it ignored how computers generated distinct electronic social environments. Further work in the study of technology and social interaction was a synthesis between the perspective of Meyrowitz (1985) and McLuhan (1964, 1969), who perceived technology not as an external agent but as an internal device that redefined how individuals presented themselves. The study of computer bulletin boards as locales of societal performance attempts to deconstruct the intricate process by which individuals present themselves via electronic media of social interaction.

While personal-computer networks are relatively new, there have always been electronic bulletin boards. The earliest E-mail programs were internal electronic-memo programs (Duranti 1986; Sproull and Kiesler 1986; Gerson 1988; May 1991; Rice 1993). Such programs, the forerunners to the present-day "Echo Mailing" systems used by bulletin boards, were mainframe message-posting bases, alternatives to conventional mail. These systems led to more complex ones under which private messages could be sent directly to individuals on the network. Such a system meant that everyone on the network was linked to everyone else electronically. The era of instantaneous communication had begun (Heise 1981). The only limitation now was institutional; to be wired in, you had to be on a network.

As a direct result of the increased number of personal computers, private electronic communications networks were established. These new systems, called BBSs (bulletin board systems), had much the same abilities as their mainframe counterparts (Shamp 1991; Makus 1990; Greenstein 1987). A BBS network allowed individuals on a net to link their home computers with each other through phone lines. Thus, they could exchange both messages and programs. Each network was run by an individual called a "Sysop," who acted as a gatekeeper, defining the scope of the BBS and deciding who could link with it. Currently, young people can participate on a wide spectrum of BBSs. The possible topics are more or less infinite.

Most public BBSs are designed to link people with common interests so that they can share ideas on certain subjects. Other systems have arisen with more illegal intent. Throughout the world there has been a great increase in the number of "pirated systems," which operate underground in contravention of communications laws. These systems deal in stolen items, in software that is not public, and in other information such as stolen calling and credit card numbers. Typically, users of such systems pay a fee and then are entitled to use the information for their own illegal activities. Many of the young people using such systems are finding out how to perform certain illegal activities, where to find other interested parties, and the locations of coming events. For countless youths, scratched messages on a wall or locker have been replaced by highly electrified and far more powerful billboards.

✱ "Getting Connected" to a Bulletin Board: An Electronic Methodology

To understand how computer bulletin boards have helped create new (and sometimes illegal) environments for youths to interact, I examined a cross-example of systems currently operating in Canada. I approached 24 electronically and selected 10 as representative of the diverse networks currently operating for young people. I selected the public (i.e., legal) bulletin boards from notices in newspapers and computer magazines such as *Computing Toronto* and *Bulletin Board Monthly*. I found subterranean (i.e., "pirated") systems by interviewing former users. I approached each system the way any new user would, engaging in all the procedures expected of a "petitioning user." Generally, this involved filling out an electronic questionnaire and having a phone conversation with the Sysop, whose approval would ensure full validation on the system. Once I was validated on the board, I experienced all areas of the system electronically. This included the message bases, file listings, and advertisements, all of which I captured in an electronic journal for later reference (Walsh et al. 1992). Doing so enabled me to learn the proper etiquette and ascertain how expectational structures differed from one system to another. Through direct participation on various computer networks, I soon learned that bulletin boards were diverse environments of social interaction. Within each board, users were able to utilize the same techniques of presentation as used in face-to-face encounters.

Even when mechanically empowered (by possessing the physical devices), an individual cannot interact on the boards until he or she has been socially accepted by both the Sysop and the other users. The process of acceptance differs greatly between public and private systems. Generally, in order to become a participating member of an electronic subculture, one must engage in many levels of acceptance and disclosure. At the beginning, an individual must call the desired board and fill out a "new user survey." Administrative and security documents such as these ask for the name, address, and phone number of the petitioning user. Most importantly, references of credible computer users are demanded. To verify this information the bulletin board may call the user's system electronically to verify the number and then in turn call the user by voice and have a brief discussion with him or her as to why validation on that specific bulletin board is being sought. After the initial process of validation has been completed successfully, the Sysop will increase the user's access level based on the new user's successful participation within the culture.

✹ Cyberskating: Interaction within Electronic Youth Subcultures

A critical examination of young adults' interactions on computer information systems clearly demonstrates that computer bulletin boards are technologically defined and mediated locales of social interaction. Computer communication electronically enhances the construction and mediation of youth culture. Further, the presentation techniques young adults use on such systems are analogous to the those which have traditionally been associated with physically intimate social environments.

It is evident that bulletin boards are defined environments of social interaction. Each board, whatever its focus, has certain specific expectations of users. These expectations are the same as those held by audiences in face-to-face situations. McLuhan noted that "man in his normal use of technology is perpetually modified by it and in turn finds new ways of modifying his technology" (1964:57). This adaptation to technology results in new electronic encounters and stages of social performance being constituted. These "environments are not passive wrappings but active processes which work over as completely, massaging the senses and imposing silent assumptions" (1964:69), mediated by barriers of language and social convention. The electronic bulletin board is a "place bounded by barriers of perception" (Goffman 1959:35), social constraints contained within the dominant expectational structure. Jeremy, a Cyberskater for eight years, notes:

> No matter what system you are on, you have to live by their rules. That means if they tell you that your chats are not liked by other users, or that you always "flame" people for no reason, then you have two choices—make them happy or be thrown from the system. It would take a fool not to know that you are in trouble, because the rules are pretty clear—you know what you can get away with and what will piss them off.

All computer systems have expectations that are dominant, and individuals are guaranteed success within the technological medium only when their actions meet the expectations of others. In computer culture, some practices are generic to all systems; others are specific to subcultures within the larger bulletin board network. Given computer systems constitute "regions" or "cultures" of performance; an individual's success on a system depends on the successful presentation of self within the audience's electronic expectational structure. On bulletin boards, individuals perform electronically in order to maintain a functional level of social acceptance within technologically defined stages of performance.

Given that electronic locales of interaction are defined by technologically imposed barriers of perception, the actor must employ electronic techniques of presentation in order to function successfully on the system. Barker (1968:11) notes that "behaviour settings are bounded by physical and temporal locales," in that in the case of computer communication, a technological barrier exists as well as a social one. Having a computer and a modem does not ensure access to a bulletin board, in the same way that having a uniform does not guarantee one's acceptance into the military. In order to succeed socially, one has to be accepted into the cultural environment, where one can learn more about the expectations of its participants. Joe, a new computer user, notes:

> I thought that once I had a system and a modem I was on my way to becoming a cyberpunk, but that was not the case. Sure I could call the systems that I knew about, but many times the minute I logged on it would hang up on me with a message not to call back. Only later did I find out that many of these systems have trick log-on questions designed to exclude the normal user from getting onto a pirated system. Just 'cause I could call a board did not mean I was accepted. It took a lot more than that for them to let me on the board.

This process of acceptance is seen with most computer systems. Before an individual can become a member of the electrified community, he or she must pass certain tests to demonstrate to both the Sysop and the users that the rules of the technologically generated culture will be followed. Validation is a technological rite of passage. "When anyone enters into a social setting, they need to know and demonstrate something about the situation and other participants" (Meyrowitz 1985:28). Thus, to become a validated user is to engage in an initial performance of acceptance that allows the user to further his or her education in the system and increase his or her scope of electronic communication within the electrified youth subculture.

The various youth subcultures found on bulletin boards are defined areas of interaction bounded by dominant expectational structures. Utilizing Goffman's dramaturgical perspective, it can be argued that the area bounded by the expectations of the computer audience constitutes the "front region" (1959:22), whereas the area outside of the view of the system users constitutes the preparatory or "back region" (1959:28). In the dynamics of computer communication, a physical site of interaction is not based on a face-to-face exchange, but rather on an impulse-to-impulse exchange, which is then translated into readable text on the computer screen. In the "front region," "settings involving furniture decor, physical lay-out and other background items are used which supply the scenery and stage props for the spate of human action played out before, within, or upon it" (1959:22). In computer interaction, props are unavailable, but items can still be "manipulated." That is, other users can electronically magnify the "miscues" of other performers.

Furthermore, in the "front region," all actions are performed in front of the audience, which observes electronically. Everything the user says and does is viewed by the system users and evaluated according to personal and collective expectations. Actions such as hanging up without logging off or typing in capitals (which is denotive of yelling) may be misread by the audience. These "miscues" can result in a failed performance and cause the individual to be thrown off the system. In face-to-face interactions, the "front region" is the area of performance in physical proximity to the audience. The computer has expanded the regions of performance to include sites of interaction that are social in nature but articulated technologically.

The computer also changed the preparatory areas of social presentation. Given that electronic interaction is not face to face, certain physical props, such as dress and facial gestures, need not be prepared. Rather, utilization of electronically enhanced gestures are utilized. When manipulating the board, computer users are in the presence of the Sysop, who is watching the system; but when reading information on the screen, the audience has no means to observe their performance. The constant changing of regions allows for a more calculated presentation, given that a response to a message may be written out beforehand and merely typed into the system. Carla, a computer user for eight months, states:

> What is so fantastic about the computer is that I can plan what I am going to say. I used to say what came to my mind when my friends were in front of me, but when I am on the system I can read what I am going to post before I send it out for everyone to see. That helps me sound like I know what I am talking about and that way no one thinks I am stupid for saying the wrong thing.

Interaction in this instance is electronically captured, static, and not easily manipulated by the individual who originally posted it. Young people who regularly "skate the boards" find that

> using the concepts of areas of performance in the study of computer communication, what is created is a new behaviour that arises out of merging situations, called "middle regions," two sets of behaviour that result from the division entitled "deep back" and "fore front behaviour." [Meyrowitz 1985:47]

The influence of the device over the locales of performance causes stages to exist independent of the actor's dramaturgical manipulation and the participation of the audience.

In an attempt to circumvent these problems, which are built into social interaction on computers, individuals utilize the same techniques of presentation as they do in face-to-face social encounters. On electronic message bases, performers try "in the presence of others to infuse their activity with signs which dramatically highlight and portray confirmatory fact that might otherwise remain unapparent" (Goffman 1959:30). To achieve this end, an individual might participate in all message bases on the board in an attempt to present him(her)self as a fully participating member of the subculture. If the board is specialized, the performer might also be very critical of others in an effort to seem very knowledgeable about the subject area. Thus, the user demonstrates to the electronic culture abilities that in his or her daily interaction would not have been visible. In order to to "dramatically realize" (Goffman 1959:30) their role on the system, individuals must first "idealize" their performance (1959:74). This process is observed on the system when the new users "in their performance tend to incorporate and exemplify the officially accredited values of the society" (1959:34), so that they appear to be functioning within the expectational structure. This social presentation through electrified media is similar to face-to-face encounters for many young people, according to John, an 18-year-old cyberskater:

> When I get on to a new system I wait a while before I leave a message on the system. It is kind of like when you go to a new school, you find those you want to hang with and then find out what and who they like and hate. Once I know what their score is I say things I know they are all right with. Same with the computer. I watch what the system likes and then give them what they are looking for. That way they like me and I have no problems.

For young people on the Information Highway, performance techniques are quite similar to those used in person. This highlights that computer communication is a direct electronic reflection of existing youth subcultural norms and values.

☀ Skating the Net: Electrifying the Deviant Youth Subculture

The computer has dramatically altered not only formal learning processes and leisure time for young people, but also the deviant subcultures within which many youths regularly interact. BBSs and other information systems can easily link youths who are interested in deviant and illegal activities. For many of these people, the risks associated with deviant activities are reduced by the computer. BBSs are highly "policed" environments that are open only to trusted members of the subculture. Years ago, rumour and word of mouth were the vehicles by which information was disseminated to group members; the computer provides a far more private environment.

Computers have enabled countless young people to expand their webs of interaction and their deviant and illegal associations and activities. Many members of these new "virtual communities" have developed electronic "clubhouses" to facilitate various illegal activities, including the sale of stolen goods and pirated software. BBSs also give the location of raves—underground parties involving alcohol and drugs. The computer is a social and political outlet through which self-professed "cyberpunks" can express themselves both as individuals and as members of a disenfranchised youth subculture (Biddick 1993; Foster 1993; Rosenthal 1991). Jack, a former cyberpunk, notes:

> When I was on the boards, I felt like I knew a secret that no one else knew. I could tell where the next wild party was going to be, where I could pick up a computer at a really good price—you know, the ones that seem to keep falling of a truck. I could also talk to my friends outside of my calling area for free, by piggyback on a mail server. Hell, I could arrange a party with people in Sudbury for free and no one could tell what was going on—the police, the school or even my family. I never had such a feeling of power before. It was addictive, everything that I did was from some system or from someone I had met from a board.

Interestingly, many cyberskaters attest to the sense of privacy they experience when using the system. They feel that this area of communication is solely their own. This intimacy becomes all-consuming. Maria, a cyberskater, commented:

> While there was a lot of shit going on—on the system—I was not as much interested in really doing the stuff, but rather just knowing about it. You know, sometimes you like to hang with a bunch who has a reputation for being wild, and while you probably would never do it yourself, you feel cool just hanging with them? Well that was what it was like for me. The stuff on the boards was *power*. I knew shit others at school did not and because of that they felt I was connected with the right gang and this made them leave me alone and respect me.

This sense of power is very important for the young computer user. The power of the communicative force allows for the construction of a new social space that few are able to traverse. Expertise translates into acceptance, and eventually into participation in a social setting for which they possess all the attributes required for success. For many, computer communication is a joyride on the Information Highway, complete with detours that both entertain and increase social status. Except for the computer, many youths would not have any contact with the deviant subculture of their age cohort.

Many young people utilize the computer merely as an outlet. Countless others have translated their deviant activities directly into the virtual community. Mark, a cyberskater for three years, notes:

> Stuff I used to do, like go to warehouse parties or pick up a stolen part for my computer or car, has become a lot easier for me since I became a board surfer. Now when I get home I log on a system and see what's happening with my friends. Shit, my parents even thought it was great that I was so interested in my homework, since I was always on the computer, and they bought me a new system and let me stay up all night on the computer. It was great. Who would have thought that I was planning my weekend party line-up or where I could score an ounce of weed without getting hassled by the cops.

Repeatedly, respondents noted that while spending time at the mall or at someone's home caused parents to become suspicious, the computer did not because computer work was conveniently associated with school. Jason, a cyberskater for six months, stated:

> I was never that good a student, C plus at best. But when I learned about the computer boards from the boys at school I was spending a lot of extra time in the computer lab. We would stay there until the monitor told us we had to leave. They thought we were doing school stuff, but we were really copying disks of "gifs" we had lifted from the various systems so we could trade with other punks. The teacher even said on my next report card that I was becoming a serious student, doing my work and spending time increasing my computer skills. Yeah, right!

Cyberskaters develop their own vocabulary as a means of distancing themselves from others. For instance, "gifs" are files that display pictures onto the computer screen; many of these, in the electrified youth subculture, are pornographic in nature.

Interestingly, many activities in youth subculture have not disappeared because of computer communication; rather, they have become calibrated according to the nuances dictated by the device. Public declarations of subcultural affiliation, and territorial claims traditionally scrolled across a bathroom wall, have become electrified. On one system, a certain group of cyberskaters claimed control over a message area. Jonathan, a seven-year cyberskater, noted:

> When I was on the boards I would always see messages addressed to certain groups of people telling them that this system was not for them and that they should get off the board. This was because there was a group of users who had taken control of the system and would only let their friends post messages or take files. If anyone else wanted to work on the system they would flame them until they got pissed and never called back. I even heard that some boards have called some people to face-to-face meetings where they planned a fight to settle their arguments.

These regular character assassinations and defamatory remarks on the computer mimic the interactions that occur in more physically intimate settings. The computer has electrified the practice of graffiti, presenting a highly technical wall upon which rebellious youth statements can be posted for the cyber community to read and comment upon. Many of the racist, homophobic, and sexist comments regularly found on the walls of schools and malls are found on youth computer bulletin boards. Everyone participating on the system regularly reads the deviant and sometimes violent sentiments. The only difference between computer posting of discriminatory views and wall graffiti is that computers reach a far greater audience and cannot be accessed by police or school authorities.

✳ Echoes from Cyberspace: Reflections on the Electrification of Youth Culture

Computers have directly affected the ways in which young people interact and script their daily lives. In the early 1980s, Heise made this forecast:

> By the end of the decade, microcomputers will have changed the way social scientists do research, the way they teach courses and the way they work in applied settings. And computers will also create new topics for social analysis as the microcomputer revolution reaches diverse sectors of society. [1981:395]

Computers have designated for young adults the mechanical, linguistic, and conceptual parameters in which they must develop and execute strategies of social interaction and articulation. The power that this new and highly technical setting provides the young computer user "reaches into the very grain of [individuals], inserting itself directly into their actions, attitudes, discourses, learning processes and everyday lives" (Foucault 1986:39).

Many young people have harnessed this new-found power to enhance their educational and social "web" of activity; others have harnessed it for deviant and illegal activities. As the world becomes increasingly computerized, youth culture will become increasingly electrified. The challenge for researchers, educators, and community advocates is to find new and innovative methods to involve all segments of the youth culture on the Information Highway and to ensure that some young people are not left stranded at the side of the road.

References

Barker, Roger G. 1968. *Concepts and Methods for Studying the Environment of Human Behaviour*. Stanford, CA: Stanford University Press.

Barr, A., and E.A. Feigenbaum. 1991. *The Handbook of Artificial Intelligence,* Volume 1. Stanford: Stanford University Press.

Benedikt, Michael. 1993. "Introduction" in *Cyberspace: First Steps*, Michael Benedikt (ed.). Cambridge: MIT Press.

Biddick, Kathleen. 1993. "Humanist History and the Haunting of Virtual Worlds: Problems of Memory and Renemoration." *Genders* 18 (Winter).

Costin, Donald. 1968. *The Design and Development of a Man–Computer Communication System*. Winnipeg: University of Manitoba.

Duranti, Alessandro. 1986. "Framing Discourse in a New Medium: Openings in Electronic Mail." *Quarterly Newsletter of the Laboratory of Comparative Human Cognition* 8(2).

Forester, Tom, and Perry Morrison. 1990. "Computer Crime: New Problem for the Information Society." *Prometheus* 8(2).

Foster, Thomas. 1993. "Meat Puppets or Robopaths?: Cyberpunk and the Question of Embodiment." *Genders* 18 (Winter).

Foucault, M. 1986. *Power/Knowledge*. New York: Pantheon.

Gaines, Brian R., and Mildred L.G. Shaw. 1984. *The Art of Computer Conversation: A New Medium for Communication*. Englewood Cliffs, NJ: Prentice-Hall International.

Gerson, Elihu M. 1988. "Electronic Mail." *Qualitative Sociology* 11(4).

Gibson, William. 1984. *Neuromancer*. New York: Ace Books.

Gibson, William. 1987. *Count Zero.* New York: Ace Books.

Goffman, Erving. 1959. *The Presentation of Self in Everyday Life.* New York: Doubleday Anchor.

Green, Bill, and Chris Bigum. 1987. "Aliens in the Classroom." *Australian Journal of Education* 37(2).

Greenstein, Theodore N. 1987. "Public-Domain and User-Supported Software for the IBM PC and Compatibles." *Social Science Microcomputer Review* 5(1).

Halal, William E. 1992. "The Information Technology Revolution." *Futurist* 26(4).

Heise, David R. 1981. "Microcomputers and Social Research." *Sociological Methods and Research 9.*

Levin, M.L. 1986. "Technological Determinism in Social Data Analysis." *Computers and the Social Sciences 2.*

McLuhan, Marshall. 1964. *Understanding Media: The Extensions of Man.* New York: Mentor.

McLuhan, Marshall. 1969. *Counter Blast.* Toronto: McClelland & Stewart.

Makus, Anne. 1990. "Stuart Hall's Theory of Ideology: A Frame for Rhetorical Criticism." *Western Journal of Speech Communication* 54(4).

May, Linda. 1991. "Sociolinguistic Research on Human–Computer Interaction—A Perspective from Anthropology." *Social Science Computer Review* 9(4).

Meyrowitz, Joshua. 1985. *No Sense of Place.* New York: Oxford University Press.

Myers, David. 1987. "Anonymity Is Part of the Magic: Individual Manipulation of Computer-Mediated Communication Contexts." *Qualitative Sociology* 10(3).

Postman, Neil. 1992. *Technopoly: The Surrender of Culture to Technology.* New York: Knopf.

Rice, Ronald E. 1993. "Media Appropriateness: Using Social Presence Theory to Compare Traditional and New Organization Media." *Human Communication Research* 19(4).

Rosenthal, Pam. 1991. "Jacked In: Fordism, Cyberpunk, Marxism." *Socialist Review* 21(1).

Shamp, Scott A. 1991. "Mechanomorphism in Perception of Computer Communication Partners." *Computers in Human Behavior* 7(3).

Sproull, Lee S., and Sara Kiesler. 1986. "Reducing Social Context Cues: Electronic Mail in Organizational Communication." *Management Science* 32(11).

Sterling, Bruce. 1990. "Cyberspace (TM)." *Interzone* 2(November).

Stone, Allucquere Rosanne. 1993. "Will the Real Body Please Stand Up? Boundary Stories About Virtual Cultures." In *Cyberspace: First Steps,* Michael Benedikt (ed.). Cambridge: MIT Press.

Tanner, Julian. 1987. "New Directions for Subcultural Theory: An Analysis of British Working-Class Youth Culture." *Youth and Society* 9(4).

Walsh, John P., Sara Kiesler, Lee S. Sproull, and Bradford W. Hess. 1992. "Self-Selected and Randomly Selected Respondents in a Computer Network Survey." *Public Opinion Quarterly* 56(2).

CHAPTER 14

"Ya Gotta Walk That Walk and Talk That Talk": Youth Subcultures and Gang Violence[1]

Gary M. O'Bireck
Lakehead University

Arguably, the year 1955 was pivotal in the development of youth in North American society. Cleveland disc jockey Alan Freed claimed to have coined the phrase "rock and roll" to describe the "new" music of youth that was sweeping Canada, the United States, and the rest of the world. (In truth, both the phrase and the roots of the music had been created by black musicians years before.) Bill Haley, a white country swing guitarist and balladeer, arranged a group of New York musicians into a backing group (the Comets) and produced "Rock Around the Clock," followed closely by "Shake, Rattle and Roll." Released on national radio, these two irresistible party songs encouraged young people to celebrate the advantages of youth.

Taking a chance on the perceived popularity of this new sound, Hollywood appropriated "Rock Around the Clock" as the theme song for *Blackboard Jungle*, a brooding and insolent black-and-white film about youth gangs and dysfunction in secondary school. Three months later, Elvis Aaron Presley, a white, greasy-haired, leather-jacketed, hip-swivelling dynamo from Tupelo, Mississippi, left audiences of young people breathless and simultaneously alienated adults. With his burgeoning popularity among youth, Presley eventually created opportunities for black artists to begin to become recognized for the music they had been creating and cultivating in previous years (Tosches 1979:33–34; Lewis and Silver 1982; White 1984).

For instance, on both radio and in person, Little Richard Penniman (and his renowned band of Upsetters) continued to electrify mixed audiences with his sexually suggestive lyrics ("Tutti Frutti," "Slippin' and a Slidin'") and infectious dance music. The masterful lyrics and supreme showmanship of Chuck Berry ("Maybelline," "You Can't Catch Me") thrilled steadily increasing youth audiences. The quintessential New Orleans performance ability of the somewhat older Fats Domino ("Ain't That a Shame," "Blueberry Hill") continued to contribute to what both society and young people collectively began to refer to as "the Big Beat" (White 1984).

Desperately wishing to capitalize on this new "youth craze" called "rock and roll," Hollywood became more deeply involved. "Teen idols" Natalie Wood and James Dean were cast with Sal Mineo and Dennis Hopper in 1955's colour feature *Rebel Without a Cause*. This tale of misunderstood youth became a beacon for young people to follow. The social "buzz" about the film suggested and confirmed in the minds of the young people of that time that (a) massive differences existed between traditional adults and young people, (b) it was more fun to be young, (c) it was very attractive and adventurous to get involved in adult activities (drinking, having sex, driving cars, staying out late, going to parties, etc.), and (d) the aggravating problems they were experiencing within their social existences (parents, school, curfews, resources, dating, sex, love, peer associations, cliques, other restrictions and constraints) were not entirely unique to themselves, but fairly universal in character.

While adolescence had always been seen as a "difficult time" for young people, this separation between adults and young people actually began at least a year before rock and roll music and its resultant style began to dominate the social frames of reference for youth. The "disturbing" black-and-white film *The Wild One* (1954) featured Marlon Brando and Lee Marvin as leaders of rival outlaw motorcycle gangs. Loosely based on an actual July 4, 1947, incident in Hollister, California, the film shows two rival gangs of angry outlaw bikers completely taking over a small town by disarming the police force; they then indulge in drinking, violence, and other forms of mayhem. According to Lowe:

> To its middle-class viewers, *The Wild One* was a metaphor, Brando's anti-heroic character representing a repellent yet fascinating symbol of iconoclasm, of what might happen when the sacred cows of their parents—the sanctity of private property and womanhood, the rule of law—were utterly swept away. [1989:81]

The addition of rock and roll music compounded the problem in the minds of adults, but increased the quest for social identity in the minds of North American youth.

The trend continued unabated. For instance, in 1956, Gene Vincent and his Bluecaps captivated youthful audiences with recordings and wild stage performances of "Bebopalula," "Race With the Devil," "Teenage Partner," and "Blue Jean Bop." Jerry Lee Lewis, the "Wild Man from Louisiana" (aka "The Killer"), had just recorded "Crazy Arms" on Sun Records and was set to challenge Elvis for rock and roll supremacy with "Great Balls of Fire," "Whole Lotta Shakin' Goin' On," "The End of the Road," and "High School Confidential." The Rock and Roll Trio (the Burnette Brothers) from Memphis, Tennessee, experienced similar success with "Rockabilly Boogie," "Honey Hush," and "Train Kept a-Rollin'." Oklahoma-born Eddie Cochran thrilled audiences with original compositions like "Summertime Blues," "Twenty Flight Rock," and "Somethin' Else." Jackie Wilson, a former Golden Gloves boxer known as "Mr. Excitement" for his dynamic stage performances, impressed capacity audiences of young people with his near-operatic vocal range on "Reet Petit," "Lonely Teardrops," and "Baby Workout" (Lewis and Silver 1982). Frequently, cash-hungry promoters would package these and other artists together into touring shows that would entertain young people in overflowing arenas and fairgrounds throughout the United States and Canada.

Again, Hollywood moguls increased the gap between adults and youths and legitimized this completely separate form of youth culture by incorporating it in feature films directed at young people. At the low end of the production scale, black-and-white films like *Don't Knock the Rock, Rock, Rock, Rock, High School Confidential, Mr. Rock and Roll,* and *Rock Around the Clock* meshed flimsy plot lines with guest appearances by a wide variety of current stars. Complete legitimization in the minds of youth was accomplished when 20th Century Fox mated Jayne Mansfield, its current sex symbol, with proven rock and roll artists (Little Richard, Fats Domino, Eddie Cochran, Gene Vincent, and so on) in the colour feature-length film entitled *The Girl Can't Help It.* While the plot lines of films of this nature were obscure, the message widely and consistently disseminated to both youth and adult society was quite clear:

> Adolescence is a stage that happens only once in a person's lifetime. It should be a fun time. To you adults, don't mess with us, don't try to control us, and don't try to understand us, because you can't.

In this chapter I will further explore the gap between adolescence and adulthood primarily created by popular music and the youthful quest for an intrinsic feeling of "cool." More specifically, I will present findings from my 1993 participant observational study of a group of working-class youths to detail the lived experiences of three mutually exclusive subcultural groups—

Hommies, Housers, and Bangers—and the specific subdivisions within each. The main purpose of these subcultural forms is not to solve problems of status frustration. Instead, inclusion serves as a social frame of reference that guides self-identity, increases a feeling of acceptance of the self, and in essence provides a guidebook that clearly indicates what to appreciate and what to disdain.

☀ Theoretical Considerations

Between 1954 and 1956, the firmly rooted and increasingly prevailing separation between the ideals of youth and the supposed responsibilities of adulthood did not escape the probes of sociologists. Prior to this time, Lee (1945) and Gordon (1947) separately envisioned subcultural involvement as a type of learned behaviour resulting from a divergence from a sense of national culture. Close attention was paid to the effects of socialization within the plethora of subgroups found within pluralist society. While these contentions only hint at what was occurring within the social consciousness of youth in the middle 1950s, other sociologists set out to attempt to understand how and why subcultures of youth are formed.

Adopting a functional strain perspective, Cohen formulated a macro theory in *Delinquent Boys* (1955), which details the way in which he believes subcultures of juvenile delinquent males are formed within a middle-class school system. Cohen did not conduct his own empirical research; he did peruse intellectually by synthesizing the theoretical positions of Edwin Sutherland, Talcott Parsons, and Robert F. Bales. He then applied these theoretical contentions to the school situations of lower-class boys.

Cohen believed that status frustration marginalized lower-class males from the status goals prominent within the middle-class school system. As a result of this strain, and through communication with others in similar situations, lower-class males began to reject these cultural goals and the legitimate ways of attaining them. Gradually they adopted a procedure Cohen referred to as reaction formation (doing the opposite of what is expected), which enabled them to attain status more effectively within their own group rather than within the larger confines of middle-class society. In this way, believed Cohen, subcultures of youth take shape. Experiencing some measure of intrinsic social success allows these new subcultural forms to be sustained; this in turn allows the tradition to be passed on to future generations (Cohen 1955).

Other functionalists, most notably Merton (1957) and Cloward and Ohlin (1960), added support to this formulation with their own contributions, which generally stressed the attainment of financial goals. Miller (1958), on the other hand, argued that working-class subcultures were merely extensions of working-class values. Matza and Sykes (1961) took another contradictory stance by arguing that the opposing values common to youth subcultures were actually shared with those of the wider culture.

An extremely pervasive influence common to youth at that time was glaringly absent in these class-based analyses of subcultural formation. The explosion of rock and roll music created a near universal acceptance by youth (and remarkable disdain by adults) that crossed existing class lines. Contained within this musical form was a sense of style gained from the adoption of a way of dressing (leather or denim motorcycle jackets, T-shirts, sweeping "duck's ass" haircuts, rolled-up blue jeans, and Wellington boots for young males; pedal pushers, flat-pointed loafers, beehive hairstyles, V-neck sweaters, cone-shaped brassieres, and heavy make-up for young females) that was quite separate from clothing styles of adults. Cues for these fashion statements were unmistakably taken from the youthful music and film stars of that time.

In essence, the message to youth of the middle to late 1950s was very clear: "You weren't cool if you didn't like rock and roll." However, appreciating the music and viewing the films invariably involved acquiring and freely displaying these easily recognizable symbols. These symbols were generally reformulated by adults as "rebellious" and "delinquent" indicators, but conceptualized by youth as pronouncements that they were simply being "cool." Social rules of inclusion and exclusion generally depended upon "the look" one adopted, and further, whether one could "walk that walk and talk that talk" in the manner displayed by the stars. Levels of immersion were decided as youth assessed themselves and each other. Perhaps most importantly, "hangin' out," "cruisin'," and/or attending live concerts of their favourite touring musical artists allowed these youth the opportunity to display their symbols of subcultural allegiance and the corresponding "attitude" which suggested that they were unique. While enjoying the music and camaraderie with like-minded peers, these subcultural groups of youth simultaneously invited negative labels from those they referred to as "L-7's" ("squares": those who stood in opposition to rock and roll culture).

The subcultural groups of middle-1950s youth formed not strictly on the basis of status frustration, and behaved differently not solely because of a process of reaction formation. Instead, the hope of gaining and maintaining acceptance within the separate cultural form of the "teenager" could only be accomplished by striving to attain a sense of style (coolness, perhaps). This "cool" factor must be considered as a strong inducement for youth to bind together collectively. Moreover, different behaviours were not solely the result of the outright rejection of middle-class and adult values, but more an attempt to emulate youth-held perceptions of the real or imagined illusions displayed by their musical and cinematographic icons.

Ten years after his ground-breaking yet class-based work on the formation of youth subcultures, Cohen expanded his theoretical approach to include a conception of style. However, in 1965, the world of popular music was not dominated by the "architects" of rock and roll music but rather by "super-groups" like the Beatles and the Beach Boys (White 1994), who projected a completely different sense of style. By taking into consideration the relationship between social structure and social interaction, Cohen conceded that the symbolic use of style is a contributing element of subcultural formation:

> An actor learns that the behaviour signifying membership in a particular role includes the kinds of clothes he [she] wears, his [her] posture, his [her] gait, his [her] likes and dislikes, what he [she] talks about and the opinion he [she] expresses. [1965:1]

Later, British scholars considered these American theoretical positions and acknowledged this addition of style in their attempts to understand youth subcultures in Britain. They augmented these American functionalist contentions with arguments primarily based on a Marxist philosophy (Hall and Jefferson 1976; Hebdige 1979; Brake 1980, 1985; Muncie 1981). With specific regard to the concept of style as a component of subcultural formation and maintenance, Hebdige reveals that

> style in subculture is ... pregnant with significance. Its transformations go "against nature," interrupting the process of "normalization." As such, they are gestures, movements towards a speech which offends the "silent majority," which challenges the principle of unity and cohesion, which contradicts the myth of consensus. [1979:18]

From this passage comes the clear indication that, to British scholars, possessing and/or pursuing a sense of style is of special and key importance in relation to subcultural formation and boundary maintenance. In addition, this excerpt further suggests that, in the youth culture of Britain, style fuels the fires of potential subcultural rebellion against the dominant class.

Brake (1980) also believes that style is of crucial importance to the formation, member maintenance, and identification of youth subcultures. Within any social context, a young person quickly learns to evaluate him(her)self and others based on their singular and collective dedication to perfecting their sense of style, since it will express a degree of commitment to the subculture, and it indicates member-ship of a specific subculture which by its very appearance disregards or attacks dominant values. [1980:12]

But what is style? Or in the vernacular of young people of the middle to late 1950s, what did it mean to be "cool" or "hip"? In an attempt at clarifi-cation, Brake delves deeper into this concept of style by including three main components in a more detailed definition:

(a) "Image," appearance composed of costume, accessories such as hair-style, jewellery and artifacts.

(b) "Demeanour" made up of expression, gait and posture. Roughly this is what actors wear and how they wear it.

(c) "Argot," a special vocabulary and how it is delivered. [Brake 1980:12]

When examined under the rubric of self-enhancement theory (Sirgy 1982), the concept of style is clarified as a critical component of subcultural forma-tion and maintenance. This theoretical perspective intimates that the entirety of human behaviour is focused on the construction, maintenance, and buttressing of a positive perception of self, idealistically resulting in high levels of personal self-esteem. This theory also contends that collective social behav-iour of all societal members reinforces positive self-perceptions for themselves and for other associated members. Commenting specifically on the inclusion of style in the formation and maintenance of youth subcultures and the resultant adoption of a new identity, Richards (1988) states:

The new identity revolves around subcultural rules and expectations which are within attainable reach of the members. Subcultural dress serves to add cred-ibility to the new identity while enhancing the unreal or escapist characteris-tics of the subcultural role. By looking like, as well as acting like, someone from outside the boundaries of the larger culture, the individual proclaims his [her] ineligibility for evaluation under the existing rule system—a system which, in some way, is perceived to be a threat to self-esteem. [1988:58]

Similarly, recent qualitative research in relation to a Canadian West Coast punk subculture conducted by Baron (1989) locates members' sense of style as crucial to the perception of authentic membership and self-identity, and allows for complete participation in group activities:

Style was not something to be embraced and discarded at certain times of the day, but represented an extension of the member ... The members were very conscious of style as a kind of self-representation, particularly an expression of attitudes and feelings regarding school, the family and politics. [1989:306–307]

Taken further, findings from Baron's research confirm that one's immersion in a particular sense of style is inextricably bound together with one's appreciation and acceptance of a specific type of musical expression. For punk subcultural members, the choice of musical expression is punk or "hardcore" (Fox 1987; Baron 1989:308), while for youthful subcultural members of the middle to late 1950s, it was, without question, rock and roll.

Young people becoming both attracted and attractive to the universal appeal of rock and roll music in the middle to late 1950s, and to the subcultural groups of youth that resulted, appears to be more reflective of the pursuit of acceptance through style than of strain and status frustration. According to Brake (1980), this contention should not be surprising to sociologists. The universal power of, and desire to attain, a sense of style is present in all social classes. More importantly, perhaps, pursuing a sense of style as a method by which one enhances positive self-perception, especially in the critical stage of adolescence, outreaches the class-specific theories that cite strain (caused by status frustration) as a major determinant of subcultural formation in youth:

Style, then, is used for a variety of meanings. It indicates which symbolic group one belongs to, it demarcates that group from the mainstream, and it makes an appeal to an identity outside that of a class-ascribed one. It is learned in social interaction with significant subcultural others, and its performance requires what theatre actors call "presence," the ability to wear costume, and to use voice to project an image with sincerity. Indeed, this form of performance skill may well be tested out by other subcultural members. [1980:14]

In partial sum, this research indicates that youth subcultures appear to be formed and maintained through some combination of both processes: (a) by some form of strain that alters the self of the individual into the self-perception that marginalization from mainstream society is occurring, and (b) by the persistent and voluntary pursuit of acceptance through the development of some sense of style. Both processes may be regarded as social inducements to subcultural formation, although the voluntary pursuit of acceptance through style seems to hold more universality. According to Frith (1984), youth subcultures in Western societies hold three common attributes: (a) they are leisure-based rather than family- or work-based; (b) organization is predicated around peer groups rather than family units, ethnic groups, and so on; and (c) the predominant focus is placed on members' style rather than on political or social doctrines.

Having a fairly concise idea from sociological literature about how and why young people become involved in subcultures is one aspect, but gaining an understanding of what type of social structure they are getting into is quite another. This leaves the final task of offering a set of working definitions in relation to the sociology of subcultures. Rubington and Weinberg (1987) characterize a subculture as "a social entity which holds beliefs, values and norms which are different from, yet supportive of, conventional traditions." By contrast, a deviant subculture, according to these authors, "usually refers to a social entity which holds beliefs, norms and values that violate conventional traditions" (Rubington and Weinberg 1987:203). Ultimate clarification of the social groupings sociologists generally refer to as subcultures may be attained when one considers the following noteworthy contribution from Vaz:

> It is an established way of life, i.e., a world of special techniques, judgements and attitudes, a way of dealing with problems, defining situations and categorizing people. It generates its own social milieux, garbed and distinguished by human overtones. It fosters its own customs and traditions, respects its own myths and legends and furnishes its own reward. It produces its own code of ethics and provides its own control mechanisms and sanctions for keeping members in line. [1976:123]

☀ Methodology

One research tradition within symbolic interactionism and qualitative methodology is the exploratory study. This developmental approach is based on a researcher's interaction with actors forming a social group, with a corresponding social life, located in and around particular natural settings. The natural order of the particular social situation under study gradually surfaces and becomes evident. Researchers are then free to decide which methodological strategies best accommodate the specific research setting and to adapt them accordingly. This approach to conducting sociological research is succinctly explained by Rock in this passage:

The abandonment of a priori reasoning brings in its wake an abandonment of the need to impose coherence and harmony on the opening stages of the quest for knowledge. Some disunity and illogicality can be countenanced before and during research because the greatest emphasis is on a flexible accommodation with the research experience itself. After all, the social life which research explains is not always understood as a clear and organized process at all ... System and interconnections may be discovered, but they lie in some strange realm behind or beneath phenomena and are not necessarily more true than contradiction and muddle. [1979:209]

Moreover, a guiding framework of "sensitizing concepts" is used as a general sense of reference instead of variables in a rigidly causal framework characteristic of positivistic inquiries. This approach is defined, differentiated, and explained by Blumer in this passage:

A sensitizing concept lacks such specification of attributes or benchmarks and consequently does not enable the user to move directly to the instance and its relevant content. Instead, it gives the user a general sense of reference and guidance in approaching empirical instances. Whereas definitive concepts provide prescriptions of what to see, sensitizing concepts merely suggest directions along which to look. [1970:58]

Once immersed in the natural settings of the actors under study, individual voices heard through informal interviews, group discussions, and relevant actions witnessed and recorded in field notes result in the acknowledgment and eventual acceptance of a series of cumulative realizations. The researcher gradually begins moving from abstract configurations, taken from a large body of previous knowledge, to more specific social scenarios guided by sensitizing concepts and supported by current developments in empirical knowledge.

The theoretical procedures of Glaser and Strauss (1967) take a similar position. For them, sociological research is often commenced with a "partial framework of 'local' concepts" (1967:45), which include some basic knowledge of features common to the setting under study. However, upon commencement of and throughout the particular inquiry, theory and methods become inextricably bound together. According to these authors,

These concepts give [the researcher] a beginning foothold on his research. Of course, he [she] does not know the relevancy of these concepts to his [her] problem—this problem must emerge ... The sociologist should also be sufficiently theoretically sensitive so that he [she] can conceptualize and formulate a theory as it emerges from the data. Once started, theoretical sensitivity is forever in continual development ... A discovered, grounded theory, then, will tend to combine mostly concepts and hypotheses that have emerged from the data with some existing ones that are clearly useful. [1967:45–46]

This present inquiry operates within and attempts to preserve the sociological tradition of *Verstehen*. In a general sense, *Verstehen* is the overall appreciation of the social worlds and prevailing concerns of others through interpretive understanding. According to Wax (1967), *Verstehen* is a mode of inquiry that leads the researcher to "the perception of action as meaningful" by grasping "the vast background of shared meanings" that assist and/or guide the organization of particular social worlds (1967:326). By undertaking the holistic experience of learning about the lives, attitudes, thoughts, and behaviour patterns of others through this tradition of *Verstehen*, fieldwork results in researchers acquiring a clearer sense of the varied meanings awarded to events and objects within a particular social setting. According to Wax:

> The student begins "outside" the interaction, confronting behaviours he [she] finds bewildering and inexplicable: the actors are oriented to a world of meanings the observer does not grasp ... the fieldworker finds initially that he [she] does not understand the meanings of the actions of this strange people, and gradually he [she] comes to be able to categorize peoples (or relationships) and events. [1967:325]

By way of this process of interpretive understanding, the undertaking of empirical research therefore becomes a deeply personal and potentially transformative experience. This occurs because the most versatile and prominent research instrument available to each researcher is the researcher's self. This sense of self is often affected by this holistic social immersion and eventually may be altered to some degree. But these effects can be quite beneficial to the development of the overall inquiry by providing researchers with new ideas, concepts, leads, hunches, and ways of seeing social life that were previously absent. According to Whyte (1955), methodological concepts and theoretical ideas "grow up in part out of our immersion in the data and out of the whole process of living ... Much of this process of analysis proceeds on the unconscious level" (1955:280).

In essence, the point of this methodological approach is to enable the researcher to understand the particular social setting from the perspective of the resident actors under study (Rock 1979:198). Actors come to know themselves, define situations, and understand others and their surroundings through "sympathetic introspection" and "imaginative reconstructions" of ongoing social situations (Filstead 1970:4). Within the setting under study, actors learn to agree on the meanings of certain symbols; and as these social symbols are manoeuvred in different situations, group members achieve a sense of social understanding (or conflict). One of the primary tasks of the sociological researcher, then, is to seek out these often hidden yet highly relevant symbols and attempt to arrive at their true meanings by observing how they are manipulated. The researcher must then attempt to interpret the social behaviour of the resident actors. An overall understanding of this approach to conducting social research is summarized by L.A. Visano:

> Social action is constructed through a process in which people interpret and assign meanings to situations. As a process being constructed and reconstructed, social action is a matter of discovery and not readily fixed in advance. Specifically, this perspective assumes that human societies are negotiated and emergent productions. It is this interactional pattern which must be understood if the nature of process and structure of phenomena are to be determined ... A study of real actors in actual settings recognizes that the activities of actors have a meaning independent of the research. That is, pre-defined categories and well-specified units of analysis are suspended in favour of learning the actors' words, language and expressions of central meanings. Only by getting close to these "hosts" and spending time on their "turf" can the investigator discover the organization of action. [1987:45–47]

In an attempt to gain accurate first-hand knowledge of the social existences of the subcultural members in this present inquiry, I adopted a qualitative methodology largely determined by the techniques of participant observation. My intention from the outset was to gain access to their social worlds, explore their social beings, accurately document their lived experiences and voices, and then subjectively interpret my findings. Participant observation seemed the only way to do this. My general goals seemed attainable because participant observation serves as

> a method in which the observer participates in the daily life of the people under study, either openly in the role of researcher or covertly in some disguised form, observing things, listening to what is said, and questioning people, over some length of time. [Becker and Geer 1970:133]

Between February 1992 and April 1993 I collected data in a working-class neighbourhood of a large Canadian city. This involved close contact with 26 male and female adolescents aged 13 to 18. "Extra" actors contributed to many informal group discussions and were often observed in social settings. I tailored my appearance to resemble a quasi-rock musician/biker (shoulder-length hair, black jeans, leather jacket, cowboy boots, sleeveless T-shirt, and so on) and projected a "tough but fair" attitude during social interaction with actors in the field.

The actors under study were initially suspicious but warmed to me after I demonstrated that "the big dude" (as they referred to me) was unmistakably on their side. They learned this gradually, as they saw me stepping forward to mediate disputes and confrontations with police, mall security, and other authority figures. I made it very clear that I wanted nothing from them but simply the chance to talk. I quickly gained the reputation as someone who always "covered my piece" (paid my own way) and occasionally "broke my wad" (paid for them). Gradually, these actors changed their perception of me from "the big dude" to a "standup dude." In sum, they came to regard me as an older brother rather than a traditional adult.

Preliminary observations informed me that many adolescents were attracted to specific "youth hangouts" at specific times and for specific reasons. These places—a convenience store and a pizza parlour—were attractive mainly because they contained a varied selection of high-quality and ever-changing video and computer games. They routinely patronized these establishments (before, during, and after school, on weekends, etc.) because they could play these games and watch others play them. During these games sessions, other socialization processes were routinely carried out (purchasing refreshments, setting up competitions, arguing, gossiping, intimidating, fighting, commencing relationships, etc.). To these actors, these commercial settings were clearly the social "place to be."

I set out to become friendly with the proprietors by repeatedly visiting each setting and purchasing products. While waiting for food items to be prepared, or processing video rentals, etc., I would start conversations with each proprietor, while keeping a close eye on the activity around the video games. Once the proprietors were familiar with me, and I with them, I presented myself as a university student and explained my research intentions in a cursory fashion. Later, I asked them for, and they granted me, permission to come by for the express purpose of conducting sociological research.

During this preliminary period of informal observations (Downes 1966:195), I also became a familiar face to many of the young actors who frequented these places. They understood me to be a "good friend of the owner" who posed no threat to their activities. I knew very little about computer video games, and I initiated conversations with many youths based on this ignorance. The vast majority were quite willing to and very patient at explaining the parameters of each game; they clearly enjoyed trumpeting their proficiency and demonstrating performance strategies. I was eager to learn, but in every competition with an adolescent foe, I was mercilessly defeated.

As I quickly learned, the accepted social norm for those who lose a match is to either pay the fee for a return match or give up their position on the game. Usually I would play (lose) two or three games, typically while a crowd watched, and then retire to become a member of the crowd. After this period of observation and participation, I would conduct informal, open-ended interviews with some of the onlookers (Becker and Geer 1970:133).

Gradually, after these young people and I grew more familiar with each other, I presented myself in the new role of a university student faced with the difficult task of having to prepare a "big essay about youth." On the basis of the acceptance they had already shown, I began asking them to help me out on this essay. In essence, I became comfortable with "creating and maintaining a series of viable roles and identities" (Manning 1972:244) as a means to getting closer to the actors. Within this new role of university student, I was able to converse and interact with these actors for great lengths of time, then retire to my own residence to "work on my essay" without creating suspicion or disturbing either research setting (Wax 1980:273).

At first, I approached familiar adolescents and asked them to complete a "youth survey" in my presence. Later, through a "snowball technique" (Inciardi 1979:73), I was introduced to other actors as a "cool guy" or "radical dude" who wanted to "hang for awhile" and "ask a bunch of questions." An interview guide was used as a prop with the express purpose of stimulating conversation on a variety of topic areas. Once engaged in conversation, each actor was allowed many opportunities, unrestricted by time, to express his or her feelings anonymously on any subject.

In most instances, these informal unfocused interviews (Harris 1973) were tape-recorded and transcribed; but in the few situations in which the tape recorder appeared to cause uneasiness (or rechargeable batteries failed), I made field notes, which I would key into my computer within 24 hours. Through these methods and over time, I was able to assemble a multitude of separate "portraits" that accurately documented the voices and lived experiences of these adolescent actors. Included in these portraits were corresponding field observations of social interactions within their respective subgroupings.

In a number of ways, I made sure the actors were "treated at all times as ends in themselves, never merely as means" (Cassel 1980:35). I guaranteed anonymity to all the actors, and never used surnames. Furthermore, I substituted pseudonyms for actual first names (Sutherland 1961:111; Heyl 1979:37), and for locations and events the actors mentioned (if I didn't simply eliminate the name).

All actors had to trust me not to "rat them out" to the police, school offi- cials, welfare agencies, and/or parental figures under any circumstances. We established this trust very early in data collection. During preliminary observa- tion in a pizza parlour, five adolescents were playing a video game when two foot patrol officers entered the premises. They quickly walked directly over to the adolescents and began aggressively questioning them about an incident of vandalism from the evening before. Coincidentally, I had been watching these same actors playing these games between the hours that witnesses were claiming they had committed the vandalism. However, the police officers did not accept their collective alibi and tried to arrest them. At that point, I stepped forward on their behalf, identifying myself as a Ph.D. student studying criminology and a published author on the topic of local policing. They immediately shifted their attention toward me, and I began substantiating the adolescents' alibi.

One officer assessed my credentials as the other summoned two squad cars for backup and/or transport. One of the arriving squad car officers recognized me as the person who had interviewed him in an earlier police study and vouched for my credentials. At that point, the five actors were informally exonerated and the police officers left the premises. Later, three of the adoles- cents came over to me at the counter and thanked me for being a "standup dude." We then slapped hands in a gesture of acceptance. Word spread swiftly through the neighbourhood that the "owner's friend" was an "awesome dude," and other adolescents, then unknown to me, began treating me with a level of respect usually awarded only to subcultural members.

✳ Subcultural Forms

In applying this concentrated yet flexible methodology, I quickly realized early in the data collection stage that, for these actors, subcultural affiliation is a major determinant of current social circumstances. These affiliations are initially based on styles of dress and preferences in music, but other factors such as drug and alcohol habits, preferred social activities, temperament, race, and ethnicity contribute as well. It soon became evident to me that each of my actors could be assigned to one of three major subcultural groups—Hommies, Housers, or Bangers. All three groups were strictly mutually exclusive. Within each of these main subgroups were further divisions.

Hommies

Strictly speaking, a Hommie is a black male who is a member of a gang (referred to in argot as a "posse" or "crew"), or who aspires to become a member of a gang. He is most often a nondrinker of alcohol but a frequent user and/or seller of crack, powdered cocaine, and heroin. Hommies are characterized by short-cropped hair and often have symbols, initials, or designs shaved onto their scalp. A common feature of gang membership is a particular type of baseball hat worn sideways or backwards. The actual placement of the hat on the head holds symbolic significance for it indicates to other Hommies the gang of affiliation and in some cases ranking within that gang. Hommies also wear baggy jeans; oversized leather, sports team, or combat jackets; leather starter shoes; and prominently displayed gold jewellery.

The music the Hommies listen to is critical to subcultural affiliation, and so is the style their chosen artists disseminate. (This is true of all of these subcultural groups.) Hommies listen to underground rap music ("gansta" rap) exclusively. This music is very pro-black, anti-white (and other races), anti-establishment, and (sometimes) pro-revolution. Hommies differentiate between their admired gangsta rap and the despised rap artists who gain commercial airplay by consciously including whites in their audience. Thus Hammer, Bobby Brown, and Tone Loc are abhorred, while Public Enemy, Sister Soldier, and Ice Cube are acceptable. Through an ever-present set of headphones connected to a portable tape or CD player, these young people are constantly in touch with their favourite musical artists.

Although it wasn't as true in the setting I observed (since it drew undue police attention), when "hangin'" on street corners, in neighbourhood parks, on school grounds, and in mall parking lots, the lowest-ranking gang member is responsible for providing music for the entire group by way of a powerful portable stereo unit. The Hommies in this setting enjoy their music while congregating at members' homes, at informal house parties, in "booze cans" (illegal nightclubs), or in the homes of female acquaintances.

Hommies are a relatively violent subculture and use tactics of intimidation on a regular basis. Fistfights and gang muggings are fairly common in the neighbourhood. Violence is carried out by heavily armed members who usually travel with concealed small-calibre guns, steel bars sewn into jackets, or (at least) brass knuckles worn in the form of separate rings. As a function of black pride, gang members become incensed when they feel that outsiders have "dissed" (i.e., slighted) them personally, or their gang, or blacks in general. When this happens, they do not hesitate to lash out verbally and physically. Hommies often commit theft, assault, extortion, and car theft; also, they often deal drugs.

In this setting, the most vicious and crime-prone Hommies adopt the name "B Boys." Hommies must be legitimate gang members in order to be included in, and seen as part of, the authentic subculture of B Boys. Taking their cues quite literally from their gangsta rap icons, these members see themselves as having elevated status among other Hommies. They make no effort to get along with other races, display aggressive tendencies at every turn, and generally conduct themselves with a proverbial "chip on their shoulder." Gang membership is signified to other Hommies by a combination of many prominently displayed gold necklaces and chains and red baseball hats worn sideways.

Female Hommies (who often refer to each other as "Home Girl") arrange themselves in subcultural groups depending upon their collective desire to become connected to an existing male gang. Those who display gang affiliations or romantic ties with authentic gang members are referred to as "Fly Girls." They emulate the toughness and aggressiveness of their corresponding male gang, listen to the same music, and attempt to mimic their fashion statements. They accentuate their femininity through make-up, hairstyles, and semirevealing upper wear; aside from that, they look remarkably similar to their male counterparts. Fly Girls often help B Boys carry out criminal activities.

White males who attempt to emulate the style, attitude, and behaviour of authentic Hommies are referred to, by themselves and others, as "Wiggers." By adorning themselves in nearly identical clothing and accoutrements, and by adopting speech patterns characteristic of gangsta rappers, Wiggers seek social acceptance from authentic Hommies. They also do this in more subtle ways.

For example, I covertly observed two Wiggers practising what they called their "n——r walk" in an alley behind the pizza parlour. Attaining proficiency with this slower, hand-slapping gait was almost an obsession for these young people. However, their main reason for this mimicry was not necessarily to be accepted into a Hommie gang, or accepted as a "solid" associate; rather, it was to establish a romantic relationship with a black female. Also to this end, Wiggers openly supported black rights, spoke out against racism, quoted Malcolm X and Martin Luther King, Jr., and displayed distaste for the company of white females. In fact, I often heard Wiggers denigrate white females as "ho's" (whores) or simply "bitches."

In this setting, white females who attempt to establish a romantic relationship with authentic Hommies are referred to, by themselves and others, as "Wiggerettes." They dress in ways they believe flatter black culture; for instance, they braid their hair in dreadlocks, wear the Rastafarian colours of red, gold, and green, and listen only to black music (both gangsta and rap). In public, a Wiggerette will openly demonstrate subservience to any black male by attempting to pander to his wishes. Quite loudly and publicly, Wiggerettes speak highly of black males as suitors ("Once ya had black ya never go back") while simultaneously denigrating white adolescent males of any subculture.

Wiggerettes and Fly Girls absolutely do not get along with each other; surprisingly, neither do Wiggers and Wiggerettes.

The term Hommie is bantered around in North American popular culture quite freely. Often, the term denotes friendship or neighbourhood familiarity. In this now-diluted context, Hommie is short for Homeboy or Homegirl. Hollywood popularized this term in the 1991 feature film *Boyz N the Hood*. Through this film and through later references on television (Arsenio Hall, Montel Williams, etc.), the term Hommie has taken root across many ethnic subgroups.

In this setting, however, the term holds special significance and is not used in the diluted manner common in popular culture. Should an authentic Hommie hear any outsider refer to another outsider as his Hommie (or her Home Girl), a violent confrontation is certain to ensue with multiple members of each subculture. I observed several incidents of this nature. Hommies believed their subculture had been "dissed" by members of a rival subculture. In effect, "taking their name in vain" is considered highly inappropriate and a serious social invasion of the authentic Hommie subculture.

It should not be difficult to imagine that I encountered a great deal of difficulty in securing interview data from any members of the Hommie subculture. As a long-haired, leather-jacketed, white, adult researcher, I was treated with extreme suspicion and kept at arm's length. (Most thought I was an undercover police officer.) Despite repeated attempts, I was unable to engage these young people in conversations of any length or substance. My persistence in a local mall resulted in me being called a "honky" by an irate Fly Girl, who then challenged me to a fistfight. Very quickly, I was surrounded by three threatening B Boys who came to her perceived defence. Only the immediate intervention of mall security guards prevented the situation from escalating further.

I did speak to some Wiggers and Wiggerettes; however, these encounters were sporadic and very brief. These actors trusted me about as much as the Hommies did. In this brief interview, 16-year-old Aretha suggested why she supports the Hommie subculture:

G.O.: You look great Aretha! What's all this about? You tryin' to make a fashion statement?

Aretha: Yeah, once you had black, you never go back.

G.O.: What d'ya mean?

Aretha: Once you had black, you never go back. [pause] Jus' wha' it says! [long pause as she glares menacingly at me] Ya don't get it, do ya? Open your eyes, man! Madonna's a Wiggerette. [long pause] After she fucked a few black guys she tol' Sean Penn to go fuck himself. You know she got it goin' on [laughs defiantly]

G.O.: Really? I didn't know—

Aretha: It's all about where you wanna be, an' I wanna be with a black guy, 'cause black guys know how to treat ya right. They like the best music, they like to dress up, they got attitude goin' on, they got money, they like to dance. Know wha' I'm sayin'?

G.O.: Yeah, I think so, but—

Aretha: Good, 'cause you sure ain't one of 'em. I'm outa here. [she leaves quickly]

Housers

The term "houser" originated in North American dance clubs in the late 1980s and early 1990s. These venues would employ a resident disc jockey to provide continuous dance music to patrons. By using state-of-the-art electronic technology to mix and remix musical selections while simultaneously inserting snippets of others artists' work into the overall sound (referred to in argot as sampling), these disc jockeys gradually attained celebrity status in their own right. The resulting musical form became known as "house music" since it was uninterrupted, produced an infectious rhythmic beat for dancing, and was fairly unique to the club in which the DJ was mixing the overall sound. The patrons of these clubs soon became known as Housers since they were attracted to these places because of their unique music. Perhaps more importantly, the accompanying styles and fashion statements generated by the music and the celebrity disc jockeys largely accounted for the patron's self-perception of social uniqueness.

In this neighbourhood setting, those young people who had become enamoured with this form of cultural expression proudly adopted the name "Housers" for their subcultural group. This racially mixed subculture is also characterized by a type of gang mentality, but Housers demonstrate more subtle behaviour patterns. Instead of presenting an angry and aggressive demeanour characteristic of Hommies, Housers present themselves as happy and carefree individuals who are securely grounded by their close ties to the group. Relations among each other are characterized by joking, gossiping, play fighting, humming, demonstrating dance moves, and discussing the latest fashions to be worn in their favourite clubs.

A sense of style determined by fashion is extremely important to this subculture. In day-to-day living, male subcultural members wear oversized sports club jackets (Chicago Bulls, San Jose Sharks, L.A. Raiders), baseball hats worn squarely on the top of the head, baggy black or blue jeans, baggy overalls with the "bib" unattached, one or two strategically torn T-shirts, and black leather tennis shoes. Hairstyles usually combine shaved sides with longer locks cascading to the collar. Personal uniqueness within this milieu is determined by one or two hair braids, the use of gel to attain the "spiked" look, and/or a short ponytail.

Female subcultural members generally mimic the fashion statements of their male counterparts in day-to-day interaction, although they accentuate their femininity more often than female Hommies. Female actors in this setting were observed to wear make-up and brightly coloured nail polish tastefully, and to construct fairly elaborate hairstyles largely absent of the shaved sides common to males. The skilful use of gel, dyes, henna, and hairspray frequently indicated to the untrained observer that these actors were "punk chics" (their term), yet this unflattering label was hotly contested by every female Houser encountered in the field. Since a sense of style is of crucial importance to these actors, appearance transgressions for both males and females are dealt with by subcultural members first in a joking verbal manner, but later in a physical and often quasi-violent manner.

Weekends and special occasions are marked by a fashion and attitude transformation for these actors. Day-to-day wear is largely supplanted by elaborate displays of a variety of leather clothing, long jackets, T-shirts, and pleated trousers for males, and skirts, tops, and dresses for females. Hairstyles remain similar although they are awarded increased attention to detail. In the self-perception of being "dressed to kill" and "OTI" (out to impress), these actors congregate en masse at dance clubs, private house parties, and after-hours clubs within the general neighbourhood.

Housers listen to a more commercial variety of rap music, often referred to as dance, hip hop, or "house" music (currently known as "techno"). However, instead of merely listening and dancing, these actors are nearly consumed by the music, the artists, the disc jockeys, and the collective sense of style generated by this combination. Favourite artists include House of Pain, Brand Nubian, Tribe Called Quest, and others on what appears to be a quickly revolving basis. Without question, social interaction for both male and female actors is premised on dancing en masse at dance clubs. Within this public context, images of self are presented, impressions are made, evaluations are undertaken, and self-identity is created, reformulated, and maintained.

Since the physical demands of continuous dancing require boundless energy, Housers have adapted their drug and alcohol habits to accommodate their passion. They prefer to drink wine coolers and liquor instead of beer and wine since the latter are "too heavy" and "take too long to get a buzz." Perhaps more importantly, these actors prefer to ingest powdered cocaine and ecstasy instead of smoking cannabis and ingesting hallucinogens since the latter "slow you down" and "put you too far out there." As was frequently related to me, these actors seek the "perfect" combination of "liquid and powder" to stimulate and prolong their ability to dance.

Especially when they are "dressed to kill," but even on a day-to-day basis, these actors believe that their sense of style draws an inordinate amount of attention. Attention from residual youth (nerds, dweebs, losers, etc.) is considered positive and is welcomed, since Housers tend to believe that these lower-status youth are envious of their status accomplishments. However, negative attention from Hommies, Bangers, the police, area merchants, and school officials is not welcomed since these actors know from experience that some level of tension will inevitably result. In an effort to deflect this negative attention, Housers generally congregate and travel in groups of five or six for "personal safety."

Outwardly, these actors show no fear of other youth and will engage in acts of violence, but only when provoked and only as a group. While in the field, I did not witness any of these actors initiating violent confrontations; but by the same token, I did not witness any indication that invitations were declined. Disagreements were usually started over minor aspects of adolescent social life (barbed remarks regarding clothing, hairstyles, ethnicity, etc.) and temporarily settled as collective action escalated to threats, slaps, fisticuffs, and (occasionally) full-fledged gang fights. As a form of protection, Housers usually carry knives and namchatka sticks instead of guns.

Crime involvement appears to be restricted to drug dealing, shoplifting, break and enter, car theft, and clothing store heists. During field work, I discovered that many of these actors regularly interacted with an adult fence who operated a buy-and-sell "store" in the neighbourhood. Proceeds from the criminal endeavours of these actors (CDs, VCRs, cordless telephones, microwave ovens, cameras, car stereos, etc.) were habitually exchanged for cash. Two of the more criminally ambitious Housers were supplying a local automobile wrecking yard with stolen vehicles ($500 each regardless of year, make, and model). Regardless of the origin, this free-flowing source of money would then be used to facilitate these actors' passion for acquiring the music of their favourite artists and, perhaps more importantly, attending dance clubs well dressed.

When queried about their initial attraction to, their passion for, and their personal goals within this subculture of Housers, Brian, Vivica, and Judy revealed the following thoughts:

G.O.: I know you Housers are a tight bunch, but how'd you get like this?

Judy: For me, like, I don't know. We like what we're into, I guess. We all love to dance, you know, dress up an' get down on the floor, get wasted, party—

Brian: When I transferred here I liked the way these dudes looked. They got attitude, and the music is righteous, you know? An' they liked me 'cause I don't put up with anyone's bullshit.

Vivica: Yeah, you're awesome, Bri! [all laugh] I think it's the tunes, at least that's what it was for me, an' struttin'.

G.O.: What do you mean, struttin'?

Vivica: We're in your face! We always look good, not like those fuckin' Hommie bitches. An' we have fun. That's all we wanna do is have fun.

G.O.: Does this make sense to all of you?

Judy and Brian: Yeah, for sure. That's it, Annie.

While members share general characteristics that guide behaviour, ethnicity and race create minor subdivisions within this subculture of Housers. Ethnicity and race had the effect of binding similarly situated youth into what I came to refer to as friendship pockets: small groups of Housers who would interact together more frequently than with the rest of the members. Although no major conflicts were witnessed among these subgroups based on their respective compositions, episodes of gentle chiding and gossip were recorded from field observations. Perhaps the best example of these chidings resides in the nicknames these actors give to and accept from each subgroup. White Housers were often referred to as "Skaters"; those of Latin descent were called "Spics"; Asians were called "Slants"; while those of European descent were usually referred to as "Ginos" and "Ginas," reflecting an Italian or Portuguese heritage in particular. By virtue of their close subcultural affiliation, the negative connotations of these nicknames common in the wider society were supplanted by a positive self-perception of inclusion.

Bangers

In direct contrast to the angry and aggressive demeanour of the Hommies and the fun-loving disposition of the Housers is the sullen and relatively quiet subculture of the Bangers. This group is exclusively comprised of white males and females who refuse to even acknowledge the presence of other subcultural groups in this neighbourhood. For these actors, personal appearance is not nearly as important as it is to Hommies and Housers, provided that all members obtain and display the basic and unchanging rudiments of fashion expression. Male Bangers display very long, unruly, and unkempt hair that is not cut in any particular style. Tight-fitting blue or black jeans are complimented with heavy leather or motorcycle timing-chain belts and heavy boots (either army, or cowboy, or construction). Plaid overshirts or black leather vests are worn under black leather motorcycle jackets or Levis denim jackets. To complete their image, male Bangers exclusively wear tight T-shirts emblazoned with their favourite musicians, cars, or motorcycles (Chevy, Ford, Harley Davidson, Triumph, Norton, or BSA). Body tattoos (skull and crossbones, devil's head, guitars, woman's head and naked torso, etc.) were observed on some members. On a few occasions these actors were observed to wear dirty baseball hats tightly on their heads and in the proper position, but this was not a regular occurrence.

Female Bangers can best be described as young women who actively attempt to closely emulate the stylings of women who appear in current rock videos, either as sexual foils for male performers or as female artists (Lita Ford, Joan Jett, Courtney Love, Sass Jordan, Alannah Myles, etc.). For instance, they pay much attention to their hairstyles, which are invariably long, sometimes teased, often dyed (usually platinum blonde), hair-sprayed and gelled, then frequently arranged and rearranged during social interaction (referred to as "hair flipping" in argot). Heavy facial make-up is complemented by black or deep purple nail polish and an array of bracelets and neck chains. A leather or denim jacket covers a tight T-shirt worn with a micro-mini or extremely tight Levis of any primary colour. A few actors proudly display body tattoos (a butterfly, a small heart, and a pair of puckered ruby lips) above breasts and in the neck area. An ever-present pair of high heels ("spikes" in argot) completes their presentation of self.

Although members appear very similar in style, Bangers are clearly divided into two distinctly different subgroups solely based on musical preference. "Strict Bangers" (usually referred to by themselves and others as simply Bangers) prefer the more current sounds of alternative grunge or thrash rock music (Soundgarden, Nirvana, Pearl Jam, Kurt Cobain, etc.), while "Rockers" prefer heavy metal (Slik Toxic, Metallica, Svengali) and music from the 1970s (Led Zeppelin, Bad Company, Black Sabbath, Deep Purple, Steppenwolf). While each subgroup varies in its specific musical tastes, both are extremely respectful of the other's musical preference and are quick to mention their camaraderie. Both Bangers and Rockers wholeheartedly agree on one aspect of musical expression: they dislike any form of rap music (with a passion) as well as the resultant cultural stylings associated with the artists and their admirers.

The commonalities among these various forms of rock music suggest a "hell bent" attitude characterized by loud amplifiers, dazzling light shows, screaming vocals, piercing guitar solos, and a pulsating beat. Unlike Housers, and to a certain extent Hommies, dancing to the music in any traditional way is of no concern to Bangers. Instead, these actors were observed to "rock" (argot for moving the head and body rhythmically to a song) while standing alone in one spot. By moving their heads to and fro very aggressively, groups of these actors may appear to be actually striking their heads on immovable objects (tables, posts, or even each other), hence the evolution of the name "Banger," which is a shortened form of "Headbanger."

Bangers generally do not carry weapons of any type and are not as involved in criminal activity as Hommies and Housers. To them, acting violently for any reason other than self-preservation is a complete waste of time. Instead, these actors prefer to frequently "kick back" by drinking beer and wine, smoking large amounts of cannabis, and (occasionally) ingesting LSD ("sids" in argot) on weekends. Social activities involve attending rock concerts, collecting the musical offerings of their favourite artists, and just "hangin' out" with other Bangers. For those actors who admitted to being involved in some criminal activity, the focus is placed on minor property crimes and drug dealing (mostly marijuana and hashish).

Although they are an extremely close subculture, Bangers do not travel in packs and generally avoid all contact with other adolescent subcultures. However, when provoked, they are considered by other young people to be the most dangerous "warriors" in the neighbourhood. Since Bangers repeatedly advised me that they avoid violence, this evaluation appears to be the result of their presentation of self as relatively silent, brooding, and mean actors, with the potential for physical explosiveness constantly present. In essence, a Banger will "intentionally and consciously express him[her]self in a particular way, but chiefly because the tradition of his [her] group or social status requires this expression" (Goffman 1959:6). The general perception that all Bangers are unpredictable warriors allows these actors to travel without the protective benefit of multiple members or weapons, and to move throughout the neighbourhood relatively unencumbered.

To illustrate with an incident I observed in a neighbourhood park late on a weekend evening: Five male Hommies were discussing the events of the previous evening as I observed them from a picnic table within earshot. Since I could hear them sniffing between bouts of loud conversation, it was clear to me that they were under the influence of powdered cocaine and were "coke ranting" (O'Bireck 1993:17). A male Banger and his female friend came sauntering through the park arm in arm. As the couple approached, one of the Hommies uttered an insulting comment about the young woman's body within earshot of both myself and the couple. As the couple stopped walking, the male Banger turned to face the five Hommies approximately three feet away from them.

Male Banger: What you say?

Hommie: Nothin'.

Male Banger: Apologize.

Hommie: [all others fell silent as the atmosphere grew tense] We didn't say nothin'.

Male Banger: [in a firm tone] Apologize to my lady.

Hommie: Sorry.

The male Banger issued a firm stare at the perceived offender, then locked arms with his female companion. They turned away from the group and proceeded on their way. When the Bangers were out of earshot, the five Hommies resumed their conversation for a brief period without commenting on the incident, then left the area.

A group discussion involving Michael, Danny, Nina, and Olivia reveals a close detailing of the process and perception of group mutual exclusivity held by most actors in this setting. Social qualities such as creative innovation, social equality, and intergroup integration, which are often advertised as good qualities in our wider society, do not seem to hold much importance for these actors. Instead, striving to live up to the expectations of the group is more important.

Michael: You asked me before an' I told ya, I'm a Banger. I'll always be a Banger. I do what Bangers do.

G.O.: What's that?

Michael: I fuckin' told ya that too!

Danny: We like heavy metal, smokin' drugs, drinkin' beer. Don't like none o' that nigger shit. Don't like rap, or dancin'. We don't like those people.

G.O.: How do you know you don't like stuff like that?

Michael: We *know*. 'Cause Bangers don't do shit like that. We do our *own* stuff. Like if I went on [a local weekly TV dance program dominated by rap music] my friends would think I was fried, big time. It would never happen 'cause I wouldn't have any friends after that bullshit move.

Nina: You can't do everything. It's one thing or another. You kinda like decide what you're into.

G.O.: What do you mean, "what you're into"?

Olivia: Like it usually happens in grade 7, or like around there, ... I don't know when, ... when you're young ... but you listen to all kinds of music and kinda decide what you like best, I guess. Like what your friends are into, like rap, hip hop, rock, metal, whatever, ... an' like follow the bands an' shit ...

Michael: You make a choice and stick with it, dude. You start hangin' with those people, and that's it. You don't fuck around. Once a Banger, always a Banger.

Danny: Bangers just like partyin' with Bangers. We don't like no one else. And fuck, man, they don't like us.

This clearly attests to a high degree of group cohesion within this subculture of Bangers. Group members respond to their acceptance and inclusion by remaining committed to the particular characteristics of the group. Furthermore, and very similar to the Hommies and Housers, peer group members are held in high regard and considered to be extremely important to each member's individual social existences. To conclude this section, a demonstration of this overall feeling is aggressively detailed by 17-year-old Brandon's fiercely direct (although somewhat dramatic) description of his own perception of subcultural life:

G.O.: Looks to me like you and your buds are really tight. Has it always been like that?

Brandon: Yeah, we're Bangers! My friends are my family, always have been, Gary. They're cool an' I don't deal with nobody else, 'cept you. My friends watch out for me, protect me an' I look out for them. These are special people, my friend! Why are you lookin' at me like I'm crazy or something?

G.O.: I didn't think I was, sorry. I guess I'm just knocked out by how quickly you got those words out. You're really committed to these people, huh?

Brandon: Yeah, these are class people I'm talkin' about. These people would lay down their lives for me an' I'd lay down my life for them, anytime. An' they know that.

G.O.: Wait a minute, man. It sounds like the Mafia or something! Is this as serious as you make it sound?

Brandon: This is a very important thing, Gary, friends, ... it's something you don't joke about around here. It's serious shit. Think about it. Friends are all we got. You can't trust your enemies.

✹ Discussion and Conclusions

The vast majority of actors in this neighbourhood frequently mentioned that their leisure time was predominantly consumed with "hangin'." Roughly defined as very loose, highly unstructured social interaction located in malls, pizza parlours, video arcades, apartment complexes, street corners, parks, and playgrounds, this activity was considered by these actors to be a prominent feature of their social existence. Although hangin' is a relatively inexpensive way of maintaining social contact, it yields very few material rewards. What it does provide is the consistent opportunity for subcultural members to remain unified and to reaffirm their self-identity by displaying their respective symbols of style (haircuts, clothes, music, etc.) and their resultant attitudes.

Most consider hangin' to be an activity they frequently enjoy, but also feel compelled to do, since they simply cannot afford to enjoy other forms of adolescent entertainment privy to more affluent youth. This feeling of perpetual denial often results in actors harbouring a sense of envy, anger, and resentment toward more privileged adolescents they may encounter in other public places. Combining these semihostile feelings with an overall atmosphere of chronic boredom common to these actors, a potential for volatility lurks as an undercurrent in their collective social being. It was within this atmosphere that most interviews and group discussions were conducted.

Moreover, the vast majority of these actors report that the bulk of their social activity is rarely monitored by their parents, stepparents, and/or guardians. Most report that they are not required to be home at certain times, do not have to specifically account for their whereabouts when away from home, and do not require parental approval for their peer associations. On many occasions, actors were observed congregating in the streets late at night, long after both settings had finished business for the day. Actual reasons for this perceived parental inattention are currently unknown to me. However, these actors generally report that their largely unsupervised and unmonitored social lives are the direct or indirect result of parental figures who "are too busy working," "couldn't give a shit," and/or "are out drinkin'."

My collective impressions of these various strains yield a fervent belief that most of these actors remain in a precarious emotional position. In essence, they are restricted by any combination of three realistic choices: either accept the self-perception of second-class status and compensate by displaying a sense of style consistent with one's chosen subgroup affiliation, and/or eradicate the images of affluence from immediate sight (by using barbed remarks, threats, violence, avoidance strategies, etc.), and/or commit acts of deviance/crime in a concerted effort to attempt to even the score in their own minds. All three strategies seem to provide only a partial solution by relieving the immediate strains caused by this sense of perpetual envy and resentment. However, regardless of what repair work is accomplished, the deeply felt pain of "not being good enough" often remains. Therefore, as I observed and experienced many times during field work, while actors in all of these subcultural groups are hangin', inside they may also be seething.

While the effects of these strains were evident within the lived experiences of the young actors in this neighbourhood, the pursuit of a sense of personal uniqueness through style was clearly more prominent. Attaining the label and self-perception of "cool" or "awesome" bolstered the self-identity of these actors and reduced the strains that may have contributed toward their sense of seething. In this setting at least, findings reveal that this attainment could only be accomplished through an affiliation with an existing subcultural group. Since Hommies, Housers, and Bangers are all mutually exclusive subcultures, rules of inclusion demanded that one's sense of style be in place or willing to be developed, complete with relevant symbols and corresponding habits and attitudes.

In order to develop their sense of style initially, actors in this setting gradually immersed themselves in the preferred popular cultural traditions characteristic of their particular subculture. Once recognized as committed to their exclusive method of conducting social life, existing subcultural members would then provide neophytes with camaraderie, emotional and physical support, and a clear frame of reference in relation to likes and dislikes, attitudes, and ways of behaving in the neighbourhood. By conforming to the cultural traditions of their particular subculture, these young actors gained a sense of belonging, constant reaffirmation of their self-identity, and confirmation, in the minds of both themselves and their subcultural members, that they had made the grade. In effect, they were cool.

The overwhelming social power of the "architects" of rock and roll music (circa 1955) is of little relevance to young people in 1995, although what they accomplished should not be discounted or forgotten. Through their exemplary work, not only did these "quasars" provide great music, but these musical artists helped provide young people with an opportunity to forge their own identity and gain acceptance, largely independent of the world of adults. The torch has been passed many times over in the ensuing years since 1955, so that currently young people have a plethora of social choices rooted in music, film, and fashion. Some choices will involve subcultural groups, while others will not, but one contention remains fairly certain: being perceived as "cool" matters to young people.

Note

1. I am deeply indebted to all of the young actors who allowed me to enter their world to conduct this inquiry. Without their approval and sharing, this study would be incomplete.

References

Baron, S.W. 1989. "The Canadian West Coast Punk Subculture: A Field Study." *Canadian Journal of Sociology* 14(3):289–316.

Becker, H.S. 1963. *Outsiders: Studies in the Sociology of Deviance*. New York: Free Press.

———. 1970. *Sociological Work: Method and Substance*. Chicago: Aldine.

Becker, H.S., and B. Geer. 1970. "Participant Observation and Interviewing: A Rejoinder." In *Qualitative Methodology*, W. Filstead (ed.). Chicago: Rand McNally.

———. 1969. *Symbolic Interactionism*. Englewood Cliffs, NJ: Prentice-Hall.

Blumer, H. 1970. "What Is Wrong with Social Theory?" In *Qualitative Methodology*, W. Filstead (ed.). Chicago: Rand McNally.

Brake, M. 1980. *The Sociology of Youth Culture and Youth Subcultures*. London, U.K.: Routledge and Kegan Paul.

———. 1985. *Comparative Youth Culture*. London U.K.: Routledge and Kegan Paul.

Cassel, J. 1980. "Ethical Principles for Conducting Fieldwork." *American Anthropologist* 82:28–41.

Cloward, R., and L.E. Ohlin. 1960. *Delinquency and Opportunity*. Glencoe, IL: Free Press.

Cohen, A. 1955. *Delinquent Boys*. Glencoe, IL: Free Press.

———. 1965. "The Sociology of the Deviant Act: Anomie Theory and Beyond." *American Sociological Review* 30:1–14.

Denzin, N. 1970. "Rules of Conduct and the Study of Deviant Behaviour: Some Notes on the Social Relationships." In *Deviance and Respectability*, J. Douglas (ed.). New York: Basic.

———. 1978. "Sociological Methods: Critical Reflections." In N. Denzin (ed.), *Sociological Methods: A Sourcebook*. New York: McGraw-Hill.

Downes, D. 1966. *The Delinquent Solution*. New York: Free Press.

Emerson, R.M. 1988. *Contemporary Field Research*. Prospect Heights, NJ: Wavelength.

Filstead, W. 1970. "Introduction." In *Qualitative Methodology*, W. Filstead (ed.). Chicago: Rand McNally.

Fox, K.J. 1987. "Real Punks and Pretenders: The Social Organization of a Counterculture." *Journal of Contemporary Ethnography* 16 (3).

Frith, S. 1984. *The Sociology of Youth*. Ormskirk, U.K.: Causeway.

Glaser, B., and A. Strauss. 1967. *The Discovery of Grounded Theory*. Chicago: Aldine.

Goffman, E. 1959. *The Presentation of Self in Everyday Life*. New York: Anchor.

Gordon, M. 1947. "The Concept of the Subculture and Its Application." *Social Forces*, October.

Hall, S., and T. Jefferson. 1976. *Resistance through Ritual: Youth 1976 Subcultures in Post-War Britain*. London, U.K.: Hutchinson.

Harris, M. 1973. *The Dilly Boys*. London, U.K.: Groom Helm.

Hebdige, D. 1979. *Subculture: The Meaning of Style*. London, U.K.: Methuen.

Heyl, B. *The Madam as Entrepreneur*. New Brunswick, NJ: Transaction.

Inciardi, J. 1975. *Careers in Crime*. Chicago: Rand McNally.

Lee, A.M. 1945. "Levels of Culture as Levels of Generalization." *American Sociological Review*, August.

Lewis, M., and M. Silver. 1982. *Great Balls of Fire: The Uncensored Story of Jerry Lee Lewis*. New York: Quill.

Lofland, J., and L.H. Lofland. 1984. *Analyzing Social Settings*. Belmont, CA: Wadsworth.

Lowe, M. 1989. *Conspiracy of Brothers*. Toronto: Macmillan.

Mann, F. 1970. "Human Relations Skill in Social Research." In *Qualitative Methodology*, W. Filstead (ed.). Chicago: Rand McNally.

Manning, P. 1972. "Observing the Police: Deviance, Respectables and the Law." In *Research on Deviance*, T. Douglas (ed.). New York: Random House.

Matza, D., and G.M. Sykes. 1961. "Juvenile Delinquency and Subterranean Values." *American Sociological Review* 26:712–719.

Mead, G.H. 1934. *Mind, Self and Society*. Chicago: University of Chicago Press.

Merton, R. 1957. *Social Theory and Social Structure*. Glencoe, IL: Free Press.

Miller, W.B. 1958. "Lower Class Culture as a Generating Milieu of Gang Delinquency." *Journal of Social Issues* 14:5–19.

Muncie, J. 1981. *Politics, Ideology and Popular Culture*. Milton Keynes, U.K.: Open University Press.

O'Bireck, G.M. 1993. *Gettin' Tall: Cocaine Use in a Subculture of Canadian Professional Musicians*. Toronto: Canadian Scholars' Press.

Richards, L. 1988. "The Appearance of Youthful Subculture: A Theoretical Perspective on Deviance." *Clothing and Textiles Research Journal* 6:56–64.

Rock, P. 1979. *The Making of Symbolic Interactionism*. London, U.K.: Macmillan.

Rubington, E., and M.S. Weinberg. 1987. *Deviance: The Interactionist Perspective*. 5th edition. New York: Macmillan.

Sirgy, M. 1982. "Self Concept in Consumer Behaviour: A Critical Review." *Journal of Consumer Research* 9:287–300.

Sutherland, E.H. 1961. *White Collar*. New York: Holt, Rinehart and Winston.

Tosches, N. 1979. *Country: The Biggest Music in America*. New York: Delta.

Vaz, E.W. 1976. *Aspects of Deviance*. Toronto: Prentice-Hall.

Visano, L. 1987. *This Idle Trade*. Concord: VitaSana.

Wax, M. 1967. "On Misunderstanding Verstehen: A Reply to Abel." *Sociology and Social Research* 51:323–333.

———. 1980. "Paradoxes of 'Consent' to the Practice of Fieldwork." *Social Problems* 27:272–283.

White, C. 1984. *The Life and Times of Little Richard*. New York: Simon and Schuster.

White, T. 1994. *The Nearest Faraway Place: Brian Wilson, the Beach Boys, and the Southern California Experience*. New York: Holt.

Whyte, W.F. 1955. *Street Corner Society*. Chicago: University of Chicago Press.

Epilogue

J. Gottfried Paasche
York University

The articles in this collection raise a great many more questions than they answer. And that is as it should be. The first three articles especially, but all of them in some way, point to the means by which answers may be found. But more importantly, they help us frame the questions. Paradoxically, it is the questions that are the most difficult to frame. Is there anything going on out there about which we need to inform ourselves? Why? And to what purpose? Can anything be done anyway?

Perhaps more important is simply the emotions involved. All of the articles assume that we care, that we are concerned, and that we can be drawn into the discussion. If you have experienced frustration, irritation, and even anger as you have read through the articles, for whatever reason, that is something you should value. We begin to delve into issues and topics when we notice them. And negative responses can be as stimulating as positive ones. Total agreement with a line of argument often results in complacency. We let down our critical guard. Unfortunately, readers often feel that if they find a line of reasoning difficult to understand or to accept, they are free to reject what they read and to move on. What I would suggest is that the emotions that were aroused in you when you read the articles are just the beginning of thought and reflection. The trick is not to suppress or deny the emotion, but to harness it for learning. Let me give you an example.

One of my own responses to the articles in this collection on the surface may seem quite irrelevant to the subject at hand. I began to think about the place of children and young people in our families and communities and the larger society. More specifically, I began to wonder whether having children is really necessary. Questions surfaced, such as, "Is anybody better off for having children?" "Do we need them?" To tell you the truth, one of my first responses to any difficulty—and these articles have often spoken about youth as difficult—

is to get rid of those seemingly responsible for the difficulty rather than to try to work out what usually seems, at least initially, a difficult problem. This tendency in my personality has sometimes led me not to notice the often simple solutions that are in fact at hand.

Notice that this initial response to the issue of difficult youth "blames the victim." If young people are difficult, something must be wrong with them. If they are difficult then let's get rid of them. The articles have in fact tried to demonstrate that young people's difficulties are part and parcel of larger societal conditions. They have argued that we cannot attempt to understand young people in isolation from the world in which they are growing up. I share this tendency to blame the victim with a great many others, maybe even with some of you. For me not to notice this would be for me to be a victim myself of a particularly human response.

But let me work a little with my initial response to the issues presented in this collection. In what sense are children and young people necessary in the world we know best, that is, our own? What difference does this necessity make for the place young people have in our lives? I want to work briefly on these questions by thinking about two issues: the economic contribution of children and youth, and the matter of choice in the issue of child bearing. These two issues seem to me to be interrelated.

It is hard for us to remember that children and youth were for most of our historical past required for the survival of individuals, families, clans, tribes, and nations. As soon as a child had the necessary mental and physical capacities, he or she was drawn into the everyday activities of the world. The economic and household activities were such that the contributions of even young children were valuable. Children were necessary in a way that is completely foreign to most of us today. We forget how radically the world has changed in the last few centuries. In fact, we respond today with moral revulsion when we hear that some children in this present world have to work. And yet that was the norm for most of prehistory and history.

Thus, references to children as an economic burden, as an *expense*, would in earlier times have been understood quite differently or not at all. Today it is common to be told, "We are going to have children when we can afford them." And at the community and societal levels we calculate what children cost us. This speaks volumes about the place of children today. Such considerations and positions would have been incomprehensible in the past. Children were necessary for their labour in the household economy.

If children today are a heavy cost, they also stimulate demand in what is so heavily a consumer economy. Where would many manufacturers, entertainment companies, and care and teaching professionals—not to speak of the whole "problem children industry"—be without a steady supply of children? And now children themselves are consumers. Apparently, children are now "necessary" in a whole new way, consistent with economic changes.

For large segments of today's population, the reasons for having children are totally different than they were in the past. Some social groups speak of children as if they were vacations, or dinners out, or opera tickets, or recreational vehicles. In other words, as if they were luxury items to be consumed. To "sensible" parents, the "necessities" of life (a house, a car, a certain standard of living) are a prerequisite for thinking about having children. Having a child becomes a matter, for instance, of personal fulfilment, or of obligations. Many come to hold in contempt individuals who have violated this understanding by having children they cannot properly care for.

The end result of all of this is that the elites in our society (and I would include most of the middle class, but especially the professional upper classes) consider having children one option among many. The trend is for people to consider having children only after they are solidly established occupationally and economically. And it is becoming increasingly acceptable not to have any children at all, and certainly to limit their number to one or two. All of this makes very good sense, given the situation of our lives today.

The other side of these social developments is that those men and women who do not conform for one reason or another are seen as deviant and morally suspect. It is thus simple to blame them for their own problems. And here we have to mention the topic of choice. When the ifs, whens, and how manys of child bearing and rearing become in some real sense a matter of choice for large segments of the society, the foundation is laid for saying that those who have children are responsible for any consequences. After all, you cannot have responsibility where there is no choice. The two go together.

So now we have a situation where children are a burden and an expense because the household economy of all segments of the population no longer accommodates children as in the past. Society as a whole no longer sees children as "units of production." Only some segments of the population, mainly the elites, have full control over this historically new situation.

Is it any wonder that abortion has become such a salient issue in all developed countries? Abortion as an issue is simply shorthand, it seems to me, for how we respond to the question of where children fit in our contemporary society. Modern social and economic circumstances have led to very different responses to child bearing and rearing, and to some very deep and bitter divisions among us.

In this historically novel situation in which we all find ourselves, some segments of the child and youth population are seen as problematic and sometimes labelled deviant. Another way of saying this is that in contemporary society, children divide rather than unite us—they are one more way in which social classes are differentiated. We still, out of our past, have the *rhetoric* of children as a universal solvent, so to speak. We tend to respond more positively to children in trouble than to adults in trouble. Appeals for help and concern are directed at us with this in mind. But the truth is that we can separate ourselves from children and young people in trouble. They are part of "the other." We have nothing in common with them.

To me, this is the challenge. I don't want to stop here. Self-interest does not allow me to do so. You and I do have to share this same world with everyone else. Our seclusion and separations are never perfect, as much as we try. We forget about the others at our own peril. If we care about the future prosperity and safety of our own children, we have to think about the prosperity and safety of *all* children. At least, that is what I have learned, both in life and through study. Where to begin?

One way that is relevant to us as readers of this collection of articles about youth in our society is to take seriously the invitation to get to know the world of young people, to listen to them and to participate in their lives. That is an essential part of any solution. It seems so simple—to share in one another's lives. And yet how difficult! We have to learn to respect one another, to value one another. But first of all, we have to find one another!

Let me end by saying that in my own youth and adolescence, a series of adults took an interest in me. Adults went out of their way to talk to me, to reach out to me. At crucial times they cared about me. My life would not have turned out the way it did if these adults had not reached out to me. I needed my friends and my peer groups, but without these adult interventions, freely offered, I don't think I could have surmounted the problems that faced me in my life. Today they stand as models for me in my interaction with young people. And I often think about young people—many of whom appear in the studies in this collection—who start life without the kinds of adults that were part of my own life.

Let me then suggest a challenge to you. Think of each article as providing a map for a journey of discovery. We invite each of you to undertake it. There will be tough moments, detours, and moments of getting lost. But the reward is contact and engagement. Those are the beginnings necessary for the growth of mutual respect, knowledge, and understanding, and for mutual change and common journeys. Social change takes place one step at a time, one person at a time. We cannot know the larger impacts and consequences until we begin.

Index

To the owner of this book

We hope that you have enjoyed *Not a Kid Anymore,* and we would like to know as much about your experiences with this text as you would care to offer. Only through your comments and those of others can we learn how to make this a better text for future readers.

School _____ Your instructor's name _____

Course _____ Was the text required? _____ Recommended? _____

1. What did you like the most about *Not a Kid Anymore?*

_____

_____

_____

2. How useful was this text for your course?

_____

_____

_____

3. Do you have any recommendations for ways to improve the next edition of this text?

_____

_____

_____

4. In the space below or in a separate letter, please write any other comments you have about the book. (For example, please feel free to comment on reading level, writing style, terminology, design features, and learning aids.)

_____

_____

_____

_____

Optional

Your name _____ Date _____

May Nelson Canada quote you, either in promotion for *Not a Kid Anymore* or in future publishing ventures?

Yes _____ No _____

Thanks!

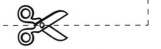

- FOLD HERE -

MAIL ➤ POSTE

Canada Post Corporation
Société canadienne des postes

Postage paid	Port payé
if mailed in Canada	si posté au Canada
Business Reply	**Réponse d'affaires**

0066102399   01

Nelson

TAPE SHUT

0066102399-M1K5G4-BR01

TAPE SHUT

Nelson Canada
Market and Product Development
1120 Birchmount Rd.
Scarborough, ON M1K 9Z9

PLEASE TAPE SHUT. DO NOT STAPLE.